HER GREATNESS PROCLAIM

HER GREATNESS PROCLAIM

The History of Girls' Latin School
Boston, Massachusetts
1878–1976

KAREN MASTROBATTISTA CURRAN

THE ALUMNAE OF GIRLS' LATIN SCHOOL

Copyright © 2014 Karen D. Curran

This book or any part thereof may not be reproduced in any form or by any means, electronic or mechanical, including photocopying, recording, or use in any information storage or retrieval system now known or to be invented, without the permission of the author.

Edited, designed, and produced by Vern Associates, Inc., Amesbury, Massachusetts www.vernassoc.com
Edited by Brian Hotchkiss and Joan Powell
Design and type composition by Glenna Collett
Production by Susan McNally

Printed and bound in China by Asia Pacific Offset

ISBN: 978-0-9906565-0-0 (cloth)
ISBN: 978-0-9906565-1-7 (paper)

Acknowledgments

I could not have written this book without the help from countless sources. First and foremost, I would like to acknowledge the hundreds of Girls' Latin School alumnae who so generously supported this book.

Unending thanks go to the various research libraries from which I coaxed back to the surface so much GLS history. I especially thank the Radcliffe Institute for Advanced Study at Harvard University for its support, in particular the Schlesinger Library staff, including Marilyn Dunn, Executive Director; Kathryn Jacob, Curator; Diana Carey, Visual Resources; and Sarah Hutcheon, Reference Librarian.

Pusey Library and other Harvard archives and libraries provided assistance, including Mary Haegert, Public Services at Houghton Library; and Edward Copenhagen, Special Collections Librarian at Munroe C. Gutman Library. I came to know Ed in 2010, and from that moment forward his support was second to none. Nanci A. Young, College Archivist at the Smith College Archives; Ian Graham, Archivist at the Wellesley College Archives; Dean M. Rogers, Special Collections Assistant at Vassar College; and the Mount Holyoke College Archives & Special Collections were all invaluable help.

From Boston Latin School, Archivist Valerie Uber helped immeasurably to discern historical facts. At Roxbury Latin School, special thanks go to its former headmaster, F. Washington Jarvis; Headmaster Kerry P. Brennan; Archivist Christopher Heaton; and several teachers who encouraged my endeavor. Roxbury Latin provided me unlimited access to the papers of Mary Sibyl Collar, a treasure trove.

A tremendous amount of my research was conducted at the City of Boston Archives and Record Management Division. I am indebted to Kristen Swett, Assistant Archivist and Boston Latin School graduate, who assisted me dozens of times over five years. The Boston Public Library's Rare Books & Manuscripts Department was equally helpful, and Sean Casey proved inexhaustible in helping me sift through its Boston Latin School collection. I also thank Jane Winton and Tom Blake of the library's Print Department for providing access to their photograph collections.

Of course I thank my colleagues at Vern Associates—Peter Blaiwas for keeping the train on track from the minute it left the station; and Brian Hotchkiss, always a gentleman, for his "gracious" guidance that turned a rough stone into a brilliant gem of writing. I am eternally grateful.

You would not be one of the 9,000 graduates of Girls' Latin School if you did not find some error, grammatical transgression, or outright misstatement of fact. It is inherent in our training to insist on accuracy, and I apologize in advance. *Mea culpa.*

Contents

	Acknowledgments	iv
	Foreword	vi
	Map of Boston, 1877	1
I	Due to the Girls of Boston	2
II	The Headmaster	40
III	A Young School Finds Its Voice: *The Jabberwock* Is Born	70
IV	Girls' Latin School Fights for a New Building	104
V	A Struggle over the Control and Direction of Girls' Latin School	128
VI	Big Changes	150
VII	The "Happy" Days	164
VIII	*Plus ça change* . . . Hitting Full Stride: The 1930s and 1940s	184
IX	The End of Our Fenway Wonderland, or *Alea Iacta Est*	200
X	The Yellow-Brick Building	220
XI	*Brevis Est Vita*: The Ironic Undoing of GLS by the Women's Equal Rights Movement	240
	Endnotes	263
	Picture Credits	281
	Index	283

Foreword

Fewer than 9,000 women graduated Girls' Latin School between 1878 and 1976. I consider myself extremely lucky to have been one of them. The ability of poor and disadvantaged students in Boston to obtain a public education equal to that offered by the best private schools in the United States was a precious legacy of the Brahmin-era devotion to education.

We have lost something valuable in Boston. Will a phoenix in the form of a Girls' Latin School ever rise again? We can only hope that at some point Boston's leaders will recognize what was lost and act in the best interests not only of young women, but of tradition, Boston history, and future generations.

I write this book so that the story of GLS, filled with so many ironies, will not be forgotten.

To the alumnae of GLS, what is our legacy? Our legacy is to stand for the future young women of Boston, that they may have the opportunity to obtain the same quality education that we were afforded. But more importantly, to stand united in support of academic excellence for all children of Boston.

Carpe Diem.

Map of Boston, 1877

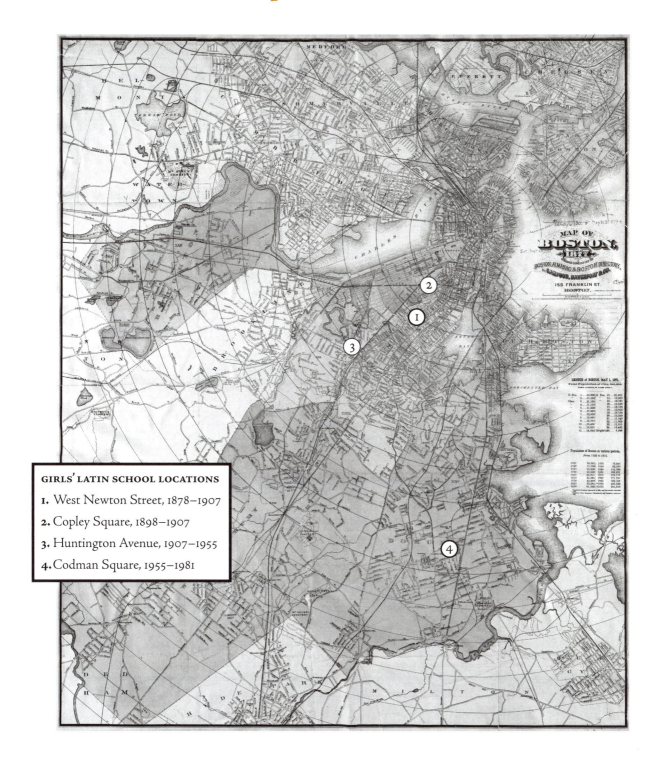

GIRLS' LATIN SCHOOL LOCATIONS
1. West Newton Street, 1878–1907
2. Copley Square, 1898–1907
3. Huntington Avenue, 1907–1955
4. Codman Square, 1955–1981

1630
Massachusetts Bay Colony is settled by Governor John Winthrop.

1635
Boston Latin School (BLS), the first school in the United States, is established.

1636 ▶
Harvard College is established.

1645
The first BLS building is constructed on north side of School Street.[1]

The Roxbury Latin School is established.

1748
A new BLS building is constructed across the street on south side of School Street.

1776
The American Revolution begins

1812
A new BLS building is built on same site.

1826
Girls' High School, the first high school for girls in the United States, is established in Boston, but is closed two years later.

1837 ▶
Mount Holyoke Female Seminary is established.

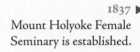

1844
A new BLS building is built on Bedford Street.

Boston Latin School Association is established.

1852
The Boston Normal School is opened to train girls to be teachers.

1853
Girls' High School is reopened and merges with Boston Normal School to create Girls' High and Normal School.

1861
Vassar College is established.

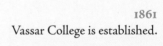

1872 ▶
The Great Fire of Boston burns 65 acres and 765 buildings.

1875 ▶
Smith College and Wellesley College open.

I

Due to the Girls of Boston

Boston Public Garden seen from the southwest, ca. 1875

In the second half of the nineteenth century, Boston was smaller than New York or Philadelphia but saw itself as infinitely more cultivated. Upper-class Brahmins—largely the descendants of the first English settlers in Massachusetts—wielded great influence over the city's customs and conventions.[2] *Brahmin sons were expected to graduate the Boston Latin School and all-male Harvard College, two of the country's most venerable institutions. Membership in this rarified academic set was as vital to a Brahmin's social status as residence on Beacon Hill.*

In 1876, a small group of Boston women began to push for the Boston Latin School (BLS)[3] *to admit girls. To BLS alumni the idea was unthinkable. After all, Boston Latin was the oldest school in the United States and had enrolled only male students for almost 250 years. In fact, BLS was older than the United States, the Commonwealth of Massachusetts, and even Harvard College.*

Allowing girls to attend BLS was as radical a proposal as the Boston School Committee had ever considered. The public was generally averse; some publicly called the idea an "intense folly."[4] *"Shall Greek and Latin compensate for badly-cooked potatoes, smoky soups and ill-done meats unless the whole machinery of domestic life is overthrown?"* asked one merchant.[5]

Emily Fairbanks Talbot was unafraid of proper Boston.

SHREDS OF OPPORTUNITY, CRUMBS OF KNOWLEDGE

By the morning of Friday, October 5, 1877, the storm signal had gone out. Only the whitecaps in Massachusetts Bay were still restless. Over the previous 24 hours, a fierce autumnal gale of almost hurricane force had dropped four inches of rain throughout New England, flooding streets, tearing up trees, and knocking out the police and fire department telegraph service. The ships docked in Boston harbor had suffered considerable damage.

It was a perfect time for a walk. Emily Talbot and Dr. Israel Tisdale Talbot left their home at 66 Marlborough Street[6] in fashionable Back Bay to attend the first public hearing on whether to admit girls to the Boston Latin School. After years of teaching, Emily had vowed to obtain the best education possible for each of her four children. In stark contrast to prevailing views, her aspirations included her daughters, Marion and Edith.

In the late 1800s, the great majority of women did not work outside the home; their primary task was to supervise their households and children. They could not vote and rarely participated in public affairs. Emily Talbot, however, did not view herself as a renegade. She simply believed women should be educated. When Mark Twain observed, "In Boston they ask, how much does he know?" Emily would have countered, "And she?"

The Talbots crossed Berkeley Street and continued up Marlborough. When they reached Commonwealth Avenue, they crossed over to the Public Garden. Through the pillared gate and fountains, they walked by the impressive bronze statue of George Washington on horseback. Over the tamped gravel path, they proceeded toward the lagoon pond. The very first swan boat had appeared that summer, a slender catamaran with sides in the shape of white swans covering the paddle wheel. Owner Robert Paget propelled the paddles by foot and could be hired to encircle the Public Garden lagoon. As they walked over the Lagoon Pond Bridge, they could see the exhausted swans waiting for Paget to remove them from the water and store them for the winter.

They entered Boston Common, which had been established in 1634 as an area for meetings and the grazing of cows and sheep and was now enclosed by a wrought-iron fence. They walked to the exit and stopped before crossing busy Tremont Street, always choked with horse-drawn carriages and omnibuses jockeying for position and moving at a snail's pace. As the jangle of horsecar bells faded in the distance, they turned off Tremont onto Mason Street and walked the last one hundred feet to the imposing building wedged between the Boston Theatre and West Street. At the main entrance was the door to the School Committee's chambers. Emily looked up to see *School Committee* in golden letters on a black wooden sign above the door.

Although it had been a short walk, the journey had been very long.

Emily Talbot had spent months researching the history of girls' education in the public schools of Boston. For her, it was a "peculiarly depressing experience."[7] Before 1780, girls could not attend the free public schools at all. "For every boy there was free education up to the very threshold of Harvard." "For girls there was not the opportunity even to learn the alphabet."[8] Mothers prevailed upon the School Committee to allow girls to use the empty schoolhouses for classes during the sweltering summer vacations. Thus, when girls were first admitted to the public schools, it was not as a right but as a concession when the schoolrooms were not in use by boys. "For many years the girls had to be content with these husks, these shreds of opportunities, and they were undoubtedly more or less grateful for such crumbs of knowledge as fell to them," Talbot noted.[9]

These summer schools were eventually abolished, and girls were extended the privileges of the grammar and primary schools. In January 1826, the Boston School Committee approved the establishment of Girls' High School, the first high school for girls in the United States.[10] The demand to attend Girls' High School was so great that there were 300 applicants for 130 seats; at the time, fewer than 300 students were enrolled at Boston Latin and Boston English combined. Parents of many who were denied admission demanded a larger school building. Mayor Josiah Quincy III, fearing enrollment by the 3,000 Boston girls attending private schools, claimed the idea was too successful and that

EMILY FAIRBANKS TALBOT—A BIOGRAPHY

Emily Fairbanks was born on February 23, 1834, in Winthrop, Maine, to parents Columbus Fairbanks and Lydia Tinkham Fairbanks. Largely self-educated, she became a teacher while still in her teens and in 1854 met Israel Tisdale Talbot, whom she married two years later. They had four children, two of them girls, the younger of whom, Edith, later wrote about her parents' meeting:

> He went to Baltimore in April 1854 to say goodbye to his sister, Susan Richards, and there met an attractive girl from Winthrop, Maine, named Emily Fairbanks, who was teaching a small group of neighbors' children in Mrs. Richards' house. . . . A late snowstorm excited the children, and their young teacher took them out at recess to have fun with snowballs. Young Talbot joined them and made a particularly good hit with a snowball and laughed heartily at his success, throwing his head back with his mouth wide open, when, quick as a flash, Miss Fairbanks picked up a handful of snow and threw it straight into his mouth. . . . Years after, he used to tell his children that he decided in that moment to try to win Miss Fairbanks as his wife, for, he said, a girl who could think so quickly . . . certainly had qualities that he wanted in his wife.[11]

> He hoped to talk to her after supper, but she retreated immediately. Mrs. Richards tried to convince her to come meet him, but she thought it highly improper. She did, however, consent to a correspondence. Slowly, through his letters, Emily began to understand that Tisdale was a man who had an extraordinary capacity for hard work, day after day and long into the night. "Life for me is no blank. It was not given for nought. . . . There is a long life of usefulness before me, and till it closes, it is for me to rise above the trials which may fall to my lot,"[12] he wrote her.

From 1854 through 1858, Talbot continued medical studies in Europe.[13] The couple was married on Tisdale's birthday, October 29, 1856. While they were on vacation in Thun, Switzerland, Marion was born. Edith, Winthrop, and Henry were all born in Boston.[14]

Education was accorded great importance by the Talbot family. Marion remembered how early she had been made to study. For example, while on vacation with an aunt in 1865, the girls received the following letter from their mother:

> My dear little daughters:
> I sent Mary to the Post Office this Sunday morning. I felt so anxious to hear from you, and the trunk, how it reached you. Your letter came and gave me much pleasure. . . .
> Tuesday & Friday mornings I want you to go into your room, or where you can be <u>alone</u>, and spend about fifteen minutes in writing. I think it will tire you less to write with a pencil. Go to

writing right after breakfast, then take the letter to the Post Office, and I will receive it the next morning. Tell Edith Mama says, she must not talk to you or disturb you, when you are busy writing. In your last letter you said 'I take my pen in hand to write you.' Now that was a waste of time & strength because of course I knew, without your telling me you had your pen in hand, else how could you write? Neither must you say, 'I will not write any more now.' Of course if you stop writing I see it. Now your next letter, <u>talk</u> to me as though I was by your side. Tell me how your dress & skirts fitted you, and if you are well & happy, then stop writing. You can do that in fifteen minutes without any hurry, and have it look neat & nice. You cannot play all the time and it is your duty to give Mama a little time twice a week, as it is your pleasure, I know when you think of it. You must tell when you want to be sent for.

Now goodbye & good night, my darling little girls.[15]

After her successful effort to establish Girls' Latin School, she helped found the Association of Collegiate Alumnae in 1882 with her daughter Marion and Florence Cushing and gave financial assistance to a great many young girls so that they could attend college.[16]

Unfortunately, Emily Talbot would not see the fruits of her labor in the form of a GLS diploma for her daughter Edith. Although Marion states in *The History of the American Association of University Women 1881–1931* that her younger sister was a member of the school's first graduating class, the records do not list Edith Talbot as a graduate of Girls' Latin School. Edith Talbot did graduate Boston University in 1883 and married Dr. William A. Jackson, a surgeon at the Massachusetts Homeopathic Hospital and professor at BU, on May 21, 1884. They had one daughter, Margaret Talbot Jackson.

Dr. Israel Tisdale Talbot had been experiencing poor health when he died of a stroke at the couple's summer home in Hingham on July 2, 1899. His funeral was held at Trinity Church in Boston's Copley Square the following day. He received both national and international recognition for his life's work.

Emily Fairbanks Talbot was 66 when she died on October 28, 1900, at The Poplars, her home in Holderness, New Hampshire.

Marion Talbot earned degrees from Boston University and the Massachusetts Institute of Technology before becoming dean of women at the University of Chicago. She died of chronic myocarditis at age 90 on October 20, 1948, in Chicago, Illinois.

History would validate Emily as a woman greatly ahead of her time. *The Boston Evening Transcript* stated, "Mrs. Emily Talbot, who soon followed her husband's death . . . was one of the active forces in Boston for years, in matters of education and charity. The establishment of the Girls' Latin school owed much to her."[17]

Left: Edith and Marion Talbot, circa 1870s

Right: Edith Talbot

the cost—$2,000 per year—was too great: "No city could stand the expense."[18] No further appropriations were made for support of the girls' school, and it "ceased to exist" after two years.[19]

The girls who could no longer attend high school of "their own free will and notion" wore black silk aprons in public as a sign of protest.[20] According to Mary Caroline Crawford, author of numerous books about Boston history and customs, "there was a great hue and cry because many young Irish girls, who had entered the High School and proved to be fine scholars, were unwilling, after enjoying this taste of culture, to become domestic servants."[21] Talbot remarked, "We can imagine the grief of those bright girls, thus compelled to relinquish their studies, and the disappointment of their parents. It was to them the death of hopes, from which there could be no resurrection."[22]

Boston claimed to spend more of its tax revenue on education than any other city on earth. So significant was Boston's influence on education standards throughout the United States that the discontinuance of the girls' school temporarily stalled the momentum in favor of secondary school opportunities for girls. But in 1851, the City of Boston elected its first superintendent, Nathan Bishop, to administer the public schools. He recommended that girls who had completed grammar school with success should have a school where they could prepare to be teachers.

The Boston Common Council, which had responsibility for final approval of the school budget, adopted Bishop's recommendation.

On September 14, 1852, the School Committee approved the creation of Boston Normal School for the training of female teachers. Despite this accommodation, public demand for a general-studies high school for girls intensified, and Girls' High School was reopened in 1853. The schools were conjoined in one building as Girls' High and Normal School so that, as the School Committee declared, "the present system of Public Instruction in the city may be rendered symmetrical and complete in all its proportions by the establishment of a high school for girls."[23] It was clear, however, that public perceptions about women's education were changing, and Talbot and other Boston women believed that the bar of "symmetrical and complete" instruction should be raised.

All four of the Talbot children had attended and graduated from Chauncy Hall School, a predominantly male private school.[24] Their elder daughter, Marion, began the study of Latin when she was 10 years of age and the study of Greek at 13, partly through private instruction as well as at Chauncy Hall.

In October 1876, Marion and Edith, then 18 and 16 years old, respectively, were enrolled at Girls' High School.[25] The school did not offer extensive courses in Greek, Latin, algebra, or geometry, so the headmaster personally supervised Marion's study of the *Aeneid* and the *Iliad*.[26] However, "so slow was the pace set for her, in even the advanced class in Geometry at the Girls' High School, that Dr. and Mrs. Talbot arranged for her to enter college."[27] Marion left Girls' High at the beginning of Boston University's winter term in 1876, making up entrance requirements and "work of the fall term which she had missed."[28]

SUMUS PRIMI

Meanwhile, Winthrop Talbot—Marion and Edith's younger brother—had been accepted to Boston Latin School for sixth grade and had started that September, 1877.[29] In the very first week, an old silver Harvard Phi Beta Kappa medal was awarded to the ten-year-old boy who had been at the top of the class. It was a gentle introduction to BLS goals and aspirations and a symbol of the scholarly heights no other public school in the country could exceed. Eventually Boston Latin would adopt the motto *Sumus Primi* ("We are first"). It was a bold statement, and uncontested for innumerable reasons.

For their younger daughter, Edith, the Talbots could not find preparation equal to Winthrop's at Boston Latin.[30] Convinced that Boston Latin School made the path to college "so clear and easy and unswerving," the Talbots believed that the doors to BLS should be opened for their daughter and all other young Boston girls.[31]

At the time, Boston Latin School was located in a simple granite structure on Bedford Street, its third location.[32] On July 8, 1844, the building had been dedicated so enthusiastically that Headmaster Epes Sargent Dixwell suggested that alumni form an association to provide continued financial support. So, on the very same day, the Boston Latin School Association was established.

By the 1870s, the now-tired building sat in the middle of a small bricked yard on a narrow street. Its exterior blocks were dingy, the windows rattled and opened with great difficulty, and the woodwork and walls were marred by years of abuse from growing boys. Public officials had become increasingly concerned with safety because of the dangerously constricted staircases, lack of exits, and overcrowding: the facility was shared with Boston's English High School, and the need for more space was becoming urgent.

Throughout the school, walls were adorned with photographs of ancient Greek and Roman monuments, including a large picture of the Roman Forum. Portraits of past headmasters Gould, Lovell, Dillaway, and Gardner occupied prominent positions. The boys were more drawn to the cork models of the Colosseum; plaster casts of ancient busts; and other projects they had fabricated in connection with their studies. Even so, none of these classic objects could relieve the gloomy feel of the building.

President Charles W. Eliot of Harvard College, who graduated Boston Latin in 1849 and was appointed president of Harvard in 1869, had attended the school on Bedford Street. Warmed by hot furnaces, the rooms were stale and ventilated by a single duct in the ceiling. "As these wooden ducts were not actuated in any way," he recalled, "the air of the rooms never hurried out of the ducts. I remember seeing my father, who had recently been mayor of Boston and a member of the school committee, testing the ventilation in the rooms of the Latin school by holding

Bedford Street, the third location of Boston Latin School, ca. 1860; the fifth story was added in 1854.

a light handkerchief in front of the ventilating exits. The handkerchief displayed not a tendency to enter the tubes."[33]

From Bedford Street, the boys would walk two blocks to Washington Street, cross over West Street, and head up to the Boston Common. There, in their navy blue uniforms, jackets with distinctive Boston school regiment brass buttons, and military caps with the initials *BLS* in silver cord, the boys still conducted military drills, a practice left over from the Civil War.[34] But allowing boys to exercise and practice on the busy Common was no longer practical.

In 1872, after a lengthy process of deliberation, the Committee on Public Instruction finally approved the acquisition of land for the construction of an enormous, brand new building to serve both Boston Latin School and English High School. The committee had negotiated to acquire multiple estates on Warren Avenue totaling 81,400 square feet, almost eight times the size of the Bedford Street lot. The Common Council signed its concurrence and sent it on to the mayor. On November 9, 1872, Mayor William Gaston signed the order to purchase land for the new BLS building.

The sunset that Saturday evening in Boston was unusually serene. There were light winds, and the temperature hovered in the low 40s over the crisp, clear night. On Summer Street, merchants closed early, and families prepared to eat their evening meals. Summer Street and its wealth of merchandise and warehouses became deserted.

Following the sinking sun, the slivered moon came up as usual into a nearly cloudless sky. At 83–85 Summer Street stood a four-story granite store and warehouse. Hours before, a spark that escaped unnoticed had ignited and slowly spread. About seven o'clock, a lone watchman smelled smoke. Looking up, he saw bright flames licking at dry goods in a darkened room. The loud blast of Fire Box 52—five blows, a pause, and then two more blows—signaled every firefighter in Boston. The blaze would last eighteen hours and require 1,700 men to bring under control.

Bostonians watched in horror as the firestorm burned 65 acres of the richest section of Boston's business district. The wall of violent flames spread so rapidly that 765 magnificent structures were torched like paper. Thousands of residents watched all night from Boston Common as the voracious flames seared a swath from Summer Street east over Devonshire, Federal, Congress, and Pearl Streets, stopping blocks from Faneuil Hall.

A reporter for the *Boston Evening Transcript* struggled to find words to describe what had just taken place. "It was a scene of incalculable destruction," he wrote.[35]

The Latin School on Bedford Street stood less than one thousand feet from the Summer Street dry goods building where the fire began. Although the wind had been blowing hard south toward Bedford Street and the entire South End, to the wonder of firefighters, the flames danced along roofs on the south side of Summer Street and then began to spread north instead. Some opined that residents of the Bedford Street area must have been more devout worshippers, but the alumni believed that their dear old Latin School had received its second blessing of the day. The city clerk noted the fortuitous timing of the $280,000 land purchase: "It is safe to say, had the order not passed *that day*, the land would not have been purchased at all."[36]

A FAIR CHANCE FOR GIRLS

Soon the holidays arrived and weeks of gentle snow had left no bare spots or cradle holes on Boston's cobblestone streets. The thump of horse hooves and skitter of sleighs resounded as fur-wrapped Bostonians filled the streets to shop for elegant gifts and practical presents. Faneuil Hall was transformed from a produce market into a forest of Christmas trees. The annual performance of Handel's *Messiah* by the Handel and Haydn Society at the Music Hall was eagerly anticipated. On Boston Common, boys sledded from Beacon down to Tremont Street and skated on the Frog Pond. The black-charred buildings downtown were now wrapped in shrouds of snow.

The New England Women's Club, located at the rear of Two Tremont Place, had also miraculously escaped damage from the fire. The club housed parlors, meeting rooms, and guest bedrooms and was staffed around the clock to receive mail, packages, and overnight guests. Boston had numerous men's clubs like the Somerset and the Union, but this was one of the first clubs in the United States to cater solely to women, and an embryonic symbol of female self-empowerment. Its importance to Boston women was extraordinary.

Emily Talbot's close friend Julia Ward Howe,[37] club president and author of "The Battle Hymn of the Republic," had invited Dr. Edward H. Clarke, a former member of the Harvard Medical School faculty and a well-known physician, to speak at the club. Clarke was chosen because he had espoused the view that women had the right to the same educational opportunities as men, and in fact should train as physicians. Because her husband had established the world's first medical college for women, Emily Talbot greatly looked forward to Dr. Clarke's speech.

By 4:30 P.M. on December 16, 1872, the room in which Dr. Clarke was to speak had filled to capacity with some of the most socially prominent, wealthy, intelligent and cultured women in Boston. The ornately decorated Victorian room had high ceilings, a fireplace with cast-iron grate, and deep burgundy oriental carpeting. Portraits of former club presidents and paintings of religious figures adorned the walls.[38]

Before the crowded room, Dr. Clarke read his paper "on the fitness of women" for college work "as influenced by the peculiarities of their physical constitution."[39] Clarke agreed that women had the right to higher education, but then went on to insist that rigorous intellectual demands like those presented by Harvard College's curriculum

Due to the Girls of Boston

would threaten their reproductive systems. Blood, diverted to the brain for study, would atrophy the uterus and ovaries, causing sterility, masculinization, insanity, and even death. The women at the meeting were stunned. The club's recording secretary wrote, "The eminent gentlemen invited to be present at the request of Dr. Clarke gave their full assent & approval to the ideas advanced by him. But the ladies were largely of a contrary opinion & regretted that the subject was not more fully treated and considered."[40]

Dr. Clarke shortly afterward published *Sex in Education; or, A Fair Chance for Girls*, in which he reported that "leucorrhoea, amenorrhoea, dysmenorrhoea, chronic and acute ovaritis, prolapsus uteri, hysteria, neuralgia"[41] and other maladies were "often caused and fostered by methods of education"[42] in New England. He recommended that women study subjects that demanded great mental exertion for only four hours a day and abstain completely during their menstrual periods.

With candor seldom used to describe the female anatomy, Clarke used as examples the extensive health problems of several young ladies he had treated. Miss G_____ had graduated valedictorian of a "Western college" and died a few years later. From an autopsy on her brain, he determined she had died from overwork.[43] Miss A___ and Miss C_____ had become victims "of hysteria and depression."[44] Miss D_____, a student at Vassar College, had started at the college menstruating healthily, but the "periodical function began to be performed with pain, moderate at first, but more and more severe with each returning month."[45]

The first edition of Clarke's book sold out in one week. *Sex in Education* proved highly influential in shaping public views on higher education for women. Members of the New England Women's Club tried to combat the rising tide of negativity, denouncing the book and pointing out that it did not have the impartiality of science. Howe, a mother of four daughters, responded in her book *A Reply to Dr. E.H. Clarke's Sex in Education* that women in college experienced greater stress from social life than from study. Not until almost twenty years after Clarke's speech would concrete statistical data be compiled to confirm that women in college suffered no more health issues than the general female population.

Although exasperated by Dr. Clarke's book, Emily Talbot, propelled by her own experiences and pioneering spirit, could easily ignore its dire prophecies. She had attended the local schools in Winthrop, Maine, and her own mother had supplemented Emily's studies with home tutoring. When Emily was a teenager, a woman did not have the slightest hope of attending college. She was not about to let this priceless opportunity pass for her daughters.

Julia Ward Howe reminded club members that on the day in 1833 that Oberlin College opened its doors to students of both sexes, a door had been forever unlocked. The women who sat in stunned silence after Dr. Clarke finished his speech decided to blaze their own path to promote higher education for young women.

"THE GREAT NEED FOR REFORM"

On a fine day in November 1876, Emily Talbot walked to 63 Mount Vernon Street, a four-story Greek revival townhouse with a classic bowed red brick façade. Square granite pillars guard the entrance and a small front yard is delineated by ornate wrought iron fencing. One of the largest homes on the street, the residence nests at the terminus of Walnut Street, which provides an unobstructed view of Boston Common.

It was the residence of William and Mary Claflin, who had purchased it in 1871 for its proximity to the Massachusetts State House. William Claflin would serve three terms (1868–1872) as governor of Massachusetts and would be elected to his first term as a U.S. congressman the following spring. It was often said that the governor's mansion, with the possible exception of 150–152 Beacon Street where Mrs. Isabella Stewart Gardner lived, had received more authors, philanthropists, and prominent citizens than any other in Boston.

William Claflin's father, Lee, had amassed a fortune in the shoe business, and in 1869 had used a part of it to cofound Boston University.[46] William Claflin issued the charter for the university and served on its board of trustees; he also had served on the Wellesley College board of trustees since that school's founding. Claflin was intent on promoting the collegiate education of women as well as a woman's right to vote.

Emily arrived at the Claflin townhome and mounted three granite stairs. After pushing through a heavy double oak and glass door, she was ushered up a long staircase to the parlor and adjoining library, which provided a warm and inviting environment for meetings.

After Dr. Clarke's speech, Emily Talbot had continued her active involvement in making a college education as much a right for girls as boys. She had attended meetings of the Women's Education Association and remained active with the educational committee of the New England Women's Club and at her daughter's school. She realized, however, that her husband's affiliation with Boston University could be her greatest asset in achieving her goals.

HENRY DURANT

Early in his career, Henry Durant had to take the unusual measure of petitioning the Massachusetts legislature to change his name from Henry Welles Smith to Henry Fowle Durant, owing to the number of Boston attorneys also named Henry W. Smith who were receiving not only his mail but his retainers as well. Although educated at Harvard, Durant never considered himself on friendly terms with his alma mater. In his opinion, its educators were staid and stodgy, and he was unabashed in sharing his perspective. After graduating in 1841, he joined his father's Lowell law practice. At 25, he moved to Boston to establish the law firm Choate & Durant, a law partnership with his childhood friend Rufus Choate.[47]

Durant gained a reputation for skilled corporate litigation. Mesmerizing before a jury, his superb cross-examinations were wonderfully clever in exploiting every legal advantage. No other member of the Massachusetts bar won more cases in the Boston courts before the age of 30. The president of the Goodrich Rubber Company came to him shortly after the company's founding to help secure the patent rights for the company's manufactured rubber. Not only was Durant successful, he also recognized immediately the commercial potential of the relatively new product and invested heavily in its stock, becoming one of the company's largest stockholders. These shrewd investments, in addition to the success of his law practice, made Durant one of Boston's wealthiest residents.

At the age of 32, after thorough consideration by all members of the family, he married his cousin Pauline Fowle in 1854. After the birth of their first son in 1855, they looked for a summer home not too far away from his demanding law practice. Twelve miles from Boston on an old Indian trail out past West Needham, they purchased a farmhouse surrounded by 300 acres overlooking Lake Waban and decided that the plain brown house would do as their homestead until they could build a more suitable summer dwelling.

Not long afterward, the Durants' infant daughter and eight-year-old son both died. To the astonishment of all who knew him, Durant gave up his law practice.

Israel Tisdale Talbot was born on October 29, 1829, in Sharon, Massachusetts, and went to Baltimore at age fourteen to help open a private school. Through teaching he earned enough money to continue his own studies, and he later graduated from Hahnemann Medical College of Philadelphia, which taught homeopathic medicine, as well as Harvard Medical School.[48]

In 1848, Dr. Talbot established the New England Female Medical College of Massachusetts, the first medical college for women in

---

Convinced that the West Needham property should be used for a higher purpose, the Durants—propelled by their experience in helping to found a library at Mount Holyoke Seminary—decided to establish a degree-granting college for women that would be the equal of the top New England men's colleges. In honor of the house of his nearest neighbor, he named it Wellesley College.

Unable to bear the memories of their farmhouse, Henry and Pauline built a spectacular summer home on Washington Street, not far from Wellesley's College Hall. There they lived during the summers with three servants, a seamstress, a cook, and a coachman, but they continued to spend winters in their city townhouse. In 1868, they moved to 30 Marlborough Street, just a few doors from Dr. Israel and Mrs. Talbot.

Henry Durant died October 31, 1881, a few years after the founding of GLS. Charles K. Dillaway, former headmaster of Boston Latin School, spoke at Durant's memorial service praising him as one of the "founders" of the Latin school for girls, to which Emily Talbot took exception. Dillaway later explained his thinking in a letter:

> February 14, 1882
> My dear Mrs. Talbot,
>
> It annoys me exceedingly that there should be anything wrong of my account of the Girls' Latin School. Certainly it was not from want of effort on my part to have everything correctly stated. I was much interested in the founding of the school and have always considered its origin and success due to the preserving energy of our Boston ladies.—The aid of the gentleman was a secondary element in the matter.
>
> The most important part of my information came from a letter you kindly sent me and a manuscript sent by Mr. Tetlow, written also I think by you. From these I gathered that Mr. Durant favored the establishment of the school but certainly I had no reason to suppose him the founder.
>
> I gave him credit for his interest in the matter although Mr. Philbrick in a letter to me said that Mr. Durant was strongly opposed to a union with the Boston Latin School.
>
> If I have done him any injustice I am sorry but cannot remedy it until another edition of the Memorial is published. I do not think any one person deserves the credit for the founding of the institution. Nothing would have been done without the aid of our Boston ladies,—Believe me.
>
> Your friend,
> CK Dillaway[49]

the world. He also served as both surgeon and secretary of the corporation for the Massachusetts Homeopathic Hospital, which was founded in 1855. When the Massachusetts Medical Society threatened to disbar anyone who practiced homeopathy, Talbot persuaded Boston University School of Medicine to absorb the women's college in 1873, and he became its dean, a position he would hold until the end of his life.

Throughout the Northeast, postsecondary educational opportunities for women had already begun to expand. Mount Holyoke College was founded in 1837, Vassar College opened in 1865, and Smith and Wellesley Colleges both opened their doors in 1875. Previously all-male New England schools had also begun to admit women: first the Massachusetts Institute of Technology in 1870, followed by Boston University in 1877. Still, only 3,000 women—just 0.3 percent of all women in the United States—were attending degree-granting institutions in 1870.[50] That same year, 1,312 women received bachelor's degrees.

Mary B. Claflin, William's wife, was interested in supporting girls who had been admitted to Boston University, and she later became the first woman ever elected to the university's board. In November 1876, she invited a small group of women to an afternoon tea to discuss ways to help girls prepare for and stay at college.

The women in her parlor that afternoon reflected on the problem that, although more colleges and universities were allowing admission to girls, only by being privately tutored could they hope to pass the entrance examinations. "The parents of few girls could afford this expenditure," Emily Talbot would later note.[51] Boston University president William F. Warren, also in attendance, was concerned that girls who could not find the necessary funds would deprive themselves of the commonest necessities of life in order to pay for tutoring. He therefore made a personal appeal to the women at the meeting: "The generous and sympathetic women of Boston would help them, did they know the pathetic histories which come within my observation."[52]

At the invitation of Mary Claflin, a second parlor meeting was scheduled for the first Sunday afternoon of the new year. The invitees included Henry F. Durant, founder of Wellesley College, and Elizabeth Palmer Peabody.[53] Born in Billerica, Massachusetts, on May 16, 1804, Peabody became a teacher and was greatly influenced by German educational theories that advocated formal schooling for children younger than six. Peabody opened the first kindergarten in Boston in 1860 and has been widely credited with establishing kindergarten as an accepted institution in U.S. education.

Warren, the main speaker, had again been invited to describe how several young women had already been forced to leave Boston University because they could not afford the preparatory courses. After carefully listening to Warren, Durant suggested that money alone would not solve the problem.

Durant was considered the most brilliant legal mind in Boston. Shrewd investments, together with the success of his law practice, had made him one of the Boston's wealthiest men. Having spent more than $1 million dollars (about $25 million in 2013 dollars) on Wellesley College and the construction of College Hall, which housed every conceivable college function. Durant had an equally substantial interest in promoting the college preparation of girls at the high school level. He explained that the entrance exam for Wellesley was set at the same level as the standards for entrance to Harvard or Yale, and told them, "It was the preliminary training of girls for college that was defective. Reform this, and time and strength and therefore *money* might be saved to the girls, and the efficiency of the colleges now open to girls be greatly increased when relieved from the responsibility of a preparatory department."[54]

Wellesley's College Hall, circa 1870. A fire in 1914 destroyed the massive building completely, but several new buildings later replaced it.

Durant was convinced that without extensive private tutoring in Greek, Latin, and other subjects, girls trained at Girls' High School would not pass the Wellesley entrance exam.[55] He knew that girls had a legal right to a public education equivalent to that offered by Boston Latin School, and as shocking as it may have seemed to those not as extensively trained in the law as he, the laws of the Commonwealth of Massachusetts enacted by the General Court in 1647 required the City of Boston to pay for it. Durant urged parents to take legal action against the City of Boston for the unequal treatment of boys and girls with this declaration: "It was the duty of the Boston Latin School to fit girls, as well as boys, for college; to permit these privileges to be withheld from the girls—inhabitants of the City of Boston—is a legal and moral wrong."[56]

"The boldness of this assertion that the citizens of Boston, the fathers of girls, had these rights, and that it was their duty to claim them, made a lively impression upon all those who listened to Mr. Durant, whose reputation for knowledge upon legal points was unquestioned," Emily Talbot later recalled.[57] "But this suggestion that a girl had the right to study Latin at the Boston Latin School seemed at first too aggressive a thing to be seriously considered."[58] In her manuscript memoir, Talbot wrote, "The first brave, outspoken suggestion of what was due to the girls of Boston to secure them a higher education came from the lips of Henry F. Durant and Elizabeth P. Peabody.... The great need for reform was so forcibly set, we acted."[59]

In the ensuing weeks, it was decided to formally incorporate the group that gathered at Mary Claflin's house. The articles of organization, filed on February 17, 1877, named 18 founding members of the Massachusetts Society for the University Education of Women (MSUEW), and William F. Warren was chosen as president. In less than three years, the group's membership would swell to almost 200 prominent Bostonians.

On May 19, the MSUEW appointed a special committee consisting of Emily Talbot, Florence Cushing, and Annie Adams Fields to secure the admission of young women to Boston Latin School. Married to editor and publisher James T. Fields and an author herself, Annie Fields was an important addition to the committee because of her connections to many Boston newspapers. Her influence spurred the publication of numerous supportive articles about the work of the MSUEW that were instrumental in changing the tide of public opinion about women's education. Florence Cushing, valedictorian of the class of 1874 at Vassar

College, was considered one of the most highly educated women in Boston. "Here a field for work seemed open," she said.[60] "Owing to the novelty and perhaps unpopularity of this movement,"[61] in the words of Emily Talbot, many men declined to participate, but three eventually became members of the committee: John D. Runkle, president of the Massachusetts Institute of Technology; James Freeman Clarke, graduate of Boston Latin School, Harvard College, and Harvard Divinity School; and attorney Robert D. Smith, who lived near the Claflins on Mount Vernon Street.

This six-person committee did much to lay the political and legal route needed to achieve its objective. Smith led their research into the relevant laws and learned that in fact what Durant said was true: The public education of girls was legally required. "This study of the principles of justice and equality, as set forth by the framers of school laws of the Commonwealth, inspired the committee to renewed diligence in the discharge of their duty," said Talbot.[62] A discussion followed about the BLS's legal framework that sought to identify the best approach to forwarding the argument for admitting girls.

FLORENCE CUSHING

Florence Cushing would continue to be actively involved in women's education her entire life. Shortly after Girls' Latin School was approved, she helped Emily and Marion Talbot found the Association of Collegiate Alumnae, which eventually became the American Association of University Women, an organization of which she was the second president (1883–1885).

The first alumna to sit on the Vassar College Board of Trustees, Cushing served on it from 1887 to 1894 and again from 1906 until 1912. In 1913, she was elected to life membership on the board, a position that she held until 1923. For her commitment and devotion to Vassar College, Cushing Hall was built in 1923. In a letter to the board she stated, "I simply cannot believe it, for I know how absolutely undeserved it all is. . . . I accept the high privilege as graciously as I can. . . . I am content to have the building bear the name of the alumna trustee first selected." She died at home in Norwell, Massachusetts, on September 20, 1927.[63]

Four members of the MSUEW special committee (from left to right): Annie Fields, John D. Runkle, James F. Clarke, and William F. Warren

The face of the MSUEW's formidable opponent would soon take shape in the form of the Boston Latin School Association (BLSA), the alumni group founded by BLS in 1844. "The status of the Latin School next occupied the attention of the committee. Many thought this school a body corporate carried on under certain restrictions," recalled Talbot. "Others believed it to be an absolutely free public school . . . subject to the laws governing other schools in the state."[64]

"FOR THE NOURTERING OF THE CHILDREN WITHIN US"

April's showers continued into May that year, and despite the wet, miserable weather, at four o'clock on May 2, 1877, BLSA members gathered for their annual meeting in the hall on the fourth floor of the Bedford Street building.[65] The fourth-floor hall extended across the front, and the BLSA's library was located in a small room off that hall.

Joseph Healy, the association's secretary and treasurer, had sent postcards to notify alumni of the upcoming annual meeting. Valedictorian of the BLS class of 1866, Healy was, at 30, considered a rising star. In his six years at the school he earned 21 Lawrence prizes for excellence in English as well as the Franklin Medal for Scholarship, typically given to the student who was first in his class. After graduating from Harvard College and Harvard Law School, he was admitted to the Massachusetts bar.

The BLSA's seven officers included Charles K. Dillaway, who had served as school headmaster from 1831 to 1836 and as president since 1860. At 73, he held privileged status as the only former BLS headmaster still living besides Epes Sargent Dixwell and the current headmaster and librarian, Moses Merrill. At the annual meeting of the alumni association that day, there would be no mention of the movement to admit girls to the Latin School, so preposterous was the idea. Most of the discussion centered on the enormous efforts to complete a new catalogue of all of BLS's graduates.

Although BLS was a democratic institution and its privileges were confined to no social class, an unmistakable strain of superiority permeated its graduates, a confidence forged and bonded by rigorous educational endeavor. BLS's high standard of academic excellence elevated the entire school system and conveyed prestige, so much so that in the late nineteenth century the headmaster of the Boston Latin School earned more than the pastors of Boston's most prominent churches and nearly as much as the city's mayor. The alumni of Boston Latin considered themselves guardians of a long-standing institution that was *sine qua non*.

The Boston Latin School was established on April 23, 1635, five years after the settlement of the Massachusetts Bay Colony by Governor John Winthrop.[66] According to Boston town records,

> The 13th of the 2d moneth, 1635.... Att a Generall meeting upon publique notice.... Likewise it was then generally agreed upon, that our brother Philemon Pormort, shalbe intreated to become scholemaster for the teaching and nourturing of the children within us.[67]

All graduates took six years of Latin, Greek, English composition, declamation, and Greek and Roman history. The Puritan fathers believed that knowledge of classical languages was a prerequisite to understanding scripture. A question put to a vote at the 1711 Boston town meeting was whether more "easy and delightful" curriculum ought to be introduced. That measure failed miserably. Bostonians believed that it was not what boys learned at school that made them men, but the amount of hard work they endured.

The school commanded public respect for its all-male traditions and powerful alumni. Boston Latin had produced five signers of the Declaration of Independence (Samuel Adams, Benjamin Franklin, John Hancock, William Hooper, and Robert Treat Paine); several

Massachusetts statesmen, including Robert C. Winthrop, Charles Francis Adams Sr., and Charles Sumner; Charles Bulfinch, architect of the U.S. Capitol building; Ralph Waldo Emerson; presidents John Leverett, Samuel Langdon, Edward Everett, and Charles W. Eliot of Harvard College; mayors Harrison G. Otis, Samuel A. Eliot, and Frederick O. Prince of Boston; and innumerable prominent businessmen. Boston Latin antedated Harvard College by three years; Harvard's first class entered in 1638, and from that year forward, had accepted almost all of the Latin School boys each year, and they made up one-quarter of any given Harvard class. As one graduate of both schools quipped, "the Latin School dandled Harvard College on her knees."[68]

Mayor Prince was sworn into office in January 1877. He had graduated Boston Latin in 1832[69] and Harvard College in 1836, and gone on to serve in both the Massachusetts House and Senate. By city charter, the mayor of Boston was also the chairman of the School Committee. Prince unabashedly used his power to favor his alma mater and was not in favor of making Boston Latin a co-educational institution.

Although land for the new BLS building[70] had been purchased shortly after the Great Fire in 1872, the three mayors who held office immediately afterward had "rather exceptionally conservative views respecting school expenditures," and the construction of the building was not funded.[71] "The incumbent who came into the office of Mayor in 1877, the Hon. Frederick O. Prince, taking a different view of the matter, lost no time in declaring himself in favor of a liberal appropriation for the building," stated Boston School Superintendent John Philbrick.[72]

The lavish new building planned for the Boston Latin and English High boys was further evidence of injustice for those supporting equal public funding for the collegiate preparation of girls. Although it could accommodate 1,645 pupils, both schools had only 696 students, leaving 949 seats unoccupied. The MSUEW saw the empty seats as an opportunity to make the facility coeducational, while the opposition claimed that the new school was "unfit for the accommodation of girls."[73] The MSUEW met with the architects of the building, reviewed the plans, and were assured that this statement "was not warranted by the facts."[74]

BLS headmasters (left to right): Charles K. Dillaway (1831–1836) and Moses Merrill (1877–1901).

"THEIR LAWFUL PRIVILEGES"

Beginning in the summer of 1877, Emily Talbot began gathering signatures on a petition to support the entrance of girls on equal terms[75] to the Boston Latin School.[76] Former BLS headmaster Charles Dillaway agreed to sign. It was a staggering break in the BLS ranks.

Seeking to understand their motives, Healy wrote Dillaway as well as other BLS alumni.

> Having seen your signature attached to a petition which request the admission of girls to the Latin School, I take the liberty asking you the following questions which I trust you will answer, pardoning me for thus troubling you.[77]
> I. Did you sign the petition under the supposition that you were asking for co-education of the boys and girls, or simply requesting that girls should have equal opportunities with the boys for classical education?
> II. Do you approve co-education? Why?
> III. Would not co-education in the Latin School have one of two results. (1) Will not the girls undermine their health, by working where nature demands physical and mental repose or resting,[78] then by endeavoring to make up arrears of work, in the remaining time; (2) or as the slowest scholars in the class always determine the pace at which instruction advances, if the girls work only, say, three-fourths of the time which the boys devote to study, will not they retard the progress of the boys?[79]

Due to the Girls of Boston   25

Dillaway, who had three daughters, no doubt felt they also should have had the advantages of a classical education. But it seemed clear that most BLS alumni would join together in opposition to the idea. Healy could not turn to Dillaway for support, so he turned directly to the mayor. In response to the MSUEW's petition, an opposing version began to circulate. Predictably, the first signature on the petition was that of Frederick O. Prince, mayor of Boston.

"It was then said, let the girls first be formally denied their lawful privileges,"[80] said Emily Talbot, who proceeded to enroll her daughter Edith and another young girl (whose identity is unknown) at the Latin School on September 9, 1877. This constituted an outrageous demand. Moses Merrill, who had been appointed headmaster in June 1877, was considered a man of high moral standards. Before he assumed the headmaster position, the school's enrollment had fallen to about two hundred students.[81] Largely because of his character, which was impressive to parents and students alike, the school had enjoyed a rebirth. Trying to strike a balance between respect for tradition and for the mother of current student Winthrop Talbot, headmaster Merrill told Mrs. Talbot politely that her request was so unusual he needed to refer it to the Committee on Latin and High Schools. The next day she met with Charles L. Flint, chairman of the committee.d

Charles L. Flint, chairman of the Committee on Latin and High Schools

Talbot recalled, "The chairman of this committee was at once seen, and he frankly stated that in his opinion there was no objection to the plan, that one young girl, Miss Helen Magill, was for some time a pupil at Boston Latin School, and no objection was ever made, to his knowledge; in fact, he remarked, 'I think we can slip them in easily.'"[82]

Helen "Nellie" Magill was in fact the first female ever to study at Boston Latin. Although she was never formally admitted to the school, she was allowed to attend classes because her father, Edward H. Magill, was the submaster there from 1859 through 1866. She left before finishing.[83] Magill was a sparkling example of what a female could achieve with a BLS education. A member of the first Swarthmore College graduating class, she earned a Ph.D. from Boston University in 1877 for her dissertation on Greek drama, thus becoming the first woman in the United States to be awarded the doctor of philosophy degree.[84] Edward Magill even expressed hope that, if indeed girls were admitted to the Latin School, "As Helen was the first girl to enter the Latin School as a student... she should be first on the list of women employed as instructors there."[85]

But Flint underestimated the skill of Mayor Prince and the opposition. The Committee on Latin and High Schools questioned the legality of admitting girls to Latin School, with some members suggesting the school was a corporate body rather than a truly public school. The MSUEW answered by citing public records that clearly proved BLS was a public school and, further, that public education was never intended to be limited to just boys. The statutes of the Commonwealth enacted by the General Court on November 11, 1647, required free, public education for all children.

Helen Magill upon her graduation from Swarthmore College

> That every Township in this jurisdiction, after the Lord hath increased them to the number of fifty Householders, shall then forthwith appoint one within their town to teach *all such children* as shall resort to him to write and read.... And it is further ordered, that where any town shall increase to the number of one hundred Families or Householders, they shall set up a Grammar-School, the Masters thereof being able to instruct *youth* so far as they may be fitted for the Universitie.[86]

The uncertainty about what the School Committee would do persisted; there had as yet been no indication of how it would handle this request. "But the cloud began to lift when, on the 27th of the same month [September], Mr. Philbrick, the superintendent of schools, issued his annual report,"[87] said Talbot, "and the surprising statements[88] made therein increased the interests not only of the citizens of Boston, but of the Commonwealth."[89] The superintendent's report spoke plainly enough: "There no longer exists in the system a school or class where a girl could fit for college."[90] Much to the pleasure of Emily Talbot and the other members of the MSUEW, after this report was issued, the Committee on Latin and High Schools scheduled a public hearing.

FIVE PUBLIC HEARINGS

The Talbots found the main hall of the School Committee building on Mason Street already filled with many distinguished Bostonians.[91] Many mothers and daughters "who had a deep personal interest" in the issue had come to the hearing.⁹² Dr. Talbot greeted several educators from Boston University. Florence Cushing motioned to the Talbots, and they were ushered to open seats.

The first public hearing on the matter of classical education for girls had drawn more interest than the Committee on Latin and High Schools had anticipated. Chairman Charles L. Flint was seated at the front of the room behind a large mahogany desk. A silver tray with water pitcher and glasses glistened in the soft glow of the gaslights.

A little before three o'clock, other members of the committee took their seats at their desks: George A. Thayer, minister at First Congregational Church in South Boston; Godfrey Morse, who had a successful law practice on Water Street and had attended Boston Latin; Henry P. Bowditch, a doctor from Jamaica Plain, who later would become dean of Harvard's Medical School; and finally, Abby W. May. Miss May was well respected in Boston due to her relation to the Alcott family and her close friendship with her cousin, Louisa May Alcott.

Loudly rapping his gavel on the table, Flint called the meeting of Friday October 5th of the Committee on Latin and High Schools to order. He explained that a petition had been received from Mrs. Israel Tisdale Talbot as well as many other ladies in Boston asking that the rules of the High and Latin Schools be amended so that young women can enroll at the Latin School. He asked Mrs. Talbot to kindly address the board about her desires.

Attorney Robert D. Smith was expected to conduct the hearing on behalf of the petitioners, but was called away on another matter unexpectedly at the last minute. Although he would have given the committee more credibility, Talbot had been eager to replace him. She rose from her seat and confidently summarized their position. Citing the laws that supported the admission of girls to Boston Latin, she made the following brief points:⁹³

Girls' High School and School Committee Headquarters Building on Mason Street

1. The statutes of Massachusetts require that every town of more than 4,000 inhabitants shall maintain a school in which Latin and Greek are taught for the benefit of all inhabitants.
2. In 1635, the magistrates voted that the master should attend to the "nourtering and teaching of *children*," not just boys.
3. Girls should be admitted to the Latin School because of its high standard of excellence in scholarship.
4. The justice of the request is that girls should not enter college too late or with improper training.

Godfrey Morse BLS NG and Joseph Healy BLS '66

Professor George H. Howison of MIT spoke next, and presented as evidence the recent results of applications for admission to Vassar College. Of the 32 applicants to Vassar College the previous summer from all over the United States, only six passed the entrance requirements. Eleven of the applicants were graduates of the Girls' High and Normal School. Not one passed the exam. Of the six who were admitted, not one was a graduate of the Boston schools.

Reverend James Freeman Clarke, as a member of the Harvard University Board of Overseers, had argued unsuccessfully in 1872 for the admission of women to Harvard. At that time, he suggested that Harvard graduates had daughters for whom they wanted the best education possible, but President Eliot prevailed by arguing that "religious tenets would be violated by the implementation of coeducation at Harvard."[94] Clarke, another man greatly ahead of his time, pointed out to the crowded room, "No newly established school can compare with [Boston Latin School's] excellence, no other school in the country can compare with it. Having the best way ready at our hands, why try any other?"[95]

Emily Talbot rose again to speak. "Five weeks ago, parents of two young ladies presented their request for admission to the Latin School. They are still waiting for the reply to their request."[96] There was obvious annoyance from some School Committee members.

Flint made it clear that the committee did not support establishing a college preparatory department within the Girls' High School. The

Due to the Girls of Boston

decision before them was whether or not to amend the rules and regulations of Boston Latin in order to admit girls or to establish a separate school for girls. In and of itself this was a weighty, complicated proposal. After asking without response if anyone opposed the issue altogether, the hearing was then closed.

In the days following the meeting, increased pressure was applied to allow the opponents of this plan to speak, and the committee subsequently decided to re-open the public hearing.[97] "For the School Committee and the opposition, some of whom were bachelors," Talbot noted, "the fascination for the continued hearings was greater than for the impatient parents of the girls, who saw the chances of a year's good work, slipping away from them."[98] Parents asked that courses be started forthwith under the masters at Boston Latin School and presented ten more petitions. Although the headmaster of BLS would have taught the girls himself, he suggested parents wait for the committee's decision. The Boston Latin alumni had been unprepared for the support this seemingly unthinkable idea had received. Headmaster Merrill had made the decision to remain neutral and removed himself from the proceedings. Someone needed to lead the movement.

Joseph Healy and many other prominent BLS alumni had not yet organized to speak. At the second hearing Healy begged, "The graduates of Latin School are opposed to a radical change in the course and management of the school. . . . I ask for a further hearing for the remonstrants on behalf of the Latin School Association."[99] Flint rapped his gavel to quell noise in the room, and explained that however thoroughly their committee may have considered the case of the petitioners, the public has so deep an interest in the matter that it may well desire to hear the evidence. The committee then moved to continue the hearing.

The U.S. sloop of war *Ossipee* had been lying off Long Wharf; on Monday afternoon, it weighed anchor and proceeded to sea. After its departure, the news of the day included a lively 28-inch freshwater eel that had been removed from a valve that provided water to Churchill & Co. on Washington Street, and a poor young South Boston woman that had toppled from a stool with a lamp in her hand and was badly burned when her clothing caught on fire. The story that occupied page one the next day concerned the classical education of girls in the Boston public schools: would the measure be approved?

At the third public hearing, Dillaway, with square face, receding hairline, and large mutton sideburns, spoke first. "I favor the admission of girls to the Latin School and hope this experiment will be tried. I see no very grave objection to it and think popular sentiment favors it. The only reason girls have not been admitted to Roxbury Latin, of which I am a trustee, is that the school cannot afford the expense of a new building."[100]

Healy countered that young girls would be compelled to overwork at the Latin School to keep their standings in class and that they would risk their health, given the physical incapacity of women for hard study. "The graduates look to the school as endowed with a certain personality, as it has been the leading preparatory school of the country. The admissions of girls would sanction the principle of coeducation at the high school age, a step which would lead to deleterious results all over the country."[101]

William Coe Collar, headmaster of the all-male Roxbury Latin School (1645)—the first private school in the U.S.—and father of three girls, was one of the most highly regarded educators in Boston. Collar supported the opposition and told the School Committee at the fourth public hearing that the admission of girls would seriously impair the efficiency of the instruction and course of study at Boston Latin School.[102] "Another aspect of this case is a moral one, for there comes a time when girls become an object of extreme interest to boys," he insisted. He believed a separate school for girls "would draw powerfully from the private schools, and in five years would have 300 girls preparing for college."[103]

Superintendent Philbrick, who spoke for over an hour, favored establishing a separate school for girls with the same standard of admission, the same course of study, and the same diploma examination as Boston Latin School. Seven presidents of the 21 New England colleges supported Philbrick's proposal, including President Charles W. Eliot of Harvard College, President Julius H. Seelye of Amherst College, and President Noah Porter of Yale College, who stated, "Boys and girls from the ages of fourteen through eighteen should not recite in the same classroom nor meet in the same study hall."[104] A letter from President Samuel D. Bartlett of Dartmouth College was read publicly.

> They [girls] cannot endure and should not attempt the same hard, unintermitted and long-continued strain to which boys may be and

Due to the Girls of Boston

are subjected. It is a wrong done to their more excitable temperaments and more delicate constitutions. One of the crying evils of many schools already is the heedless and culpable disregard of the health and strength of the girls. . . . I should as a parent seriously object to the opportunities for constant intercourse, direct and indirect . . . which create an air of romance . . . at an age susceptible, inexperienced and inconsiderate.[105]

Joseph Healy criticized the validity of signatures on two of the petitions submitted by the MSUEW. "Out of 73 names on two petitions, 24 were women [who could not vote], 1 lived out of town, 12 were not in the directory, and many others were clerks and salesmen." He then went on to imply that Dr. Talbot had "openly declared" that if the Latin School were opened to girls tomorrow, he would not send his daughter there.[106] The fight had suddenly turned personal, but would have to wait to continue for four days.

Dr. Talbot had in fact met Godfrey Morse on Beacon Street and had discussed the unsanitary, near-squalid conditions of BLS's Bedford Street building. When asked if he would like his daughter to attend school in that building, he had merely replied, "No, I would not."[107] That both these young men had misrepresented his remark irritated him. He was determined to correct the public record.[108]

Storms threatened Boston all day on November 5. That afternoon, an uncharacteristically impatient Dr. Talbot was seated deep in the crowded School Committee offices on Mason Street. Finally he rose to speak.

> I did not propose to appear before you at this public hearing, for I had confidence your committee would do full justice to the requests and petitions which in good faith I have made to you, but when, during these long hearings, you have patiently listened three times to one young man, who, for the want of anything better to say, has seen fit to define my positions, I think it but proper that I should be allowed to speak for myself.
>
> I am informed, and Mr. Healy acknowledged, that at the last hearing he said: "The husband of a lady who has been very prominent in this movement, when asked by one of the committee, 'If the Latin

School be opened to girls tomorrow, would you send your daughter there?' replied, 'No, I would not.'"

I could not believe it when told that this statement referred to me, and applied to Mr. Healy, who said that I was the person intended. Now this statement implies and was intended to convey one of two things: first, that I was acting falsely toward the committee, in that although I had applied for the admission of my daughter to the Latin School, yet if the request were granted I would not let her go there; second: that I opposed my wife's actions in signing this petition. Now I appeal to each and every member of this committee to know whether any word or act of mine could possibly justify them in the slightest suspicion that I was playing a false part in this matter. . . and that I did not want my daughter educated where, with the greatest satisfaction, my son now is, in the Boston Latin School.

For my own part, I do not hesitate to characterize the statements and implications made by one of the remonstrants, as far as it regards me, to be entirely and unqualifiedly untrue. . . . My attention was, perhaps, directed to the education of my daughter in the Latin school by the fact that Miss Helen Magill attended this school for three years, and attested to the courtesy and kindness she received from the teachers and scholars.

I fully support my wife's actions in signing this petition. It was at my request that Mrs. Talbot called upon the master of the Latin school and asked that my daughter and another young lady might be permitted to enter the special class fitting for college. She received the courteous answer that 'personally, he should esteem it a privilege to receive the young ladies into the school. . . .' My wife was referred to this school board for an answer to our request. Two months went by without any answer having been made to her and others desiring the same privileges for their daughters. It was then we formally submitted a petition to this board formally asking for the admission of girls to the Latin School. Consequently four hearings have taken place.[109]

Dr. Talbot surveyed the room, making eye-to-eye contact with as many of the notable gentlemen of Boston in attendance as possible.

> The petitioners for a general opening of this school to girls did not expect to be obliged to listen to a discussion of the physical disabilities of women or homilies about classical education nor have their cheeks burn and their ears tingle by the indecent expressions and absurd ideas of a mere youth.... The petitioners ask only for equal rights in this matter.[110]

Morse replied, "I did meet Dr. Talbot on Beacon Street, and while talking about the wretched condition of the Latin School building, I asked whether he would be willing to have his daughter attend. He responded as I recall, 'No, I would not.'" Morse then took exception to Talbot's criticisms of fellow BLS alumnus Healy. "You have not treated Mr. Healy fairly, Mr. Talbot."[111]

Healy defended himself. "It was the conversation as reported to me by Mr. Morse, and Dr. Talbot's advocating this petition, which were decidedly inconsistent. I know very well my youth. I have not advanced any ideas of my own, but only presented a view of a leader in medical science."[112]

President William F. Warren of Boston University would be the final speaker of the afternoon. Warren rose from his chair and strode to the front of the room. Impeccably dressed in a severe black suit, white shirt, and bow tie, he waited for silence, and then began to rebut the twenty different arguments that had been used by those opposing opening up the Boston Latin School to girls.

He countered that the mothers of Boston are "better guardians of their daughter's modesty and better judges of maidenly propriety" than the presidents of the 21 New England colleges who opposed the petition. He expressed good-humored surprise that one former academic "reports that Greek literature and Greek civilization are not fit to be taught to girls. This distinguished ex-professor we turn over to the tender mercies of . . . his old friend of Latin School days, Dr. Helen Magill, who is abundantly able to debate this astonishing thesis with him in Greek."

In conclusion, Warren outlined ten reasons "for granting a separate department under the Latin School masters," including the following: "It is precisely what these parents of daughters ask. Because it is the only arrangement which affords any reasonable guaranty of fair play . . . because it postpones the necessity of deciding whether a separate Latin school for girls is called for . . . because I am persuaded that your own fair mindedness prompts you to remove the existing injustice."[113]

Everyone expected the final vote at the November 13 School Committee meeting. Instead, School Committee chairman Mayor Prince, because he felt rules would have to be suspended to establish the school, referred the matter to the Committee on Rules and Regulations. The BLS alumni were pleased with this unanticipated turn of events and hoped the committee would find a legal premise on which to deny the admission of girls. The parents who had sent petitions to the School Committee weeks ago were outraged.

AN ANNUAL DINNER AND A FINAL DECISION

Parker's Hotel, opposite City Hall on School Street, was a natural choice for the annual BLSA dinner both due to its great size and because it occupied the former site of the third and fourth Boston Latin Schools. Standing eight stories high on the corner of Tremont Street, the hotel's white marble façade and lobby and deeply coffered ceilings gave its interiors an air of dignity and refinement. Horsehair divans, thick carpets, and huge potted palms filled the public rooms. Both the public dining rooms for men and women on the first floor and the private men's-only dining rooms on the second floor had beautiful arched windows overlooking the street.

Mayor Prince chaired the meeting of more than one hundred alumni and guests. The evening began at six o'clock with a social hour for all alumni, after which they gathered in the great hall for an elaborate seven-course dinner. At about half past eight, Robert C. Winthrop, direct descendent of Governor John Winthrop, rose to speak. He talked of his fellow graduates listed in the 1821 catalogue of Boston Latin School before saying, "But there is another void in this old catalogue. . . . It is the entire absence of the feminine gender! These 206 names are all boys' names, and I know not what would have been thought if the proposal for a mixed school had been suggested at that period. . . . We all know that it would not have been seriously entertained for an instant. . . . We do not undervalue their capacities. We are only too sensible to their attractions. But we are persuaded that boys and girls will study better and learn more and have fewer distractions in separate institutions."[114] His remarks were met with applause.

Parker's Hotel, Boston, site of the annual BLSA dinner

The next day, *The Boston Globe* dubbed the evening "A Feast of Reason"[115] and printed a poem read by Harvard professor William Everett, the last stanza of which was:

> One verse more! This meeting's private:
> Some things won't be said outside,
> Many an outward stroke and inward
> Has the dear old school defied.
> Boys or men: we'll stand unflinching
> Every bolt that malice hurls;
> But, by all her ancient honor,
> Fill not up our ranks with girls![116]

Superintendent Philbrick was caught between two strong forces and admitted that the School Committee was struggling to decide whether to "admit girls to Boston Latin on equal terms" or "to establish a separate and independent Latin School for girls. . . . The question, however, was one of considerable difficulty," he said. [117]

What remained an irrefutable fact was that the reputation and academic achievement of the Boston Latin School was superior to that of any co-educational school in the nation. Opponents of mixing girls and boys at the Latin School argued that it would lower the standards of purity and morality that had produced such results. Philbrick summarized the arguments for and against as follows: "On one hand it was contended that justice to the girls required that they should have the advantage of classical instruction identical with those enjoyed by the boys, or, what amounted to the same thing, they should be admitted to boys' Latin School, thus rendering that ancient institution a mixed school. On the other hand it was maintained that this arrangement would not be doing justice to either the girls or the boys; that it would render the Latin School less efficient as a preparatory school for boys, and that it would not give the girls as good a chance as they might have in a separate school for girls."[118]

On November 27, 1877, the School Committee met yet again, and the subcommittee chairman started off by reporting back on the order sent to them by the full Boston School Committee to establish a Latin School for girls. He read the following statement: "Committee on Rules and Regulations report . . . as the order was presented by the Committee on High Schools after much deliberation and a number of public hearings on the subject of classical education for girls, it is thought desirable that action be taken by the board directly on the subject. They therefore report back the order without recommendation."[119] Whispers could be heard among the 24 members of the School Committee. After five weeks, the committee had yet to come to a decision.

The committee's indecision, however, was no match for Emily Talbot's determination. "This order, after being referred from one subcommittee to another, was finally brought before the full board," she wrote. "One of the committee, Miss Abby May, favoring the admission of girls to the old Latin School, opposed the adoption of the order, on the ground that economy and immediate efficiency should be first considered, when meeting fresh demands upon the resources of the public schools . . . that to unnecessarily duplicate schools was a 'perversion of authority.'"[120] "Perversion of authority" was an important term because it formed the legal basis on which the court could overturn a decision of the committee. "To unnecessarily duplicate schools" was a reference to

Due to the Girls of Boston

the numerous available seats in the new BLS building. Faced with this potential legal challenge, the committee decided to vote on the order after all.

Knowing that the full School Committee was about to vote, May and Edward Hutchins offered substitute motions, with Hutchins asking that the separate classes for girls be held under the direction of Headmaster Merrill and May asking that girls be taught together with the boys in the new school building. Both these motions failed.[121] (After her term expired in 1878, May was not re-elected to the School Committee and refused to run again. She did, however, serve on the state board of education from 1879 through 1888.) The School Committee finally took action on November 27, 1877:

> **ORDERED** That the Committee on High Schools be authorized to organize a Latin School for girls under the direction of a principal with the rank of Master and with such assistances as the exigencies of the school may require, the school to be located in whatever building the committee may direct.[122]

In his superintendent's report for March 1878, Philbrick said of the new school, "The establishment of this institution, which went into operation the early part of last month, is an important event in our educational history. It is intended as a classical High School for fitting girls for college. It is the first and only institution of the kind within my knowledge.... That the physical and mental differences of the sexes... require separate education for pupils between the ages of twelve and eighteen, especially in a large city, in order to secure the *best results*...if the aim is to maintain *the highest standard of excellence yet known*, then, for pupils between the ages mentioned, the period of High-School education, provision should be made for the *separate* education of girls and boys."[123]

Emily Talbot and her courageous friends had, in the words of her daughter Marion, "made a determined assault upon the Boston Latin School hoping to make a break in its walls.... But tradition was too strong and conservatism was too stubborn, and the wall held. It was pointed out to Mrs. Talbot that the traditions of Boston Latin School were too precious to be sacrificed.... The struggle had been brave and vigorous, but inevitably hopeless, and reluctantly Mrs. Talbot and her friends accepted a substitute for their far-sighted and idealistic plan."[124]

The Girls' Latin School would be the first college preparatory high school for girls in the United States.[125]

Talbot had exerted all her strength to overcome the objections to allowing girls into Boston Latin School. As she prepared to enroll her daughter Edith in the new college preparatory school, she vowed to continue the fight.

◀ 1878

John Tetlow is hired as headmaster of Girls' Latin School (GLS).

First entrance exam at GLS (February 4)

First day of classes at GLS (February 11)

1879

Harvard Annex begins instruction for women.

The Massachusetts legislature grants women the right to vote for School Committee candidates.

Emily Talbot runs for the Boston School Committee, but is not elected.

◀ 1880

The first six women graduate from GLS; five are accepted to Smith College.

John Tetlow marries Elizabeth Proctor Howard.

◀ 1881

The sixth BLS building is completed on Warren Avenue.

The Roxbury Latin School Alumni Association is founded.

Henry Durant dies of kidney failure October 31.

1881 ▶

Boston Symphony Orchestra and Filene's Department Store are established.

1882 ▶

The Society for the Collegiate Instruction of Women, Harvard Annex, is incorporated in October.

1883

The first class graduates from Harvard Annex.

◀ 1885

John Tetlow becomes headmaster of both Girls' High School and Girls' Latin School.

II

The Headmaster

Museum of Fine Arts, Copley Square, built 1876, demolished 1911

THE HEADMASTER ARRIVES

John Tetlow, the newly hired headmaster of Girls' Latin School, looked out at the snow-encased streets of Copley Square. Luckily, he had arrived in Boston a few days before from New Bedford, Massachusetts. The 15 inches of wintry mix that had fallen the night before had been the heaviest since the Great Storm of 1867.

From his warm boarding house on St. James Avenue, a well-bundled Tetlow stepped out into the cold and walked briskly down the street. Most of the city's horsecar lines were down, and 500 men navigating 25 snowplows and 2,300 horses were at work on the task of clearing Boston's streets and dumping snow on Boston Common.

The sun peeked out, melting the snow, and causing him to slice between slippery puddles and steaming piles of horse dung like an obstacle course. In the distance the clop and skitter of horse teams on the cobblestones could be heard, along with the constant tap of shovels and ice picks. Everywhere he looked the streets were choked with men shoveling snow into pungs, large, wooden rectangular boxes on smooth iron runners or tipcarts. The air smelled of the salt of Boston Harbor and the tang of dirty snow.

In December, William H. Finney, on behalf of the Joint Committee on Nominations and High Schools, had presented Tetlow's name as a candidate for headmaster of the new school, and the 24-member School Committee elected him unanimously. When he received the handwritten letter from the Boston School Committee, he thought about it carefully overnight before making his final decision. In the morning, on January 6, 1878, he wrote:

> I received last evening your note informing me of my election by a unanimous vote to the principalship of the new Latin School, and desire to thank you and your associates for this gratifying, though, of course, provincial, expression of confidence. I have sent my resignation to the Trustees of the school with which I am now connected, and have every reason to believe they will release me in time to enter your service on the fourth of February.
>
> The intervening time, however, will be so crowded with work that I shall have no leisure to give to preparation for my duties in the new position. If I am to be the only teacher for the present, and if a course of study prepared under the direction of the Committee is to be furnished to me ready made, so that I shall simply have to classify the pupils who present themselves in accordance with its requirements, I can begin instruction on the above named date... I shall await further instructions, keeping myself in readiness to begin service with you on the 4th.[1]

Because the new Latin School was largely viewed as a trial of the as-yet-unproven proposition that girls had the ability to study a college preparatory curriculum, and because few men with Tetlow's educational qualifications had sought the position, many felt it was a great risk to his professional career to leave Friends Academy, one of the finest small private schools in Massachusetts. "The position of master . . . was considered entirely unworthy of a lettered man, so that when John J. Tetlow became master of the school . . . he was severely criticized for giving his talents to such an unworthy cause."² But an inward voice had challenged Tetlow to accept the headmaster's position at a school that few people believed could be the equal of Boston Latin School.

Tetlow had been asked to take a look at two prospective buildings for the new school. His options were to share a building with Girls' High School on West Newton Street in the South End or to take a portion of another school building on Exeter Street.

He arrived on West Newton Street to find that the school was situated not on cobblestone but on a wide dirt road that had become snow clogged and almost impassable. The Church of the Unity stood to the left of the school, and to the right was a row of brick townhouses with double-bowed fronts. Tetlow proceeded to the front door.

At the time of its dedication on April 19, 1871, Girls' High School was the largest in New England and the most expensive school built in the United States.³ At the street level, the school was constructed of granite blocks, and the upper three stories were of pressed red brick. It contained 66 rooms, of which only 26 were classrooms; 7 provided seating for 100 students, and the smallest rooms would hold 75. Said Lucy Woods in her history of Girls' High School, "The autumn of 1870 saw the school [Girls' High School] established in the new mansion on West

West Newton Street entrance to Girls' Latin and Girls' High Schools; Church of the Unity is seen just past the school.

The Headmaster

JOHN TETLOW: EARLY YEARS

Born on April 1, 1843, in Providence, Rhode Island, John Tetlow graduated from Providence High School in 1859 and then enrolled in Brown University. Tetlow could recall vividly the day he graduated from Brown. Families flocked to the trains on September 5, 1864, for the graduation, which coincided with the festivities for Brown's centennial celebration. A classmate wrote of Tetlow, "He was, as is not always the case in a college class, not only our first scholar, but the most popular man in our class. He was so, not only on account of his scholarship, which was preeminent, but also because of his genial, frank, attractive character."[4]

The graduation was held in First Baptist Meeting House, tucked at the base of the college. When the valedictorian of the class was announced, all eyes turned to Tetlow. In a clear voice and with eloquent diction, he spoke about the true glory of a college, and his words were enthusiastically received.

After college, from 1864 to 1865, Tetlow was principal at the Maple Street Grammar School in Fall River, Massachusetts, and then was a teaching assistant in nearby New Bedford at Friends Academy, where he became headmaster in 1869. Friends Academy, established in 1810 by wealthy Quakers as a private, classical school, had added a separate girls' school in 1855, and it merged with the boys' school nine years later. A graceful two-story brick building with a bell tower at its northwest corner had been built in 1856, replacing the original buildings. There, approximately 80 children of the well-to-do were taught Latin and Greek in preparation for Harvard and Yale.

Through Henry F. Harrington, superintendent of the New Bedford Public Schools, Tetlow met Henry's daughter, Elizabeth Vincent Harrington, with whom he soon fell in love. They were married on July 5, 1870, he at age 27 and she at 21. Their first daughter, Elizabeth, whom they called Elsie, was born March 31, 1875. When she was almost two, a second baby, Helen, was born on February 1. Over the weeks after Helen's birth, Elizabeth fell ill from blood poisoning brought on by childbirth. Despite her husband's vigilant prayers, she died of septicemia on March 18, 1877. Tetlow mourned her loss deeply.

John Tetlow, Brown University graduation photograph, 1864

Tetlow returned to Friends Academy in September to teach, but he was restless and dissatisfied. In December he heard about the new position in Boston through Henry Harrington, who had once taught at English High School. Partly to help Tetlow escape his memories, Harrington encouraged him to relocate to educationally more progressive Boston, and Mrs. Harrington agreed. The most difficult decision was to leave Elsie and Helen behind in the care of the Harringtons. As a single man, Tetlow could not possibly care for an infant and a toddler in Boston. But Elizabeth's sisters, Frances and Mary, assured him that they would all love and care for the girls as their own.

With that difficult decision made, he wrote back to accept the position at the new Latin school for girls.

Newton Street, substantial, dignified and large enough, it was believed, for all future needs. It was the pride of the city, the show school."5

Tetlow carefully made his way up the snowy gray granite slabs that formed the stairs, and pulled open one of the heavy paneled doors. Up a short flight of interior stairs, he saw on his left a reception room for visitors furnished with black walnut furniture and a number of lovely works of art. Immediately after the reception area was a corridor leading to the headmaster's office. The spacious office was neatly furnished, and the walls were lined with bookcases. The room that would be assigned to Girls' Latin on the first floor was located on the westerly side of the building and overlooked the Church of the Unity. Tetlow walked to the main hall and into his classroom, which was approximately 30 by 45 feet.

He also toured the rest of the immense building. On the third floor, he was struck by the cavernous assembly hall. At the front of the hall was a stage, and around the entire perimeter of the ceiling was a white-plaster copy of the Parthenon frieze that once adorned the Temple of Athena at the Acropolis of Athens. The impressive frieze was a reproduction made from molds created by D. Brucciani & Co., London, from the original in the British Museum and given by Mr. and Mrs. James Barnard, Bostonians then living in London. The frieze represented the great procession of a national festival called Panathenaea and included chariots, maidens bearing baskets, and other tributes to Athena. In the middle of each of the wall panels was a bust balancing on what seemed to be a precariously small, scrolled pedestal. Six full-sized statues,

The Assembly Hall at Girls' High School

The Headmaster

including those of Diana, Venus, Polymnia, and Demosthenes, occupied the front, sides, and rear of the room.

Although Tetlow also had been offered a different building on Exeter Street, he knew he would choose this new building with its classical assembly hall. But it would still be an inauspicious start. He would have just enough students to fill half of the 75 seats. He finished his inspection and closed the door behind him. That evening he met with members of the Committee on Latin and High Schools, and they agreed the West Newton Street building would be more suitable. Room 1, on the first floor of the Girls' High School building, together with an adjoining recitation room, would constitute the entire school.

THE FIRST ENTRANCE EXAM

The temperature at sunrise on Monday, February 4, 1878, was 12 degrees. All eyes in Boston were on John Tetlow, particularly those of the 43 hopeful young girls, averaging 15 years of age, who braved the naysayers, the frigid temperatures, and the snow-mounded streets to apply to this new school that they were certain would allow them a far greater chance of going on to college.

To allay concerns that the new school might become confused with the Public Latin School of Boston (which at the time was the formal name for BLS used by the Boston School Committee), Girls' Latin was prohibited from including the word *Boston* in its title. The name of the Latin school for girls was shortened to Girls' Latin School (GLS), and the two Latin schools now represented both the oldest and youngest schools in the city.

When the girls arrived to register at the Boston School Committee offices on Mason Street, they were warmly greeted by Abby May, Charles Flint, and other committee members before being seated at the members' desks. The room buzzed with excitement, and many parents, including Emily Talbot, recognized each other from the weeks of hearings.

Flint, rising to speak, welcomed everyone and introduced the new school's first headmaster. John Tetlow, five feet nine inches tall, had a high, broad forehead; ice-blue eyes; and a medium frame. His most distinctive characteristics, however, were his potent intellect and effusive personality. An 1891 *Boston Daily Globe* article offered its own

Left to right: Alice Mills, Mary Mason, and Vida Scudder, class of 1880

description: "Tetlow . . . has a reddish beard that resembles in color and in shape that which was so familiar a feature of the personal appearance of Gen. Grant. He has a courtly and distinguished bearing. His conversation has a fine vein of gentle humor. He looks like a man born to command and his features . . . are indicative of great resolution."[6]

As John Tetlow surveyed the roomful of girls and young women ranging in age from 12 to 18, he noticed they wore outfits usually reserved for church or special occasions. The younger girls wore heavy cotton calico or plaid prints to just below the knee. The older girls wore ankle-length dresses of rich velvets and wools in bright greens, reds, and blues elaborately looped, draped, and layered over a dark underskirt. On top, they matched tight-fitting bodice jackets fastened with quarter-size buttons over fancy shirts with bows, lace collars, and chokers pinned tight at the neck. They had on gloves, hats, leather button-up boots, and heavy sealskin capes against the cold.

From the applications he had already received, Tetlow knew that the girls came from both public and private schools, and that some had even returned from European travel to apply to GLS. Boston's 20 grammar schools as well as Girls' High School had presented their best and brightest for testing. All were "allured by the fame of a new experiment—sound college preparation for girls, offered by the city."[7]

Tetlow asked the prospective students to answer on paper eight questions about their age, previous schooling, and the college they wished to attend. Glancing over the completed forms, he saw that an

The Headmaster

Abby C. Howes had applied to enter the eighth grade, or Fifth Class. "Miss Abby Howes?" he called out. A shy girl, who was the just the "merest mite" of a student, stepped forward with her eyes cast down. Her skin was porcelain white.

"Why do you want to come to the Girls' Latin School, Miss Abby?" he asked of the Lilliputian-sized youngster as softly as he could.

"Because I want to go to college," she replied crisply.[8] He had all he could do not to laugh at her unexpected determination.

"The object of this preliminary meeting was to determine by examination who among the applicants were qualified to pursue the course of study to be adopted for the school," he told a news reporter.[9] The following morning, at Girls' High School, Tetlow met the approved applicants and administered the entrance exam he had prepared personally. The students were required to write test essays on three subjects. Over the next few days, Tetlow reviewed papers and occasionally chuckled.

John Tetlow, ca. 1880s

> One of these questions was, "On what grounds did the American colonies resist the mother country?" When I came to examine the papers, I was amused to find that one of the applicants, with a literalness of interpretation that foreshadowed the need of classical training, if not the ability to profit by it, had written, "Their grounds extended all the way from Lake Superior on the north to the Gulf of Mexico on the south."
>
> Happily, however, I had also assumed . . . there would be some whose training were in less familiar lines. . . . In answer to this invitation . . . one of the candidates, who has since become widely and favorably known as a writer on literary subjects, gave an account, in excellent French, of her study and travel in France.[10]

Of the 41 applicants, one did not meet the eligibility requirements and three were placed on probation. For a retrospective article on the early years of the school some 20 years later, Tetlow would recall, "As a result of this preliminary examination, the committee admitted thirty-seven pupils; and this number, by subsequent withdrawals for one reason or another, was reduced, before the end of the school year, to thirty-one."[11] Tetlow could now introduce a speech that he would repeat many times in the years to come, always with the same components but varying slightly in wording—something like this:

You are the first young ladies to have the honour of being accepted to Girls' Latin School. As pioneers, you must bear the burden of setting the example for all of those young women who will follow your path to college. You must give yourselves over to the standards and methods of which the sum and substance are educational excellence. My rules for this school will not be moderated to suit the indolent. You will not forslack the learning process in these classrooms. Let me also say, this school is not solely for the aristocratic class, but for any girl who desires it and has the brain. It comes with great commitment, at great sacrifice, and with the God's help, it will become the greatest blessing of your life.[12]

CLASSES BEGIN

The city had paid $2,000 a day to snow handlers during the week preceding the first classes at Girls' Latin School. Two-thirds of them had been let go by Monday, February 11, 1878, but a smaller force continued to clear paths throughout the city. As the accepted students made their

REGULATIONS, GIRLS' LATIN SCHOOL

Section 00—This school is established for the purpose of giving girls a thorough preparation for college.

Section 00—The principal shall have graduated with distinction at some college of good standing. He shall have a first assistant, and as many other assistants as may be necessary, provided the whole number of teachers exclusive of the principal shall not exceed one for every thirty pupils.

Section 00—This school shall be organized in six classes, and the course of study shall be for six years.

Section 00—Candidates must be at least twelve years of age, and must each present a certificate of character from the principal of the school last attended, and a written statement from the parents or guardians of their intention to give such candidate a collegiate education. They shall also pass a satisfactory examination at such time as the committee in charge may direct.

Section 00—The requisites for the admission to the sixth class shall be the same as, or equivalent to, the requisites for admission to the third class of the Grammar Schools.

Section 00—The Board of Supervisors shall examine the graduating class of each year; and the standard of examination shall be that of admission to colleges of the highest grade. Pupils who have completed the course of study to the satisfaction of the Committee on Examinations shall be entitled to a diploma.[13]

way to West Newton Street for the first day of classes, it was cold and cloudy, the winter refusing to lessen its vise-like grip.

An editorial had appeared in the *Boston Daily Globe* the previous week that lobbed a familiar shot at the new school. A merchant and former member of the Boston School Committee wrote, "Of all of the intense follies of the present hour, this scheme of a Latin School for girls seems to us to be the crowning folly."[14] But a brave new student rebutted the Boston statesman: "A crowning folly to furnish the girls of Boston with an opportunity, by establishing a 'Girls' Latin School,' by and through which they may be permitted to assist in winning honor for Boston, for if there is any institution of our city of which she has reason to be proud, and from which honor has arisen, that institution is the Boys' Latin School."[15] The merchant tried to resurrect the belief that women belonged at home: "Shall we educate girls so that they can't be domestic and so force husbands to do the housework?"[16] Public opinion was largely still opposed to the idea of higher education for women; most believed that girls belonged at home, that they could not meet the physical or mental demands of such an arduous course of study. And if they did, who would find them suitable for marriage?

After walking or taking the horsecar lines, 37 students gathered expectantly in Room 1. It appeared both stark and inflexible, a harbinger of the world into which they entered, but it was undeniably warm, and soothing to their frozen hands and feet. John Tetlow assigned each girl to a wooden desk that would become her small bit of personal sanctuary. The dark cherry desks with cast iron supports, bolted to the floor in ten rows of six each, had tops that sloped from front to back and were coated with shellac, the faint scent of which permeated the room. At the upper righthand corner of each was a Best glass inkwell, and a hollow for ink styli and pencils crossed the desk's top edge. The floors were hard southern yellow pine sealed with hot linseed oil.

Covering all four walls was a vast expanse of blackboard. Chalk clouds had turned the black surfaces to gray, and the ledges were caked white with chalk dust. Three large oak teacher's desks on a raised platform fronted the room and were neatly stocked with enormous dictionaries some six inches thick, large blue world globes in dark walnut cradles, and rows of leatherbound textbooks. The most inviting feature of the room was the window seats, wide stretches of wood that bridged the radiators. Outside the panes above these berths was the boisterous world of West Newton and Pembroke Streets.

The course of study at GLS ran six years, from what is known today as seventh to twelfth grade, and was identified by the number of years a student had remaining. The Sixth Class had six years, the Fifth five years, and so forth. Tetlow had divided the first group of students into three classes according to aptitude: sixth, fifth, and third.[17] The youngest class was seated at the front so he could command their shorter attention spans more easily.

The School Committee's regulations for Girls' Latin School stated, in part, "This school is established for the purpose of giving girls a thorough education for college. Candidates must be at least twelve years of age, and must each present a certificate of character from the school last attended, and a written statement from parents or guardians of their intention to give such candidate a collegiate education."[18] A classical education is rooted in the belief that study of the classics is the basis of an educated mind. Like the curriculum at Boston Latin School, the courses at Girls' Latin included the classics (six years of Latin, three years of Greek, ancient history) as well as modern fields of study (English, geography, mathematics, natural sciences, history, and French). The courses were considered extremely difficult.

Apart from the curriculum, the school was distinctive for the amount of homework that was required. When the school was approved, Superintendent Philbrick had commented, "It should be remembered that preparation for college, either of a boy or of a girl, is no light undertaking. . . . The work cannot be adapted to the pupil, as it can in all other schools, but the pupil must be adapted to the work."[19] Two-and-a-half hours of daily home studies were assigned. The ability and strength to take on any amount of work and accomplish it would be an integral factor in each girl's success at Girls' Latin School.

Obstacles remained. Tetlow had been trained to teach Greek and Latin, and he was, first and foremost, an outstanding teacher of the classics.[20] "At that time girls studying Greek was a novelty even in Boston," recalled Tetlow. "At the beginning of this period the prevailing opinion in the social and perhaps educational world was that girls' minds were not fitted to cope with so severe a subject as Greek; and yet Greek was almost universally held to be an essential part of the preparation needed for a collegiate education."²¹ He had even read a comment in the *Boston Globe* regarding whether it was advisable to burden young minds with such a demanding curriculum. Tetlow knew that, although it would take time, he would be able to remedy this false perception.

He quickly came to be regarded as strict but fair, and his reputation for accuracy was legendary. He believed that this value underpinned all strong, disciplined learning. "Accuracy in each least detail was to him a matter of extreme importance," noted one new student.²² The rigor of his lessons is apparent in a story he told his students: "*Endorse*, from the Latin word *indosare*.²³ *In* meaning 'in or upon,' *dorsum* meaning 'back.' So there is no need to say, 'Endorse the check on the back,' it is redundant. It is an inaccurate statement. A mind which condones these slight inaccuracies of speech will tolerate mistakes in other lines. This will lead to poor workmanship."²⁴

Even for someone far less demanding, both leading the school and serving as sole teacher would have been impossible. In an interview in 1898, Tetlow allowed as much: "Although the number of pupils for the first year was small, the number of classes was too great to be taught by one person; and Miss Lucy C. Elliott was appointed to serve as temporary teacher until a permanent assistant should be chosen. At the end of a few weeks Miss Sheldon, who was then teaching in the West Roxbury High School, was appointed as the first permanent assistant."²⁵

The inaugural term was short, less than five months long, and in June, Tetlow again oversaw the admissions examination for 35 new applicants.

Three early GLS graduates who went on to earn degrees from Smith College (from left to right): Elizabeth S. Mason, GLS class of 1882 (Phi Beta Kappa at Smith '86); Martha E. Everett '84 (Smith '88); and Fannie Goodwin '86 (Smith '90; Radcliffe College '94)

He then closed his room and dismissed his students, knowing that the following September he would fill 50 of the 75 desks in the room.

During the first week of September 1878, the public schools of Boston prepared for the new school year, and many families who had escaped from the hot summer of the city to the cool countryside now returned. On Beacon Hill, two servants finished opening the house at 86 Charles Street while its owner Harriet Dutton Scudder prepared to enroll her 16-year-old daughter Vida Scudder in the Girls' Latin School. Hand-sewn dresses had to be washed, shoes cleaned, and school supplies put in order.

Born Julia Davida Scudder in Madurai, India, in 1861, Vida's missionary father, David Coit Scudder, had drowned when she was an infant, after which she and her mother returned to the United States. Both the Duttons and Scudders were old Yankee families. Vida grew up in a well-educated, upper-class environment surrounded by aunts, uncles, and grandparents. At age six, her mother took her to Rome for four years, where she learned to love Italian culture. Upon their return, they moved to Boston's Charles Street. Many years later, Vida wrote,

> I honor my mother for entering me, in the autumn of 1878, at the much heralded and just organized Girls' Latin School in Boston. She made her decision, so far as I remember, without consulting me; for her daughter never had confided to anyone the private fairy tale wherein, disguised as a boy, she crept into Harvard.[26]

She also recalled her first day of school.

> In the room of the old high school building, where the candidates for the new Latin School for girls were assembled, a very frightened small girl found herself confronted by a cheerful, decisive, red-haired gentleman, whose demands for definite knowledge on her part were a new phase in her experience.[27]

Girls' Latin School enrolled an eclectic mix of girls from every part of the city and each layer of the social strata. Worldly Scudder was a self-professed snob and not quick to warm to some of her classmates from working-class families. Her Second Class included Alice M. Mills,

Charlotte W. Rogers, Mary L. Mason, Alice S. Rollins, and Miriam S. Witherspoon. Mary Mason lived in the South End, on West Chester Park, about ten streets from West Newton. Alice Rollins was a West Roxbury resident. Miriam S. Witherspoon lived on Eden Street in Charlestown, and her father was a ship chandler. Charlotte Rogers lived at 38 Melville Avenue in Dorchester with her widowed mother, Maria. Scudder reflected:

> To begin with, I found myself with girls who seemed, though they weren't, much younger than I. Most had come through the Public School system; they were unsophisticated, they had no contact with the society buds with whom my former school life had been cast. They lived, astounding fact to me, at the South End. They seemed almost like little girls. Especially Mary M., the class phenomenon, her black curls tied at her neck, her plaid dress, ugly to my eyes, up to her knees. I now did my hair up; I wore skirts uncomfortably long, touching the ground, as was deemed decorous for all but children.[28]

Alice Mills described that first group of girls to enter the school as "so prim, so straight-laced, so altogether different," retaining in their attitudes "a sort of timid awe—awe of teachers, of each other, of the still rather unusual path ahead of them."[29] Surprisingly, their intellectual skills were greater than even Tetlow could have imagined. His biggest challenge would be to motivate this group to their fullest capability. Scudder was ranked fourth, although she would later be one of the first American women admitted to Oxford University. Their final grades for that first term were as follows: Mary Mason, 99.3; Alice Mills, 91.78; Charlotte Rogers, 87.2; and Vida Scudder, 81.29. Scudder observed, "They knew how to study . . . oh! the grades of Mary M., compared with mine!"[30]

Scudder became an early object of Tetlow's attention; her aloofness, bordering on arrogance, needed reining in. On the other hand, he had learned quickly that Mary Mason was too fragile to treat roughly. After correcting her more than once, with his hand on the enormous dictionary that sat on his desk, he had warned her in a stern voice, "Miss Mary, I am greatly tempted to throw this book at your head if you make that mistake again."[31] She had so cowered before him he feared she might never return to school.

The young Scudder, on the other hand, had iron in her veins. Tetlow, fully conscious of the last-name basis headmaster Moses Merrill employed with his boys, rebuked her. "Miss Scudder, it is hard for me to conceive how a young woman of your intelligence can recite so like a fool." She recalled her response: "Miss Scudder, not mouse-like at all, broke into a laugh. He had struck her funny spot; and they were friends from that minute."[32] Even so, she would soon find that careless work was no laughing matter for the headmaster. For the fiftieth-anniversary of the GLS, in *The Jabberwock*, a student recalled his bearing in the classroom:

> We were all a little afraid of Mr. Tetlow in those early days. He was a young man, though we did not realize it. There was an honest scorn of stupidity, still more of laziness in him; there was an occasional vehement outbreak when our work was slipshod, which kept us, to tell the truth, perennially scared. When those kindly blue eyes flashed, and the red ran swiftly up to the roots of his hair, his class held its breath anxiously.[33]

And in a memoir, Scudder recounted a personal remonstrance.

> The evident bewilderment of our Head that we could be so stupid ... tempered by that warm kindliness on which, through all difficulties, we soon came to rely, were more effective than any reprimands.... After a week or two, during which I had rather scornfully surveyed my schoolmates, and condescended with amused distaste to a machine-made system, Mr. Tetlow summoned me. I don't know what I expected—not promotion, for we seven big girls had been put into the First Class, that famous "first class" to be graduated from a deservedly famous school. But I did not expect what I got. For none too gently I was told that my inaccuracy of mind and my blunders in parsing poor Caesar were so blatant that I must be put down to a lower class—the third, for no second class had been organized—with girls much younger than myself.... The intolerable shame! I tingle to this day. And what little capacity for close application or for scholarly precision I may have, I trace to that conversation with Mr. Tetlow. Salutary sting, blessed discipline! When I hear casual talk about Progressive Education and the need to indulge the aptitudes

of the dear children, and to encourage their "self-expression"—sacred phrase!—by letting them follow the line of least resistance and do what they enjoy, I wonder what would have happened to me if my young nose at that critical point of adolescence had not been rubbed in the Latin subjunctive.[34]

Scudder insisted that that first GLS class did not have an easy time.

I believe ease is never a characteristic of the Girls' Latin School training. . . . We were not treated like future young ladies: we were handled like boys. The old exhilaration comes back to me at this moment as I think of it. And with all our woes—they seemed many to us then—we had one great compensation. To us was given the thrill of the pioneer. You cannot feel it now. Women will rarely, if ever, feel it again.[35]

THE SEED FOR RADCLIFFE COLLEGE IS SOWN

The thrill of being a pioneer was shared by another brave young woman, who would not only give rise to the most prestigious women's college in the United States but also establish the bar of excellence for a GLS teacher. Abby Leach was born on May 28, 1855, to Marcus and Eliza Paris Bourne Leach. She graduated from Brockton High School at the age of 14 and from Oread Collegiate Institute in Worcester at 16, where she taught from 1873 to 1878. That fall, she moved to Cambridge.

Leach had developed an enormous interest in ancient languages as a young girl. Although she would not be allowed to enter Harvard Yard for classes, Leach managed to persuade two Harvard professors, James B. Greenough in Latin and William M. Goodwin in Greek, to take her on as a private student. At first Goodwin had smiled at her request but politely declined to teach her. She looked so crushed with sadness that he reluctantly pulled a Greek book from a shelf and asked her to translate, certain her inabilities would be revealed and his decision confirmed. After the first page, he rose from his chair, extended his hand, and agreed to accept her as his student.

Her requests cleverly evaded Harvard rules. In his inaugural speech of 1869, Harvard president Charles Eliot had stated, "The Corporation

Abby Leach

will not receive women as students into the college proper, nor into any school whose discipline requires residences near the school."[36]

Leach studied voraciously during the day and, as dusk fell, retreated to a boarding house, as no dormitories were available to women and the area around the college was only dimly lit by flickering gas street lamps. As the first woman to be taught by Harvard professors, she aroused considerable curiosity: who was this young lady who believed she was as smart as the Harvard College men? No one had seen her yet. One young man reportedly opined in scorn, "She is an x, a missing quantity!"[37] And in true Harvard tradition, "an x" became "annex"—Harvard Annex.[38]

After Leach's tutoring had begun, Arthur Gilman, director of a Cambridge school for girls, invited Professor Greenough and his wife to spend the evening in his library. There he outlined his plan to offer a small group of women the same Harvard courses offered to men. Greenough agreed to support the plan after his experience of teaching Leach. With the encouragement of Gilman, Greenough, and Goodwin, seven women proposed this plan to President Eliot. Although he made it clear that women would not receive a diploma equivalent to an official Harvard credential, Eliot approved the idea.

Candidates for study at Harvard Annex would take the same entrance examinations and tests as Harvard-bound men and, after the completion of coursework, receive certificates that they had fulfilled the requirements of a degree from Harvard College. These certificates were awarded based on the recommendation of the Academic Board, a group of Harvard professors.[39] However, Harvard students and professors alike largely remained opposed to coeducation. Eliot had, after all, insisted that the college would never enroll women.

Abby Leach, along with 26 other young women, presented herself for examination on September 24, 1879, and was accepted as a special graduate student. Classes were held in two rented rooms at a private residence at 6 Appian Way (the present location of the Monroe C. Gutman Library). Compared to the stately buildings of Harvard Yard, a clapboard colonial-period house may have seemed a pedestrian beginning. But it was another important step forward for women aspiring to higher education.

The Society for the Collegiate Instruction of Women, the formal name of Harvard Annex, was incorporated in October 1882 and become Radcliffe College in 1894. Leach was invited back to speak at the 25th commencement of Radcliffe College in 1903 and President LeBaron Briggs introduced her. "No one can speak more fitly at a Radcliffe Commencement than she who was the Commencement of Radcliffe College."[40]

EMILY TALBOT FIGHTS ON

On November 15, 1879, Emily Talbot hurried to a meeting at Park Street Church near the Boston Common. Three days earlier, a group of women had met at Freeman Place Chapel on Warren Street, where they discussed the future of Boston's public schools. At the conclusion of the meeting, it was resolved that they must place women on the ballot for School Committee and encourage all women to exercise their newly acquired right to vote when committee elections next occurred. Then they formed a committee to organize and inform women voters.

The 19th Amendment giving women the right to vote would not pass until 1920, but in 1874 the Massachusetts legislature gave women the right to serve on Boston's 24-member School Committee. Four women were elected in 1874, but the committee refused them their seats, a ruling that was later upheld by the Massachusetts Supreme Court. This episode resulted in the enactment of the new legislation, supported by the Women's Education Association, that gave women the legal right to serve.

In December 1875, four women were elected: Abby W. May, Lucretia B. Hale (grandniece of the Revolutionary War patriot Nathan Hale, and daughter of the owner and editor of the *Boston Daily Advertiser*), Lucia M. Peabody (one of the ablest educators in New England), and Lucretia Crocker (who revolutionized math and science teaching in Boston while working with scientists at Harvard and the Massachusetts Institute of Technology), all of whom were strong advocates of girls' education and greatly favored by many mothers. May was elected for three years; however, she was not re-elected by male voters when her term expired in 1878. "The failure to re-elect Miss May was the immediate cause of the movement to secure school suffrage for women," reported a close friend.[41]

A petition was sent to the state legislature asking that women be allowed to vote for School Committee members. On April 10, 1879, legislators approved the measure with surprisingly little opposition: 129 in favor to 69 against. Abby W. May had been elected chairman of the new committee to organize women voters, and Talbot had agreed to become secretary. Now the committee began the search for candidates.

Emily Talbot's regret that girls could not attend Boston Latin School had persisted even after the founding of Girls' Latin School. Regret eventually solidified into resolve, and she decided she would continue to fight to open the doors of the Boston Latin School to girls. After lengthy consideration, she decided to run for School Committee herself, and on November 28, she was nominated for the School Committee ticket as a Republican. May refused to run again; the two other women candidates were Lucretia Hale and Sarah Lane. Only Talbot was publicly denounced as a radical. Public schools superintendent John Philbrick wrote an open letter to the editors of the *Boston Home Journal* opposing her candidacy.

> In your issue of Saturday you say that Boston Girls' Latin School was established through the efforts of Mrs. Talbot, who has been nominated by the Republicans as a candidate for school board. This seems to have been stated as a reason for her nomination. But the truth is that Girls' Latin School was established not through the efforts of Mrs. Talbot, but in spite of her persistent and strenuous opposition. During the whole time the establishment was under consideration by the School Board, something like three months, she was the organizer and leader of the opponents of the measure in six or seven hearings at the School Committee rooms. She was, it is true, strongly in favor of providing, at the public expense, for the instruction of girls in Latin and Greek as a preparation for college, but her plan for doing this was to admit girls to the public Latin School for boys, thus converting that institution to a mixed school. And it is precisely because she is an *extreme* advocate of coeducation of the sexes, and will doubtless, if elected, exert herself to change all our schools, both high and grammar, from separate to mixed schools, that I should not favor her election.[42]

The *Boston Daily Advertiser* replied the next day.

> This statement does great injustice to Mrs. Talbot, as will be seen by everyone who recalls the circumstances . . . on every side Mrs. Talbot was congratulated on the success of her efforts, and today the girls'

Latin school, which but for her strenuous exertion in its favor would not have existed, is giving classical training to more than one hundred girls. It seems strange that, after two years have passed, Mr. Philbrick should desire to place Mrs. Talbot in such false light before the citizens of Boston.[43]

Talbot and her daughter Marion, who was now a senior at Boston University, returned on Friday to the vestry of the Park Street Church, where May's committee had arranged another meeting of registered women voters. Marion helped Emily with her secretary's responsibilities, and despite the opposition from Philbrick, "the committee's nominations were confirmed after amusing questions on the views of the candidates in temperance, women's suffrage, etc."[44]

The city elections were held on Tuesday, December 9, a clear, cold, and crisp slice of late autumn. At the polls, men showed great courtesy to the women who were voting for the first time, stepping aside to allow them to cast their vote, not smoking until noon, and removing their hats. They gave their attention to any women who needed assistance. Although carriages had been arranged for women who felt they might lose their courage to come vote, the female turnout of 862 was considered light.

Accompanied by her husband and daughter, Emily prepared to vote for the first time in her life. Voting ticket in hand, she entered the polling room. Men stood behind a large wooden box, and police were stationed as supervisors. She was asked to confirm her name, and then a slide on the box was opened and she dropped her ticket in. Marion Talbot recalled, "Papa and Mama and I went to the polls, cast our ballots. Everything went on very naturally, no remarks were made, and everyone was perfectly polite."[45]

Emily Talbot received 10,262 votes, leaving her in fifteenth place for eight seats. "At 6 P.M. we heard Prince was elected by 2,700 votes, so we knew that Mama was not elected," stated Marion Talbot, who also recalled, "A great day for the women of Boston. It remains to be seen whether they are equal to their great responsibility. . . . No women elected, alas!"[46]

The New York Times reported:

> Mrs. Dr. Talbot, who was defeated, was one of the most active women in educational reform, and has done much to bring about

the Girls' Latin School and raise the standard of female education. She was especially marked for sacrifice by those opposed to women on the School Board and to the new methods in the conduct of school affairs.[47]

May assured her committee that their efforts would pay off in the long term, although the immediate sting of defeat had been great. Emily Talbot had not given up.

CHANGING OF THE GUARD

When Philbrick resigned in March 1879, Tetlow had the chance to meet with the new superintendent of schools, Samuel Eliot, who had served as headmaster of Girls' High School from 1872 through 1876.[48] He found Eliot quite sympathetic, saying that "the Girls' Latin School is at the opposite pole. Its purpose, its course, its details, its means, are all of our own day. It begins without a tradition to either check or inspire its

A photograph taken in September 1880 when these students entered the Smith College class of 1884; it is believed to show five of the six members of the first GLS graduating class. Left to right: (seated) Annie Amelia Allis; Alice M. Mills, GLS 1880; unidentified student; (standing) unidentified student; Vida D. Scudder, GLS 1880; and Mary L. Mason, GLS 1880. The two unidentified students are presumed to be Charlotte Rogers and Miriam S. Witherspoon (both GLS 1880).

members."[49] Eliot went on to quote John Milton's *Paradise Lost*: "The world all before them, where to choose their place?" Eliot would remain in office only two years before being replaced by Edwin Seaver in 1880.

At the end of June 1880, John Tetlow had much on his mind—not only the first graduation from Girls' Latin, but his own impending nuptials as well. Tetlow was pleased that five of the six members of the class had applied to Smith College. For each candidate he had written out a recommendation confirming that the student was ready for the Smith College entrance exam and sent them off to President L. Clark Seelye. Now he sat in his office signing the last few diplomas and considering just how much these girls had accomplished. After all, only about a thousand women went on to attend college each year in the United States. A few days later, Tetlow handed out diplomas in the classroom without pomp or circumstance. Five of the graduates then took the train to Northampton, Massachusetts, and a horse-drawn buggy from the train to Smith College. It was great news when all of them were accepted to the class of 1884 and became part of only the second class to graduate from Smith College.

The heat wave had started in mid-June, and the 90-degree weather had persisted for ten days. The grass on Boston Common was so dry and yellow that a horse-drawn Boston fire steamer was ordered to soak the park lawn with water after the sunset. But thankfully, the weather would cool in time for the many events planned for the coming Independence Day weekend. The city had organized professional scull races on the Charles River, sailing regattas off City Point, canoe and tub races on Jamaica Pond, and bicycle races on Commonwealth Avenue. Thousands would gather to watch a hot air balloon fill and then take flight from Boston Common, and the much-anticipated fireworks display would be set off at eight o'clock that evening.

On July 1, in the hot summer sun, Elizabeth Proctor Howard wed John Tetlow.

Howard never could have imagined she would marry 18 months after starting to teach at GLS in January 1879 as only the second teacher appointed. One of the most beloved teachers at the school, the 27-year-old Miss Howard was received warmly. "One of my pleasantest memories is of their open-hearted receptions of me when I came to the school as a young, rather inexperienced teacher," she recalled later.[50] According to Charlotte W. Roger, "Miss Howard was not only a good teacher, but she was also a real friend to the girls, smoothing out many difficulties, even those outside her own department.... As we have learned much from Mr. Tetlow's passion for accuracy, so we have learned from Miss Howard the meaning of *suaviter in modo* [sweetly in way] which her gentle manners always illustrated."[51]

Almost immediately upon meeting her, Tetlow had felt an affinity for the new teacher. After a suitable courtship period, which the students embraced as a welcome romantic diversion from their "dry years of college preparation," the couple announced their engagement.[52] Appropriately, the ceremony was officiated by Reverend James Freeman Clarke, who had fought so valiantly to establish GLS. Women could not marry and continue to teach for the Boston Public Schools, so Howard retired after the June graduation. Tetlow immediately brought Elsie and Helen to Boston so they could reunite as a family.

GLS AND HARVARD ANNEX CONNECT

John Tetlow knew that building Girls' Latin School's reputation and standards would require a cadre of obsessively dedicated teachers. Almost all of the masters and junior masters at BLS were Harvard graduates. In addition to the first two teachers, Jane Sheldon and Elizabeth Howard, he brought on two more—Augusta Curtis in January 1879 and Jessie Girdwood the following September. Boston School Superintendent Edwin Seaver informed Tetlow the following year that he could replace his new wife by hiring one new teacher for the 107 students. With little hesitation, he selected a remarkable young woman brought to his attention by the professors at Harvard Annex, who said she was as adept in Greek and Latin as any of the advanced male Harvard students.

In September 1880, 25-year-old Abby Leach was hired to teach Latin and Greek at Girls' Latin, where she impressed her students with her scholarship and depth of learning. While at GLS, she met Florence Cushing, who may have persuaded her to leave the school in September 1883 for a teaching position at Vassar College. Although she was never formally enrolled or took a course at Vassar, she received an A.B. and A.M. in 1885 on the basis of her certificate from Harvard Annex and her scores on Vassar's examinations. She went on to teach Greek and Latin at Vassar for more than 30 years.

William M. Goodwin, Eliot Professor of Greek Literature at Harvard, later wrote this letter of recommendation for her.

> Miss Abby Leach studied Greek with me during the three years from 1878 to 1881 and half of the following year. She did as difficult work as that which is done by the most advanced students at Harvard College, and did it as well as they do it. I am confident that if she had been a male student of the College, she would have graduated with the highest honors in Classics.[53]

John Tetlow learned one of the most important lessons of his professional career from Leach: To produce the best and brightest students, his classes must be taught by the best and brightest teachers. In an essay,

MARY J. FOLEY

Born in Roxbury in 1864, Mary Josephine Foley's father, Matthew, a credit bureau clerk, wanted his children to enjoy the advantages of the formal education he lacked, and he shared with his children his great love of books. At Lewis Grammar School, Mary was so far advanced that she was promoted a grade ahead of her classmates, and when the school presented no further challenge, its principal enrolled her in eighth grade at Girls' High School in September 1878.

With Tetlow's encouragement, she transferred in April 1880 to Girls' Latin School as a ninth grader. In his first two years of teaching, Tetlow never taught a young lady with Foley's brilliance, but she was daunted.

> I first saw Mr. John Tetlow when I was a pupil in the Girls' High School on West Newton Street. He was then Master of Girls' Latin School, which occupied a large corner room on the second floor of that building, Room 4. Every morning, promptly at sixteen minutes of nine, he came up the stairs from the office and made his way into Room 4. He was a man of medium height, dark complexion with a closely cropped beard, and rather stern in appearance, but with a twinkle in the corner of his eye.[54]

She found much to admire in Tetlow's teaching as well. "He was an inspiring teacher, and we were eager to please him, and to take advantage of every word that

Among the first faculty members at GLS were (from left to right): Jane Sheldon (Latin and physics), Jessie Girdwood (French and Latin), and Abbie Leach (classics)

fell from his lips," said Foley. "We went into the fourth class. This class was taking Latin with Mr. Tetlow. We sat amazed at their recitations. Our hair stood on end, and our hearts sank into our boots at the thought of competing with its members, for it was a brilliant class."[55]

She completed the four years of study at GLS in three and graduated in 1883 with her sister, Rosanna, who was three years older. Foley entered Harvard Annex in 1884, one of the first four from GLS to pass the entrance exam, and became known immediately for academic excellence, especially in mathematics.[56]

From September 1887 to September 1888, enrollment at GLS increased by 30 girls, which entitled the school to an additional teacher. On September 11, 1888, the Boston School Committee appointed Foley to Girls' Latin School as a temporary teacher. "I was very proud when Mr. Tetlow asked me to teach under him, for I felt he had confidence in my scholarship and my character," said Foley.[57] That temporary position evolved into 40 years of teaching Latin at GLS.

In a Radcliffe alumnae survey taken just months before Foley's death in 1928, she was asked, if she could choose to go to college again, whether she would choose Radcliffe. Her response suggests she considered herself an equal to men: "Yes . . . I had hoped for a Harvard degree, and there were no sectarian limitations." When asked if a woman could successfully manage a career and marriage simultaneously, she answered, "I doubt it."[58] Alice Cunningham Lacey '14 wrote of her, "In her character there was a deep spirituality which inspired others with much of her high idealism. . . . Her memory will always be fragrant in the hearts of those who knew her as a teacher or a friend."[59] The Alumnae Association established the Mary Josephine Foley Student Aid Fund in her honor and stipulated that the interest on the fund "may be used each year to assist a member of the school, preferably in the First Class, who is temporarily in need of financial assistance."[60]

he wrote, "Much as I value the knowledge of the principles that underlie the art of teaching, I set a far higher value on the thorough mastery of the subject taught.... And so I say that the first duty of a teacher, and the one that demands special emphasis at this time, is the duty of scholarship."[61]

After reluctantly accepting Leach's resignation in 1883, it was not surprising for Tetlow to select Mary Foley to come back to teach once

THE FIRST GRADUATING CLASS

Of the five students from that first GLS class who were accepted to Smith College, only Scudder and Mason graduated. Although each followed different paths, they remained loyal and supportive to their high school alma mater their entire lives.[62]

Vida Dutton Scudder (December 15, 1861–October 9, 1954)
Vida Scudder, who did not feel academically challenged at Smith, graduated Phi Beta Kappa as part of the Smith College class of 1884, only the second class to graduate from the college. One of the first American women to be accepted at Oxford University, she was greatly influenced while in England by the lectures of John Ruskin. It was then that she began to consider her life of privilege and think seriously about her responsibilities to the less fortunate.

Scudder taught at Wellesley College from 1887 to 1927. A leading expert on Franciscan history and author of sixteen books, she was a devout Anglican and committed socialist her entire life. Scudder's paternal uncle, Horace, was an editor with the *Atlantic Monthly* and later at Houghton Mifflin. E. P. Dutton, her maternal uncle, founded the publishing company that bears his name. She was also a good friend of author Louisa May Alcott.

She founded the first settlement home in Massachusetts, Denison House at Upham's Corner in Dorchester, and addressed women strikers during the Lawrence Textile Strike of 1912.[63] She was also instrumental in helping many GLS graduates go on to Wellesley and Smith Colleges.

A few years before her death, Scudder wrote in *Wellesley Magazine*, "My last word shall be one of reassurance. I have had a happy life; but I am finding my ninth decade the happiest yet."[64] When she died just a few months short of her 93rd birthday, Scudder was the last surviving member of the GLS class of 1880. Her death was reported by Florence Converse, a former editor of *The Atlantic Monthly* and her companion of many years.

Mary L. Mason (1862–June 24, 1934)
Mary Mason was the valedictorian of the class of 1880, scored highest on the Smith entrance exam, and graduated from Smith College in 1884 with Vida Scudder. Mary was a tutor in Boston from 1884 to 1886 and taught at Miss Sewall's School for Girls in Indianapolis in 1886.

On June 5, 1887, Mary, her older sister, Katie, younger sister, Elizabeth, and Smith classmate Carrie Day left on a three month vacation to Europe, an account of which is contained in her diary, now at Smith College. Upon her return, she taught at a private school in Boston from 1888 to 1889. She received an MA in Greek and philosophy she graduated—the first Catholic to do so—from Harvard Annex in 1888. Foley was also the first GLS graduate to become a teacher at her alma mater. "The School Committee of the early days gave him free hand in the selection of teachers, and they were wise in so doing. Teachers came to visit the school from all over the country. They felt sure they would see excellent teaching," Foley said. "His sense of duty was remarkable. He never asked his teachers to do disagreeable things.

from Cornell in 1892 and taught Latin at Columbus High School in Columbus, Ohio, from 1892 to 1917. She returned to Northampton and lived at 53 Crescent Street, teaching at the Mary A. Burnham School from 1917 to 1931. She died at Northampton Hospital on June 24, 1934.[65]

Alice Mountfort Mills (June 13, 1862–March 12, 1944)
After attending Smith from 1880 to 1883, Alice Mills taught music and worked in a settlement home. She went abroad to Leipzig, Germany, in 1892 to study and travel. In 1911, the Smith College alumnae catalogue has her residing at 17 Park Vale in Brookline and listed her occupation as a music teacher. In 1924, she sailed with her sister Harriet aboard the *Acadian* from New York to Bermuda on vacation. She was also the first president of the GLS Alumnae Association, which was organized in the late 1880s, and was a speaker at the GLS 50th anniversary celebration in 1928. She died at 81 years of age.[66]

Alice S. Rollins Brewster (May 8, 1861–December 30, 1901)
Alice Sophia Rollins entered Radcliffe College in 1892 when she was 31 years old and studied there for three years. Rollins was the only member of the class to marry; in later life she went by her married name, Mrs. Edwin T. Brewster.[67] She died on December 30, 1910, at the age of 48 in Andover of chronic arthritis, from which she had suffered for 10 years.

Charlotte W. Rogers (b. May 1862)
Charlotte Rogers attended Smith for one year and was an active GLS alumna; she also attended Radcliffe.[68] In 1920, Charlotte was living at 38 Melville Avenue with her sister Helen and sister's husband Edward Farrell.

Miriam S. Witherspoon (January 15, 1860–March 12, 1949)
Miriam Witherspoon attended Smith for two years—1880 to 1881 and 1882 to 1883—and from 1881 to 1882 she attended Radcliffe. She taught in Malden, Massachusetts, between 1885 and 1886 and in neighboring Everett from 1886 to 1892. She was an assistant at the Associated Charities in Boston (founded by Annie Fields) from 1892 to 1894 and served as the executive secretary of the Associated Charities in Worcester from 1894 through 1929. Witherspoon died in Worcester on March 12, 1949, at 89 years of age.[69]

He did those himself, and always stood back of his teachers. First in his mind came the good of the pupils, next the good of the teachers, ending with himself."[70]

GLS ESTABLISHES A REPUTATION FOR EXCELLENCE

Following the resignation of Girls' High School headmaster Homer Sprague in 1885, Tetlow was appointed headmaster of Girls' High School as well as Girls' Latin School and took charge of 815 girls, 653 at Girls' High and 162 at Girls' Latin.[71] There were only nine high schools in Boston, and Tetlow presided over two of them. His annual salary was increased to $3,700, and he reluctantly reduced his presence in the classroom. The headmaster's office, which he had inspected on his very first visit, was now his alone.

From 1880 through 1884, 42 girls graduated from Girls' Latin and 32 were accepted to college: 15 to Boston University, 11 to Smith College, 4 to Harvard Annex, and 2 to Wellesley College. The acceptance rate of GLS graduates to the Seven Sisters colleges was greater than 50 percent, setting a high standard for future classes.

Four of them were named to the Phi Beta Kappa honor societies of their respective colleges: Vida Scudder '80 and Elizabeth Mason '82 at Smith College; Sarah Elizabeth Briggs '83 and Mary J. Foley '83 at Harvard Annex. In 1880 and 1884, a GLS graduate achieved the highest score in the class on the Smith entrance exam, and each was awarded a $200 scholarship, a substantial sum at a time when the annual college tuition and board was $350.

The *Annual Report of the Boston School Committee 1885* reported these statistics, demonstrating its strong interest in the academic achievement of the school. By 1882, only about eight hundred women attended colleges in Massachusetts. By comparison, between 1880 and 1884, 127 students graduated from Boston Latin School, and 100 percent of them were accepted to Harvard College.

After Harvard Annex was established, President Eliot softened his stance on the education of women and began to share many educational ideologies with Tetlow. A deep professional respect and friendship grew from their meetings. Eliot reviewed the GLS curriculum, marked it up in pencil, and returned it to Tetlow, who implemented his changes.

These changes helped to ensure many a student's future entrance into Harvard Annex, so much so that it was jokingly referred to in later years as the Girls' Latin School Annex.

After assuming the dual headmastership, Tetlow would teach one Greek class for seniors only. By then, the girls of both schools had nicknamed him Zeus, for the Greek god of sky and thunder. Foley wrote, "I thought the name exceedingly appropriate. The lightning still struck on the instant, and on the spot, but as time went on the thunder rolled less loudly, and the lightning struck less frequently. He became more softened, partly of his having charge of two schools, but mostly because of the influence of his wife."[72]

1881
Marion Talbot, Ellen Richards, and others meet to discuss the needs of college-educated women.

1882
Association of Collegiate Alumnae (now American Association of University Women) is formed.

◀ **1882**
George Santayana and other Boston Latin School students found *The Register*, one of the first high school papers in the U.S.

1886
Frances Tetlow is born on June 17.

Elizabeth Tetlow and Mabel Hay Barrows enter the Sixth Class at GLS.

1887
Mary Sibyl Collar enters the GLS Fourth Class.

◀ **1888**
The first issue of *The Jabberwock* appears February 14, and Lewis Carroll gives GLS students permission to use the name.

◀ Carroll writes "A Lesson in Latin" for *The Jabberwock*, the only poem he ever published in a U.S. periodical.

1889
The Tripod is founded at Roxbury Latin School.

BLS Headmaster Charles K. Dillaway dies on May 2.

◀ **1891**
Abbie Farwell Brown, Mary Sibyl Collar, and Virginia Holbrook (first editresses of *The Jabberwock*), graduate from GLS.

◀ **1892**
Mabel Hay Barrows (*pictured, left*) and Elizabeth Tetlow graduate from GLS.

III

A Young School Finds Its Voice
The Jabberwock Is Born

Tremont Street with Park Street Church in the background, 1890–99

THE SCRIBBLERS HAVE AN IDEA

On a bright September day in 1887, Mary Sibyl Collar climbed the stairs of the West Newton Street building to start ninth grade at Girls' Latin School. Her father, William Coe Collar, had been the headmaster of the Roxbury Latin School since 1867. Collar had met John Tetlow while serving on the Boston School Committee and discovered that they both shared a passion for academic excellence and an abhorrence of inaccuracy. This meeting of minds had substantially contributed to Mary's arrival that morning at Girls' Latin School.

A steady stream of students mounted the gray granite stairs along with her. She could pick out the youngest girls, who were entering the Sixth Class, taught by Miss Sheldon; they appeared unsure of what was about to happen to them. Collar hoped that, although she too was nervous, she showed more poise than her younger schoolmates, at least outwardly. As she looked around at all the strange faces, she also wondered if she would eventually come to know every one, as the older girls seemed to. She finally found the room to which she was assigned and, with great trepidation, began high school.

Collar, who would be called Sibyl at GLS, soon made a special friend, Abbie Farwell Brown.

> My first memory of Abbie Brown takes me back as far as 1887, when Destiny decreed that I should enter Class IV of G.L.S. The only school I had known, up to that time, comprised two floors in a suburban private house, and the change was a shock. The West Newton Street building, of which the Latin School claimed only a corner, seemed like a vast unfriendly Ark, with a code—almost a Constitution—of its own; and the competence, the assurance, the resourcefulness of the girl whose name I learned was Brown, who furthermore charmed the eye with her thick golden braid and her merry blue eyes, was the first of the seven wonders of that world. For some days—it might even have been weeks—I was rebellious and intolerant. The smell of chalk and varnish, varied by wet umbrellas, used to depress me each morning, as I opened the big street door—always attacking it the wrong way, in spite of printed directions. But before long, by a mysterious attraction, I was drawn into a group of girls.[1]

Both Brown and Collar loved to write, and they quickly learned they were not alone—so did Mabel Hay Barrows, a girl from the Fifth Class, and another member of their Fourth Class, Virginia Holbrook. These new writing friends called themselves "The Scribblers" and encouraged each other's literary endeavors. Sibyl became the novelist of the class, writing romantic tales that were passed from girl to girl and read with great enthusiasm.

The oldest students, those in First Class—who were not to be referred to as "seniors," but as "Class I"—made it clear to the younger ones that they reserved the right to make all the important decisions in the school. But one day in algebra class, Collar passed a note to Barrows that read, "I've had an inspiration. Let's have a class paper."[2] They shared the note with Brown, who thought the idea brilliant, and the three immediately made plans to proceed. Brown recalled, "It was an unheard of proceeding for these insignificant under-graduates to start anything so radical as a school paper, without consulting their seniors; and the upper classes looked with scorn upon the proceedings. But the dauntless and self-confident class of '91 was not to be discouraged or snubbed."[3]

Collar agreed. "Always we must be hatching something: every recitation room was an incubator. The *Jabberwock* germ first conceived in an Algebra class, and passed on as a scrawled note, was the monopoly of Class IV, with no shadow of self-consciousness about what our 'elders' in the school might have to say. We were the goddesses on Olympus—creation was our métier. The fact was, that Abbie was the darling of the Muses, and her genius overflowed and dyed us all in purple."[4]

The name *Jabberwock*, inspired by "Jabberwocky," Lewis Carroll's famous nonsense poem in *Through the Looking Glass*, was picked from a list Brown submitted.[5] "I remember well what an exciting meeting that was wherein the new paper was to be named," she later said. "Different girls brought in lists of titles which seemed suitable, and they were all written on the blackboard. It is one of the proudest recollections of my life that the name JABBERWOCK was on the list which I submitted, and was voted by the class to be the best one. I was a fond friend of 'Alice' and knew her chronicle by heart."[6]

The girls threw themselves into publishing the paper despite the fact that they had never published anything before. Brown recalled, "One of the three editors elected by the class, Mabel Barrows, was the daughter of a really-truly editor and knew all about the business. It was a simple matter to have the paper printed—why not?"[7] Mabel Barrows did enlist the help of her parents, Samuel and Isabel Barrows, in guiding the paper's publication. "My Father and Mother, experienced and sympathetic editors, were always ready to give advice and encouragement when needed, and from them we would have our first lessons in copy revision, proof reading and making up the paper."[8]

The following flyer was sent to fellow students:

THE JABBERWOCK

A NEW SCHOOL PAPER

Conducted by the Fourth Class of the Girls' Latin School, will appear in February. It will contain spicy editorials, pithy poems, interesting anecdotes and sketches, notes from the Girls' Latin School and its brother schools, home and foreign correspondence—in short, all that goes to make up a readable and entertaining paper.

Now is the time to subscribe![9]

MARY SIBYL COLLAR

To William Coe Collar, headmaster of the Roxbury Latin School, it was a matter of utmost importance where his daughter, Mary Sibyl, would attend ninth grade. Initially, Collar argued against admitting girls to Boston Latin School, but later, as a member of the Boston School Committee, he met John Tetlow, with whom he developed a close professional relationship, and his attitude changed. "I came to know Dr. Tetlow almost immediately after his coming to Boston... and from the time that I made his acquaintance I felt his sympathetic interest in his work in the school he was founding, in its growth and in its success."[10] Collar had come to strongly favor women's suffrage and wanted an enlightened setting for his daughter's education.

His wife, Hannah C. Averill Collar, gave birth to Mary Sibyl on October 29, 1873, and her father wrote to her family in Connecticut the following day.

> I suppose you are waiting to know a few particulars about the advent of our third daughter. Hannah passed a very comfortable night and has had a good day. Her sickness lasted only about two hours, but she suffered a great deal. I went to school at 8:30, and then she was not very sick, but at the end of an hour and a half they sent for me to come home.
>
> The baby is uncommonly large for us—weighed 10 lbs. She seems very healthy and strong and our chief anxiety is likely to be to provide her with food. The baby is white haired with a very pretty head and looks, Hannah thinks, like dear Willie. Hannah has an excellent nurse.
>
> Heaven seems to refuse me a boy.
> Truly yours
> W.C. Collar
> P.S. Hannah will probably name the baby "Mary."[11]

William Coe Collar

Mary Sibyl had two older sisters, Mildred and Alice, and eventually a younger brother, Herbert. Two older brothers had died, Frederick in infancy and Willie in 1867 at the age of three as a result of an accidental drowning in an excavation hole near the family's home. In 1876, Collar bought a half-acre on Maple Street in Roxbury and built a large mansard-roofed home. To the left of the front door was Collar's library, and it was here that Mary Sibyl received her father's early lessons. "We were not 'made' to read anything as I remember, but we were definitely encouraged," she later said. "He started me at the age of six by a birthday present of a book of Shakespeare Stories, simply told, bound in green and gold, and profusely illustrated."[12]

As Sybil neared secondary school age, Collar was increasingly absorbed in writing his latest text, *The Beginner's Latin Book*, the earnings from which he hoped would provide resources for her college education. He frequently took sabbaticals to write, and teaching time with his "Sibylla" was becoming more and more limited. Collar found Tetlow's work with his girls' school inspiring and knew in his heart that GLS would provide the best classical training for his daughter's future path, and once enrolled she became known simply as Sibyl. Once Tetlow agreed to accept her, Collar helped Mary Sibyl as much as he could.

Mary Sibyl Collar, ca. 1905

I alone used to have Latin lessons with him, rather unsystematically at first in a little conversation-book that used to embarrass me by its plain-speaking, but later, when in the Girls' Latin School, I used often to read at sight my entire assignment of Ovid or Virgil to him. Not the help only over the hard spots, but the encouragement to express the meaning accurately, neatly and "beautifully"—to use one of his favorite words—was of inestimable value in setting a standard of English for me.[13]

Mary Sibyl Collar enrolled at Smith College in the fall of 1891. Over the Christmas vacation of her freshman year, her mother died at the age of 54. Soon her father would begin a relationship with a young female teacher from Roxbury Latin who was just eight years older than Sibyl.[14] Their wedding took place on January 5, 1893, about a year after Sibyl's mother's death.

Upset by these events, Sibyl left Smith College and, with fellow GLS alumna Virginia Holbrook, applied as a junior to the Harvard Annex. Although some school officials thought the two girls should enter as sophomores, they were able to obtain junior year status and graduated from Radcliffe College two years later in 1895. (The name change from Harvard Annex to Radcliffe occurred in 1894.) That summer Collar traveled to Natchez, Mississippi, where she taught Latin and English at Stanton College, a school for girls.

She returned to Dorchester a year later and married Pinckney Holbrook, Virginia's brother, on June 30, 1896, at the First Church in Roxbury. *The Boston Globe* reported, "The ceremony was witnessed by a brilliant assemblage of prominent people of Roxbury and vicinity."[15] After a short trip to western Massachusetts, the couple returned to Boston.

Sibyl Holbrook had five children, three of whom survived into adulthood,[16] and she later returned to Radcliffe to earned a master's degree that was granted in 1921.[17] Holbrook, another Scribbler, would eventually write and translate plays in French. The Holbrooks moved to Florida shortly before 1945, where Pinckney died in 1953. In 1957, Sibyl would send her father's collection of letters to the archives at Roxbury Latin with the following note:

Mr. Collar, Headmaster of the Roxbury Latin School for almost half of last century, was my father, and the author of several text-books. He also wrote many letters, and some years ago I compiled and edited a bookful of these, but have not been able to find a publisher for them. To make a long story short, I am now over eighty years old myself, and disposing of my possessions, including my literary productions which represent years of work. I hesitate to commit to the flames the MS of "The Intimate Letters of William C. Collar", and it was suggested to me the Archives of the school would be a natural repository.[18]

Finally, after much deliberation about exactly what they should publish, the first issue of the paper was ready, but the exact meaning of the word *Jabberwock* was still a mystery. "I did not know, however, *why* I had selected that particular name,"[19] said Brown. So the first three elected,

ABBIE FARWELL BROWN

At 41 West Cedar Street on August 21, 1871, an Irish servant hurried back and forth to care for a new baby. Benjamin Brown, then nearing the age of 44, had hoped that his firstborn would be a boy, but the baby girl he and his wife bore offered some consolation—she looked just like him. Benjamin and his wife, Clara, named the baby after her father's maternal aunt Abigail Farwell. The new father wrote to his mother-in-law in Hampton, New Hampshire, the next day.

When I came home to dinner yesterday (Monday 21st) I found Clara feeling unwell, that was a little past two o'clock, and I asked our next door neighbor, Mrs. Fields, to come in to see her, and I went for the Doctor and Nurse. Doctor came about half past three, and I got the Nurse there about four o'clock. The child was born, before five. Clara got along very well indeed and both are now doing nicely.

The <u>Baby</u> is a nice strong, healthy looking little <u>girl</u>, and weighs eight (8) pounds and if her appetite continues as it is, <u>she must</u> do well. So you see, <u>we</u> are doing well. Our "kitchen gal" is also doing well and taking it, all in all, we find ourselves kindly favored, and blessed, and are very grateful.

I have scratched these few lines off in a hurry so as to get the letter in-to an early <u>mail</u>, and you may have some trouble to decipher my writing, but I think you will understand that, we have got a <u>Baby</u>, and may tell that fact to all whom it may interest.

Respectfully,

Benj

P.S. Clara would be glad no doubt to add a postscript, but I should not at present of course <u>let her</u> add a letter.[20]

Abbie Brown was of Brahmin parentage. Mr. and Mrs. Benjamin Brown were listed in *Clark's Boston Blue Book*, a directory of prominent Boston families. A descendent of Isaac Allerton, an original passenger on the *Mayflower* who became assistant governor of Plymouth Colony, Benjamin owned B. Brown & Co. Oils, a wholesale dealer in whale oil, candles, drugs, and medicines, established in the 1840s. He married Clara Neal, who was 14 years his junior, on October 13, 1870.

In June 1886, when Abbie was 14, she was valedictorian of her class at the girls-only Bowdoin Grammar School.[21] After graduating, she received a handwritten letter from John Tetlow accepting her as a student at GLS. Clara Brown was pleased: as a writer who had published some of her own work, she wanted the best for her daughter.

self-dubbed "editresses"—Virginia Holbrook, Abbie Brown, and Mabel Barrows—wrote to Carroll in London asking for an explanation of, and seeking permission to use, the name. They waited for a reply as long as they could, and then went forward with printing.

After graduating GLS in 1891, Brown entered Harvard Annex but left three years later without a diploma. She also chose not to marry. "Abbie's first and last love was writing—story-telling—or verse-making. With her sweet face, merry wit, and quick sympathy, she always attracted men as well as women, and I know at least one decision—against marriage—that was slow and difficult in the making," remembered Collar.[22] Brown would lose her father, Benjamin, in March 1897; and her mother, Clara, and younger sister, Ethel (who also attended GLS) stayed on together in their home at 41 West Cedar Street.

Brown's visit in 1899 to Chester Cathedral in England inspired her first and most highly regarded children's book, *The Book of Saints and Friendly Beasts*. When it was published by Houghton Mifflin in 1900, she remarked, "It is all the *Jabberwock*'s fault that I wrote any book at all. For in four years' care of you [*The Jabberwock*], I acquired a taste for scribbling, which is rarely cured and which has broken out at last in this awful way."[23] Although Brown continued to write poetry, she never achieved the success she desired and aspired to as a *Jabberwock* scribbler. She was, however, a leading literary figure in Boston and a charter member of the New England Poetry Club in 1915 along with Amy Lowell, Caroline Ticknor, and Josephine Preston Peabody.

In 1919, Mabel Daniels, Brown's old friend and fellow GLS alumna, set to music Brown's World War I poem "Peace with a Sword." The piece was sung by the Handel and Haydn Society and played by the Boston Symphony Orchestra. Brown herself remained an active alumna: at the 1915 meeting of the Alumnae Association, she read from poetry she had written. "Her interpretation of her own words held the audience spellbound and called forth many encores," wrote an attendee.[24]

In June 1925, she had had a mastectomy of her right breast, but the cancer metastasized and traveled to her brain. Early in 1927, Brown began to lose her sight. Her friend Caroline Ticknor, granddaughter of William D. Ticknor of the publishing house Ticknor & Fields, wrote, "The sudden failing of her eyesight, always so keen and so fine, came as a staggering blow."[25] Abbie Brown succumbed to breast cancer on March 4, 1927, at the age of 55 and was buried at Mt. Auburn Cemetery in Cambridge. She gave GLS a signed copy of her first book, *The Book of Saints and Friendly Beasts*, shortly after its publication. On the first page she wrote, "Girls Latin School Dec. 1900 Presented by the author Class of '91 G.L.S." It is one of the school's most treasured possessions, as is the bound set of *The Jabberwock*, volume 1, which was inscribed by her and includes the inaugural issue.

"THE JABBERWOCK" HITS THE STANDS

On Valentine's Day 1888, as postal workers delivered the love notes in their bags, the temperature hovered at freezing. Because of the cold temperatures, extra straw had been placed on the horsecars' floors for warmth, and the deliverymen made sure the small stoves inside each car were filled with wood. That day, the first that *The Jabberwock* was in print and distributed, also saw delivery of an important letter to GLS.

That morning, the mail was placed upon Tetlow's desk as usual. Mail on Valentine's Day may well have seemed to send his young students into a swoon, but for the headmaster it was likely just school business. A small, white envelope measuring two by three inches poked out from the pile. Addressed simply "Girls' Latin School, Boston, Massachusetts, U.S.A.," its return address was Covent Garden, England. He opened it, read the letter slowly, and then, pushing back from his desk, asked Miss Sheldon to deliver it at recess to Abbie Brown, Mabel Barrows, Sibyl Collar, and Virginia Holbrook. Dated February 6, it read:

> Mr. Lewis Carroll has much pleasure in giving the Editresses of the proposed magazine permission to use the title they wished for.

The Jabberwock's *founding editresses (left to right): Mary Sibyl Collar, Abbie Farwell Brown, and Mabel Hay Barrows*

He finds that the Anglo-Saxon word "wocer" or "wocor" signifies "offspring" or "fruit." Taking "jabber" in its ordinary acceptation of "excited and voluble discussion." Whether this phrase will have any application to the projected periodical, it will be for the future historian of American Literature to determine. Mr. Carroll wishes all success to the forthcoming magazine.[26]

"I remember well the excitement with which his first letter was received by us, the editors and promulgators of that earliest number of *The Jabberwock*," said Brown. "We were a little society of wonderlandists. There was not one of us who was not ready to accept the White Rabbit as her guide through thick and thin. Not one of us but knew by heart, 'Twas brillig and the slithy toves.'"[27]

Beginning with that first issue, *The Jabberwock* was published monthly from September through June "by the Fourth Class of the Girls' Latin School, Boston."[28] Its first editors were Abbie Brown, Virginia Holbrook, and Mabel Barrows, and an annual subscription cost 50 cents. The first editorial stated, "We would have our subscribers to know that it is wholly for *their* sakes that this paper is published in English. Were it for ourselves only, we should of course print in Latin.[29]

Abbie Farwell Brown's notebook cover

Abbie Brown bought a brown paper notebook much like the notebooks she had always used as a young girl in which to keep a collection of stories for *The Jabberwock*. She entitled it "Contributions" and drew a Jabberwock on its cover. That drawing would later become the school's logo.

The Boston Latin School's *Register*, established in 1882, was one of the very first high school papers in the nation. Initially published twice a year and later every month, it was founded by George Santayana, then a BLS senior, who went on to become a poet, philosopher, and Harvard professor. The March 1888 *Register* reported:

> The young ladies of the fourth class in the Girls' Latin School have started a paper under the interesting but rather queer title of "The Jabberwock." Despite this name, the paper is bright and very readable, and has our heartiest wishes for its success. We have often wondered why the young ladies did not start a school paper, for who ever yet heard a girl acknowledge that her sex was in any way inferior to the sterner one? We are glad to see that the "Jabberwock" has at last taken the field and is determined to stay.[30]

John Tenniel's original drawing of the Jabberwock

The Roxbury Latin School's *Tripod* was established in March 1889 at the urging of Headmaster William Coe Collar, who noted that other schools were able to publish successful papers. *The Jabberwock* welcomed the newcomer: "We heartily congratulate *The Tripod* on its first appearance. Surely there must be a great deal of interest in the school to start such a large paper."[31] Rather than sharing the literary focus of *The Jabberwock*, however, the papers established at both boys' schools were geared heavily toward sports and filled with photogravures of athletes.

The format of *The Jabberwock* (which, remarkably, remained unchanged) resembled that of *The Register* in both layout and content. Each issue consisted of an editorial; student stories and poems; and school notes from GLS, Girls' High School, BLS, Roxbury Latin, and even Boston University. It carried advertisements for calling card printers, corsets, and caterers. Later it would include sections with the headings *Domi* (a listing of school events), *Alumnae* (which reported on the successes of GLS graduates), and *Ridenda* (jokes and comical moments of a GLS education).

The Jabberwock also included accounts of daily student life that showed how singular a GLS education could be. One such report read, "At Thanksgiving, when a Fifth Class member was asked what her class was thankful for, she replied, 'The Fifth Class will be thankful that Latin is a *dead* language, and they don't have to speak it all the time; that there are only five declensions; that they are no longer the 'infant' class; and they know *lots* more than the Sixth Class.'"[32]

The expense of *The Jabberwock*'s publication was the sole responsibility of the students. Barrows explained, "It was a pioneer enterprise. . . . Mr. Tetlow and teachers helped us by keeping their hands off. . . . Financial terror was our heaviest burden. How often it seemed our next issue would be our last . . . we dug the ballast to keep the ship steady, even

The Jabberwock *masthead, 1888*

VIRGINIA HOLBROOK

Although delicate and sickly in her early years, Virginia Holbrook, born in 1871, blossomed into a strong young adult. Virginia was considered the brains of the Holbrook family, and her parents thought she should attend GLS. By the time he was 64 years old, Silas Pinckney Holbrook and his wife Eliza, age 41, had four children in addition to Virginia: Pinckney, Ridgeway, Elizabeth, and John. Virginia and her siblings were raised in comfort, having both servants and an extended family of grandmother, aunt, and cousin living with them.

Virginia's grandfather had become wealthy through his investment with the Boston & Sandwich Glass Company. Her father was a real estate broker, developer, and land auctioneer who co-owned Holbrook & Fox, one of the most prestigious real estate development firms in New England. The two-story Holbrook mansion at 56 Crescent Avenue was one of Dorchester's earliest houses. A wisteria vine grew over the front door and wrapped around to the side porch on the left, and attached to the right was a large ballroom. The turret room on the roof afforded views of "the Old Harbor and an expanse of salt marsh known as The Calf Pasture."[33] In 1880, when the total valuation of the homes on Crescent Avenue was $68,000, the Holbrook estate alone accounted for $25,000, a price that rivaled those on Beacon Hill at the time.

Virginia's older brother, Pinckney, graduated from English High School in 1887, the same year Virginia started at GLS. After graduating from Radcliffe in 1895, she studied from 1900 to 1901 at the Franco-English Guild in Paris. From 1903 to 1905 she taught at Miss Ingall's School in Cambridge, and the following year she taught at Miss Alice Brown's School in Boston. Then Virginia decided to take a risk. Sibyl Collar recalled:

56 Crescent Avenue, designed by Edwin J. Lewis

Virginia had become engaged through correspondence with a young Swiss teacher in an English School, introduced by the irreproachable Mrs. Pender originally for the sake of language practice between "Lui et Elle." She left us in June [1906],[34] planning to travel abroad with an intimate woman friend, and her lover, Ernst Dick, to meet her in Paris. If they felt as much drawn to each other in the flesh as they had been for two years drawing in the spirit, they would plan a marriage (not a wedding) as soon as possible. She was to cable, and I was then to be the town-crier, and hasten announcements through the engraver.... The marriage took place in Berne, on August 7,[35] and the Dicks set up housekeeping in Basel, where Dr. Dick has a high school post.[36]

The Dicks had one daughter, Elizabeth, in 1907. Virginia Holbrook Dick died in Basel, Switzerland, on June 7, 1958, at the age of 87.

MABEL HAY BARROWS

In 1867, Isabel Hayes Chapin, who had been widowed at age 19, married Samuel June Barrows in New York. They then moved to Washington, D.C., when Samuel was offered a position as private secretary to Secretary of State William H. Seward. Isabel had studied medicine in New York and Vienna and, after earning her degree, opened an ophthalmology practice in Washington, one of the first women in the United States to do so; once she filled in as a stenographer while her husband was ill, thus also becoming the first woman employed by the U.S. State Department. After a few years, the couple left Washington for Cambridge, where Samuel enrolled in Harvard Divinity School and their daughter, Mabel Hay Barrows, was born in 1873. Upon completion of his studies, Samuel was ordained as a Unitarian minister and became pastor of the First Parish Church in Dorchester in 1876, only to resign in 1880 in order to become editor of *The Christian Register*, a Unitarian weekly periodical. In 1897, however, Reverend Barrows returned to government service when he was elected to the U.S. Congress.

As a young girl, Mabel traveled extensively with her parents. In a biography of her husband, Isabel wrote, "In September, 1875, we sailed for Germany, my husband, my sister and little Mabel, now a delightful child running about and chattering like a magpie.... We settled in Leipzig for a year."[37] Mabel often quipped, "I was born in Cambridge, learned to walk in Kansas, and to talk (both English and German) in Vienna."[38] In 1885, the Barrowses adopted their nephew, William B. Barrows—in Isabel's words, "the child of my brother, whose beloved wife died, leaving the poor little mite but a week old."[39] Born in June 1885, he was twelve years younger than Mabel. Isabel's sister and a servant often cared for Mabel and Willie when their mother's work took her away to out-of-town meetings and conferences.

The Barrows family (left to right): Mabel, Isabel, William, and Samuel

Both Reverend Barrows and Isabel Barrows were advocates for African American and Indian rights, women's suffrage, and prison reform. Isabel, now an associate editor at *The Christian Register*, was an independent and progressive woman. Mabel was strongly encouraged to excel academically, and the Girls' Latin School seemed a natural fit for her. She started the Sixth Class in September 1886 and quickly became one of the most popular girls in the class. "Joyous and original, she instilled color into the drab routine of our daily work," said a classmate.[40]

The Barrows family soon learned, however, that Headmaster Tetlow made rules and set the bar of expectation high. Tetlow was intent on dispelling once and for all the notion that girls were not physically equipped for college preparation. At a morning assembly, he lectured his students about the need to attend school every day unless they were sick enough to require a doctor's care. He had read off the names of the girls who were absent the day before, a list that encompassed about one-fifth of the school. The day after his speech, he found placed on his desk a letter from Samuel Barrows explaining that Mabel had been absent because Mrs. Barrows had been traveling and that he disapproved of Tetlow's criticism of his daughter. Tetlow wrote the following in response:

> I hardly think I deserve the censure which your note of this morning implies, though I must thank you for the kindly and courteous manner in which you convey the censure. I knew that Miss Mabel was in no way responsible for her absence ... what perhaps Miss Mabel did not quote ... that I did not wish to be understood as blaming all those whose names I had read, because I had not yet learned why they had been absent. I added, it is true, that, whatever the cause of the absence had been, girls could not expect to succeed in our course of study, and to qualify themselves for admission to college, without being regular in attendance.... But when the percentage of attendance in a class sinks to 81, which means that, on average, one-fifth of all the girls in that class are absent all the time, then I know that the instruction must be suffering seriously, and that, unless a corrective be applied, the work which we must do cannot be done.
>
> You will not, I hope, forget that I have charge of about nine-hundred girls; and that, while it is obviously my duty to give censure in private rather than a more formal way, yet, when the progress of an entire class is injuriously affected by a growing evil, ... I may find a different way more effective as well as more expeditious.[41]

The potential rift was replaced by a great friendship, and from that point onward Barrows supported the headmaster.

After graduating from Girls' Latin, Mabel Barrows left for Europe in September 1892 and studied in Leipzig, Germany. In 1893, she traveled to Greece with her father, who worked for a year with the German archeologist Wilhelm Dörpfeld to excavate the city of Troy. After this year-long experience, Mabel and her mother traveled to Sweden to study Swedish gymnastics.[42] Her experiences in Greece inspired in Mabel a keen interest in ancient Greek drama. Upon returning to the United States, she entered Radcliffe and composed a highly praised play in the style of Homer. Barrows became a stage director and dancer and coached Latin and Greek plays at many colleges and high schools.[43]

In 1905, Mabel Barrows married Henry Raymond Mussey, professor of economics at Columbia University, at Cedar Lodge, the Barrows's Vermont home on the shores of Lake Memphremagog, with eighty guests in attendance.[44] In April 1910, Mabel gave birth to a son whom she named June Barrows Mussey in honor of her father. She would travel all over the world with her husband and son, visiting China and Japan as well as Europe. In 1931, in Neubrandenberg, Germany, for a year's sabbatical with her husband, she died on November 30 at age 68. Former classmate Sarah Tappan Coe wrote a memorial article for the January 1932 issue of *The Jabberwock* in which she recalls her as "a master in the joy of living."[45]

though she careened frightfully at times. It would have broken our hearts to have the *Jabberwock* shipwrecked."[46]

In November 1888, *The Jabberwock*'s appearance changed when a block-printed image from an engraving of a Jabberwock and a boy was added to the top of the first page. The engraver had precisely copied Brown's notebook rendering of the Jabberwock. This image later became the school's logo and remained in the banner of every issue until November 1937. Brown wrote, "Although like its relative, Latin School *Register*, *The Jabberwock* cannot yet afford an entire outer garment, it can boast of a new hat, the pattern of which was designed specially for it, by a kind friend. . . . We have not yet discovered the name of the rash youth, who, armed with a pen, is trying to subdue the Jabberwock; but, whoever he is, let him remember the warning words—'Beware the Jabberwock, my son.'"[47]

In the November 1888 *Register*, editor F. G. Jackson noted the paper's design change and led off his editorial with the following: "We congratulate the Jabberwock on its new 'hat'. Instead of an innocent bird with tropical plumage, its chief ornament is a soul-appalling dragon with a limited supply of teeth, but with an enormously elongated tail. This, we presume, represents the visible incarnation of our contemporary. We shall 'beware.'"[48]

CARROLL LOSES PATIENCE

Carroll took a great interest in the magazine from its inception. From the beginning, the school forwarded every issue to him. He expressed disapproval about a piece in the first issue called "A Clerical Wit," which was a story told by George Washington in his diary about a young scholar at the University of Oxford who poked fun at a vice chancellor who kept falling asleep during the sermons at his church.

> Mr. Lewis Carroll is sincerely obliged to the Editresses of "The Jabberwock" for having kindly sent him two numbers of it. He trusts they will not take it ill, if he ventures to add a remonstrance on the admission of such anecdotes as involves jests in texts of the Bible. The one to which he alludes, is a specially solemn one—recalling, as it does, a scene quite unique in the history of the world for its intense pathos. Surely words that have been, all through these years, "dear as sacramental wine" to sorrowful hearts, are not fit vehicle for jesting? He would be very glad

to think that no other such anecdote will be admitted to the pages of this magazine.⁴⁹

The following reply was printed in the June 1888 issue of *The Jabberwock* under the title "A Friend Worth Having":

> THE JABBERWOCK has many friends, and perhaps a few, (very few, let us hope) enemies. But, of the former, the friend who has helped us most on the road to success is Mr. Lewis Carroll, the author of "Alice in Wonderland," etc. Our readers will remember his kind letter granting us permission to use the name "JABBERWOCK," and also giving the meaning of that word. Since then we have received another letter from him, in which he expresses both surprise and regret at an anecdote which we published in an early number of our little paper. We would assure Mr. Carroll, as well as our other friends, that we had no intention of making light of a serious matter, but merely quoted the anecdote to show what sort of a book Washington's diary was.⁵⁰

In May 1888, Carroll made amends by composing a poem especially for GLS. Abbie Brown wrote, "But now a third letter from our kind friend has come, enclosing, to our delight, a poem, 'A Lesson in Latin,' the pleasantest Latin lesson we have had this year."⁵¹ The first two letters from Carroll were handwritten whereas the third was composed on a typewriter, and he referred to this fact in the third letter.

> Dear Young Friends: After the Black Draught of serious remonstrance which I ventured to send to you the other day, surely a Lump of Sugar will not be unacceptable? The enclosed I wrote this afternoon on purpose for you.
>
> I hope you will grant it admission to the columns of THE JABBERWOCK, and not scorn it as a mere play upon words.
>
> This mode of writing is, of course, an American invention. We never invent new machinery here: we do but use, to the best of our

Lewis Carroll's original handwritten letter to the editresses of The Jabberwock, *1888*

A Young School Finds Its Voice

ability, the machines you send us. For the one I am now using, I beg
you to accept my best thanks, and to believe me

    Your sincere friend,
    Lewis Carroll[52]

"Surely, we can patiently swallow many Black Draughts, if we are to be rewarded with so sweet a Lump of Sugar!" replied *The Jabberwock*.[53]

A Lesson in Latin
By Lewis Carroll

Our Latin books, in motley row,
    Invite us to the task,-
Gay Horace, stately Cicero;
Yet there's one verb, when once we know,
    No higher skill we ask;
This ranks all other lore above,-
We've learned "amare" means "to love"!
So hour by hour, from flower to flower,
    We sip the sweets of life:
Till, ah! too soon the clouds arise,
And knitted brows and angry eyes
    Proclaim the dawn of strife.
With half a smile and half a sigh,
"Amare! Bitter One!" we cry.
Last night we owned, with looks forlorn,
    "Too well the scholar knows
There is no rose without a thorn"-
But peace is made! We sing, this morn,
    "No thorn without a rose!"
Our Latin lesson is complete,
We've learned that Love is "Bitter-sweet"![54]

Lewis Carroll (Charles Lutwidge Dodgson), ca. 1880

The poem is the only piece Lewis Carroll ever published in an American periodical. Unfortunately, he did not think that the girls heeded his attempts to guide them regarding proper reporting tenor, as demonstrated by his fourth letter.

Dear young Friends,

With many thanks for your kindness in sending me the Numbers of "The Jabberwock," I must beg you to discontinue sending it. Our ideas are too far apart as to what is proper matter to make fun of. In a recent Number was a stanza—meant to be comic—about "Confession of Sin," one of the very saddest of all thoughts in human life.

    Your sincere friend,
    Lewis Carroll.[55]

John Tetlow was impressed with his younger students and the success of their literary endeavor. Despite the rebuke from Lewis Carroll, their headmaster believed they should be extremely proud of their accomplishments. He also appreciated the way Mabel's mother, Isabel Barrows, helped with the publication of *The Jabberwock*. He thought the paper beneficial as a social outlet and a conduit for school loyalty and identity, and insisted it remain the full domain and responsibility of the girls. Mrs. Barrows's involvement had assured him that the girls' course was proper. She came to mind immediately as he planned the 1888 graduation program, and he wrote to her.

Letter dated June 27, 1889, from Lewis Carroll to The Jabberwock

The closing exercises of the Girls' Latin School, as you doubtless know, are to occur Tuesday, June 26, at 9 o'clock A.M. Our closing exercises are always simple, consisting mainly of ten-minute addresses to the graduating class from three or four friends of the school specially invited to render this service.

    I hope you will agree with me in thinking that, as you are one of the mothers, we have a special claim on your favorable consideration, and so I write to ask if you will gratify us by consenting to be one of the three or four friends to say a few words at the closing exercises to our graduating class.

    Earnestly hoping you will not disappoint us.[56]

A Young School Finds Its Voice

Initiation party at the Barrows residence, January 26, 1889. From left to right: (seated on floor) Mary Sybil Collar; (seated in middle row): Virginia Holbrook, Belle Smith, Abbie Brown, Annie Young; (standing): Mollie Fox, Josephine Sanborn, Bessie Waite, Alice Howard, Grace Brooks, Saddie Tappan, Nan Myrick, Mabel Barrows

MY DEAR MAMMA: MABEL BARROWS WRITES HER MOTHER

During the last few months of her senior year, Mabel Barrows wrote to her mother constantly. Isabel Chapin Barrows was a stenographer and editor, which required her to attend numerous national conferences, and frequently took her away from Boston. Her daughter's letters offer a unique and intimate glimpse of the life of an exemplary GLS alumna.

>Wednesday May 18th
>My dear Mamma,
>Your dear postal card came this morning. I was glad to hear even a word from you.
>Mr. Tetlow yesterday extorted a promise from us that each member of the first Class would come to school every day after the exams are over until graduation day! I think it is a shame. We shall have to have prepared lessons everyday, just the same. I should think the teachers would want that time to use for the exams of the other classes. I suppose we shan't have to work very hard, but I don't want to have to go to school at all then. I should like to have some time to rest before starting off alone for the "wide, wide, world." . . .
>We have to hand in on paper today the colleges we are going to go to next year, or what we are going to do. I wanted desperately to say "Leipzig University" and "Central Institute" but I contented myself with saying "Leipzig and Stockholm." I thought even that was quite impressive.
>Give my love to little William. I miss you both very much.[57]

>June 26, 1892
>Oh! such a beautiful time as we had, Mommy dear, at Class Day! The day was perfect after all. All sunshine and not too warm. I want to begin at the

A TORCH IS PASSED—A SUMMER BEGINS

At three o'clock on Saturday, January 26, 1889, thirteen girls arrived at the Barrows residence to initiate *The Jabberwock*'s new officers. After the paper's first successful year, Virginia Holbrook would be stepping aside as an editor and Sibyl Collar would be leaving the business committee. As hostess, Mabel Hay Barrows made a brief speech and asked the new officers to take their oath. Veteran editors Brown and Barrows were joined by Annie Young, class of 1892.[58] Barrows had hidden a camera behind a screen and persuaded a young man from English High School to take a group photograph as well as individual portraits. A reporter from the BLS *Register* sent in his card asking to call, and he too was invited to join the group.

With the first year of publication under their belts, the girls prepared to take leave of GLS for the summer. While Abbie Brown usually vacationed in New Hampshire, both the Holbrook and Barrows families spent their summers at Lake Memphremagog, which extends from

Left to right: Virginia Holbrook, Annie Young, Mabel Hay Barrows, and Abbie Brown at the initiation party in January 1889

very beginning.... My class day costume seemed to be very successful. I carried my little Glenn shawl, but even then I was outshone by my gorgeous relative.... There were several Gym girls there, who? Grace Brooks was one of the most exquisite girls we saw. Abbie [Brown], too, was a perfect picture in a very quaint gown and bonnet. Poor Sadie [Tappan] shadowed by the everpresent swans was no belle. I felt very sorry for her.... Come home soon! We have not heard from you for three days.

Your very love Lassie,
Mabel[59]

June 30, 1892 [postcard]
Dear Mamma,
All over at last! Thank fortune. My diploma is waiting for you to unroll it. I have not looked at it.

We had a pretty stupid time at the exercises. Mr. Lyon's speech was nice, and Papa's was lovely, but the others were long and slow. Papa's poem was beautiful. Will Glover and I drove in very early & decorated the room. Grace Brooks invited eleven of the girls to her house to luncheon, directly after the exercises. From there we went to the class reception at the Tetlow's and had a lovely time. Then I went across the street to the Smiths and took dinner. Joseph came for me at nine. Yesterday I took lunch with Sibyl.... Mr. Williston has invited our class to his house this evening. Isn't that lovely? Everyone asked for you at school & sent their goodbyes. Love to all.

Your grown up daughter,
Mabel[60]

During summer 1889, Mabel Barrows (seated, lower left) visited the Holbrook family—including fellow Jabberwock editor Virginia Holbrook (seated on stairs, second from right) and her brother Ridgeway (bottom, center)—at Hemlock, the family's summer home in Georgeville, Quebec, Canada.

northern Vermont into Quebec, Canada. The two families spent the entire summer together, visiting back and forth. Mrs. Virginia Holbrook and Mrs. Isabel Barrows called each other "sister," and the girls called each other's mother "aunt."

Sibyl Collar spent the summer of 1889 in Pomfret, Connecticut, at her mother's family's home. But unlike the other girls, she was not returning to GLS. That July, William Coe Collar had been granted a 14-month sabbatical from his duties at Roxbury Latin School to visit Europe and had informed his daughter that she would be spending a year traveling abroad. Her father had already been gone a few months, and the family were to meet him in England.

Sibyl traveled with her family to England on the *Saale* in mid-September. The children were placed in school in Bremen, Germany, and in December, they traveled to Dresden, Germany, where 18-year-old Mildred, 16-year-old Sibyl, and 15-year-old Herbert spent five months apart from their parents in the care of a German family they had only recently met. Sibyl later remembered

> On the 21st [January 1890] they left for Dresden after buying photographs, . . . and after ten days with us, again departed for Munich and points south. It was an adventure on both sides, and I have wondered many times at their confidence in us and the comparatively new friends to whose nominal charge we were confided. But nothing ill came of it, and several life-long friendships developed. My father could read people at sight as well as languages.[61]

Jane Sheldon, the first teacher appointed to the GLS faculty, had also taken a leave of absence that September to care for her ailing mother in Waterville, Maine. A letter to Barrows of January 27, 1890, makes plain her attachment to the school and to the students.

> I was very glad to get your letter. Never think again that you don't "dare" write to me. You could not have given me a greater pleasure.

I miss you all so much and think of you all so often that it is really delightful to know that you miss me too. I shall be very glad when I can take up my work again with you. Sometimes I dare to cherish the hope that I may be with you again next Monday, but I cannot say positively yet....

I have received a long and interesting letter from Sibyl Collar since I have been here. I suppose you girls hear often from her, but if I have any later news from her than you have, I shall be glad to share my letter with you when I come back. I'm glad you are getting on so well with your English, French and Latin lessons. I felt sure you would enjoy working with Miss Dix.[62]

FUNDRAISING: *THE FEAST OF DIDO*

High printing costs necessitated finding ways to supplement *The Jabberwock*'s income, and the girls sold subscriptions not only to classmates but to students in other schools, prominent Bostonians, family members, and friends. In January 1889, the magazine staff held its first Jabberwock Dance, which took place on January 22 at Lyceum Hall in Dorchester and was superintended by Miss Sheldon and Miss Luce. Tickets were sold and dance cards distributed, and the event "proved a great success."[63] The truly adventurous fundraiser, however, would appear in another form: an original play written and performed in Latin by GLS students.

The girls had discovered that the Roman festival of Lupercalia fell on the day after *The Jabberwock*'s birthday. To celebrate the anniversary, Mabel Barrows suggested they raise money by putting on a dramatic production, entirely in Latin, for the general public, and she herself wrote and directed a play called *The Feast of Dido*. The Reverend Edward Everett Hale of South Congregational Church agreed that the students could perform the play at the church (encouraged, perhaps, by Barrows's father, an associate reverend there).

By mid-morning on the day of the play, the church's parlors were a carousel of activity. Twenty students participated, including Sarah Tappen as Queen Dido, Annie Young as her sister Anna, and Mabel Barrows and Abbie Brown played Helenus and Andromache, respectively. Mabel Smith played Venus, and Elizabeth Tetlow was Fidus Achates. The girls had made almost all of the costumes by hand. For stage sets,

A Young School Finds Its Voice

butter-dish bottoms became silver plates; small lampshades stood in for large goblets; old Christmas trees created a beautiful grove; boxes and cushions covered with velvet drapes became couches; and the characters reclined on borrowed fur rugs of tiger skin, leopard, monkey, fox, and gray raccoon. They even shook tin sheets and banged on the furnace in the basement with a coal shovel to simulate thunder.

Shortly before the play was to start, Barrows pulled back the curtain and looked out. "I little thought, when I looked out from the stage, across the crowded audience and, with a thrill, saw the great Phillips Brooks [minister of Trinity Church] sitting in the window, as there were no seats left, that my own career was decided that night."[64] Samuel Barrows introduced the evening, joking that, although he was quite sure everyone in Boston would understand the Latin, on the chance that some in the audience might be from Cambridge, Governor John D. Long would provide the English translation in advance of each scene.

The play opened in Queen Dido's Carthage palace with the arrival of Aeneas, played by Josephine Sanborn. In the second scene, two stage assistants simulated the noisy battle of Troy in the background by knocking on wooden boxes. The dressing room bustled with confusion just prior to the third act. Ascanius, played by Annie Young's little sister, had disappeared. Young whirled around the dressing room in her blue costume, a hairbrush in one hand and a Greek robe in the other. Sarah Tappan, the dignified queen, searched in earnest, and ushers, attendants, and slaves joined in the hunt. As the bell announced the final scene, they groaned and headed to their places, and there on stage, settled into her place upon an elephant's foot, was little Miss Young. Scolding, laughing, and crying, they had barely enough time to compose themselves before the curtain swept open for the final act. The play closed with a lyrical dance by the slaves.

A tableau from The Feast of Dido *(from left): Annie Young, Mabel Barrows, and Abbie Farwell Brown*

Henry Schuecker of the Boston Symphony Orchestra played the harp; John P. Fox of Boston Latin School—a good family friend of the Holbrooks—drew the stage sets; and Mary Frances Brown, class of 1892, choreographed the slave dance. *The Jabberwock* quoted from the review in the *Boston Globe*: "The costumes and stage setting, and dance of the slave girls in the last act, were all excellent." The *Boston Post* also mentioned that "Girls' Latin distinguished itself on Saturday afternoon by a performance of 'The Feast of Dido.'"[65]

Edward W. Capen, editor-in-chief of the BLS *Register*, reviewed the play in March 1890.

> We do not desire to draw any invidious comparisons between the acting of any of the young ladies who took part; all did remarkably well, and recited the Latin lines as if Latin were their mother tongues. We must say, however, that we were most charmed with the scene at New Troy and with the extremely 'beautiful dance of the slaves.' . . . We feel sure that we voice the sentiments of all who were present, when we congratulate the Jabberwock, those who took part, and Girls' Latin School, on the great success of their entertainment.[66]

The Roxbury Latin *Tripod* wrote, "It was very well done and remarkably pretty, especially the scene of the feast and the rhythmic dance of the slave-girls at the close. Its success was equal to its merits, the *Jabberwock*, to which the returns went, probably 'chortled in its joy' at the financial results."[67]

The Church of Unity on Pembroke Street asked the girls for an encore presentation in May,[68] and Mabel Barrows wrote about the performance to her mother soon after.

> This morning Florence and her mother went to the dentists', so I went to the [*Christian Register*] office and studied until lunchtime. . . . How funny to think you do not know anything about what is in this Jabberwock. Can you wait until you get home to see it, or had I better not mail you a copy? . . . What do you suppose one of the business committee did the other day? Went to get "ads" instead of going to school! <u>Please</u> don't tell, for if you should the dear Jabberwock would probably meet with a violent death. It happened this way. She wanted to go to

the English High Declamation, and knew they would not dismiss her from school to go, so she decided not to go to school at all, and the time before going to the Dec.[lamation] she might as well put to good use.

I got a letter from Alice Holbrook tonight about the "Feast of Dido." I sent her a ticket to it. The poor girl did not hear a word, but enjoyed seeing it greatly.... I had a letter the other day from Miss Cox.... She thought the play was lovely,—said I was very <u>dignified</u>,— the only one that was! Wasn't that funny? I think Josephine [Sanborn] and Abbie [Brown] were both very dignified.... I am glad you are coming home soon. Willie says he shall steal all the kisses from you so that I can't have any. Don't get homesick.[69]

The interaction among the various Boston high school periodicals, through their "Exchange" columns and in supportive comments on endeavors such as *The Feast of Dido*, no doubt contributed to the calling of a meeting on March 29, 1890, at *The Jabberwock*'s publication office. Abbie Brown invited the editors of the Boston Latin School *Register*, Roxbury Latin *Tripod*, English High School *Record*, Cambridge Latin School *Review*, and Girls' High School *Distaff* to form the School Editors' Club (SEC); Edward W. Capen, BLS class of 1890, was elected president. Shortly thereafter, invitations to join the club were extended to the Chauncy Hall *Abstract* and Newton High School *Review*. Three editors from each school met monthly to discuss topics of mutual interest, such as how to obtain advertising, how to get students to write for the papers, and how to increase alumni participation. In 1905, the SEC was renamed the Boston Interscholastic Press Association.

"LET DOWN HER DRESSES AND ROLL UP HER HAIR"
In the June 1890 issue of *The Jabberwock*, Abbie Brown wrote, "One more summer of fun and frolic for the Second Class girl, and then she must come back to the school as a sedate and dignified member of the First Class. Then she must not run races in the street or vault her neighbor's fence. She must let down her dresses and roll up her hair and speak condescendingly of the 'children' of the Sixth Class."[70]

Before they could advance to their final year, however, they had to contend with the crush of examinations. As exams loomed on June 6, 1890, Mabel Barrows wrote to her mother.

I must take a "breathing spell" from my studying. I have done nothing but cram since you left, on history. I had to let everything else go. I have prepared my Greek & Latin at school, but I haven't done anything outside of school except history. I studied pretty late on Tuesday night, but I went to bed last night at nine, and I'm going to tonight, for otherwise I am afraid I will give out before the exam is over, tomorrow. I only went to school today for unprepared Greek & a French examination. I don't think I shall go in at all tomorrow, except for the examination in history. I <u>must</u> keep up through that, then never mind what happens. I have put in a little over five hours today, on Roman history, and I am exactly half through. I think I shall have time for three hours more,—two at any rate, and possibly two hours tomorrow morning. I have finished Grecian history, but I don't know <u>anything</u> about it I am afraid. If I don't pass in Greek I shall have to leave the Latin school. They don't allow anyone to stay 3 years in one class.[71]

Brown, Holbrook, and Barrows returned to school for their senior year; happily, so too would Sibyl Collar. The entire Collar family had embarked at Liverpool, England, on August 28, 1890, and returned home to Boston on September 8 aboard the Cunard Line ship *Catalonia*. Edward Atherton, a teacher at the Roxbury Latin School, sailed with them on the return voyage. *The Jabberwock* reported, "We were all glad to welcome back our friend, Miss Sibyl Collar, to school. She has been in Germany a year and has now returned and joined the Second Class."[72] Nonetheless, Collar was able to make up the coursework she had missed in order to be promoted up to the class of 1891. When the Collars left on sabbatical to Europe, they rented out their home for the year, and it still was not available for them to occupy. Sybil later recalled, "From September 1890 to June 1891 we continued to be exiles from the Maple St. house. We occupied most of 6 Centre St., Roxbury, which was conveniently near the Roxbury Latin School, and walking-distance for me from the Girls' Latin, where I finished my preparation for Smith College, covering in one year (with a concession allowing me to substitute German for Physics) the work of the last two years."[73]

At the beginning of her final GLS year, Brown would meet Josephine Preston Peabody, and they became instant friends. Like Brown,

Peabody was attracted to *The Jabberwock* circle of writers and was recognized almost immediately for her talent. The two girls often greeted each other "with whoops of inexplicable mirth" and "fantasticalities and huge stretching laughter."[74] When Peabody wrote a three-act comedy called *En Masque*, *The Jabberwock*'s present and former editors—Brown, Holbrook, Collar, and Barrows—all performed in the play, which was presented in the big hall at West Newton Street.

Josephine Preston Peabody, born in 1874 in New York, was the daughter of Susan J. Morrill and Charles Kilham Peabody. After her father died when she was young, the family moved to King Street in Dorchester with her grandparents. Peabody began to write lyrical poetry in grammar school. At age 14, she submitted a poem to *The Atlantic Monthly*, and editor Horace Scudder was impressed by the verse and asked her to call at his office. When he met her he was astounded to learn her age.[75]

GRADUATION FOR THE GLS CLASS OF 1891

On June 23—Graduation Day—the sky was overcast but temperature was warm as the members of the class of 1891 made their way from all parts of the city to the West Newton Street building, and then to the second floor assembly hall. In the June issue of *The Jabberwock*, her last as editor, Brown had written

> 'Vale' At last the long-dreaded hour has come... when we, who guided the first tottering footsteps of the infant JABBERWOCK and watched over him with a mother's love and tenderness,—for he is, surely, our child, the child of '91—must leave him, and sever the ties which bind us to him most closely,—ties which no other class can ever feel so strongly or know such pain in breaking.... It is not, then, for his sake that we dread the end of our course here and separation from him forever, but for our own that we grieve.... The JABBERWOCK seems to us like a real being for us to love and work for and protect, and we really feel in parting from him that we are leaving behind us, with all the rest we shall miss hereafter, another person, dear to us as the others, and with a peculiar claim upon our love and protection in that for us he would never have been.[76]

JOSEPHINE PEABODY

In 1893, at age 19, Josephine Preston Peabody left Girls' Latin School due to poor health and therefore never graduated with her class. But she continued to write, and *The Atlantic Monthly* and *Scribner's Magazine* published many of her short stories and poems. *The Wayfarers: A Book of Verse* (1898) contains a poem that was first printed in the December 1891 issue of *The Jabberwock*; she later recalled that the poem "was actually written in school, on a slip of 'practice paper,' within a book, within a desk, within a dream."[77]

Peabody was accepted at Radcliffe College in September 1894 as a special student, and there her writing flourished. She graduated Radcliffe in 1896 and taught English literature at Wellesley College from 1901 to 1903. An active member of the GLS Alumnae Association, she read some of her prose to about 125 attendees at an alumnae meeting held at the Hotel Vendome in 1904. Her poetic drama *Marlowe* was performed at the dedication of Radcliffe's Elizabeth Cary Agassiz House in 1905.

"Josephine... yearned for the deepest experiences of human passion and was not qualified for the single life," said Sibyl Collar.[78] When she was 24, she attended an art exhibition where the photographer and mutual friend F. Holland Day introduced her to Kahlil Gibran, known for writing *The Prophet*. The young Lebanese American had drawn a sketch of her, and she began corresponding with Gibran while he lived in Lebanon. When he returned to Boston a few years later, they became romantically involved and he proposed marriage, but she refused him. In 1906 she married Professor Lionel S. Marks, an Englishman teaching at Harvard University, and had two children: a daughter, Alison, born in 1908, and a son, Lionel, born in 1910.

In February 1910 Peabody learned that one of her plays had been included in the top 7 of 115 submitted for England's Stratford-on-Avon prize. Sibyl Collar Holbrook recalled, "This play of *The Piper*... and as the rest are never tired of hearing, was in 1910 awarded the Stratford Prize, and performed at the Shakespeare Memorial Theatre in Stratford-on-Avon, Warwickshire."[79]

In addition to her poems, Peabody wrote and published two one-act plays and five full-length dramas. In 1911, she read some of her poems as a special guest at GLS's Christmas exercises, and in the early 1920s, despite failing health, she returned to the school for another reading. In the last decade of her life, she struggled against an illness that hardened the arteries leading to her brain and left her extremely fatigued. She died on December 4, 1922, at age 48.

On Class Day, the girls had gathered on the school lawn to listen as a classmate read the class will, prophecy, poem, and quotations. In her class prophecy, Esther Sanborn predicted that Abbie Brown would become an editor or a drawing teacher, Claire Hammond a violinist, and Sibyl Collar a missionary in Turkey. The prophecy also foretold that Mabel Smith would graduate from Smith College after graduating from Wellesley College; that others would become mothers, New York society ladies, or the wife of an English nobleman; and that two would have "pleasant estates side by side in some suburb of Boston."[80]

Even after graduating from GLS, Abbie Farwell Brown remained an active contributor to *The Jabberwock*, writing "The Jabberwock Genealogy," an article for the October 1891 issue. As if to validate Sanborn's prediction, she also continued to serve as a member of the executive committee of the Boston School Editors' Club. From her humble beginning as an editor of *The Jabberwock*, she ascended to become the author of several children's books and the editor of the Boston publishing company Hall & Locke's Young Folks Library series.

On the morning of June 26, Brown looked through the wealth of finery in her closet and removed the pure white dress made especially for her graduation day. Before the long glass in her bedroom, she slipped on the dress of white cotton and lace with puffed sleeves and delicate lace trim along the V-shaped neckline. She removed the single strand of graduated pearls from her jewelry box and clasped them around her neck, and carefully swept the dark brown hair up on her head. She was ready.

At West Newton Street, with parasols fluttering in the breeze and voices rising in excitement, class members were filing into the school in their white gowns. For the last time as students, they climbed the steps to the second floor. William Coe Collar, Vida Scudder, and Mrs. Charles Ames all sat in the first row as special guests.[81] At nine o'clock, the exercises commenced. Josephine Sanborn sang and Claire Hammond performed a violin solo. Speeches were made, and the class presented a bust of Homer to John Tetlow as its gift to the school. The graduates then received the much-coveted diplomas from their headmaster.

As the girls walked out under the overcast sky for their pictures, Brown looked at her lovely classmates, all splendid students, elated at having in their hands a Girls' Latin School diploma.

Only 13 of the 24 students who began with the class of 1891 had just graduated. Abbie Brown and Elizabeth Waite had been accepted to

Abbie Farwell Brown at her graduation in 1891 and her GLS diploma

98 Her Greatness Proclaim

Harvard Annex; Claire Hammond, Virginia Holbrook, and Sibyl Collar were to attend Smith College; Helen Wilder, Mabel Smith, Ethel Rogers, and Isabella Moore were headed to Wellesley College; Esther Sanborn to the University of Michigan; and Lucy Warren to Boston University. The remaining two—Josephine Sanborn and May Willis—did not go to college but, respectively, studied voice in Germany and stayed at home. Of this revered class, Florence Gragg, class of 1895, wrote, "They were peerless in our eyes. I can still see them acting in Josephine Peabody's play. Sadie Tappan was all that was beautiful and charming; Sibyl Collar, all that was dashing and gallant."[82]

Collar and Holbrook became roommates at Smith. "With a parent apiece, my chum Virginia Holbrook and I spent a day of spring vacation in Northampton mud, and picked out a newly-built detached house on West St. as most suitable for our very definite plans of college-life," Collar wrote later in life. "We were partly influenced I am sure by the fact that the street number corresponded with our class numeral—95!"[83]

No other single class left a more indelible mark upon GLS. Tetlow was truly sad to say goodbye to this group of girls who had reshaped school life with their initiatives. He and his wife invited the entire class of 1891 to their home in Roxbury for a party after graduation. Plans were made almost immediately to bring everyone back together at a dinner the following September. "The class intends to hold many reunions, for '91 will never be willing to allow its members to become scattered," said Brown.[84]

THE HARVARD ANNEX CLASS OF '91

The day before the Girls' Latin School graduation, John Tetlow had attended graduation ceremonies at Harvard Annex, now in its thirteenth year and growing rapidly. Elizabeth Agassiz, president of the college, posed for a photograph in Fay House's wide hall with the graduates in a circle around her. There Tetlow was proud to see Helen A. Stuart, class president and GLS alumna, receive the Maria Denny Fay Scholarship, and fellow GLS alumnae Ellen C. Griswold and Ida Mott-Smith receive diplomas tied

Among the Harvard Annex graduates, class of 1891, were three GLS alumnae: Helen A. Stuart (seated at left, in white dress); Ellen C. Griswold (at Stuart's left, in dark dress); and Ida Mott-Smith (at right, holding a cat).

A Young School Finds Its Voice

with brightly colored satin ribbons and a cluster of flowers. Cake and ice cream were served during the social hour. Tetlow made the trip with staff recruiting in mind, and two of these graduates later returned to GLS to teach.

THE LAST OF THE ORIGINAL EDITRESSES GRADUATES

Beacon Hill's Chestnut Street was lined with leaded, scalloped windows and door transoms filled with delicate lavender panes of glass, brass door knockers, wrought-iron lanterns, and slender Corinthian columns punctuating entryways to the red brick, Bulfinch-designed townhouses. It was widely regarded as the finest collection of Federal-period architecture in the city, and this single street seemed to embody the Boston Brahmin more than any other street on Beacon Hill.

On an overcast day in June 1892, at 12 Chestnut Street the cloudy sky cast no shadow on the party about to take place. Reverend and Mrs. Charles G. Ames and their daughter, Edith, prepared to receive guests. Edith Ames, class of 1892, had finished her year as *The Jabberwock*'s editor. John Tetlow, Mabel Barrows and her parents, and all of the previous year's editors were passing on the baton. On the dining room table, atop a centerpiece of moss and flowers, was a stuffed Jabberwock, its red mouth open and black wings spread in flight. The table was laden with chocolates, sherbets, cakes, candies, and pastries.

The few weeks ahead would be filled with final exams, class day, and graduation for the class of 1892, and the girls chatted excitedly about all that was about to unfold. They also granted an interview to a young *Boston Globe* reporter who was writing an article on the high school newspapers of Boston. A member of *The Jabberwock*'s business committee recalled:

> Do you know the first time I tried to get an advertisement I was frightened, awfully frightened, and I literally shook in my shoes as I went into one of the large stores and asked for a member of the firm. Why, experience taught me that I meet with greatest success when my victim is a jovial bachelor of 40. I always wear my prettiest dress and sprinkle my best smile through the conversation, and the result is something surprising . . . I can do nothing at all with women. They say "No I will not." And that ends it . . . but a

man,—if you stay and talk fast enough and look awfully shy and appealing and let your eyes grow moist as though you were going to cry when he frowns, he will give you twice what you ask and tell you where else to go, besides.[85]

Following final exams, Tetlow prepared the following recommendation letter for Mabel Barrows on June 20, 1892: "Miss Mabel H. Barrows is recommended for examination at the Harvard Annex in the following subjects: English, Elementary Greek, Advanced Greek, Greek Composition, Elementary Latin, Advanced Latin, Latin Composition, Elementary German, Elementary French and Plane Geometry."[86] For years

KINSHIP AMONG THE FOUNDING EDITRESSES

As their Class 1 year was drawing to a close, the inaugural editors realized that only six more editions of *The Jabberwock* remained to be published. As 1890 was turning into 1891, Brown wrote,

> I am so glad you liked my little Jabberwock. I was afraid I did not do him justice—and that his—"what do you call him?" foster pa—would eye my poor attempt with scorn. I fear that even the "cracker jar" will not appease his wrath when he sees—that is, I hope he won't, but if he does,—my beastie. The "Three Jolly Editors" grace my mantel shelf and ever as I open my morning eye and gaze with languor on the new born day, I strive to decide which is the other and who is which of us.
>
> I shall be happy to help you dogs ear the first leaf of the volume of '91—"Our" year! Just think the class of '91 is morning star now, or will be in two days, and a Happy New Year to it say I.
>
> Between the three of us I think on New Year's afternoon we ought to be able to turn over the new leaf even if it is pretty heavy, vellum or parchment or sheepskin—as seem appropriate to me, a graduate. Annie seems to have begun already in her truly Christian spirit of cracker-jarring. If we three give it together, will it be an "editorial jar"? I'm sure I hope not. Family jars are bad enough—I've heard.
>
> And now "vale",
> With a Happy New Year,
> —Abbie—[87]

Despite their close relationship, however, they sometimes struggled to decide which among the articles would be published, as can be seen from this letter Barrows wrote to her mother in March 1891:

> We had our compositions given back to us yesterday, and Bessie Waite and Sibyl read theirs. Miss Sheldon said that she wished especially to commend Misses Barrows, Brown and Holbrook! I was amazed. Virginia is very anxious to have mine published in the Jabberwock. Abbie hasn't read it yet. . . . Abbie has written an editorial that will take up the first column and a half <u>about</u> Spring! It is meant to be funny, but it fails utterly in that direction. Virginia and I are distressed. We don't know what to do, for Abbie said that it is "plenty good enough" and almost insists on having it. It is a puzzling matter.[88]

Tetlow had enjoyed the close friendship of Samuel Barrows, and as an indication of how special the family was to him, he invited Barrows to speak on graduation day.

> Miss Mabel has probably told you that the closing exercises of the Latin School will take place on Tuesday, June 28 at nine o'clock A.M. As a special friend of the class, you will be glad to learn that the marks for the recent examinations, which were made up today, warrant me for "recommending" all the class for diplomas. It would have been a sore disappointment to me if they have been obliged to withhold the recommendation in any instance.
>
> I am writing this note to say that I am counting on you being present at the closing exercises and saying a few words to the class when they have received their diplomas. I am extremely sorry that Mrs. Barrows is to be away at that time. If she were to be here, I should send her a message in this note to the effect that I should "nod" again this year in her direction.
>
> Please give her my warmest regards, and thank her for the kind note she wrote the other day; also in your own behalf, please send me word by Miss Mabel that you will accept this invitation.[89]

On graduation day, showers, sometimes heavy, could not dampen the atmosphere. Samuel Barrows said a few words to the class. Mabel looked upon her classmates and could sense their air of confidence and strength of purpose as they embarked on the next phase of their lives.

Of the 24 graduates, seven were accepted to the Harvard Annex: Mabel Barrows, Blanche Bigelow, Eleanor Hammond, Grace Lane, Edith Nickels, Kathrina Sanborn, and Elsie Tetlow.[90] Five others attended Smith, and as many went to Wellesley. The class of 1892 also produced the first GLS graduate to attend Vassar College—Clara Barnes. Hannah Myrick was the first alumna to become a doctor, Annie Young enjoyed dramatic success at Smith, and Blanche Bigelow went on after completing studies at Radcliffe to attend Oxford University.

This particular class had special meaning for Tetlow for another reason: it included Elizabeth "Elsie" Tetlow, his firstborn, and the first of his daughters to graduate GLS.

Mabel Hay Barrows

Girls' Latin School class of 1892. Left to right: (front row, seated on ground): Elizabeth Tetlow, Emma Jutten, Hannah Myrick, Marion Lincoln, and Prudence Thomas; (second row, seated on chairs): Annie Young, Grace Brooks, Sarah Tappen, Mabel Hay Barrows, and Kathrina Sanborn; (third row, standing): Alma Whitman, Emily Lovett, Blanche Bigelow, Clara Barnes, Annie Ziegler, Frances Jones, Grace Lane, Nellie Jones, Edith Nickels, Carrie Harper, Edith Wheeler, Eleanor Hammond, and Mary Frances Brown.

The classes of 1891 and 1892 did much to raise the profile and advance the goals of Girls' Latin School, but their greatest legacy remains the founding of *The Jabberwock*. Initiated by young women with no training in journalism, *The Jabberwock* is one of the earliest examples of Girls' Latin School students entering a public forum with a confidence nearly unknown in its era, and the paper's story is one of young editors and writers finding their voices through a self-initiated venture—an unusual achievement in any place and time.

◀ 1881
Boston Latin School's building on Warren Avenue is completed.

late 1880s
The Girls' Latin School Alumnae Association is founded.

1894
Harvard Annex is incorporated as Radcliffe College.

1895 ▶
Boston Public Library opens in Copley Square.

1895
Helen I. Tetlow graduates from GLS.

1897 ▶
First Boston Marathon is run on April 19.

Tremont Street Subway, first subway in the United States, is opened September 1.

1898
Lewis Carroll dies.

◀ 1898
Girls' Latin School moves four upper classes to the Chauncy Hall School building in Copley Square.

Mary Antin enters GLS.

1899
Israel Tisdale Talbot dies on July 2.

1900
Emily Talbot dies.

Abbie Farwell Brown's *Book of Saints and Friendly Beasts* is published.

1902
BLS Headmaster Moses Merrill dies and is replaced by Arthur I. Fiske.

1903 ▶
Isabella Stewart Gardner completes Fenway Court.

◀ 1903
GLS celebrates its 25th anniversary; the class of 1903 gives the school a statuette of Joan of Arc.

The Girls' Latin School Alumnae Association is formally incorporated.

IV

Girls' Latin School Fights for a New Building

Bela Lyon Pratt's bronze allegorical figure of Science in front of the main entrance to the Boston Public Library

GROWING PAINS: THE SCHOOL SEARCHES FOR MORE SPACE

With great clarity, John Tetlow could recall the day in 1881 when, seated at the dedication of the new Warren Avenue building for Boston Latin School and English High School, he vowed to obtain a new building for Girls' Latin School. Fifteen years had gone by, and the well-deserved new building had proven an elusive goal. Tetlow called a meeting of approximately 150 parents and friends of the school to bring attention to the matter, and on December 10, 1897, he headed to the second floor assembly hall with a prepared speech, hoping that Athena, Greek goddess of intelligence, skill, and battle strategy—whose likeness towered at the front of the hall—would impart to him some of her powers. The West Newton Street building had become far too small to accommodate both Girls' Latin and Girls' High Schools. Built for 925 girls, its occupancy now approached 1,200 students.[1] Every available recitation room was filled with desks, the drawing and music rooms in the attic and basement had become classrooms, and even the cloakrooms were converted for use. Many of these spaces were not properly ventilated or heated. Tetlow knew that the overcrowded conditions were rendering the building unsafe.

Both he and Boston Latin School headmaster Moses Merrill remained strongly in favor of separate education for boys and girls. When asked by the *Boston Evening Transcript* to provide an opinion on coeducation in the public schools, Tetlow replied, "In towns and small cities . . . coeducation works well. . . . I am inclined to think that, for large cities like Boston, the former [single-sex schools] are to be preferred."[2] Merrill agreed:

> Several years ago, a protracted and exhaustive hearing was given by the school board on this very question, so far as the Latin school is concerned. A happy solution of the question, as it has always seemed to me, was made by the school board in the establishment of a separate school for girls. . . . I have always had considerable sympathy with the objectors to the co-education of the sexes in a classical course of instruction. . . . Under the present peculiar and favorable condition of the two Latin schools in this city, I should consider it unfortunate to have them united.[3]

Tetlow walked into the assembly hall and was comforted to see so many old friends; Samuel and Isabel Barrows, Florence Cushing, and many former students were in attendance. To those gathered, he said, "I think a city that can expend $12 million for public parks, $2 million for a library, and pay $50,000 to one artist for mural decorations is able to provide a suitable building for the Girls' Latin School."[4] Amid general agreement that the drive for a new school building would require organization, tasks were allotted: Florence Cushing agreed to serve on the executive committee; Isabel Barrows signed on to the subcommittee on speakers and arguments; and Ellen C. Griswold, an alumna and new teacher, chose to serve on the subcommittee for petitions.

Several new school facilities in the city had been delayed for years. The previous spring, Mayor Josiah Quincy had asked all city departments to submit their loan requests for the upcoming fiscal year. The borrowing capacity of the city was limited to $1.7 million (which would have amounted to about $50 million in the early 2010s). Approximately $300,000 was needed to fund the construction of a new Girls' Latin

School. But there would be staunch opposition from East Boston and South Boston residents who were without their own high schools and desperately needed them. Residents of these neighborhoods pressed the point that the overcrowded conditions at Girls' High School would be lessened if new neighborhood high schools were built. Boston School Superintendent Edwin Seaver, on the other hand, ardently supported a new building for GLS. According to the *Boston Globe* in September 1897, "Superintendent Seaver believes that Girls' Latin has become so large, it is entitled to a separate building and its own corps of teachers. He says removal from the West Newton street building is absolutely necessary."[5]

BOSTON LATIN SCHOOL'S SIXTH BUILDING

On February 22, 1881, young men of Boston Latin School and English High School, dressed in their formal military uniforms, were ushering in the immense crowd assembling for the dedication of the massive new building that now housed both schools.[6] Located about six blocks south of Copley Square, the Latin–English building consumed almost an entire city block and was as spectacular in architecture as in size.

More than 3,000 guests had already filled the enormous drill hall, a space meant to accommodate 2,500, and the latest arrivals were jamming the doorways, the stairs leading to the gymnasium above, and the corridors. Many others, though awed by the size of the new schoolhouse, could not find a place to view the proceedings and reluctantly departed.

The drill hall gleamed with decorations and was crammed with Boston politicians. The viewing galleries above the main floor were draped in stars-and-stripes banners. In front of the Clarendon Street cavalry entrance, the large platform erected to seat the dignitaries was also elegantly festooned. Portraits of past headmasters were proudly displayed around the room.

On the temporary stage were seated John D. Long, governor of Massachusetts; Frederick O. Prince, mayor

Boston Latin and English High School Building, Warren and Montgomery Avenues; completed in 1881

Drill Hall, Boston Latin School

of Boston; lawyer and philanthropist Robert C. Winthrop; author Ralph Waldo Emerson; former headmaster Charles K. Dillaway; and current headmaster Moses Merrill as well as 20 or so other dignitaries, including School Committee and Common Council members.

Also on the platform was Girls' Latin School headmaster John Tetlow, who had removed his attention from the crowd to his own students. A student choir from Girls' Latin, together with vocal groups from BLS, Girls' High School, and English High School were singing "The Heavens Are Telling" by Beethoven. Tetlow was struck by the wonderful tone and harmony of the girls' and boys' voices. He found it somewhat ironic that these students were not allowed to occupy the same building.

Tetlow recognized from the outset that his growing school would need its own home. Yet once he saw the new Latin–English building, the need seemed more immediate than ever. The huge structure was a great contrast to the few classrooms occupied by GLS at Girls' High School or the simple wooden structure on Kearsarge Avenue that housed the Roxbury Latin School. Several times that morning he had heard someone say, "It is the largest and most expensive school building in America, if not the world."[7] The edifice had indeed cost $820,000 and could accommodate 1,645 pupils.[8] Each time he heard the statement, he became more resolved to obtain a commensurate building.

Former superintendent Philbrick took the occasion to tell the large crowd that Boston now had the ideal high school system: Boston Latin and Girls' Latin for classical and college preparatory education, and English High and Girls' High for those who wished to enter the business world or teach. "I trust that, in due time, the Girls' Latin School will be provided a building to match that of the Latin School for boys,"[9] he asserted, providing Tetlow with the greatest comfort and encouragement of the day.

In the months following the dedication ceremony, however, public opinion began to sour. The Latin–English building's underutilization and cost continued to be a point of contention with taxpayers. In January 1882, several prominent officials suggested that the new building be converted to a public library and a smaller building be constructed for the school. Discussions were renewed on the subject of whether its occupancy should include GLS,

Entrance hallway (top) and library, Boston Latin School

but BLS alumni and faculty remained firmly opposed.¹⁰ At their annual meeting, the BLSA offered the following resolution and moved its adoption:

> Whereas it has been suggested on several occasions that the building occupied by the Latin and English High Schools should be diverted to other uses, and the schools at the present therein, should be removed to other quarters. Resolved—that the Boston Latin School Association at its annual meeting May 3, 1882, desires to express itself as being strongly opposed to such ideas or any movement which shall change the present positions of the schools. Resolved that the officers of the Association are authorized and requested to present the views of the Association whenever occasion may require. The motion was seconded by Dr. Merrill.¹¹

Moses Merrill made clear his feelings about the prospect of girls occupying the Warren Street building. "The Boys' Latin School is large enough already. The schoolhouse is constructed for boys alone.... I have never heard of any parents expressing a preference for mixed classes in the Latin schools."¹²

The idea of using the facility to its capacity continued to gain traction. On November 29, 1882, the School Committee ordered that the cost to provide Girls' Latin School with accommodations in the new Warren Avenue building be evaluated.¹³ Tetlow's hopes rose that his girls would share the advantages of the new facility. On December 12, the Committee on Schoolhouses reported back to the School Committee:

> Mr. Chapin, to whom was referred an order instructing this committee to report a plan for providing

Boston Latin School masters at the Warren Avenue entrance with Headmaster Moses Merrill on first step at center.

> accommodations for the Girls' Latin School in the Latin-School building, and to report an estimate of the cost of the same, reported that seven rooms, six on the second floor and one on the third floor, can be fitted up for the accommodation of the Girls' Latin School, in the new building. The two schools can be entirely disconnected by separating that portion to be used by the Girls' Latin School from other parts of the building, by the erection of suitable partitions, and by assigning a separate entrance to each school. One of the large lecture rooms on the second floor could be used by Girls' Latin School as an assembly hall.... The estimate costs of arranging these furnishings is two thousand dollars, fifteen hundred of which would be for furniture."¹⁴

The recommendations were accepted, but there was insufficient support to pass the measure. Tetlow was disappointed again, and it seemed that the door to sharing the building with the Latin school for boys remained closed.

For a headmaster of lesser stature, the fight for a new building likely would have been an exercise in futility. Tetlow, however, commanded respect from some of the most important educators in the United States. In 1897 he edited an edition of the eighth book of Virgil's *Aeneid* for use in high schools. He had attained recognition through active membership in the Headmasters' Association of the United States, the Association of Colleges and Secondary Schools of New England, and the Massachusetts Schoolmasters' Club. The GLS faculty regarded Tetlow as "a mixture of President Eliot of Harvard—and God."[15]

Above all, Tetlow achieved significant national prominence in the summer of 1892, when the National Education Association appointed a committee of ten educators "to prepare a report on the uniformity of high school programs and the requirements of admission to college."[16] Chaired by Harvard University president Charles W. Eliot, the Committee of Ten included William T. Harris, the U.S. Commissioner of Education, as well as several U.S. college presidents. John Tetlow was one of three high school principals appointed to this committee. The committee's final report was considered "the most important educational document ever issued in the United States."[17] The committee emphasized the importance of a standardized liberal arts–oriented curriculum for all students through high school; its work resulted in what is known today as the College Entrance Examination Board (CEEB), and the CEEB in turn created the Scholastic Aptitude Test (SAT), of which Tetlow, William Coe Collar, and Ray C. Hurling are considered the founders.[18]

Dr. John Tetlow, headmaster of Girls' Latin School, at the blackboard in Room 5A

In 1893, Brown University conferred upon Tetlow an honorary doctor of science degree, after which he was often referred to as Dr. Tetlow. In 1895, the Roxbury Latin School asked him to serve on its board of trustees. Headmaster Collar said, "Dr. Tetlow was a neighbor of mine for many years in Roxbury ... I knew that for myself I would have a strong and sympathetic supporter, and I knew that in every vital concern of the school he would think and judge and act without bias, and without prejudice."[19] In April 1897, S. P. Marble of New York wrote a letter to Tetlow, offering

Her Greatness Proclaim

him a salary of $5,000 for taking the helm of the New York City public schools. Although the sum represented a significant increase in pay, he declined. After all, he had a new building to chase.

MARYASHE ANTIN: AN IMMIGRANT'S JOURNEY TO GLS

Mary Antin dressed and readied to leave the cramped, dark room of the three-story tenement house on Dover Street where she lived with her family in Boston's West End. She had excelled in grammar school and was determined to make her future path as bright as possible. After being told that Girls' High School was the oldest high school for girls in the United States but that the brightest girls attended Girls' Latin School to prepare for college—and keenly aware that her parents could not afford college—Antin was determined to find her way somehow. During the summer of 1898,[20] as she debated whether she could be "fitted" for college at Girls' Latin School, she decided to discuss the matter directly with Headmaster John Tetlow. From Dover Street, Antin walked to the electric trolley and boarded a green car with gilt lettering. The fare was one cent, an enormous sum to Antin, but she was determined to reach her destination.

> It was just like me... to go in person to Mr. Tetlow, who was principal of both schools, and so get the most expert opinion on the subject. I never send a messenger, you may remember, where I can go myself. It was vacation time, and I had to find Mr. Tetlow at his home. Away out to the wilds of Roxbury I found my way—perhaps half an hour's ride on the electric car from Dover Street. I grew an inch taller and broader between the corner of Cedar Street and Mr. Tetlow's house, such was the charm of the clean, green suburb on a cramped waif from the slums.[21]

Room 18, the Physical Laboratory

Her full name was Maryashe Antin, and she was born in Polotzk, Poland, on June 13, 1881. Antin had come from Europe to the United States without knowing a

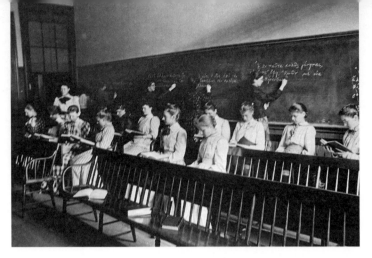

A Greek class in Room 5B, ca. 1892

word of English. In the late nineteenth century, Jews were emigrating to the United States from Russia and Eastern Europe in vast numbers to escape persecution and poverty, and Mashke, as she was then called, left Polotzk with her mother, two sisters, and a brother to join her father, who had been in Boston for three years. Arriving in Boston on the *Polynesia* on May 8, 1894, the family moved to a three-story tenement house on Union Place, "two imposing rows of brick buildings, loftier than any building I had ever lived in . . . [under] the May blue of an American sky!"[22] Union Place was in truth an alley formed by two brick buildings separated by only a narrow shaft, blocked off at the back and overlooking brick sidewalks, but to Mashke, it was the symbol of a new beginning.

The family soon moved to Arlington Street in Chelsea so her father could sell lemonade, peanuts, and pink popcorn during summers on Revere Beach. Now using the Americanized name Mary, Antin started school there in 1894 and, after just four months of studying English, was able to write so beautifully that a teacher sent one of her essays to the local newspaper, which published it. Both Antin and her family took great pride in her accomplishments.

The Antins moved back to Boston to a tenement on Wheeler Street in the South End, and Mary completed her courses through ninth grade at the Winthrop School, where she was widely considered a prodigy, and from which she graduated in June 1898. The family moved once again, this time to Dover Street, and although her father sought work, he could not, in her words, "earn enough to pay the rent in full and buy a bone for soup."[23] Her father continued to shift from job to job, and his inability to earn a stable income for his family perpetually haunted Antin. "My father had not lost a whit of ambition for me," she recalled. "Since Graduation Day, and the school-committeeman's speech, and half a column about me in the paper, his

The First, Second, and Third Classes in Room 5, ca. 1892

ambition had soared even higher. He was going to keep me at school till I was prepared for college."²⁴

When Antin reached Tetlow's home, she walked up to the door unannounced.

The Sixth, Fifth, and Fourth Classes in Room 4, ca. 1892

> My faded calico dress, my rusty straw sailor hat, the color of my skin and all bespoke of the waif. But never a bit daunted was I. I went up to the steps to the porch, rang the bell, and asked for the great man with as much assurance as if I were a daily visitor on Cedar Street. I calmly awaited the appearance of Mr. Tetlow in the reception room and stated my errand without trepidation. And why not? I was a solemn little person for the moment, earnestly seeking advice on a matter of great importance.²⁵

John Tetlow was working in his home office when a domestic servant summoned him. He was a bit surprised to learn that a young visitor had arrived alone and wished to discuss whether she should attend Girls' Latin School or Girls' High School in the fall. When he saw her apparent poverty, he was sure she had been misdirected; however, a few minutes of conversation made clear that she was not only intellectually gifted but also mature beyond her years. Antin recalled, "That is what Mr. Tetlow saw, to judge by the gravity with which he discussed my business with me, and the courtesy with which he showed me the door. He saw, too, I fancy, that I was not the least bit conscious of my shabby dress; and I am sure he did not smile at my appearance, even when my back was turned."²⁶

That September, Antin entered GLS as a sophomore of the Third Class and part of the graduating class of 1901. She regarded her schoolmates as an "aristocratic set"²⁷ who dressed well and came from fine homes, and were either intellectually gifted or incredibly hard working.

> By all these tokens I should have had serious business on my hands as a pupil in the Latin School, but I did not find it hard.... To remain unconscious of my shabby and ill-fitting clothes when the rustle of silk petticoats in the schoolroom protested against them was a matter still

Girls' Latin School Fights for a New Building

While attending GLS from September 1898 to April 1901, Mary Antin met Hattie Hecht, a Jewish community leader and philanthropist. Hecht knew Antin was eager to earn money in order to attend college. The *Boston Evening Transcript* had already published some of Antin's poems—Antin had approached the editor herself and asked him to print them. Antin had showed Hecht the letters she had written in Yiddish to her Uncle Moses about her long journey by land and sea from Polotzk, Poland, to Boston. Why not publish these letters?

Hecht arranged for her to correspond with Israel Zangwill, who would later become her benefactor. Zangwill read the letters and was struck by their lyricism and eloquence. The recent Jewish immigrants to the United States had at the time published few books, and Zangwill saw great potential in Antin's writing. He persuaded Philip Cowen, editor of the magazine *The American Hebrew*, to publish the letters in book form, and in 1899, Cowen published *From Plotzk to Boston*.[28]

Antin was thrilled when the book was published and gave a copy to John Tetlow, who praised her writing. She sent him this letter in response.

> As I do not wish to intrude upon your busy moments more than I can help, I write these few lines instead of seeking you again in person. Accept my sincere thanks for your very kind opinion of my little book. I need not tell you that your words are an encouragement to further efforts as well as a reward for this my first.
>
> You are very kind in noticing what you choose to term "my aptitude for learning." I believe it to be the fruit of my keen appreciation of an American girl's advantages; which appreciation is the natural result of my having been deprived of those advantages so long, that when I began to understand what it meant to call education and progress one's <u>right</u>, I determined to make the best of it. . . .
>
> If you think it would be a pleasure for us to read Homer together some day, what shall I say? The time when I shall be more directly your pupil appears, in my dreams of the future, like one beautiful holiday. . . . Your hint of what there is before me swells my formerly-anticipated pleasures, and would, perhaps, even make me impatient of their realization were not my present studies so dear to me. I am content to arrive at them by the route mapped out for me.
>
> Hoping that I may ever merit to retain your present kindly interest, and that I may someday have the right to subscribe myself your friend, I am
>
> Respectfully yours,
> Mary Antin[29]

In September 1899, Antin returned to GLS. "Instead of leaving school, I have entered another year, with the addition of Greek and English to last year's Latin, French, Algebra, and history," she wrote Zangwill. "If the present state of my health continues, I hope to make a good year of it."[30]

Antin became active at Hale House, a settlement house established in Boston by Edward Everett Hale. Through the Hale House's Natural History Club, Mary escaped the city to the lush nature preserves that encircled Boston, like Nahant Beach and Cuttyhunk. On one of these trips she met Amadeus William Grabau, a geologist and doctoral candidate at the Massachusetts Institute of Technology. Over the summer of 1900, Antin was hired for three weeks as Grabau's secretary at the Bayville Summer School of Natural History in Bayville, Maine.

Although she returned to GLS in September 1900, by the beginning of March 1901 she had informed her family she was unable to continue at school and went to New York to stay with the Cowens for a month. "The facts are these: my teachers and my physician having agreed between them that Mary Antin was 'run down' and needed a change (unless she was willing to put up with nervous prostration later on), and Mary Antin packed her grip at once and made a beeline for 123 W. 111th Street, New York."³¹ She returned to Roxbury in May and, sadly, dropped out of GLS before graduating.

On October 5, 1901, at age 20, Antin was married to Amadeus Grabau. Eleven years her senior, Grabau became a professor of geology at Columbia University, and they moved to New York. Her new circle of friends there encouraged her to write her autobiography. In 1911, *The Atlantic Monthly* first published excerpts of *At School in the Promised Land, or The Story of a Little Immigrant*, and when Houghton Mifflin published the full book in 1912, it became a national bestseller. Regarded as a love letter to the promise of America, the book recounted the story of the "waif" who had walked to Tetlow's house to ask to be admitted to Girls' Latin School. In her book, Antin wrote, "Education was free. That subject my father had written about repeatedly... the essence of American opportunity, the treasure that no thief could touch."³²

Many of the young Jewish girls who arrived at Ellis Island and other immigrant ports in the United States came without their parents and were therefore exposed to both sexual and economic exploitation. On December 8, 1912, Antin spoke at New York's Waldorf-Astoria, delivering an impassioned plea for more support of Jewish immigrant girls arriving alone in the United States: "A girl worth letting into the country is worth looking after to see what becomes of her."³³ Between 1912 and 1918, Antin crisscrossed the country giving lectures on immigration issues to large audiences. GLS headmaster Ernest G. Hapgood invited Antin back to GLS to speak on October 22, 1914, and Antin donated signed copies of her several books to the GLS library.

After the United States entered World War I in 1917, Antin's support of the Allied cause led to an estrangement from her German husband. By 1919, she had suffered a nervous breakdown, and the couple had separated permanently. Grabau moved to China, where he remained until his death in 1946. Antin retired from public life and lived once again very modestly. She died May 15, 1949, in Suffern, New York, of cancer.

In 1997, Penguin Books published a new paperback edition of her book, retitled *The Promised Land* and edited and with an introduction by Harvard professor Werner Sollors. In an article in the *Harvard Gazette*, Sollors said, "Her book really established the genre of the immigrant autobiography.... But it's also a great stylistic accomplishment. She's a very good writer, which is remarkable considering the fact that she came here at the age of 13 without knowing a word of English.... I think *The Promised Land* helped to redefine what it means to be an American. It's an important book, especially now that immigration and multiculturalism have become such significant issues for our own time."³⁴

The Boston Public Library holds the original manuscript of Antin's autobiography. Her book remains a pinnacle example of how education can change a life.

within my moral reach.... To stand up and recite Latin declensions without trembling from hunger was something more of a feat....

Everything helped, you see. My schoolmates helped. Aristocrats though they were, they did not hold themselves aloof from me. Some of the girls who came to school in carriages were especially cordial. They rated me by my scholarship, and not by my father's occupation.... And it was more than good breeding that made them seem unaware of the incongruity of my presence. It was a generous appreciation of what it meant for a girl from the slums to be in the Latin School, on the way to college. If our intimacy ended at the steps of the school-house, it was more my fault than theirs.[35]

Antin admired her classmates for their beauty, manners, and poise. She readily perceived that a girl from Dover Street had little in common with a young socialite from Commonwealth Avenue, but they shared a mutual respect nevertheless: "they guiltless of snobbishness, I innocent of envy. It was a graciously American relation, and I am happy to this day to recall it."[36]

In the summers, many wealthy families left Boston for the seashore or the mountains. But she had discovered her own oasis that to Antin was a sanctuary more luxurious than any Newport mansion: the Boston Public Library. In later life, she remembered looking at the triple-arched main entrance and soaking in the inscription above it: FREE TO ALL. Inside the vaulted entrance, the ceiling was covered in marble mosaic, and the marble floors were inlaid with a brass scorpion and other zodiacal signs. Just beyond the entrance, a staircase of Echaillon marble was guarded at each of its two turns by a lion. The paintings by John Singer Sargent and the detailing in Bates Hall were enthralling. Within the library lay another haven: the courtyard garden, a replica of the arcade at the Cancelleria Palace in Rome. While there, she felt lifted out of the strictures of poverty and outsider status, and she soared.

> I felt the grand spaces under the soaring arches as a personal attribute of my being. The courtyard was my sky-roofed chamber of dreams.... Everything I read in school, in Latin or Greek, everything I read in my history books, was real to me here, in this courtyard set about with stately columns.... That an outcast should become a privileged

citizen, that a beggar should dwell in a palace—this was a romance more thrilling than poet ever sung.[37]

LEAVING THE NURSERY

With a quick, noiseless step and downcast eyes, John Tetlow walked down the hall past crowded classrooms and entered the inner sanctum of his office. He sat at his desk and, referring to the ledger-sized volumes in which all GLS admissions and discharges were recorded, he carefully wrote a report to the School Committee documenting the number of girls in attendance at the school for the last 19 years. The nib of the pen was the only sound that could be heard as he listed the information.

Between 1878 and 1897, enrollment at GLS grew from 48 to 326 students. The school that started as an experiment was now an integral part of the Boston school system, and its reputation had grown so tremendously that many parents moved to Boston for four to six years so that their daughters could attend. Although the population of the City of Boston had increased by only 25 percent, the number of students at both Latin schools had increased by 69 percent.[38]

In January 1897, Major Henry Lee Higginson, partner in the prestigious firm of Lee, Higginson & Co., joined the fight for the new school

Enrollment at Girls' Latin School, 1878–1897[39]

YEAR	NUMBER OF STUDENTS	YEAR	NUMBER OF STUDENTS
1878	28	1888	158
1879	75	1889	196
1880	104	1890	191
1881	140	1891	204
1882	141	1892	219
1883	141	1893	225
1884	145	1894	220
1885	147	1895	255
1886	146	1896	297
1887	155	1897	326

for GLS. Higginson was born on November 18, 1834, and had entered BLS in 1846. After graduating in 1851, he served in the Civil War, and afterward began a very successful career in banking. He became one of Boston's most generous philanthropists, donating Soldiers Field to Harvard College and acting as founder and patron of the Boston Symphony Orchestra. Higginson organized a petition that was signed by more than 3,000 citizens asking the School Committee to appropriate funds for a new building. A public hearing was held on January 27, 1897,[40] at which much support was expressed; however, the School Committee lacked the funds and took no further action.[41]

After considering Tetlow's report, the School Committee decided it had to find GLS additional space. Renting was the least expensive temporary option, and in January 1898 the committee entered into an agreement to lease the former Chauncy Hall School in Copley Square, which had been vacated two years earlier. In February, the First through Fourth Classes, approximately 240 students, were moved to the new location. "The present transfer of the main part of Girls' Latin School to an independent building is rightly viewed by the friends of the school as a subject for congratulations," Tetlow observed. "But let it be remembered that this transfer is only one step toward the consummation to be striven for. . . . The school needs—for the adequate performance of its mission in the community—a new and well-equipped building."[42]

Gideon F. Thayer established the Chauncy Hall School in 1828 exclusively to prepare boys for entrance to the Massachusetts Institute of Technology and other science schools. When the original building on Chauncy Place burned to the ground in 1873, the decision was made to relocate and erect a new building at 259–265 Boylston Street between Dartmouth and Clarendon Streets, directly across from the Museum of Fine Arts, which opened in 1876; Trinity Church, completed in 1877; and the new Boston Public Library, which opened in 1895. The stone edifice with three spires was best known for its beautiful ivy-covered façade. The third floor had a 400-seat hall, and 12 classrooms occupied the first two floors. The 8,064-square-foot building, assessed for $113,000, had been put up for sale in 1896 but still sat vacant two years later. The City of Boston would rent the building from the Chauncy Hall Association for two and a half years at $8,708 per year.

From the beginning, the school was thought to be unsuitable and located too far from West Newton Street. As noted in the February 1908 issue of *The Jabberwock*, "At Copley Square was dust and darkness and noise, the continuous roar of street-cars, in front and in the rear; the glare of electric lights inside; and outside all kinds of distracting noises: shoveling of coal, beating of rugs, pounding of tin cans, clatter of empty bottles, cries of fruit peddlers, playing of hand-organs."[43] Twice each month, the hundred or so students in the Fifth and Sixth Classes that remained at the West Newton site walked the two-mile round-trip to attend school assemblies. GLS teachers complained constantly of the difficulty of keeping the girls moving past store windows on these trips. Mr. Tetlow, a bicycling enthusiast, preferred to travel between the schools on bike. Many students immediately missed the large library at Girls' High School as well as the statues that were gifts from graduating classes.

However, the new school also presented some advantages. The students felt the refining influence of being close to the new Boston Public Library and the art museum. Most important, the new location afforded a private area for *The Jabberwock*'s office. "Yes at last we have just what we needed,—a large commodious closet, in which we may have absolute possession," noted the March 1898 issue, which continues,

> Here we are at last, comfortably settled in our new quarters, and ready, after Easter vacation, to buckle down to hard and earnest work. . . . By the way, it is very awkward, in speaking of the girls we left behind us, to mention them as "those now occupying a portion of the West Newton Street building"; and we wonder if they would mind occasionally being alluded to as "The Nursery."[44]

From that point forward, the West Newton Street building was known as the Nursery.

As time went on, the younger students greatly anticipated the day they got to move from their incubator to the building with the four upper classes. One of the students recalled:

> I remember the first year I spent at the school. How shy and timid I felt in the presence of the dignified upperclassmen! They wore long flowing skirts and high laced shoes and piled their hair in puffs on their head. . . .
>
> Our social life began to broaden then. There were high school drill competitions, and we watched our various heroes parade through the streets while our hearts fluttered and we whispered among

Girls' Latin School Fights for a New Building

ourselves as they passed. There were Mechanics Fairs, luncheon and card parties; but most fun of all were the "sets" of dances we as young ladies were allowed to attend.... Oh yes, there was that first eventful day when we first rode those dangerous horse cars to Roxbury Crossing in the company of several dashing Roxbury Latin boys.[45]

The first graduation after the move took place at the Copley Square school in June 1898. The 34 graduates, in soft white gowns and dainty ribbons, presented a magnificent bust of Athena to Tetlow, who was presiding over his eighteenth graduation ceremony. In its coverage of the occasion, the *Boston Evening Transcript* quoted him as follows:

> A friend in congratulating me in the early days upon having received the mastership of the school said: "It will always be a small school, but it will always be made up of choice girls." He was wrong in the former surmise, but in the latter he was distinctively right. Next year we expect to have four hundred pupils. They will still be, however, "choice girls." The duty that this school owes to others is a large and deep one. When we were pleading our cause before the Legislature not long ago, the dean of Radcliffe College and the president of Boston University both spoke for us and testified that this school's graduates are among the best students in their institutions. To this Wellesley has lately added its unsolicited testimonial by announcing our lesser certificate is sufficient for admission there.... The girls will meet with a cordial welcome wherever they may go to college. It remains for them to see that welcome continues to be cordial as other classes go forth from this school.[46]

BECOMING A RENTER AT COPLEY SQUARE

To economize and move the relocation project forward, the School Committee began to look for ways to consolidate Girls' Latin with a second school in 1899. On the motion of committee member John A. Brett, it was ordered that the Committee on High Schools consider the advisability of establishing both Girls' Latin School and Boston Normal School in the same building. Some School Committee members pointed out that a single lot and heating system would save money, but member Samuel H. Calderwood called the plan "open to many and serious objections," and thus began a long, protracted negotiation.[47]

Girls' Latin School, formerly Chauncy Hall School, circa 1900

On February 13, 1900, the School Committee approved a request to acquire land for Girls' Latin School, but the necessary bond issue of $250,000 was not approved for months. With little choice, the Board of Schoolhouse Commissioners approved renewing the lease at the Chauncy Hall School for $7,000 in November 1902. Shortly thereafter, the Committee on High Schools ordered that the board of commissioners "purchase a site and erect a building for Girls' Latin, at the earliest possible date."[48] However, at the end of the year, the Committee on Schoolhouses reported that funds to erect a building for either Boston Normal School or Girls' Latin School remained unavailable, and the matter was referred to the next school board.

By November 1902, the crusade for a new building had entered its fifth year. During that time, Boston's school-age population had increased by ten thousand children, and the pressing need for more schools was unanticipated. Tetlow implored the School Committee to move forward with a new building.

The Girls' Latin School . . . was established for the express purpose of fitting girls for college, and has held strictly to the purpose for which it was established, its standards for promotion and graduation have been largely determined by the admission requirements of the best New England colleges. Although, therefore, its growth has more than justified the expectations of its founders, it has not become a large school. . . . For twenty years from the organization of the school, in 1878, all classes were housed in the building in West Newton Street appropriated to the Girls' High School. This arrangement, which had been viewed from the first as a temporary makeshift, became at last physically impossible, owing to the growth of both schools, and in 1898 the Chauncy Hall building in Copley Square was leased by the city for the use of Girls' Latin School. . . . This division of the school into two parts, although made imperative by the congested condition of the West Newton Street building . . . should be discontinued at the earliest possible moment; for a school, to accomplish its best work, should have the unity of spirit and purpose that comes from a common participation on the part of all its pupils in its general exercises. . . . Now that the needs of the suburban school districts have been met, and the pressing needs of the Girls' Latin School are frankly acknowledged, it is hoped that money will speedily become available for the purchase of a site and erection of a new building for that school.[49]

A BIRTHDAY IS CELEBRATED

The atmosphere in the assembly hall at West Newton Street was electric. The Alumnae Association, responding enthusiastically to Tetlow's request to decorate the hall for the evening's ceremonies, brought in armloads of flowers and greens. The stage was filled with chairs for dignitaries, and 25 students from the First Class, dressed in evening gowns and carrying wands of white satin ribbon, hastened about helping the teachers ready the hall for visitors.

Girls' Latin School, still very much a young lady, was celebrating its 25th birthday.

At the same time, Tetlow was witnessing the passing of a wonderful era. BLS headmaster Moses Merrill, the man to whom Emily Talbot had directed the request that her daughter be allowed to attend Boston Latin

School, had died. After taking a leave of absence beginning in September 1900, Merrill retired from his position due to ill health on December 11, 1901. Headmaster for more than 43 years, Merrill was widely respected for reorganizing the curriculum and for authoring several textbooks. After two months of serious illness, he died at home on April 26, 1902. Submaster Arthur I. Fiske was selected to take his place.

Tetlow had invited the presidents of Smith and Radcliffe Colleges and President Warren of Boston University to speak at the celebration. Yes, he had accomplished what he had hoped for. GLS had 350 students and BLS had 500, but—most importantly—they had become academic equals. Each speaker recalled how difficult it was to believe, 25 years after the fact, that a city as cultured as Boston would be reluctant to support the classical education of women. Smith College president L. Clark Seelye praised Tetlow for his "high moral courage and prophetic insight"[50] in aligning himself with a liberal studies school for women, a move that, at the time, could have seriously jeopardized his professional career. "But Mr. John Tetlow... had more faith in women's intellectual capacity and did not shrink from hazarding his reputation," stated Seelye.[51]

Tetlow was the last speaker of the evening. Friends who filled the hall gave him a standing ovation, and it was several moments before he could begin. When at last he could be heard, he said, "I question whether there is any teacher to whom the genuine and sincere expression of appreciation gives more pleasure than to me."[52]

He was deeply touched when Abby C. Howes, former student and now teacher, presented him with a beautiful silver-mounted cut-glass loving cup containing 25 ten-dollar gold pieces. The cup was inscribed, "John Tetlow Girls' Latin School February 4, 1878 Graduating Class of 1903"; the gold coins were a gift from alumnae. The class of 1903 also presented the school with a statuette of Joan of Arc, a copy of the famous sculpture by Henri Chapu prepared in plaster in 1870 and in marble in 1872.[53]

The next day, Superintendent of Schools Edwin P. Seaver, a staunch supporter of GLS, sent Tetlow the following letter:

> I wish to offer you my sincere congratulations on the pleasant affair which took place at the Girls' Latin School last evening. Your twenty-five years of service in that school are epoch-making. The

school is now mainly what you have made it and for a long time to come it will continue to feel the directing impulse you gave it during its earliest years.[54]

As Boston turned the page on the previous century, the honor of GLS's graduates had risen to new heights. Between 1880 and 1900, 16 GLS graduates became members of the Phi Beta Kappa Society at their respective colleges.[55] Between 1901 and 1910, 55 percent of the GLS students accepted at Radcliffe graduated with distinction.

THE ALUMNAE INCORPORATE

The Girls' Latin School Alumnae Association was founded sometime after 1885, and reportedly Alice Mills '80 served as the first president, to be replaced by Elizabeth Briggs in 1887. To mark the school's 25th anniversary, the association decided to file its formal incorporation papers in 1903. One act of kindness extended by the association in its early years was to offer an honorary membership to Helen "Nellie" Magill, the only girl to have attended Boston Latin School. Upon the 25th reunion of the BLS class of 1870, she wrote from Florence, Italy, to the Boston Latin School Alumni Association:

> It gives me much pleasure to send a word of greeting to my old class of the Boston Latin School. It is true, I had not the advantage of remaining with you long enough to graduate. Still I feel as if I were one of you in a manner, as I studied and recited with you, though I left the school in '67 when my father's connection with it ended. So I did not have a chance to see, as I had always hoped in my youthful dreams, whether the doors of old Harvard would really remain fast closed to a girl who had gone through the old Latin School. . . .
>
> I can hardly tell you how much I was pleased and touched by your communication. Sometime ago the Girls' Latin School Association, in view, I suppose, of my homeless condition, and of the fact that I may be regarded as having comprised at one time the whole Girls' Latin School in my unworthy person, kindly offered me a place among its members, and this recognition gave me pleasure. But a lingering regret has been ever in my mind for memories and associations and traditions which can have no meaning to them

Helen Magill, ca. 1895

[GLS], and which we therefore cannot celebrate together. But if I could look in upon your gathering, how many a single word or name I should doubtless hear which for me, as for you, would touch the source at once of smiles and tears. . . .

Indeed the very place [Bedford Street] is gone, as to its outward appearance. But I believe we can all say, as I know I can, that I have few things to be more thankful for than that almost chance experience. . . .

You do me the honor to ask me to send my photograph to my class . . . which I have finally decided to send you. After all, why should you not have the great privilege of seeing the only daughter's daughter of the old school? Moreover it seems to me that this portrait may perhaps serve to emphasize the truth that whatever her schools or schoolmasters, a woman whom nature has made truly a woman, will never think she can find a worthier occupation than that in which you see me proudly engaged.[56]

MIRABILE DICTU!

The School Board expressed a desire to keep the school in Copley Square. On May 6, 1903, the *Boston Globe* reported that the schoolhouse commissioners had advertised for sealed-bid proposals for a 30,000-square-foot parcel of land in the vicinity of Copley Square. At the last instance, this order was expanded to include within the same complex Boston Normal School and a new grammar school. Finally, the Massachusetts legislature authorized approximately $1.5 million of new loans within the debt limits of the City of Boston, and the Boston Schoolhouse Commissioners finally had the funds to move forward with the Girls' Latin School project.

Land in Copley Square proved to be too expensive, and the search turned to newer outlying neighborhoods of the city. In 1903, Isabella Stewart Gardner, one of the first to purchase land in the marshy Fenway area, completed work on Fenway Court—referred to as Mrs. Jack's Palace—which she designed to emulate Venice's Palazzo Barbaro. Shortly thereafter Simmons College purchased land for $180,000 for its first permanent building, which opened in the fall of 1904. Within two more years, Harvard Medical School would construct five gleaming white marble buildings nearby.

The Schoolhouse Department scoured the area and found a suitable parcel just a stone's throw from Mrs. Jack, which added to the cachet of the potential site. On May 26, 1904, the department requested that the Board of Street Commissioners take land on the Tremont entrance to the Fenway and Worthington Street. This taking would provide access to a 110,000-square-foot parcel owned by Charles G. and N. W. Rice. The city paid $165,580 for the parcel—roughly $3.5 million dollars in 2013 dollars. Three schools were to be located in this complex, and the Board of Schoolhouse Commissioners selected three different architectural firms to collaborate on the design of the buildings—Coolidge & Carlson were awarded the designing of Girls' Latin School, Peabody & Stearns were to create the plans for Boston Normal School, and Maginnis, Walsh & Sullivan got the nod for the model grammar school.

In his superintendent's report of March 1904, Seaver wrote: "The efficiency of the two Latin schools cannot be too highly praised."[57] Tetlow had always deeply appreciated Seaver's support, and when the School Committee's election for superintendent of schools took place that year, Tetlow had no reason to believe that Seaver would be leaving his position. On June 1, 1904, however, Tetlow received the following letter:

> A committee of the Boston School Board... has been appointed to present nominations for the office of Superintendent of Schools and Supervisors in this city. Your name has been suggested as eminently qualified to fill any of the above positions. If you desired to be considered in this respect, will you kindly advise me and submit such testimonials and records of your educational career as you may deem advisable?[58]

He replied:

> In answer to your communication of yesterday, permit me to ask you not to use my name in any way in connection with the Superintendent or Supervisor. I much prefer to remain in my present position. Thanking you for the confidence implied in the invitation contained in your letter, I am
> > Very respectfully yours,
> > John Tetlow[59]

At the GLS graduation exercises on Saturday, June 25, 1904, the stage at the Copley Square building was decorated with a yellow shield with *1904* emblazoned on it and mountain laurel, syringa blossoms, and pink roses. As he presided, John Tetlow took great satisfaction in knowing that the number of subsequent graduations that would take place at Copley Square was finite—no more than two or three, he hoped. His youngest daughter, Frances, would graduate the next year, however, and he lamented that none of his children would have had the advantages of the new building.

The new Girls' Latin School under construction on Huntington Avenue in the Fenway would be ready for the start of the 1907–1908 school year. Many students were thrilled, and all looked forward to occupying the brand new building. From Chauncy Hall, *The Jabberwock* reported:

> *Mirabile dictu*, it has come true at last! The rattling windows, where one has to ascend by feeling rather than by sight, the din of Boston's traffic, the settees of varying height and comfort, the alley with its coal wagons and "musicians"—all of these—are to give place to the well-equipped, beautiful new building to which we have so long looked forward and for which we have so often yearned.[60]

1905
Frances H. Tetlow graduates from GLS.

◀ 1906
Stratton D. Brooks is appointed superintendent of the Boston Public Schools.

1906 ▶
Albert Einstein introduces the Theory of Relativity.

1907
◀ Girls' Latin School moves from the buildings on West Newton Street and Copley Square to a brand new building on Huntington Avenue.

Headmaster William Coe Collar retires from Roxbury Latin School.

1907 ▶
Julia Ward Howe is first woman elected to membership in the National Institute of Arts and Letters.

1908
The *Christian Science Monitor* is first published.

◀ 1908
GLS faculty member Ellen Chase Griswold '87 is transferred to Dorchester High in January; she dies unexpectedly on December 13 of that year.

V

A Struggle over the Control and Direction of Girls' Latin School

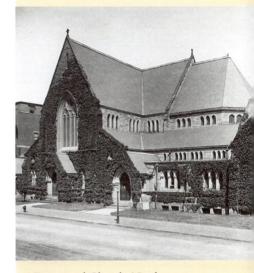

Emmanuel Church, Newbury Street, Boston, ca. 1900

STRATTON D. BROOKS BECOMES SUPERINTENDENT

On June 1, 1906, Boston Public Schools Superintendent Stratton D. Brooks took a seat on stage at the Boston Latin School on Warren Avenue. One of the guests invited to declamation and prize day by BLS headmaster Arthur Fiske, Brooks had occupied the office of superintendent for just over two months, and his appointment had been accompanied by both tragedy and controversy.[1]

The event was well attended by family and friends. Although the day was cloudy, temperatures had reached into the seventies, and the auditorium was becoming warm. The semicircular stage's small podium was centered at the front, and a piano stood to the left. A row of chairs for dignitaries was arranged at the back of the stage. Five enormous brass chandeliers hung from the coffered ceiling. The theatre-style, wrought-iron chairs had punched into their leather backs the initials PLS, for Public Latin School. Dozens of elegant oil portraits hung on the walls.

Brooks glanced down at his program, written entirely in Latin, to see his name listed with such other honored guests as philanthropist Robert Treat Paine and Senator Daniel W. Lane. Some of the declamations included "The Song of the Wreck" by Dickens and "The Fall of Cardinal Wolsey" by Shakespeare. More than 50 prizes were to be awarded for excellence in the classics, modern studies, and conduct.[2] There was little doubt that the scholarship of these young students was impressive, but Brooks continued to question the cost at which it had been achieved. In his estimation, too many students failed to graduate the Latin schools, and with graduation time around the corner, he was

BLS HEADMASTER FISKE DOES NOT FLINCH

Arthur I. Fiske was appointed headmaster of the Boston Latin School after Moses Merrill died in 1902.[3] Highly regarded as a scholar of Greek, he had a gentle, sensitive nature that contrasted with the spirited group of young men over which he presided. He ruled more with love than with fire and brimstone, but he was also known to be firm.[4] "Pa" Fiske was courageous in the execution of his duty as headmaster. As was his nature, he quietly absorbed the controversy concerning Boston Latin's graduation rate and then carefully considered his best option.

School Committee chairman Storrow, as a matter of respect and in an effort to increase the percentage of students graduating from BLS, met personally with Fiske.

"Mr. Fiske, we have granted six diplomas," explained Storrow, naming each student.

"Yes," said Fiske in his pleasant manner, "I thought you might, but the trouble is, Mr. Storrow, that I cannot bring myself to sign the diplomas for those boys."

Storrow, assuming this mild-mannered man would eventually do what he asked, made no further comment. Fiske assumed the meeting was ended and quietly departed.

Storrow told Brooks about their meeting and what Fiske had said. Brooks started to laugh.

"Why are you laughing?" asked Storrow.

"I am laughing at you."

"Why?"

"Because the boys will not get their diplomas."

"Did we not grant them?"

"Yes," replied Brooks, "but Fiske will not sign them."

Brooks was correct. Fiske did not sign them, and the boys did not graduate. Later Fiske told Patrick Thomas Campbell BLS '89, who would become the school's headmaster in 1920 and Boston school superintendent in 1931, about his meeting with Storrow, and said, "Mr. Campbell, I shall never give an order that is the first step in making the Public Latin School a second-rate school."[5]

intent on ensuring that this point was understood.

Born in Missouri in 1869, at 37 Brooks was still relatively young. He had graduated from the University of Michigan and his master's degree was granted by Harvard University. He and his wife, Marsila, had three daughters, Helen (born in 1892), Marion (1894), and Dorothy (1900).

When Girls' Latin was established in 1878, the Boston School Committee consisted of 24 members elected from Boston's 12 wards.

Auditorium of Boston Latin School on Warren Avenue

The Board of Supervisors had been created in 1875, and consisted of six supervisors selected by the School Committee to serve two-year terms. The supervisors visited schools, examined teachers and pupils, and acted as the executive arm of the School Committee.

Edwin P. Seaver had been Boston's superintendent of schools from 1880—in short, for most of Girls' Latin School's history—and was an ardent supporter of both the school and John Tetlow.[6] In 1902, Brooks became a supervisor, and during his tenure was as critical of GLS as Seaver had been supportive. Brooks later told the School Committee that, from the time he was appointed, he perceived teacher Ellen Griswold to be "a dominant spirit" at Girls' Latin School and her influence was not in the best interest of the pupils.[7]

Stratton Brooks, ca. 1915

Girls' Latin School was considered the best classical education available to girls in the United States. The report of the National Education Association's Committee of Ten advocated that career educators—rather than lay boards of citizens—design high school curricula. Tetlow, who staunchly subscribed to this view, bristled from any assault on his high curriculum standards, especially by the Boston School Committee.

GLS faculty constantly implored lazy students to return to the neighborhood high schools. High attrition—with students vanishing overnight and classes losing as much as half their original members—was a constant in its academic routine. The competitive coals flamed, fanned brighter by the high dismissal rate.

A Struggle over the Control and Direction of Girls' Latin School

But Tetlow came under scrutiny from Brooks and others, who suggested that students were either forced to leave the school "by tyrannous overwork" or graduated due to "overwhelming perseverance and undaunted courage."[8] In the Boston School Committee's 1903 annual report, Seaver included Tetlow's response to these allegations and defense of his standards:

> The school now sends almost thirty-five girls to college every year. Approximately half of this number go to Radcliffe College, and, in order to be admitted, must pass satisfactorily the Harvard College entrance exam.... As, therefore, the standard of graduation from the school is largely determined by the requirements for admission to Harvard College, those who enter other colleges by certificate, having received the same training and having been subjected to the same tests of proficiency as their classmates, are as well prepared for collegiate work as those who go to Radcliffe College.... On the other hand, it is not the policy of this school, as is sometimes assumed, to *over*-prepare its pupils for collegiate work, so that they will have little to do during the Freshman year at college....
>
> There have been times in the history of the school when parents and others interested in its welfare have felt that it demanded unduly strenuous work on the part of its pupils; and doubtless the school has suffered somewhat in reputation from this cause in comparison with the high schools of the city. But the probable explanation of the popular impression that the Latin School course of study is relatively severe is that all the girls attending the Latin School are intended for college, whereas only an insignificant part of the pupils attending the high schools have college in view.[9]

Edwin Seaver, who was Protestant, lost the June 1904 election for superintendent and was ousted by vote of the School Committee in favor of the Catholic George H. Conley, who had been a supervisor since 1886 and had also served on the Massachusetts Board of Education.

Stratton Brooks, who had also lost his bid to become superintendent, decided to seek employment elsewhere. In November 1905, he was selected to be superintendent of the Cleveland Public Schools in Ohio and resigned his position in Boston effective January 1, 1906. His two oldest daughters were enrolled in Girls' Latin, and the family decided that

Mrs. Brooks would remain at a boarding house in Brookline to permit 13-year-old Marion and 15-year-old Helen to finish the school year.

In 1905, in a move spearheaded by committee member James J. Storrow, the Boston School Committee was reorganized by a special act of the state legislature. It now comprised five members, each of whom were elected at large rather than by ward and would serve staggered three-year terms. This move effectively centralized power to a much greater degree with the superintendent and school department officials. A former schoolmaster recalled, "Under the old regime, when I was a supervisor, I could go into a school and I might advise as much as I liked, but I could not enforce anything. . . . Now that is all changed; they have given us a quantity of duties and the power to discharge those duties."[10] The new five-member School Committee consisted of George E. Brock, David A. Ellis, Thomas J. Kenny, William S. Kenny, and James J. Storrow.

Unfortunately, Conley died suddenly in December 1905, just a month after Brooks accepted the position in Cleveland. The Boston School Committee voted to replace Conley the following March. Storrow, Brock, and Ellis voted for Brooks, a decision that ultimately became unanimous. Storrow said, "I have exercised my most careful judgment, and am thoroughly convinced that the best man in the United States for up-building the Boston School system is Stratton D. Brooks."[11] At a March 22 meeting, Common Council member Leo F. McCullough criticized this appointment:

> The public was startled yesterday morning by the announcement that Stratton D. Brooks, our newly elected Superintendent of Schools, was accused by the president of the Cleveland School Board of "jockeying" and threatened him with dismissal from the position of the Superintendent of the Cleveland Public Schools. . . . This is the man placed in his present exalted position by three members of the present [Boston] school board but really by the will of that master, millionaire politician, Chairman James J. Storrow. If ever a political deal was consummated, if ever one-man-power was exemplified,—if ever educational interests were set aside and personal desires substituted, it was the election of Stratton D. Brooks.[12]

After the announcement became public, the School Board of Cleveland, Ohio, would in fact dismiss Brooks from the superintendent's position there without waiting for his formal resignation.

TETLOW ALMOST RESIGNS

Immediately upon becoming superintendent, Brooks appointed a special council to evaluate and submit recommendations on the high percentage of students in the Boston Public Schools who were unwilling or unable to complete their high school studies and graduate. At the center of this controversy was the high dismissal rate at the Latin schools. The School Committee expressed concerns that too many students left the Latin schools because the work was too difficult. Brooks explained, "When twenty-five percent of all the pupils in the high schools of this city fail. . . . These pupils are justified in demanding high school instruction adapted to their needs."[13] Brooks insisted high marks were proven by the "science of psychology" to lead to better work.[14]

Superintendent Brooks met with the teachers at the Girls' Latin School to explain his new policies and the five recommendations made by his new council as to how students should be graded and taught. The new policy was based on Brooks's declaration that "a school conducted exclusively for the best students is not justifiable as a public school."[15] Of that meeting, Tetlow would later say, "The superintendent administered to us, as a body, severe and, as I believe, undeserved criticism."[16] Holding to their high standards, the teachers disagreed, and the proposed changes were met with great resistance. At the end of the meeting, Brooks warned that "unless the teachers were able to modify and improve their methods, it would be necessary to transfer some of them to other schools."[17]

In a letter dated April 19, 1907, Tetlow wrote Brooks:

> I send this note to assure you that you may confidently count on the earnest desire of the teachers of the Girls' Latin School to respond to your wishes and expectations in the matters which you brought to our attention last Monday. I beg you not to allow your present unfavorable opinion of our work and spirit to crystallize into permanent convictions, but to make every possible effort, in light of such evidence that may come under your observations or be brought to your knowledge, to believe, and to show that you believe, that we deserve your confidence.[18]

Although the note was conciliatory, Tetlow strongly disagreed with Brooks's desired mission for the Latin schools. Earlier he had decided to give up his position as headmaster of Girls' High School when Girls' Latin moved to its new building that fall; however, he was in such vehement disagreement with the new superintendent's vision that he changed his mind and drafted the following letter the very same day:

> You will remember that some months ago, when I talked with you about the advisability of my retaining the headmastership of Girls' High School and Girls' Latin School after the removal of the latter to the new building, I expressed a desire to do so for at least another year. I wish to say now that I think the interests of the two schools would be best served if each should be placed under the care of a separate head master at the close of this present school year.... If you agree with me in thinking it better that the joint management of the two schools should end now rather than a year hence, I should like to be relieved of the care of the Girls' Latin School at the close of the present school year.[19]

Before sending the letter to Brooks, he shared his decision with several family members and teachers at the school. One of them was Ellen C. Griswold, who had graduated from Girls' Latin in 1887 and Harvard Annex in 1891, and had been appointed as an assistant teacher on September 5, 1894. She taught briefly in New York and New Jersey before coming back to Boston to teach Latin and Greek.

As a member of the Radcliffe Alumnae Association and American Association of University Women, Griswold was dedicated to helping prepare girls for both college and life, which made her incredibly popular among the students. When the *Boston Globe* ran a contest to award a trip to the teacher with the highest number of votes cast by students, Griswold led all voting for Girls' Latin. Tetlow, who had the utmost respect for her and had asked her to serve on the Girls' Latin School Board of Trustees, shared his decision with her, to which she immediately responded.

Ellen Chase Griswold in her Radcliffe (class of 1891) graduation photograph

> In reference to your resignation as master of the Girls' Latin School, I know you will want me to speak frankly, in view of the fact that it has been my privilege to know you for some twenty-five years ... I can't believe that you are now going to desert us. If we ever needed you, we need you now. Do not let the graduates feel that in this crisis you failed them.... The trends of the time are against us, and

A Struggle over the Control and Direction of Girls' Latin School

we may have to yield, but do not let us lose our identity before we
have to do so.... Therefore I hope you will write Mr. Brooks such
a manly letter as you can write saying that the best interests of the
school require that you devote all of your time restoring the Girls'
Latin School's to a place in his favor, and that you are willing to sever
your connection with the Girls' High School next September.[20]

Another alumna who had returned to teach at GLS, Abby C. Howes '82, also wrote to Tetlow.

> Your proposed letter to Mr. Brooks has made me sick at heart, and I have not known how to write you on so painful a subject.... Should you desert the Latin School at this crisis in its existence, I fear in a few years we would ... cease to be a college preparatory school. We do not enjoy the historical prestige of the Public Latin School, nor have us a body of voting graduates to defend our interests.... If you should desert us now in these dark days, your resignation would be regarded as a virtual admission that these charges made against us are true.[21]

Mathematics teacher Mary C. C. Goddard wrote

> May I allude to the other matter you spoke to me about? Can you guess at the utter consternation and dismay that overwhelmed me? To me, and I know that to the other teachers as well, the Girls' Latin School has always been the embodiment and expression of your personality. Without you there is no Girls' Latin School. You began it. You have made it what it is. I love this school.[22]

The near unanimity of words from his family, friends, and teachers convinced Tetlow to change his mind. On the letter of resignation draft, he crossed off "Latin" and wrote over the top of his marks "High." Brooks accepted his resignation effective September 1, 1907. Albert Perry Walker assumed the headmaster position at Girls' High School with Tetlow's full support. On May 9, 1907, Walker wrote to his predecessor:

> I thank you heartily for your cordial note regarding my appointment to the Girls' High School. Nothing in connection with my promotion has given me more pleasure than your own attitude towards it. I feel

that to succeed you is in itself a ground for pride, and that it will be no light task to keep the school worthy of the name that you have won for it.... I shall have many questions to ask you about your scheme of organization and administration, for I want to have the school go on—as far as may be—as if no new hand were at the helm. You must answer only so many of them as you have time and inclination to answer. Your assurance that the teachers are kindly disposed towards me is very gratifying indeed.[23]

AN UNWELCOME SURPRISE

At the beginning of the new school year in late summer of 1907, Brooks remained determined to substantially lower the high dismissal rate. He sent a letter to the parents of each of the girls who had left Girls' Latin School the previous June and elected not to return to the school in September. The letter stated in part, "If your reasons for the withdrawal of your daughter . . . were based on the conditions in the school I should be pleased to have a full and frank reply to this letter, stating what these conditions are, as you understand them."[24]

Before the inauguration of the new five-member School Committee in 1906, no teacher had ever been transferred from a Boston public school without the consent of both the teacher and the headmaster. One Friday evening in December, however, Tetlow attended an event at which he met Charles J. Lincoln, headmaster of Dorchester High School. Lincoln told his colleague that he had been informed that Ellen Griswold had been transferred to his school. Tetlow had not been informed, much less consulted, about the pending transfer. Griswold was his finest teacher and president of the Girls' Latin School Alumnae Association. Brooks could not have selected a more loyal supporter of Tetlow and GLS.

Brooks had met with Lincoln on Friday, December 6, 1907. He had also asked that Tetlow meet with him on Monday, December 9, at his Mason Street office. In that meeting, Tetlow took exception to the superintendent's decision as well as to the manner in which Brooks had made it known to him. After a long discussion, Tetlow told Brooks that he would appeal his decision to the Boston School Committee. "Such an appeal is entirely proper under the rules and regulations, Mr. Tetlow," the superintendent replied. "I shall abide by the result of your appeal whatever it might be."[25]

Brooks then sent the following letter to Miss Griswold:

I have given long and careful consideration to the ideals of instruction and the methods of administration as carried forward in the Girls' Latin School. I am of the opinion that you are so decidedly out of sympathy with the ideals and standards that I consider proper and advisable in that school, that you cannot render efficient service therein. I therefore enclose an official transfer of yourself to the Dorchester High School, said transfer to date from Jan. 1, 1908.[26]

Upon reading the copy of this letter, which had been sent to him by Brooks, Tetlow let it drop to his desk. He had feared this possibility when he accepted the superintendent's daughters Helen and Marion at Girls' Latin School. Griswold, who had been a teacher for over 13 years, had a reputation for being strict. Both girls were in her classes and had failed to obtain high marks. Tetlow went home that evening and gave great consideration to what he should do. The next day, he placed a call to Brooks and asked him to provide a specific illustration of the defiant spirit the superintendent said was shown by Griswold. Brooks replied by telling Tetlow he was not going to get into a discussion of the matter with him. Tetlow hung up the phone more frustrated than he had been in 30 years of service.

Closing his eyes, he wondered if the entire world had gone mad. What becomes of achievement when teachers blur together good and bad work? What becomes of excellence when poor work is graded dishonestly? The grading system at Girls' Latin was consistent with the standards needed to achieve entrance into Radcliffe College. He felt compelled to challenge the superintendent's decision.

The headmaster had always striven to administer the school with his students' scholastic advancement foremost in mind. Superior instruction by the teachers and hard work by the students contributed to the school's high standards. Although Brooks insisted that the transfer was entirely about the number of students who failed to graduate, Tetlow did not believe him: the low marks of the two Brooks girls must have played a role in the superintendent's crusade. When Brooks had been a district supervisor, he had no power over educational standards. Now, it was clear, he intended to make his point.

On December 10, Griswold wrote Tetlow, "If I were alone in the world my resignation would already be in the hands of the Superintendent. . . .

If he really thinks that my influence is harmful to the school, I do not wish to stay in it, for I care too much for its success. Therefore I ask you to make no more protests in regard to my transfer."[27] Tetlow met with Griswold and explained that, although he had tried, Brooks had not wished to discuss the matter with him. Tetlow could only advise her to meet with Brooks in person and inquire what he had found wrong with her work. On December 13, Griswold did meet with Brooks, hoping their conversation might lead to a better mutual understanding. Once again, however, Brooks refused to discuss the matter.

Soon, Griswold's supporters began to make public allegations that Superintendent Brooks had personal motivations for penalizing the school. Former Boston School Committee member John D. Bryant, who held Tetlow in higher respect than almost any other person in the Boston public schools, sent the following letter to Chairman Storrow:

> The transfer of Miss Griswold is, as I view it, but an episode, although a very important one. Rightly or wrongly, the belief among the parents is that Ms. Griswold and Mr. Tetlow are the object of Mr. Brooks' dislike because his two daughters, when in that school, were not marked as high as he would have liked to have them.[28]

Brooks exploded that the allegation was "too contemptible to be worthy of a denial from me."[29] Apparently the argument was also meaningless to Storrow, who was intent on seeing his recently conceived five-member School Committee survive the first serious test of the powers granted to the superintendent. Bryant, a BLS alumnus, met with Storrow on behalf of Girls' Latin on December 13, 1907. Afterward, Bryant provided Tetlow some legal insight into the conflict:

> I am confident you will pardon this confidential communication from a stranger. . . . I have had this morning a conference with Mr. Storrow. . . . I think Mr. Storrow feels that the School Committee . . . having some time since given the Superintendent power to make transfers, ought not interfere with the Superintendent in the exercise of that power unless for special and urgent reasons. . . . If the committee could be made to see the transfer would be detrimental to both schools. . . I think they would advise the Superintendent to revoke his proposed transfer.[30]

A Struggle over the Control and Direction of Girls' Latin School

Three days later, Tetlow was given an opportunity to address the School Committee and change their minds. But the committee was unmoved by Tetlow's arguments, stating that his reasons did not seem sufficient to change the superintendent's mind, and voted to support Brooks. Alumnae and friends of Girls' Latin were not prepared to acquiesce to this decision, however. After the School Committee's vote to transfer Ellen Griswold, other committees formed vowing to fight the decision.

PARENTS AND ALUMNAE UNITE AGAINST THE SCHOOL COMMITTEE

The Parker House Hotel, just across School Street from City Hall, had long been a favored watering hole of politicians and power brokers. The hotel's Crystal Parlor, so named for its ornate crystal chandeliers, was an elegant setting. At noon on Monday, December 30, 1907, 150 parents filed into the banquet hall hoping to reverse the actions of Superintendent Brooks. It had been over two weeks since the School Committee had backed him, and sentiment in favor of reinstating Griswold had only intensified. One of the parents, Max White, made a plea to "unmask the school board" and reaffirmed the belief that the matter originated from the failure of Stratton's daughters to succeed in Griswold's classes.[31]

Another parent in attendance was A. Lincoln Filene who, along with his brother Edward. A. Filene, owned Filene's Department store. Lincoln's daughter, Catherine, who had graduated from the Prince Grammar School in June, received a letter of acceptance from John Tetlow and had started that fall at GLS.

Indignation on the part of the assembled parents made it difficult to maintain order in the Crystal Parlor. In the end, they appointed a committee made up of Edward A. Filene, Duncan Russell, Dr. Charles H. Winn, William C. Crawford, and Mrs. M. C. Stanwood to meet directly with Brooks. The committee agreed to convene again the next day at the Hotel Bellevue. Many of the parents departed confident that Dr. Brooks would reverse his decision.

The following week Brooks met with the committee of parents, to whom he said that the attitude of the Girls' Latin School was hostile to his educational policy and that Miss Griswold was transferred "because she was not in sympathy with certain fundamental plans" essential to the improvement of Girls' Latin School.[32] He also told them that,

nonetheless, he would take their request "under advisement."³³ Brooks told the *Boston Herald*, "I had a conference with the committee of parents at the Parker House, at which the general policies involved were discussed. I invited them to a second meeting with me and the board of superintendents and others, at which these policies could be more completely explained, and the details presented."³⁴

Left to right: Cora Crawford, Dorothy Stanwood, Sibyl Young, and Catherine Filene. Crawford, Stanwood, and Young's parents all served on the Parent's Committee, as did Filene's uncle. Of them, only Filene supported Brooks.

In an effort to quell the conflict, Chairman Storrow also met privately with Tetlow. The chairman asked Tetlow if he thought the transfer of one teacher "warranted an extensive public agitation" and encouraged him to go along with Brooks. Storrow suggested further that it would be in the best interests of the school "to acquiesce to the Superintendent's decision."³⁵ Tetlow refused.

On New Year's Day 1908, Ellen C. Griswold, assistant teacher, was transferred to the same position at Dorchester High School, and Adeline G. Simmons was transferred from Dorchester High to Girls' Latin School. Simmons had graduated Girls' Latin School in the same class as Griswold. Tetlow extended a gracious welcome, offering to meet with her at his home before she assumed her new position. Simmons commenced her duties at Girls' Latin, where she was shown "every mark of respect."³⁶

Meanwhile, newspapers flooded their readers with news about the story. "Pupils Petition for Miss Griswold" trumpeted the *Boston Herald* on January 3. The article stated, "Miss Griswold has been teaching at the Girls' Latin School for 13 years and is also a graduate of the institution. She is extremely popular."³⁷ As evidence, a handwritten petition begging the School Committee to reconsider its decision and signed by more than 300 students was printed in the paper.

A Struggle over the Control and Direction of Girls' Latin School

Adeline G. Simmons, Smith College graduation photograph, 1891

A second parents' meeting was held at the Parker House Hotel, this time with more than 200 in attendance. The next day, the front page of the *Boston Herald* charged that Brooks had made this a personal issue. The explanation? In addition to not marking his two daughters as high as he would have liked, Griswold was accused by Brooks of insubordination because she had violated Tetlow's order that no home lessons be given to the girls over the Thanksgiving holiday. "Who told Superintendent Brooks about the home lesson?" demanded GLS parent Royal B. Young. Someone in the room cried out, "Marion Brooks!"[38]

Griswold spoke to a *Herald* reporter about the allegation.

I did give out a home lesson to be done during the Thanksgiving vacation. I was teaching several sections. The section to which the lesson was given had been given the lesson the Friday before. There was no school Monday because of a storm. Then, instead of requiring the children to turn in their papers the Wednesday of Thanksgiving week, as I might have done, I told them they could have until next Monday. The other sections had turned in their papers the week before. I had consulted Mr. Tetlow before telling this section that it might do the lesson during the Thanksgiving recess. He had assented. The girls themselves made no complaint.[39]

But in fact one student had complained to Tetlow.

I thought it was some girl who had been absent before Thanksgiving on account of illness and inquired of one of these girls. She said she had not complained but told me that Marion Brooks, daughter of the superintendent, was the girl who had gone to Mr. Tetlow. Miss Brooks was not one of the girls in the section who was to do the lesson during the recess. I asked her why she had gone to Mr. Tetlow and she gave me no reason. I did not scold her. I did tell her I was always glad to talk to the girls about their lessons and would cheerfully excuse any girl from her lessons that could advance a good reason.[40]

In the meantime, after meeting with Brooks, parent committee members Filene and Crawford rescinded their support of Griswold. They issued a minority position to the committee: "When we came to talk over the matter with Mr. Brooks, it became evident to us that certain large questions of educational policy were so closely interwoven with her [Griswold's] removal that we could not tell whether the transfer was or was not justified."[41] Tetlow responded:

> The superintendent's "policy" of which so much is said... and its relation to the standard scholarship hereafter to be maintained in the high and Latin schools of this city, are interesting educational questions on which I have a professional opinion; but as, in my judgment, this policy has only a remote bearing on the transfer of Miss Griswold from the Girls' Latin School, I will not discuss it here.[42]

On January 11, Tetlow told the *Herald*, "The implied statement that at one time 62 percent of the pupils were notified their work was unsatisfactory has no foundation in fact.... The attitude of the teachers at the Girls' Latin School toward the superintendent has never been insubordinate or hostile."[43] The *Herald* continued its detailed coverage the next day when it reported Filene and Crawford's perception of their meeting with Brooks:

> At the hearing before the school committee, which we suppose will be held soon, the facts supporting the statements contained in our report will be fully gone into.... As to the necessity for a change in the methods in operation in the Girls' Latin School, Mr. Brooks invited us to consult the assistant superintendents, who had recommended a more rational and humane system of marking. Mr. Brooks told the committee of five when he tried to put this system into effect he became convinced by the results that Miss Griswold was so hostile to the new policy that it would never be carried out by her.[44]

Three days later, the *Herald* reported that Duncan A. Russell, chairman of the parents' committee, had formally asked the school board to reinstate Griswold. They drew up a petition stating, in part, "[we] ask that our children not be arbitrarily deprived of this valuable teacher without just and sufficient cause." It continued:

> This committee will prepare a formal petition to present to the school board. They intend to go before that body with the request that they be granted a private hearing and that they be given specific reasons as

to why Miss Griswold should not be reinstated. In the event that this private conference does not result satisfactorily, the committee will ask for a public hearing.[45]

A letter from the Girls' Latin School Alumnae Association had been sent to Brooks on January 3 in which he was asked to reconsider Griswold's transfer. Although Brooks expressed a willingness to meet with them, they were unable to secure an appointment. A committee including Abbie Farwell Brown '91, Caroline B. Shaw '97, Blanche Bonnelle Church '98, and Carrie V. Lynch '90 was appointed to present a petition to the School Committee. The *Herald* relayed their concern:

> Mr. Brooks' apparent discourtesy in omitting to acknowledge the letter of Jan. 3 is disappointing to the alumnae because of the friendly relations which have heretofore existed between them and Mr. Brooks. The alumnae feel sure, however, the attitude of the school committee is considerate, realizing as they must, that the request comes from intelligent and public-spirited women, who have at heart the best interests of the public school system."[46]

A letter written by Brooks on January 16 replied:

> At the meeting of the Girls' Latin School Alumnae Association a year ago... I told alumnae some material changes in the Girls' Latin school must be made in order to adapt it to the present conditions.... Especially it is not true that I am planning to lower the standards of the school... my attitude is not that of one who is determined to carry out regardless of the detrimental consequences to the school system... because of personal or selfish motives.[47]

When the parents and alumnae were finally granted a public hearing on January 20, some 500 to 600 people crowded the School Committee offices on Mason Street. Brooks, Tetlow, and Griswold were absent. The committee began by reading the following statement from Brooks:

> In answer to your request for a statement of the reasons underlying the transfer of Miss Ellen C. Griswold.... Miss Griswold was transferred because she was not in sympathy with certain fundamental plans and

policies essential to the improvement of the Girls' Latin School. Her dominant influence in the school was such that the transfer was necessary in order to render possible the more rapid correction of the serious defects in the spirit of the school and the methods of instruction therein.

From the beginning of my service as supervisor in 1902 ... I have always found the GLS school less responsive to suggestions ... than any other school under my supervision.

The instruction given in a school should be constructive not destructive, positive not negative. ... Many teachers in the High and Latin Schools take pride in the superior quality of the students that survive what is called "the weeding out" process. This process has, in my opinion, been carried out to an extent not justified in schools supported by public taxation.[48]

Brooks went on to criticize the school because one-quarter of all students received failing grades. He went to great lengths to point out that some of the failed pupils went on to secure admission to the best colleges, from which they graduated with honor.[49] Next, Chairman Storrow read a letter he had received:

As a citizen and former member of the school board I wish to express my appreciation of the courteous stand taken by Supt. Brooks. ... He deserves the thoughtful commendation of all thoughtful citizens who feel the public schools supported by all people, are not the property of any clique or faction, social or political, who believe that the daughter of the immigrant, fighting up to college, should receive ... the same measure of sympathy and help that is accorded to the maiden of approved ancestry.[50]

WHATSOEVER THINGS ARE TRUE

At the January 27 School Committee meeting, the superintendent's decision was "unanimously endorsed."[51]

The School Committee has been requested to reverse the decision of the Superintendent of Schools in transferring Miss Ellen C. Griswold from the Girls' Latin School to a position of equal salary and equal rank in the Dorchester High School. ... We think the judgment of

> the Superintendent was correct, and we see no reason to doubt it was arrived at upon sufficient grounds. We wish to say, furthermore, that we think the Superintendent's judgment was arrived at without any personal bias or partisan or improper motives of any sort. We regard this action as an administrative act, calculated to aid in putting into effect a desirable change of educational policy in the school.

The committee's report then goes on to chastise Tetlow personally.

> There is another aspect of this case which has given this committee more concern than the original cause of the controversy . . . the master, who thereupon took the attitude of vigorous opposition . . . and proceeded to encourage a violent public opposition. . . . We are of the opinion that if the course pursued by Mr. Tetlow since the first decision of the Board in this case were followed by the other 80 school principals in this city . . . it would lead to administrative anarchy in the school system. . . . Mr. Tetlow has become too fixed in the idea that his school cannot be improved . . . and that he is the sole judge of the methods to be used in the school; and we feel it is our duty to express specifically our disapproval of his attitude in regard to this transfer.[52]

The teachers of GLS immediately sought to reassure him of their trust in his leadership.

> We wish unitedly and from full hearts to express to you our confidence and our affection, and we wish to assure you that you have our most loyal support.
>
> | | |
> |---|---|
> | E. H. Atherton | Mary D. Davenport |
> | Mary C. C. Goddard | Sybil B. Aldrich |
> | Abby C. Howes | Julia K. Ordway |
> | Florence Dix | M. Eloise Talbot |
> | Helen A. Stuart | Rosalie Y. Abbot |
> | Fred H. Cowan | Mary R. Stark |
> | Mary J. Foley | Alice M. Smith |
> | Matilda A. Fraser | Clara A. Hawthorne[53] |
> | Jacob Lehmann | |

Tetlow replied to his faculty in a letter addressed to Miss Goddard:

> Will you accept for yourself, and convey to the other teachers, my most grateful appreciation of the cordial expression of esteem and good will I received from you and them? In a sense I did not need the written assurance, for there has never been any lack of unmistakable evidence of the mutual trust existing between us; but it will always be a pleasure, whatever the future may have in store, to have something to remind me that those who knew me best gave me their complete confidence.[54]

Clearly Tetlow felt his character had been impugned by the School Committee's rebuke, and he wrote one last letter concerning the Griswold affair to School Committeeman David Ellis:

> Now that the School Committee, the supreme authority, have by unanimous vote after a public hearing sustained the Superintendent at every point and administered to me personally a severe rebuke, the matter of the transfer of Miss Griswold is of course closed. It would manifestly be improper for me to make further demonstrances or appeal.
>
> There is one point, however, in the published statement of the School Committee, which, as doing me an injustice, I trust I may, without giving offense, bring to your attention in a personal note. It is assumed in that statement that my "grievance" was that Mr. Lincoln was informed of the proposed transfer before me. That was not my grievance. It would be impossible for me to make so petty and preposterous a complaint. The point of my appeal to the School Board, so far as it was personal, was that the Superintendent had interfered with the internal communication of the Girls' Latin School by transferring without warning of any sort a teacher who enjoyed my full confidence without personally consulting me as to the necessity or advisability of making the transfer. To consult the principal of a school as to the necessity or advisability of a contemplated transfer is one thing; to notify him without previous consultation that such a transfer has already been consummated is quite another.[55]

Tetlow had also reached out to former Superintendent of Schools Edwin Seaver, who wrote back from his home on Nantucket on February 3:

> At this distance, I do not feel I understand very well the matters in controversy between you and Mr. Brooks. In particular, I fail to gain a clear idea

THE UNTIMELY PASSING OF ELLEN CHASE GRISWOLD

In early November 1908, Ellen Chase Griswold took a leave of absence from her duties at Dorchester High School. She had been teaching there for less than a year and hoped to be gone only through the Christmas holidays, expecting her health would improve with some rest.

Instead, her condition rapidly deteriorated. She died of breast cancer on December 13, 1908, at the age of 38. The news spread quickly through Girls' Latin and Dorchester High Schools and was met with disbelief and great sadness.

Her funeral was held the following Tuesday. That morning, John Tetlow forwent the usual morning exercise in the assembly hall to remember the girl who had been his pupil and the woman who had worked for him as a teacher for thirteen years. After reading several passages from the scriptures, he admitted, "I cannot trust myself to speak at length of the life and character of Miss Griswold.... In the trying experiences of her life, she showed a courage, a dignity, and a self-control that were beyond praise."[56]

Emmanuel Episcopal Church, the first building to be built on Newbury Street, was where Griswold had worshipped since she was a young girl. Reverend Elwood Worcester presided over the service. Although the funeral mass was very simple—no music, pallbearers, or ushers—the pews were filled with the teary students to whom she had devoted her life's work. All of her pupils from Dorchester High School and a great number of students from Girls' Latin School were present. Both John Tetlow and Charles J. Lincoln as well as a number of her fellow teachers and Radcliffe College classmates came to pay their respects.

Her mother Adelaide, older sister Loren, and younger sister Kate accompanied the funeral to Forest Hills Cemetery in Roslindale. Ellen Chase Griswold was laid to rest on December 15 in a private family service. She was buried next to her father, Daniel Chase Griswold, and a stone's throw from the grave of James Freeman Clarke, an original member of the Massachusetts Society for the University Education of Women.

After her death, a leather-bound, English-Greek dictionary published in 1876 was found at Girls' Latin School. On the first page, the neat, looped signature of E. C. Griswold was inscribed in pencil. The book was placed in the school library, where it was preserved in perpetual care.

In February 1909, the Radcliffe College class of 1891 presented a reading desk and chair to the Agassiz House theater in memory of Griswold, "whose beautiful character and noble life may well be an inspiration to future students of Radcliffe College."[57] The college also named a room at Cabot Hall in her honor.

Front and back views of Ellen Chase Griswold's gravestone, Forest Hills Cemetery, Roslindale, Massachusetts

of his "policy" or of the "ideals and standards" with which Miss Griswold was said not to be in sympathy. Something about the methods of marking pupils for their recitations he seems to be enforcing with a "big stick."

I was not surprised the public hearing failed to change the determination of the School Committee. Their report, apparently written by Mr. Storrow, was just what I would have expected from him. But what I did not expect, and what stirred hot indignation in me, was the unnecessary addition to the report proper, in which Mr. Storrow goes out of his way to upbraid you for remonstrating against the removal of one of the very best teachers in the city from your school. You would be wanting in your duty as master if you did not remonstrate; and it is surely no part of your duty to keep a knowledge of the facts in the case from the public. How could a man of Mr. Storrow's knowledge of affairs expect to have such an action as Mr. Brooks undertook kept away from the public? Such things cannot be done in corner and covered up. You need not take the trouble to answer this. I only felt the impulse to express myself and wanted you to know you have my full sympathy.[58]

Arthur Fiske of the Boston Latin School was absent from all proceedings, and no teachers were transferred from Boston Latin School in order to increase graduation rates or to reform the school's grading or selectivity processes. Tetlow received many letters of support from GLS alumnae, which lifted his spirits through those dark days. "Letters kept coming from all over the country. They cheered him and really kept him from a nervous breakdown," said Mary Foley.[59] Mary Underhill '09 said afterward:

> I knew at the time, with an emotional child's sense of the dramatic, that I should never forget Miss Griswold's last day in school, when she looked down from one of those semi-circular windows on us, assembled to sing the Christmas hymns. But I did not know how deep, how equally ineradicable would be the memory of the voice of John Tetlow, just and kind, scholarly and wise, reading [Philippians 4:8]: "Whatsoever things are true, whatsoever things are honest, whatsoever things are just, whatsoever things are pure, whatsoever things are of good report; if there be any virtue, and if there be any praise, think on these things."[60]

1906
Iola D. Yates is first African American student to graduate from GLS.

◀ 1907
Girls' Latin School moves to its brand new building on Huntington Avenue in September.

1908 ▶
Fire devastates Chelsea, Massachusetts.

1909 ▶
Museum of Fine Arts, Boston, opens on Huntington Avenue.

◀ 1910
BLS headmaster Arthur I. Fiske dies and is replaced by Henry Pennypacker.

John Tetlow retires as headmaster of Girls' Latin School effective August 31; Ernest G. Hapgood takes the helm.

◀ 1911
John Tetlow dies on December 9.

1912
Mary Antin's *At School in the Promised Land* is published and becomes a best seller.

Fenway Park opens on ▶
April 20.

1912
John Tetlow's memorial service is held at Arlington Street Church, April 8.

1914 ▶
Tower on Boston Custom House is built.

VI

Big Changes

The shopping hour, downtown Boston, 1910

NEW HOME ON HUNTINGTON AVENUE

Ironically, in September of the year the Ellen Griswold affair boiled over, John Tetlow finally achieved what he had hoped to accomplish for almost 30 years: the opening of the new Girls' Latin School building, situated on a beautiful swath of lawn on Huntington Avenue.

In late August 1907, after returning from vacation on Cape Cod, Tetlow arrived at the site of the new school to review the construction crew's finishing touches. He and Elizabeth had purchased a new home in Brookline, making his new commute no longer—and arguably easier—than the ride from Cedar Street in Roxbury to West Newton Street had been. Tetlow was now almost 65 years old, and his life's work crystallized as he pulled up to the beautiful building before him.

The total cost for the new building was just over $296,000, a modest amount by Boston public school standards. GLS had 375 students, and the new 17,382-square-foot building could accommodate up to 600. The 9,000-square-foot common building in the middle held the gymnasium, lunchroom, and lockers and was adorned with a beautiful clock tower. The south building was to house the city's Normal School, and the west building was reserved for the 17-room grammar school, the P. A. Collins School. (The total project cost for all three schools was $1,044,298.)

Limestone blocks, each bearing a single letter, had been inserted on a ledge atop the building to spell out *Girls' Latin School*. Over the main entrance, within a rectangle of terra cotta guarded by a winged eagle, had been inscribed LET THY LIFE BE SINCERE. This phrase rendered in Latin—*Vita sua sincera sit*—became the school's motto.

Another inscription surmounted the door leading from the courtyard back into the building: *Hic patet ingeniis campus: certusque merenti stat favor: ornatur propriis industria donis* (Here is an open field for talent; appreciative recognition is assured to the deserving; diligent application is honored with due rewards).

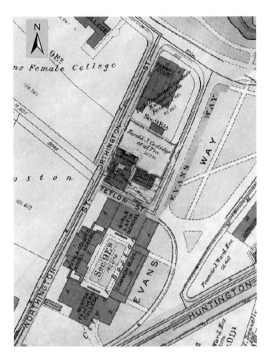

A detail of a 1931 Bromley atlas shows the newly created Boston schools complex, with GLS situated approximately at right, facing Tetlow Street; across from GLS is Tetlow Hall; Near the top of the map Isabella Stewart Gardner's recently built Fenway Court can be seen.

Tetlow recalled the hours he had mulled over these inscriptions:

The inscriptions over the entrances to our school building express the ideals we should cherish and the purposes we should aim to realize in our daily work. The leading inscription over the main entrance, is in English, and is comprehensive enough in its suggestiveness to embody all the essential virtues of personal character: let thy life be sincere. The second inscription, the one over the court entrance to the building, is in Latin, as is appropriate for a classical school and is taken from the poet Claudian. . . . Such an inscription is full of encouragement and cheer, and we shall do well to reflect the spirit of it in our work and conduct.[1]

The floors were a yellowish crushed marble aggregate, trimmed on the outside and divided into squares by granite. In the spacious entry vestibule, the ceiling was made of fifteen glass skylights that flooded the interior with light when the sun shone. Transoms over each classroom door let in more light. Every street-facing wall had a set of three huge Palladian windows with panes more than 16 feet high. Atop the windows were plaster carvings of fruits and flowers. The four buildings of the complex framed an inner courtyard with a lawn, a bench, and a water fountain on the GLS side. By Tetlow's visit, the masons had hooked up the system, and refreshing cold water filled the limestone basin.

The school sat at the very edge of the Back Bay Fens, a park system along the Muddy River. The Fens made up part of Frederick Law Olmsted's Emerald Necklace, a chain of interconnected green spaces that stretched throughout Boston. The rear of the school was bounded by Worthington Street, which later would be renamed Palace Road; to the north it was bounded by Tetlow Street, named for the headmaster.

Although construction continued in the form of fine detail completion and cleanup, school started on Wednesday, September 11, 1907. Books, blackboards, and desks were in place, but too few chairs had been ordered, forcing some girls to carry chairs from one classroom to another. The new Girls' Latin School housed 22 classrooms, two physics and botany laboratories, an assembly hall, a library, and offices for the headmaster and teachers. One room had even been set aside as a nurse's office for students who had been taken ill.

The eagle-crowned plaque set into the pediment above the main entrance proclaiming the GLS motto

Classrooms were on average much smaller than those in the previous school building: each held about 56 desks. New features were introduced, such as charts, wall maps, and battery blackboards with two panels of natural slate that slid up and down like windows. The new chemistry and botany labs included soapstone sinks and vent hoods to remove odors. Completely electric buildings were still something of a novelty, but the new school's systems included all the latest advances in electricity and heating.

For the first time, Girls' Latin had telephones as well as its own switchboard. A "telephone in the four-party coin box service"—an early pay phone—also had been installed.[2] During the early days of the school year, teachers were calling each other on the intercom in their classrooms to verify the extensions they had been assigned.

Another eagle protects the Latin inscription over the door into the school from the courtyard.

Concerning her new room, one teacher, Mary Goddard, observed:

> There is a pleasant outlook from the windows of the room where I am writing. As I glance up from my desk, I see the splendid buildings of the Harvard Medical School gleaming white through the branches of intervening trees, while away off to my right stretches a broad pasture in which, during the autumn, cattle graze peacefully.... Beyond the pasture, and bordered by tall elms, is Brookline Avenue, along which

Big Changes

an occasional street-car glides noiselessly. Still farther in the distance, rises from among surrounding trees the square tower of a little church. How charming and restful it all is.[3]

Most girls loved the new light, airy, and quiet building and were glad to leave the cramped, dingy, dark, and noisy rooms in Copley Square. A

AFRICAN AMERICAN STUDENTS AT GLS

Anita Hemmings, ca. 1897

Although we probably will never know for certain, the issue of race may have delayed enrollment of the first student of African American descent at Girls' Latin. Anita Hemmings, valedictorian of the Prince School's class of 1888, was not accepted at GLS, unlike previous class leaders from this school, perhaps due to her race. Instead, she attended Girls' High School during the time Tetlow was its headmaster. Upon graduating in 1892, Hemmings enrolled at Vassar College, from which she received her diploma, despite an uproar that ensued when the school discovered that she was of mixed-race heritage.

The first African American graduate of Girls' Latin School is not known with certainty. According to the *Boston Globe* of April 4, 1891, John Tetlow reported that Girls' Latin School had two "colored" pupils (of 200 students).[4] It is unclear if the two black students to whom Tetlow referred actually graduated—no GLS graduate surnames from 1891 through 1897 appear to match those of any Boston-area black families—but U.S. Census information confirms that Girls' Latin graduated at least three African Americans between 1906 and 1908. Thus, Iola D. Yates, class of 1906, is the first black graduate known with certainty.

Yates was born to Nicholas and Lucy Yates in Virginia in September 1888; in Boston the family lived on Savoy Street in the South End. Iola graduated from the Everett School for Girls in 1902 and entered Girls' Latin in the ninth grade. Following graduation, she attended the two-year teaching program at the Normal School and was eligible to teach in 1908. She became a teaching assistant in grade two at the Tileston School on Norfolk Street in Mattapan and was one of the first five black teachers hired in Boston.

Both Ethel Johnson and Ethel Caution-Davis were graduates of the class of 1908. Johnson, born in Maryland in June 1888, appears to have moved to Massachusetts with her widowed mother, Eletha, to live with her father's sister Jennie. Eletha had married at 16 and given birth to Ethel when she was 17. The Johnsons boarded in Jamaica Plain, where Eletha worked as a cook and laundress, and Jennie worked as a waitress and cook. It is remarkable that Ethel Johnson, from impoverished circumstances, was the first African American GLS graduate to be accepted at Radcliffe College, from which she graduated in 1912.

Two of the first ten African American graduates of Radcliffe College (Ethel Johnson in 1912 and Frances Olivia Grant in 1917) and three of the first ten African American graduates of Wellesley College (Ethel Caution-Davis in 1912, Adelaide Sears Robinson in 1917, and Katherine Naomi Robinson in 1922) were GLS alumnae.

report in *The Jabberwock* later in the year read, "Many gay little groups were formed at Dudley Street and other stations, and all were excited by the novelty of being the first to occupy the beautiful new school house. The large, bright, building filled them with delight, but they lingered longest in the library, with its cozy arm chairs, fireplace and long rows of tables and shelves."[5]

Ethel Caution-Davis

In the late nineteenth and early twentieth centuries, the long artery of Washington Street was downtown Boston's commercial heart. Colorful striped awnings and large black wooden signs with gold letters adorned its buildings. The neighborhood's department stores sold everything from clothing, dry goods, fabrics, and shoes to housewares and candies. Trollies and omnibuses with open bodies and bench seating moved slowly down the middle of the street on tracks. Outside the trolley lane, both horse-drawn carts and covered wagons transporting every conceivable good maneuvered from store to store. Pushcarts parked on the side streets sold fresh fruits and vegetables weighed by scale. Several of Boston's daily newspapers were printed nearby, within a multi-block stretch of streets known as Newspaper Row. The latest news was often written in chalk on blackboards that stood directly in front of each paper's offices, congesting the busy street even more.

Filene's Department Store on Washington Street was a vital part of this busy district. Rising five stories, it was the largest specialty store for women's apparel in the country. There a young African American woman named Ethel Caution-Davis would report to the executive dining room where she waited tables, serving food and picking up plates after wealthy businessmen had finished eating. The slight-figured woman worked diligently, seemingly absorbed in her work. But she would listen discreetly when the men discussed where they intended to send their daughters to college.

Ethel Caution was born on April 18, 1887, in Williamsport, Pennsylvania; the family later moved to Ohio. Both her parents died when she was young, and in 1892 Ethel was adopted by a white woman surnamed Davis, who became her guardian. As a young black girl she knew she had already broken an important barrier when her white foster mother enrolled her at Girls' Latin School in 1904: at the time it was still highly unusual for black students to attend GLS.[6] Only two other black girls were enrolled at GLS at the time—Ethel E. Johnson was in the same class as Caution-Davis, and Iola D. Yates '06 was two years ahead.

As Caution-Davis waited tables at Filene's, she noted that Wellesley was mentioned prominently when the discussion turned to women's colleges. She decided that that was the college she would attend, and she applied and was accepted. To earn money for tuition, she prepared an elocution program, a series of memorized poems and speeches that she would deliver as an event to which she charged an admission fee at black churches around Boston. Caution-Davis eventually saved $175, enough for Wellesley's tuition at that time.

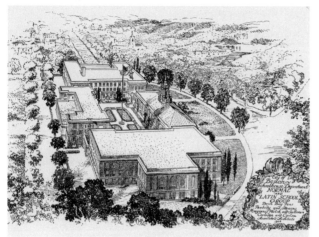
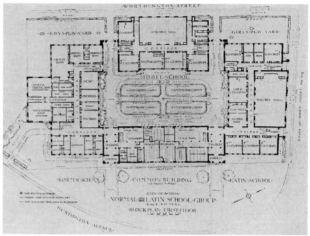

Left: Architect's rendering of the exterior of the Normal and Latin School Group
Right: Plan of the first floor.

The new building did not live up to expectations of a few students, however; some expressed disappointment because "it was not as wonderful as everyone had hoped for, but not even as good as the one lost."[7] Something important was missing. In December, the Girls' Latin Alumnae Association donated a replica Parthenon frieze to the school assembly hall that was very similar to the one that had adorned the hall at the West Newton Street school. It encircled the room at the top of the wall, and it remains there today as part of the Pozen Center at the Massachusetts College of Art. The alumnae erected a bronze tablet dedicating the room as John Tetlow Hall. "We now have an acoustically perfect assembly hall, in which we meet twice a week for an opening exercise," Tetlow reported.[8]

More than a hundred gifts had been given to GLS over its three decades of existence, and each item found a home in the new building. Photographs of the interior and exterior of the Colosseum at Rome, a gift from the inaugural graduating class of 1883, were hung in Room 27. The bust of Cicero donated by the class of 1885 went into Room 30; the bas-relief *Apollo and the Muses* from the class of 1888, of Apollo playing his lyre while nine muses dance, was placed above the door to Room 26. In the lobby was a tablet that reproduced the caryatids from the Acropolis at Athens. The frieze of the three caryatids—two at either end supporting the roof and the other seated between them—had been a present from the class of 1893.

The reproduction of the *Cantoria* by Luca della Robbia remained a favorite. The frieze had been donated to the school by Mrs. Katherine E.

Left: Tetlow Hall, the assembly hall at the new GLS
Right: GLS gymnasium

Stillings as a memorial to her daughter Elise Kemp, who died while in high school but would have graduated in 1896. Perhaps the piece dearest to the school was the statuette of Joan of Arc from the class of 1903, which came to occupy the second landing of the east staircase at Huntington Avenue. Later, the classical vase given by the class of 1907 was placed in the reception room, where it commemorated the last class to graduate from the old building in Copley Square.

TETLOW RETIRES

February 4, 1908, marked the thirtieth anniversary of the school's founding, and as the date drew near, John Tetlow reflected on the school's history and, for the first time, seriously considered its future without him. In an article published in the February 1908 edition of *The Jabberwock*, he put some of his thoughts on paper.

> As I sat last Christmas morning before a table piled with books that had come the evening before . . . my eye was attracted to one of the new books by the familiar name of a former pupil on the back and title page. . . . The author was Professor Vida D. Scudder of Wellesley College. . . . The thought which her name suggests . . . is that she was one of the group of thirty-one girls, to which Miss Howes also belonged, who constituted the entire Girls' Latin School during the first half year of its existence.
>
> The difference between a school of thirty-one girls, occupying two small rooms in a building belonging to another institution, and

Big Changes

Exterior façade showing Girls' Latin School *spelled out in limestone blocks*

a school like ours today of five hundred pupils in the independent possession of a building of its own, planned and equipped to meet its exact needs, is so great that it is difficult for the imagination to grasp the development of one out of the other; but the two are as naturally related as the seed and the matured plant.

This thirtieth anniversary of the founding of our school may fittingly remind us that we have a history in which we may justly take an affectionate interest and pride. Perhaps it may prompt us to hope the future of the school gives promise to still worthier service.[9]

At the end of the 1910 school year, the 67-year-old headmaster finally made the painful, bittersweet decision to retire effective August 31. Tetlow had been at the helm of Girls' Latin School for more than three decades, and during that time he had guided it through the difficult first years of its infancy to a position of respect and renown. GLS now had 620 students, making it almost 25 times its original size. Just a year earlier, his good friend Charles W. Eliot had retired after 40 years as president of Harvard. William Coe Collar, former president of Roxbury Latin, had taken his leave two years earlier, in September 1908. Tetlow had already resigned as a trustee of Roxbury Latin School, and Arthur I. Fiske had just died, weeks after his resignation from the headmastership of Boston Latin. Tetlow did not wish his life to end without seeing through some of his personal plans. It was time.

"His resignation from the Girls' Latin School came as a surprise," said one former Brown University classmate, "as he has not shown any lack of physical or mental strength; and at the recent reunion of the Sons of Brown during the past winter, he seemed as well and vigorous and vivacious as usual."[10] Publicly, he said that he wanted time to enjoy traveling and study; more personally, he also wanted to spend time with his wife, Elizabeth, who was ten years younger than he was. Nevertheless, it remained difficult for him to leave.

Letters with good wishes and great thanks began to pour in from past students, teachers, and colleagues. Mary Coes, recently appointed dean of Radcliffe College, wrote to say how sorry she was to hear of Tetlow's retirement "because you have always held your students to a very high standard of work and have given us much satisfactory college work from your pupils as a result of their early training."[11] Former student Sibyl Collar Holbrook wrote:

It is a source of deep regret to me to find the news of your retirement from active service confirmed and authentic. I had hoped to hear someone had blundered. You know I intend to have my daughter Carolyn a Latin School girl and I had cherished the hope that she might have at least one year in the school as I knew it and loved it looking to you as its head. May I not bring her for one morning's visit this week? Indeed, since we are going to Provincetown on Wednesday to stay until the 25th, tomorrow will be our one day to see any school work. If for any reason it would not be convenient or agreeable for us to visit the school tomorrow Tuesday, perhaps you can send us a telephone message before quarter past eight when we should be starting. Otherwise this note will need no reply since I shall hope to see you tomorrow and express more fully my regret at leaving your flock shepherdless.[12]

Classical vase, a gift of the class of 1907, the last class to graduate from the school in Copley Square

The outpouring of gratitude was incalculable, but the highest form of praise for this man of sterling character was that he was considered the only educator in Boston who "could confront Charles W. Eliot with an opinion divergent and continue to function."[13]

Under Tetlow, the GLS Alumnae Association had grown into a strong and well-organized support group for the school. The record for 1910 states: "The GLS Alumnae Association feels that the school has met with an almost irreparable loss in the resignation of its beloved Headmaster, Dr. John Tetlow, by whose vision, efficiency, and determination a high standard of scholarship was established and has been steadily maintained in this institution for the thirty-two years of its existence."[14]

The association voted to make a gift to the school of an oil painting of John Tetlow. On June 3, Helen A. Stuart, chairman of the portrait committee, unveiled the portrait of Tetlow, which was hung in the library. The artist, Ernest L. Ipsen, a highly respected portraitist, had also painted Charles James Capen, senior master of the Boston Latin School, a few years earlier. In *The Jabberwock*, Tetlow reported, "When I was asked, some months ago, to sit for my portrait . . . I will not deny that a momentary feeling of disinclination and reluctance flitted through my own mind. . . . On presenting myself at the Fenway Studios and introducing myself to Mr. Ipsen, the artist, I found . . . I had the most agreeable prospect before me."[15] Tetlow spoke at his last graduation in 1910 to 62 graduates. Many honors followed: the Boston School Committee, perhaps in atonement for

Big Changes

the Griswold controversy, voted to grant him the honorary title of headmaster emeritus, and he chose his successor, Ernest G. Hapgood.

In September, Tetlow applied for passports for himself and Elizabeth in preparation for traveling abroad for twelve months. The Tetlows sailed for Greece in October 1910 to begin an extensive European trip that included stops in Rome, Perugia, Florence, Pisa, Genoa, Milan, and Como in Italy as well as Switzerland, Germany, Holland, and France. Daughters Elsie and Frances joined them, and Helen received several letters with the details of her parents' daily travels:

> [February 10, 1911] If you should look in on Mamma and me at this moment, I'm afraid you would think we were living beyond our means. We have an elegantly furnished room, with windows that reach nearly from the floor to the ceiling on two sides, in a hotel [The Royal Hotel] that is in the middle of an orange grove on the edge of the Sorrento shore opposite Naples. From one of the windows we look right across at the Vesuvius.[16]

Headmaster John Tetlow, ca. 1910

When Tetlow returned from the trip of a lifetime, he was anxious to share his travels with his former students.

> Brookline, October 25, 1911
> Dear Readers of the Jabberwock,
>
> I should have appeared there to greet you long ago but for a persistent cold and cough, which have left my voice unequal to the strain of a thirty-five minute talk in a large hall.... How disappointed I am that I have not yet been able to visit the school. I had looked forward to my first visit to you as one of the greatest satisfactions waiting for me on my return home.... I visited Pompeii and Vesuvius; and at Vesuvius I actually sat on the edge of a crater, and looked down into the smoking interior. It was a well behaved volcano at the time, but a month later ... I learned from the newspapers the volcano had become active again, and that edge of the crater on which I sat—had fallen in and been swallowed up in the seething mass of molten matter....
>
> But this letter has already gone beyond the limits of a mere greeting.... I will stop here ... and sign myself, with warmest affection,
>   John Tetlow[17]

TRAGEDY STRIKES

Tetlow loved to ride his bicycle in the cold invigorating air of late autumn, and one day in late November 1911 he decided to ride from his home in Brookline to Jamaica Plain and circle around Jamaica Pond, a much-loved haven for ice skating in the winter and boating in the summer.

As he started down Perkins Street alongside the pond, a car suddenly appeared. In a split second, Tetlow had been hit hard and thrown from the bike. The driver, Dr. George H. Francis, pulled over and, after a brief examination, told Tetlow that fortunately he did not appear to have any broken bones or other injuries. The doctor apologized and offered to drive him home. Tetlow went to bed to rest from the bruises he received in the crash. The newspaper report filed several days later stated, "He seemed to be recovering from his fall and on Saturday left his bed to exercise in the house a little. On returning to bed to rest, he sank into a deep sleep and never regained consciousness."[18] Tetlow did not know he had fractured his pelvis and suffered a subperitoneal hemorrhage, which led to a heart attack. He passed away on December 9, 1911, at the age of 68.

When Headmaster Hapgood made the announcement at assembly hall, "it seemed as if an invisible black pall had fallen over the school, shrouding it in gloom and sorrow."[19] On December 12, the day of the funeral service, classes were cancelled for both Girls' Latin School and Girls' High School. Among the 200 or so funeral attendees were almost every Boston public and private school principal, the complete faculty of Girls' Latin, and twelve GLS students who were chosen to represent the student body. Reverend James DeNormandie—father of Sarah DeNormandie, class of 1887—presided over the services. Tetlow was cremated at Forest Hills Cemetery, and his ashes were interred in New Bedford in the grave next to that of his first wife, Elizabeth Harrington Tetlow.

Many members of the GLS community had hoped Tetlow would provide advice and guidance to the school for many years to come, and his sudden death changed the character of the Alumnae Association's annual meeting on December 28. Letters attest to the heartfelt outpouring of regard for the man who had led the school for so many years. Vida A. Scudder, class of 1880, wrote Mrs. Tetlow:[20]

> My heart has so often turned tenderly to you since the news reached me of your great loss; and memory of the dear old

Big Changes

girl-hood days has been vital within. How we girls adored you, and how eagerly we followed your husband's splendid guidance! He was a very large part of my life for several years and I always say he gave me more help than any other teacher I ever had, except Professor York Powell at Oxford. In your loss and in your sorrow you must be comforted, I think, by the knowledge of the noble service which for so many years he faithfully rendered the city, and of the deep honour in which he is held by thousands. As we grow older, the pilgrim way stretches brief ahead, and the waiting love grows brighter. May you ever walk in its light.[21]

Resolutions honoring Tetlow were adopted by unanimous vote at a regular meeting of the Boston School Committee on January 1, 1912. In its annual report, the committee noted, "Dr. Tetlow was a scholar of singular breadth and accuracy, essentially a teacher who could tolerate none but the highest possible standards in the work of pupils and teachers. . . . In him the schools of Boston had a principal of national reputation who well deserved the high esteem in which he was universally held as the organizer and builder of one great classical school."[22]

A memorial service organized by alumnae was held at the Arlington Street Church on April 8, 1912. A dozen esteemed colleagues spoke about Tetlow's life. Superintendent Brooks opened the event by saying, "We are assembled this afternoon to pay tribute to a man. . . whose steadfast integrity and insistence upon those things he believed to be right has done much to place the schools of Boston in the position they occupy in the minds of the educated of this country."[23] James Greenleaf Croswell, headmaster of the Brearley School in New York and representative of the Headmasters' Association, said:

> Your teacher was a great man. . . . The first impression that he made on me was one that I am sure you all know. In the first fifteen minutes of my acquaintance with him I said, "This man loves work." The next I am sure you know. In my next fifteen minutes of my acquaintance I said, "This man would love me to work." In the third fifteen minutes, and from that time on, my feeling of him was "I should love to work with him." He had that natural leadership. He conveyed that ideal almost irresistibly, relentlessly. He was a worker, and he spoke of work. He loved accuracy. He loved efficiency. He loved good work.[24]

One attendee described Tetlow's role in protesting the transfer of Ellen Griswold, noting that he came forward prominently to defend his teacher. Another said of him, "Exact scholarship, clear reasoning, and well balanced judgment have characterized all his work. . . . He has taught his pupils to be governed by principle rather than impulse, stimulated to do their best, and imbued them with a strong love of learning."[25]

Next, Ernest Hapgood, Tetlow's successor as headmaster of Girls' Latin School, addressed the audience. "Never was a man more generous to a young man entering upon opportunities of a great career than to me his successor. He unfolded to me his heart—I saw written on it the name of the school which he had founded, which he nurtured in its infancy and brought to maturity. . . . I think he loved that school with a love that was surpassing the love of human mind."[26]

With Tetlow's departure and death came the end of an era, one in which the young women attending GLS could look to few role models of college-educated women for inspiration. They were pioneers at a time when women's opportunities for employment and public service were almost nonexistent. Even so, the memory of the man and his contributions lived on. In 1953, in honor of the 75th anniversary of the founding of Girls' Latin School, Tetlow's daughter Helen wrote the following: "It is still an experience to meet people who remember my father. They speak of him with bated breath, deep appreciation, and pride that they have been his pupils. With them his influence remains a living guide."[27]

Ralph Waldo Emerson observed that every institution is the lengthened shadow of one man, and in many respects, Girls' Latin School in its early years was the shadow of John Tetlow. There is little doubt he was the man who set its standards and established its reputation. The educational accomplishments of his students earned him deep respect, but present-day recognition of his role in the success of GLS cannot be underestimated. John Tetlow was one of the country's first oracles for girls' educational excellence.

The gravesite of John Tetlow and his first wife, Elizabeth, Forest Hills Cemetery in New Bedford, Massachusetts

1914
James Michael Curley is elected mayor of Boston for the first of his four terms.

1922
The Athenian Club is founded at GLS.

1920 ▶
Women in the United States win the right to vote.

1920
BLS headmaster Henry Pennypacker resigns and is replaced by Patrick T. Campbell.

1922
Curley is re-elected mayor of Boston.

◀ 1922
A new BLS building on Avenue Louis Pasteur—the school's current home—is completed.

1924 ▶
The Normal School changes its name to the Teachers College of the City of Boston.

◀ 1926
GLS adopts "Hail, Girls' Latin School!" as its school song.

1927
◀ Roxbury Latin School relocates from Kearsarge Avenue in Roxbury to West Roxbury.

Abbie Farwell Brown dies on March 4.

1928
GLS celebrates its fiftieth anniversary.

◀ Maribel Vinson '28 participates in the Winter Olympics in St. Moritz, Switzerland.

VII

The "Happy" Days

Arlington Street Church near the southwest corner of Boston's Public Garden, with Boylston Street in the foreground

When school began at eight o'clock, it was already 77 degrees, and the mercury would climb steadily until it reached 90 degrees at 12:30 P.M. Only an afternoon rainstorm would temper the heat of the first day of school, September 11, 1912—the hottest in 40 years.

The headmaster's office at Girls' Latin School was tucked to the right of the vestibule inside the Huntington Avenue entrance. Seated at his desk, Headmaster Ernest Hapgood was a big bear of a presence. The top of his desk was lined with books. The cubbyholes just beneath were stuffed with pending correspondence. One chair, for visitors, was placed to the immediate left of the desk, at the edge of which sat a black candlestick telephone. The silver cast iron radiator hissed constantly in the background during winter, but was silent on this hot first day of school.

Hapgood had been born during the week of February 11, 1878, the very same week the first class commenced at GLS. Whether through karma or fate, he and GLS were destined to share their lives for 70 years. Standing more than six feet tall, he towered over students and teaching staff alike, and though of medium build, his height made him seem imposing. He had soft brown eyes, wore distinctive oval rimless glasses, and parted his

Ernest Hapgood at his desk

hair in the middle. Students regarded him as handsome, and more than one "fainted" to attract his attention. He joined the faculty in 1905, which made him one of only four male teachers at the school. Marjorie Taylor Sanderson '11 recalled Hapgood's first day after he became head of the mathematics department: "On September 9, 1908, it was as if a fresh breeze swept through the classic calm of Girls' Latin School. A tall, purposeful form strode through our corridors, brooking no obstacles; and to upper classmen mathematics became a joy . . . and our joy knew no bounds when on September 14, 1910, Mr. Hapgood became our headmaster."[1]

In short order, the girls had nicknamed him "Happy."

Hapgood reviewed in his head the points he wanted to make as he prepared to give his third speech as headmaster. It was the first time a new school year had begun after John Tetlow's passing, but in many ways Hapgood was even more resolute about upholding and improving academic standards. The corridor outside his office was packed with students, hushed by rule, filing into the assembly hall.

Assembly hall conduct followed strict regulations; the student handbook at the time read: "On the way to the Assembly Hall in other than silent passing periods, pupils are to observe the Assembly Period Quiet of 8:55 to 9:00 AM. AFTER ENTERING THE HALL PUPILS ARE TO REFRAIN ENTIRELY FROM COMMUNICATION."[2] The warning bell had sounded at five minutes of nine, and when he heard the nine o'clock gong, he knew all students would be in place. He stepped out of his office and headed to Tetlow Hall only yards away. The air inside the school was rapidly growing warmer, unseasonable for the new school clothing many had worn.

Hapgood entered the hall through its double doors, walked slowly and purposefully up the middle aisle, and mounted the three steps to the stage. As he reached the podium, assisted by penetrating stares from the faculty, the hall fell into complete silence. The rule of silence upon the headmaster's appearance was a sign of respect that Tetlow had admonished him never to relinquish. Only when the room was completely quiet did he begin to speak, acknowledging the incoming Sixth Class, delineating the school's strict standards, and reminding students of their role in upholding the GLS traditions of rigor and discipline. He concluded by assigning each class to its respective rooms. A Sixth Class student recalled Hapgood's speech: "He tells what is expected of Latin School Students and sends a little frightened shiver down your spine that you will be weighed and found wanting. After his talk you are sent to various rooms. . . . When this ordeal is over, you are allowed to go home with a very vague idea of what has happened."[3]

A CHANGING BOSTON

When Ernest Hapgood became headmaster, John F. "Honey Fitz" Fitzgerald, grandfather of President John F. Kennedy, was serving his second term as mayor of Boston (1910–1914). Fitzgerald, an 1880 graduate of Boston Latin School, would readily tell you, "I came from the streets of the North End. . . without any father or mother or brother or sister who knew anything about Greek or Latin and could give us no help at all in our lessons like most other boys."[4] Fitzgerald was not Boston's first Irish-American mayor, but his narrow defeat of old-guard Brahmin James J. Storrow in the 1910 election signaled the ascendancy of the city's Irish political organization as well as the growing electoral strength of the city's immigrant groups.

ERNEST HAPGOOD

Born in Windham, Vermont, to parents Ephraim and Catherine, Ernest Hapgood grew up in a strict Yankee Protestant environment. As a young boy, he was often up by 5 A.M. so he could complete his chores before walking several miles to school. His father had graduated from Brown University in 1874 and attended the Newton Theological Seminary, where he was ordained. At the time Ernest was born, Ephraim was the pastor of the First Baptist Church in Windham. From 1878 through 1883 the family lived in Nebraska; in 1889 they moved to Boston, where Ephraim took the position of field agent for the Massachusetts Total Abstinence Society.

Ernest Hapgood had attended Brown University from 1888 to 1890, where he played football. He graduated from Tufts University in 1901, and received master's degrees from Tufts in 1905 and Harvard in 1907. Later, in 1911, he was awarded an honorary degree from Brown. After teaching at West Newbury High School, the Volkmann School, and Mechanic Arts High School, he started teaching at GLS in 1905 and became head of the mathematics department in 1908. He was married in 1904 to Edith Kinney, his college sweetheart at Tufts, and they lived at 4 Chester Street in Newton Highlands. Hapgood and his wife would have four children: Virginia, Ernest, Richard, and David. He was elected a Newton alderman and served for a time as chairman of the Athletic Committee for the High School Masters' Club of Massachusetts.

Boston was quite a different city than when Girls' Latin School was established in 1878; by 1910 its population had almost doubled, to 670,585. The Puritan-Brahmin stronghold had melted into a city of Irish and Italian, Catholic and Jewish immigrants. According to the 1910 census, almost 36 percent of Boston's population was foreign born and about 38 percent were native-born children of immigrants. By 1920, the city's population was 32 percent Irish, 16 percent Jewish, and 14 percent Italian.

In response, Boston's wealthiest families began to retreat from the educational fabric of the city, removing their children from enrollment in the public schools. Private schools for boys, like Phillips Exeter and Phillips Andover Academies, attracted increased interest from affluent Bostonians, who considered them the "new" prestigious institutions. Frederic Jaher described this shift:

> Antebellum bluebloods were usually educated at the Boston Public Latin School and Harvard. By the late nineteenth century many patricians, disenchanted with the influx of poor immigrants and supplanted in city government by the Irish, moved to the suburbs ... the Brahmins no longer considered Boston Latin a desirable place to educate their young. They turned, instead, to the boarding school to insulate their children from city vices and pressing immigrant masses.[5]

Private schools for girls including the Winsor School and Miss May's of Boston, formerly considered "debutante dispensaries," suddenly were elevated in esteem.[6] Immigrants without the resources to attend the private schools, however, sought out the public Latin schools in greater numbers. In his history of Boston public schools during the twentieth century, Joseph Cronin wrote, "All of the high schools attracted more students, but the two Latin schools remained the 'jewels in the crown,' the most prestigious public schools in New England."[7]

Succeeding John Fitzgerald in the mayor's office at the City Hall on School Street, was his longtime Irish rival James Michael Curley. Curley, who was elected mayor of Boston for the first time in 1914, had four children at that time, and would go on to have five more; five of his sons would be enrolled in the Public Latin School and two would graduate. His daughter Mary also eventually was enrolled at Girls' Latin.[8]

The laws did not permit the City of Boston to raise taxes or float bonds for new schools. Extra money to be spent beyond the city's tax revenues would require a special act. Curley lobbied the Massachusetts legislature, which passed a bill authorizing the City to expend $750,000 to build a new Public Latin School.

> ORDERED: That in accordance with the provisions of Chapter 199 of the Special Acts of 1919 the sum of $750,000 to meet the expense of building a Public Latin School in City of Boston and the treasurer of said city is requested to issue and sell bonds the proceeds to be expended by the schoolhouse commissioners in accordance with the Chapter 473 of the Acts of 1901.

On March 8, 1917, the school board appropriated $940,947 from the tax levy for this purpose.

The energetic lobbying of four-term mayor James Michael Curley helped ensure that between 1920 and 1925 a total of $14.5 million would become available for the construction of new public schools in Boston. Dedicated in 1923, Boston Latin School's new building on Avenue Louis Pasteur in the Fenway—now directly across Worthington Street from Girls' Latin School—would allow it to grow from 1,592 students in 1923 to 2,000 by 1928, the largest expansion the school had seen in its history.

In the 1920s only 50 percent of Boston students graduated from high school; in an era when mechanical and industrial jobs were comparatively plentiful and farm-related work more common, many young

Greenough's bronze statue of Benjamin Franklin stands in front of Boston's Old City Hall. From 1865 until 1969, this landmark building was home to the City Council and 38 mayors, including James Michael Curley.

BABY DAY

The tradition of Baby Day started sometime after the school moved to Huntington Avenue. On Baby Day, students in the First Class could dress in baby clothing and act like children for the entire day of classes. A 1919 account says the seniors came to school with their hair in curls and large bows on the top of their heads, and "there was no order in your class during that day, but much tittering and even out-right laughing."[9] This tradition would continue until 1976.

Baby Day 1970

169

people entered the workforce without high school diplomas. More than 90 percent of Latin school graduates, however, continued their studies at the college level. Close to one-tenth of the total freshman class—96 boys in all—entered Harvard University in 1925 from Boston Latin.[10] This compares to 19 BLS students being accepted for admission by Harvard in 1916.[11] Likewise for GLS: of 117 graduates of the class of 1925, 17 were accepted to Radcliffe.[12]

HAPGOOD TAKES CONTROL

Hapgood knew that the politics of running a school in Boston had been altered after Tetlow's run-in with Brooks. In 1909, Boston voters had revised the city charter, eliminating the eight-member Board of Aldermen and transferring the board's powers to a strong mayor with a four-year term. The 48-member Common Council was replaced by the 9-member Boston City Council. Hapgood wanted to prove effective not only in navigating this new political system but in calming the waters with the School Committee and superintendent of schools. He recognized that the public wanted to participate in decisions about education. "The old method has been education within the sheltering walls of the cloister in which an occasional peep-hole has been cut, to satisfy the parent and silence the taxpayer. The new method proposes education in the open and under the clear and penetrating rays of the search light," he said.[13]

Hapgood was regarded as a stern disciplinarian and maintained a strict set of rules. He realized that Tetlow's success hinged on one underlying educational premise: discipline. Strict mental discipline was the key ingredient of both academic excellence and a successful life. Without discipline, laziness crept into schoolwork. Every single day he demanded discipline in his students, urging them to be thorough, to concentrate, and to apply what they learned. Student transgressions were noted on their records in pencil; if the girl's behavior improved, the comments were erased, but if she did not, the notes were rewritten in ink.

The annual School Committee report of 1911 restated GLS's singular purpose as well as an important caveat about the number of students the school would admit: "This is exclusively a college preparatory school and offers the standard classical course approved by leading colleges and universities. . . . Pupils are admitted from all parts of the city in so far as the seating capacity of the school permits."[14] That same year, the School Committee formalized the requirements of study at both Latin schools. Pupils whose scholarship allowed them to complete the required courses in six years or longer would receive a diploma from the school; those who completed only a portion of the course of study would receive a certificate of proficiency.

TEACHING AT GLS

Hapgood readily admitted he enjoyed teaching, and he was known to slip into a mathematics class occasionally and take over the recitation when a teacher was absent. Tetlow had left him an outstanding cadre of teachers. Mary J. Foley, who had started teaching in 1888, had the longest tenure, followed by Florence Dix and Edward Atherton, both hired in 1891. Abby C. Howes, Helen A. Stuart, Mary Davenport, Matilda Fraser, Sybil Aldrich, Jacob Lehmann, Julia Ordway, Fred Cowan, Rosalie Abbot, Mary Stark, Adeline Simmons, and Alice Smith all preceded Hapgood in tenure on the teaching staff. Most of them were unmarried, deeply devoted to their work, and mindful of the school's reputation. He made sure he thanked and encouraged his strongest teachers and quietly helped usher those not in step to the door.

In the early 1900s, the pay schedules for all female teachers in the City of Boston lagged significantly behind those of their male counterparts. While men could be masters, women were rarely appointed above the rank of assistant. Boston Latin had set the precedent of hiring only Harvard-educated men as teachers. As of June 1908, a teacher with the rank of master (just below headmaster) earned an annual salary of $3,780; junior masters earned $3,204. Teaching instructors earned $2,340, and starting salaries for assistant teachers were set at a maximum of $1,620. Boston Latin had eleven masters, eight junior masters (all male), and no assistants; Girls' Latin had one master, Edward Atherton, and thirteen assistants, ten of whom were female. Between 1907 and 1917, Hapgood oversaw the doubling of the GLS teaching staff, from 14 to 28. In 1917, the total salary for all 30 teachers at the Boston Latin School was $74,796 compared to $45,326 for the 25 at Girls' Latin School.[15]

Some GLS teachers were aloof, sharp-tongued, and infamous for their attitudes. Behavior deemed unladylike rarely escaped harsh rebuke. Certain teachers wielded like a club the view that few students, if any, could ever be worthy of GLS academic standards and would reprimand students with their own uniquely adapted phrases:

"You will never get into Smith . . ."
"You will fall by the wayside of Girls' Latin School. . ."
"The neighborhood high school beckons you . . ."[16]

Hapgood had every intention of doing a better job of promoting the accomplishments of his students to colleges and the general public

LOUISE BOGAN

Louise Bogan was born on August 11, 1897, in Livermore Falls, Maine. Her parents, May and Daniel, shared a tumultuous relationship, and May's many affairs and indiscretions caused the family to move to Milton, New Hampshire, in 1901, then to Ballardvale, Massachusetts, three years later, and finally in 1909 to a red brick apartment building on Harold Street in Roxbury. The following autumn, her mother enrolled Louise in the Fifth Class of Girls' Latin School. Even then, at thirteen, however, Bogan already had been significantly tempered by the hurt of her parents' relationship, later describing herself as "the semblance of a girl, in which some desires and illusions had been early assassinated: shot dead."[17] In describing Bogan's GLS years, her biographer Elizabeth Frank writes:

> [She] received the best classical education available to girls in this country. Strictly college preparatory, the school saw to it that students were given thorough training in English composition, classical languages, history, mathematics, and science. Louise took Latin, Greek and French and by the time of her graduation had read Xenophon, the *Iliad*, and had a good deal of Latin poetry and prose. She was a member of a literary and debating society called The Athenian Club, and had the good fortune to come under the influence of Miss Carolyn M. Gerrish, A.B., who. . .

read George Herbert to her students, as well as A. E. Housman, a poet who, as Bogan later recalled, was considered "very far out" in 1915. By that time she had already been writing poetry for three years. "I began to write verse from about fourteen on. The lifesaving process then began."[18]

After school was out for the day, Louise would work on her own poetry. "Hours were spent in the branch of the Boston Public Library where she read *Poetry: A Magazine of Verse*, from its very first issue. Her apprenticeship was steady, and by the age of eighteen she had accumulated a 'thick pile of manuscript, in the drawer of the dining room—and had learned every essential of my trade."[19]

as well as to the politicians. When Tetlow retired and spoke at his last graduation in 1910, of the 620 GLS students, 90 percent would go on to college at a time when fewer than 3.8 percent of all female high school graduates in the United States did so.[20] Hapgood made a point of noting on his graduation program the number of students accepted to one of the Seven Sisters colleges; when he assumed the role of headmaster, the number accounted for about one-third of the graduating class, causing him to consider that the school had room to improve. Every year, he marked beside the names listed in his graduation program *R* for

Bogan's first real audience was her fellow classmates and readers of *The Jabberwock*, the pages of which she filled with her writing. Her classmate, Martha Foley, recalled that Headmaster Hapgood sent for Mrs. Bogan to tell her to warn Louise not to expect to become editor of *The Jabberwock*, since, as he explained, "'no Irish girl could be editor of the school magazine.'.... The tall, thin girl from Roxbury, despite the headmaster's bigotry, managed to fill issue after issue with her writing.... All the girls at school knew Louise had great talent, and she was designated Class Poet."[21] The poem she wrote for her graduating class in 1915 reads, in part:

> Who holds to beauty conquers fear,
> Grasps with quick hands temptation's spear,
> Quenches the flame of anger's brand,
>   Fights but one fight, and, if he fall,
>   Rises unvanquished after all,
> Nor asks the world to understand.[22]

Bogan attributed her flair for style to Gerrish: "She taught me that style was the important element, in work of any kind, and that style depended on sincerity and a sense of form, which should grow with the writer. I owe her more than I can say."[23]

After graduating Girls' Latin School in 1915, Louise Bogan spent one year at Boston University; she won a scholarship to Radcliffe, but left school altogether in 1916 to marry Curt Alexander, a corporal in the U.S. Army, with whom she had one daughter, Maidie. The couple divorced in 1918, and Bogan left Maidie in the care of her parents. After spending a few years in Vienna, she returned to New York and published her first book, *Body of this Death: Poems*, in 1923.

At age 31, Bogan submitted two poems for inclusion in *The Jabberwock*'s March 1928 issue, which marked the fiftieth anniversary of the founding of Girls' Latin School. She went on to become one of the most accomplished poets of her time, and in 1945 became the first woman and the first New Englander to be named to the post of poetry consultant to the Library of Congress, a role later renamed poet laureate. For 38 years until 1969, she reviewed poetry for *The New Yorker*, and her poems were published in *The New Republic*, *The Nation*, *Scribner's*, *Atlantic Monthly*, and *Poetry*, among other literary journals. She died of a heart attack on February 4, 1970, in New York.

THE CLUBS OF GIRLS' LATIN

In 1894, German teacher Jacob Lehmann helped organize GLS's first official club, *Die Deutsche Gesellschaft* (The German Society), to encourage girls to speak German outside of class time. In 1903, *Le Cercle Français* was founded to provide a forum outside of class for exploring various aspects of French culture. Without a doubt, however, the Athenian Club was the most important. It was founded by Julia Steere, class of 1915, who later described its founding for *The Jabberwock*:

> On a spring afternoon in 1914, some twelve or fifteen GLS students gathered around the long, and to them impressive, table in the library of the building that then housed our school. There, in the shadow of Mr. Tetlow's portrait that hung above the fireplace, the first meeting of the Athenian Club was held. I entered the school in the third class after having spent a year as a freshman in the Cheyenne High School, Cheyenne, Wyoming, where there had been a literary club, called of all things, in that bronco-bucking land, the Athenian Club. So it may come as a shock to generations of GLS alumnae that the name of the revered club could be called a "steal" or a plagiarism.
>
> After I became accustomed to the Latin School and it to me, I wanted to do something in the extra-curricular line. I conceived of a debating society and literary club. Miss [Carolyn] Gerrish and Mr. Hapgood encouraged me—and when it came to naming the group, a classical name seemed appropriate so why not the Athenian Club?
>
> We took ourselves seriously. We had a grip, à la a fraternity, a secret signal as we passed one another in the halls. Among the other charter members was Louise Bogan, who was to become a poet of note, and Rena Flannagan who, I believe, took over her father's Charlestown newspaper.[24]

S.T.A.C. members guiding students in the 1950s

Within a decade, the Athenian Club had become an umbrella organization for most of the school's extracurricular activities. It had a literary department, nature club, and debating section and sponsored athletic, dramatic, musical, and community activities.

In 1928, the Student Teacher Advisory Council (S.T.A.C.) was formed. Encouraged by Hapgood as an opportunity to expand the role of students in school responsibilities and to foster a more cooperative attitude between teachers and students, STAC members supervised fire drills, provided lunchroom duty, and oversaw assembly hall procedures and other administrative activities. Students elected to STAC wore black armbands with the council's initials in gold letters. Reportedly, young students entering the school for the first time often were confused, too afraid to ask what it meant, and many assumed that the girls with these armbands were being punished or were in mourning.

Radcliffe, *S* for Smith, *W* for Wellesley, and so forth. By 1912, 23 of 86 GLS graduates were accepted to Radcliffe alone, and almost half were admitted to one of the Seven Sisters colleges—a marked improvement in just two years. Of the 140 graduates in the class of 1928, 33 were accepted to Radcliffe. That same year, although enrollment at Girls' Latin had grown to 1,021, it still was just half the number of students attending Boston Latin School due to the sizes of their respective buildings.

Although GLS had moved to a much larger building with the expectation of growth in the near future, the curriculum stayed true to its classical roots, eschewing the manual and practical courses—typing and home economics, for example—common at other high schools. The most significant curricular change was that girls now had the opportunity to take physics and German as electives instead of Greek.

THE SCHOOL SONG

Ruth and Barbara Lynch lived at 238 Metropolitan Avenue, a long crossover street in Roslindale between Washington Street and Hyde Park Avenue. They were pretty girls, both with short dark bobs crimped with waves in the front. Ruth would be graduating in just weeks. Barbara, who was a junior, huddled with her sister trying to collaborate on words to a new anthem for their school contest.

In 1924, the GLS Alumnae Association began to plan for the school's fiftieth-anniversary celebration in 1928. The need seemed greater than ever for a song or anthem that would represent Girls' Latin School. A petition was signed and presented to Mr. Hapgood asking that he call a competition. The cover letter read:

> Dear Mr. Hapgood:
> The names signed on the accompanying sheets of paper signify those students and teachers of the Girls' Latin School who desire and feel the need for a school song. We propose at the beginning of the 1924–25 school year a contest be opened under your supervision, every girl from the first through sixth class being eligible. We suggest that the words and music may be original or original words may be set to adapted music. Let the judges be chosen from the faculty and the best song be selected on its own merit, regardless of the age of the girl by whom it was submitted.[25]

The "Happy" Days

The Jabberwock of February 1924 printed the contest rules:

1. The contest shall be open to all present and former members of the school and to all present and former members of the teaching staff.
2. The song may be serious, a good marching song, or a song of good fellowship.
3. Either words or music, or both may be submitted on or before May 1, 1925.
4. The name of the author or composer should not appear on the manuscript but should be in a sealed envelope which should accompany the manuscript.
5. Communications should be addressed to the
   SONG CONTEST COMMITTEE
   Marion C. Moreland, Chairman
   Girls' Latin School, Boston 17.[26]

The deadline for submissions was eventually extended to May 1, 1926, and Ruth and Barbara Lynch, sisters in the First and Second Class, respectively, were keen to finalize their entry as the deadline drew near. They had decided to set the lyrics to the Irish ballad "O'Donnell Aboo," a favorite of their father, P. J. Lynch, a *Boston Post* editor who had passed along his deep love of Irish music to his children. In fits and starts they arrived at the wording, and one more time they both raised their voices and sang it from beginning to end. Yes, they agreed, this was it!

Ruth and Barbara waited on pins and needles for the winner to be declared the following November. The song committee at last recommended "that the first stanza of the song submitted by Ruth and Barbara Lynch be accepted as the school song."[27] (The Lynch sisters' lyrics were originally three stanzas long.)

The large assembly hall was packed on the Friday afternoon when P. J. Lynch arrived to help with the presentation of his daughters' song to the school. Hapgood opened the exercises and invited him to the stage. Lynch explained the song's origin as a traditional melody of Ireland handed down from generation to generation by Irish minstrels and bards, and he noted that several of these rich, Irish melodies had been appropriated by well-known composers—Beethoven, for example, had adapted an old Irish air in his Seventh Symphony. Sung at the assembly by Elizabeth M. O'Connell, the song was enthusiastically received by the whole school.

> Hail, Girls' Latin School, fair Alma Mater
> Whose fame fills the land, nor e'en stops at the shore.
> Far flung her call, her benign invitation,
> To drink deep the cup at her fountain of lore.
> Ring out your joy and pride,
> Sing paeans glorified.
> Stand by your school and rejoice in her fame.
> Stand by her valiantly,
> Fight for her gallantly,
> In all times and places her greatness proclaim.[28]

School song with original lyrics and revised tune from 1940

Unsurprisingly, the *Boston Post* ran a feature story on December 5, 1926, with the headline "Roslindale Sisters Write New Song with Irish Air for Girls' Latin School."[29] In 1940, Daniel D. Tierney, director of music for the Boston Public Schools and music director at GLS, revised the music to more of an American march tune. Through the years, bandleaders played the tune at proms, and its popularity among students increased. In 1952, copyrights were obtained by the GLS Glee Club from the U.S. Library of Congress for a fee of $4.00.

THE FIFTIETH-ANNIVERSARY CELEBRATION

Alice Cunningham Lacey '14, president of the GLS Alumnae Association, had invited Sibyl Collar Holbrook to speak at the ceremony marking the fiftieth anniversary of the school's founding. The Golden Jubilee celebration was to take place over March 30 and 31, 1928.

Holbrook had been asked to provide a memorial tribute to Dr. Tetlow as well as to speak to the student body about early days at the school. In her speech she recalled how at school she had laughed at Josephine Peabody's humor "till I fell limp at a desk or doubled dangerously over a banister" and how Abbie Farwell Brown's writings provided the initial impetus for *The Jabberwock*'s creation and, in time, gave the paper wings.[30] She told them, "It is not that the past is roseate through distance, for dry and drab stretches are unforgotten, but as I look back and re-read the early tales of our doings, the excitement of those years flames up

Class of 1926, Girls' Latin School

brightly."[31] Her words were warmly applauded. She had done her best to bring her old friends alive for the students who had come after them, but it was clear that a new era was about to dawn. She could only hope her words would inspire future generations to care for *The Jabberwock*.

GLS INTERCLASS GYMNASTIC MEETS

In May 1909, Girls' Latin School competed for the very first time in a citywide gymnastic meet, and the students loved it. The following year, Mabel Morse, the gym teacher, organized GLS's first intraschool gym meet. Students from the upper three classes—each class wearing bows in its assigned color—competed in ball relay, four corner relay, giant volleyball, wand exercises, floor drills, and apparatus work. One of the highlights of the school year, the meets continued through the 1950s. An account of the 1928 meet appeared in *The Jabberwock*:

> On Friday, May 11, the event so long awaited by Class I, Class II and Class III took place. To anyone acquainted with the school the ill-suppressed

excitement and the bows of the upper class girls betokened the Gymnastic Meet. Each girl flaunted her own color, and each teacher impartially wore between one and three bows. At two-thirty the three classes participating in the Meet marched proudly

On Saturday, more than 600 alumnae attended a series of class reunions, and a dinner in the gym was followed by a program in the assembly hall. The event included speeches by Dr. Jeremiah E. Burke, superintendent of Boston schools; Dr. William Faunce, president of Brown University; and Alice M. Mills, a member of the first graduating class in 1880. Superintendent Burke stated, "Girls' Latin School was opened . . . with the express purpose of giving girls a preparation for college equivalent to that offered by the Public Latin School for Boys. . . . For many years these [Latin] schools have been the single largest source of supply to Harvard and Radcliffe Colleges."[32] Ada Comstock, president of Radcliffe College, noted that Radcliffe was founded one year after Girls' Latin and had since enrolled a steady stream of GLS graduates in its freshman classes, many of whom returned to the school as teachers—Mary J. Foley, Abby C. Howes, Ellen C. Griswold, Helen A. Stuart, Cora Roper, Rosalie Y. Abbott, and Marion C. Moreland, to name a few. "You see, we return an original investment with interest!" she said.[33] *The Boston Daily Globe* commented, "At the time the Girls' Latin School came into existence . . . Smith and Wellesley were only three years-old and collegiate education of women was considered to be an altogether unnecessary and even an undesirable thing."[34]

into the Gym before an audience of friends, relatives and lower class girls. How fine the rows looked with each girl in clean sneakers and blouses, and neatly pressed bloomers! . . . Then the various gymnastics drills and exercises were performed. . . . Last, but far from least, ensued wildly exciting relay races and ball games. What a wild din resounded throughout the (?) [sic] usually (?) quiet gymnasium! Now came the climax. Like the Pied Piper of Hamlin, surrounded by a throng of excited followers, Mr. Hapgood made his way to the center of the gym. Amid great noise, with a single instant's hush, Mr. Hapgood announced the winner, Class I!"[35]

In the early years of the school, the girls wore long skirts to gym class. Eventually skirts were shortened from the floor to just below the knee and evolved into balloonlike navy blue knickers. In the 1920s, the uniform was changed to a white middy top with a black bow, black stockings, and somewhat less baggy black bloomers. These bloomers in turn set the precedent for the new uniform pants adopted in the 1930s, which were of heavy bright blue cotton with a fitted buttoned waist and short balloon pants with elastic gathers at the cuffs. Each girl had to embroider her last name in white across the left leg. From the 1910s through the 1950s, each class wore a tie of a distinct color.

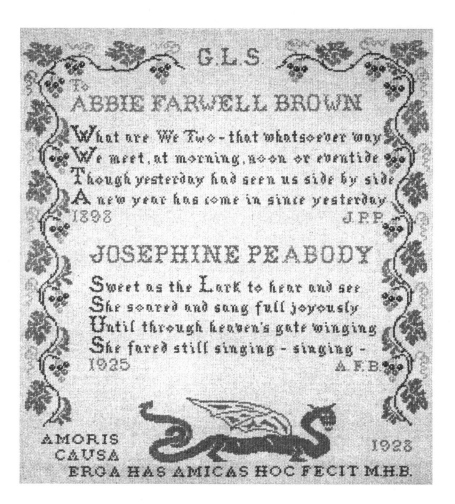

During the Golden Jubilee celebration, Sibyl Collar Holbrook presented Girls' Latin School with this sampler—which is more than five feet tall—Mabel Hay Barrows stitched to mark the founding of The Jabberwock.

Hapgood was presented a purse of gold from alumnae. Holbrook was touched when he announced the establishment of the John Tetlow Memorial Scholarship.

In a foreword to the fiftieth-anniversary number of *The Jabberwock*, Hapgood wrote:

> Congratulations are due to all... particularly the 2,276 graduates whose names are on the muster roll of Alma Mater and whose scholarly achievements have helped to keep alive the torch of classical learning for which this school has always stood. May the next fifty years be still more fruitful in rounding out a full century of growth, of dreams fulfilled, of kindling contacts with the stored up wisdom of past ages, of service to future mothers and stalwart women of the race.[36]

MEMENTOS OF A CLASSICAL EDUCATION

Cover of the 1927 Girls' Latin School yearbook, the first year it was published

Left: A GLS school pin, first issued in the late 1800s; right: GLS 1956 school ring

Throughout Boston, school lapel pins came into vogue in the late 1800s and rapidly grew in popularity. Girls' Latin's pin took the form of a black enamel scroll with curled edges outlined in gold; the initials GLS were on one side, and the center sported a gold Jabberwock. The sentimental importance of the school pin is described in the November 1923 issue of *The Jabberwock*:

> We are all justly fond of our school and its standards. We are proud to realize that our Alumnae have attained and are attaining success and varied honors.... The black and gold pin with that fabled beast, the dear old Jabberwock, has found its way into many a corner of the world. Through this medium, graduates have renewed acquaintances or found new friends. We, too, should treasure it as something more than a mere ornament. It is the symbol of our ideals. Wear it and be worthy of it!.... Then, when the motto over our front entrance is firing the ambition of future students, your pin will still whisper to you, "Let Thy Life Be Sincere!"[37]

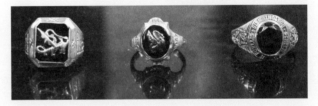

GLS school rings belonging to (left to right): Barbara Cross (1937), Barbara G. Beaman (1947), and Diane M. Dickerson (1971)

The first Girls' Latin School class rings were designed by the Boston firm of Dieges & Clust on Tremont Street. From 1913 through 1927 each class selected its own unique ring style, but the design always featured the Jabberwock in some way. In 1928, the school voted to adopt a standard ring, and that design was used through

In the 1950s, GLS printed gold-and-black book covers (left) and issued bright-gold crests for blazers (right).

the 1950s, after which it became one with a plain oval stone and was produced annually through the closing of GLS in 1976.

MARIBEL VINSON OWEN

The February 1928 issue of *The Jabberwock* reported, "On Thursday, January 19th, Maribel Vinson, of our own First Class, sailed from New York to compete in the Olympic Skating Contest to be held at St. Moritz in February. We are all proud of Maribel and are wishing her all the good luck in the world."[38] Vinson would just miss medaling at the 1928 Olympics, placing fourth in the women's singles competition, but she had already won one U.S. Figure Skating Championship as a singles skater and over the next decade would win eight more—a record equaled only by Michelle Kwan in 2005. Vinson earned a bronze medal at the 1932 Olympics, silver and bronze medals at the 1928 and 1930 World Championships, and a North American Championship in 1937. She also won seven national-level pair-skating competitions before retiring from amateur status in 1937. She then turned her talent and attention to touring in professional skating shows and eventually became a highly respected coach.

Born to Thomas and Gertrude Cliff Vinson in 1911, Maribel exhibited a remarkable sense of balance from her earliest steps. She got her first single-blade skates at four, even though the boots were too big, and she had to stuff cotton into the toes at first. Vinson didn't go to formal school until she was nine years old—"I don't think I missed a thing. Mother taught me for an hour a day and the rest of the time I was out in the fresh air and sunshine or at the Cambridge rink skating," she said.[39]

Both Vinson's mother and aunt had attended Girls' Latin, and it was practically preordained by Gertrude that her daughter would enroll at her alma mater. She and Thomas felt the school built confident, determined women, in a way no other school could match, and they wanted their daughter to feel she had a place in sports that was the equal to those held by men. The discipline and focus for study helped in honing Maribel's skating skills. In fact, if any two words described Maribel, they were *tough* and *determined*. She was an excellent student and went on to graduate Radcliffe in 1933.

The 1928 Olympics in St. Moritz, Switzerland, was only the third Winter Games in which women were permitted to compete. Vinson placed fourth, just out of the medal winners' circle. Sonja Henie of Norway took the gold and began the string of "firsts" for which she became world-renowned. At the age of fifteen, she was the youngest person ever to win Olympic gold, and that distinction remained with her for nearly 75 years. Although Vinson privately remarked that she thought her own program had a higher difficulty than Henie's, she also said, "Henie rarely made a mistake."[40] Vinson told anyone who was critical of Henie that she would have been an Olympic champion no matter what sport she had chosen, because she was so fast, strong, and athletic.

Although competitors, their near-pioneer status created a bond among the women skaters at St. Moritz. The friendship between Vinson and Henie would last over the years, and was rekindled when they competed once again at Lake Placid, New York, in the 1932 Winter Games. This time Henie took gold once again, but the bronze went to Vinson.

After graduating from Radcliffe in 1933, Vinson became a sports writer for the *New York Times*—the paper's first female sports reporter—at a salary of $45 per week, and she remained in that post from September 1934 through July 1937.[41] Her "Women in Sport" column covered events in multiple fields, including golf, tennis, and squash as well as skating. When her skating show came to Boston in 1938, she told *The Jabberwock*, "You may quote me as saying that outside of directing and producing this show, the hardest thing I have ever done was get through Latin School on five home lessons a night. What a grind! But it's good for you."[42]

In 1938 she married Canadian skater Guy Owen, with whom she had two daughters, Maribel and Laurence, both of whom she coached and helped to become elite skaters. Maribel, the eldest daughter, was enrolled at Girls' Latin School in the tenth grade, making her the third generation to attend GLS. (Together, grandmother, mother, and daughter attended GLS at all four of its locations. In 1957, young Maribel graduated and was accepted to Boston University.)

After the couple divorced in 1949, Vinson Owen supported her children through coaching, and she taught hundreds of young skaters at rinks in and around Boston.

In 1961, for the first time, the U.S. National Figure Skating Championships were televised. In late January CBS brought the event from World Arena, Colorado Springs, into living rooms around the country. Laurence won the singles—"Golly, I feel terrific right now," she said in a post-win interview.[43] This same year, her older sister Maribel and Dudley Richards, both silver medalists in 1960, took gold. The girls' mother now had two national-champion daughters, and was in a position to share with them Olympic gold, an honor that eluded her in her own career.

The girls were featured on the cover of the *Boston Herald Sunday Magazine* on February 5, 1961, and a week later—Laurence, in her bright red skating outfit, became the cover girl for *Sports Illustrated*. Through the whirlwind, they went on to compete in the North American Championships in Philadelphia, where Laurence won gold and Maribel and Dudley Richards both took silver. Richards had confided to a close friend that he and Maribel were planning to announce their engagement the following month, upon returning from the World Championships in Prague.

In February 1961, Vinson Owen and her daughters, both of whom were to compete, boarded an airplane to Prague. Their plane crashed outside Brussels, Belgium, just before landing. The entire U.S. figure skating team, along with accompanying family members, coaches, and officials, died in the crash. In their honor, the U.S. Figure Skating Association established a memorial fund that continues to provide financial assistance to generations of skaters.

◀ 1929

BLS headmaster Patrick Campbell is appointed assistant superintendent of the Boston Public Schools; Joseph L. Powers replaces him as headmaster.

1931

Campbell becomes superintendent of the Boston Public Schools.

◀ 1932

Addition to BLS building on Avenue Louis Pasteur doubles its size.

1935

Boston Latin School celebrates its Tricentennial.

◀ 1936

Portrait of Headmaster Hapgood by Claxton B. Moulton is completed.

1941 ▶
The United States enters World War II.

1945
World War II ends.

 ◀ 1945

Roxbury Latin School celebrates its 300th anniversary.

1948

GLS headmaster Ernest Hapgood retires and is replaced by Louis McCoy.

BLS headmaster Powers retires and is succeeded by George L. McKim.

VIII

Plus ça change . . .
Hitting Full Stride: The 1930s and 1940s

Commercial Street, Boston, 1930

On May 1, 1928, Ernest Hapgood reluctantly headed to an open public hearing at the School Committee's chambers. He already had been called into private session with the School Committee the previous Monday evening, but now he was being asked to provide his testimony in public. He could not help but think back to the spectacle Tetlow had experienced over Miss Griswold.

The School Committee had relocated its offices to 15 Beacon Street on the flat crest of Beacon Hill, east of the Massachusetts State House and west of King's Chapel. The ornate Beaux Arts building was built in 1903, and its first two stories were clad in an elaborate cast iron façade with gilded shields. A third-story band of limestone gave way to a curving copper-capped roof.[1]

The School Committee had established a position known as "advisor of girls" whose role was to provide counseling and advising for personal matters to female students.[2] For Girls' Latin, Mary R. Stark had been given that responsibility. Teachers taught 42 periods a week, but Stark taught 10. She was also chairman of the lunchroom, S.T.A.C., *The Jabberwock*, and, in causes of failure or misconduct, she was responsible for investigation and reporting.

Public sentiment held that this role should be a parental prerogative primarily, and both a vote of the School Committee on January 16 and a ballot vote in the April 29, 1928, municipal election determined that the advisor position was to be abolished. Hapgood openly expressed his displeasure over the referendum, however. School Committeeman Joseph J. Hurley called the headmaster at home on the weekend to discuss the matter. When asked if Miss Stark had stopped performing all "advisor" functions, Hapgood told Hurley it was none of the public's God damn business. Hapgood bristled at the political reproach, which he understood well from his role as alderman in Newton.

Now, in a public open forum, Hurley's very first question was confrontational.

> *Hurley*: Did you tell me on Saturday that it was none of the public's blankety-blank business. . . ?

> *Hapgood*: I cannot answer that question without you revising it, you asked over the telephone on which you were making a friendly conference call."[3]

"No teacher performs any function now that has anything to do with the morals of their life," stated Hapgood near the end of his testimony.[4]

At the close of the cross examination, Hurley asked the School Committee to vote to order Hapgood to assure that Stark had ceased all functions related to the post of advisor of girls and to instruct "teachers," implying Miss Stark, to teach an average number of periods. But the committee was exasperated and voted 4–1 against the measure. School Committeeman Joseph Lyons lashed out, stating that, after seven hours of meetings, the charges leveled against Hapgood and others were no better understood than before. On a second motion the School Committee voted down Hurley, and Hapgood was cleared, much to his relief.

In great measure, by 1928 Hapgood was held in very high regard. The academic reputation of Girls' Latin School had soared. In 1925, the Harvard chapter of the Phi Beta Kappa Society established a scholastic prize, which it awarded to the school with the highest standing in the college entrance examinations of any public or private school in the United States. In 1925 the Public Latin School placed first with 89 percent, ahead of the Taft School in Connecticut, which scored 88 percent. In 1926, it placed first again, ahead of the Hotchkiss School, also in Connecticut; similarly, in 1927, with an average of 90 percent, it bested Phillips Exeter Academy in New Hampshire, which scored 89 percent.[5]

For four straight years, from 1925 through 1928, Boston Latin School received the highest marks on the College Board Entrance Examinations of any school, public or private, in the United States. In 1927 Boston public-school officials proudly also reported that the students of Girls' Latin School had achieved the third-highest average score of any U.S. school on these tests. No other private or public school for girls approached GLS's record for excelling before the College Entrance Examination Board or for the number of scholarships and honors won by its graduates. That two public schools of Boston could top the most exclusive, expensive, and selective private schools in the United States was extraordinary.

The consistently high achievement of GLS and BLS students on college entrance examinations would vastly enhance the profiles and reputations of both schools, and outside events would soon challenge

HONORING THE HEADMASTER

Ernest G. Hapgood's portrait had been completed more than a decade before he retired. It was presented to him at the 1936 annual meeting of the Alumnae Association, when 250 members filled the assembly hall to surprise him with the completed canvas. This was also the twenty-fifth anniversary of his service to Girls' Latin, a particularly apt occasion for the painting's unveiling, which was done by Marjorie Taylor Sanderson, president of the portrait committee. The portrait was painted by Claxton B. Moulton, who also was present. Measuring approximately six feet high by four feet wide, today the painting is in need of restoration and is kept in the library of Boston Latin Academy.

them to grow rapidly. The U.S. stock market crashed on October 29, 1929, and the nation spiraled into the Great Depression. The percentage of Boston workers on welfare ballooned to 35 percent.[6] On New Year's Day 1931, men in overcoats and wool caps huddled in long bread lines on the North End's Hanover Street, desperate to begin the year without hunger. The city's resources to replace antiquated schools evaporated like water in a frying pan. When the papers wrote about the spectacle in the corridors, they were referring to the thousands who lined the hallways of City Hall on School Street looking for work. Mayor Curley, who served a third term from 1930 through 1934, contended that bread lines did not exist in Boston. He even tried to stop a minister from handing out free sandwiches on Boston Common, as if the mayor alone could hold back the tide of national economic collapse.

As a result of the dramatic increase in enrollment, by 1930 Boston Latin School was housed in four buildings: their own on Avenue Louis Pasteur, one across the street at Commerce High School, in seven portable classrooms set up in their yard, and in the old Sharp School on Beacon Hill.

Under the law, the School Committee could only propose orders to construct buildings, and had to wait for the order to be approved by the Board of Commissioners of School Buildings. There were four projects in the pipeline: a new Girls' High School, a new Dorchester High School for Girls, a new West Roxbury High School, and the proposed addition to the Public Latin School. However, only $2 million was available for building all four projects. Although Superintendent Campbell strongly supported the addition to the Latin School, the School Committee remained divided by their partisan interests, and could not reach agreement on which projects to fund.

Two of Mayor Curley's sons were attending BLS—Leo, who would graduate in 1932, and Paul, a member of the class of 1936. Curley called a conference of the School Committee, the Finance Commission, and the Board of Commissioners of School Buildings at his office at City Hall. The following day, the Board of Commissioners of School Buildings approved an $850,000 annex to the existing Boston Latin School that would add 40 new classrooms. Upon completion of the addition, Boston Latin had 81 classrooms and a total seating capacity of 2,500 pupils. The total cost of the building on Avenue Louis Pasteur was now almost $2 million.

Many citizens, even some among the comparatively wealthy, no longer could afford private school tuition for their children. And if the best education were in fact free, many decided to take advantage of it. By 1933, Boston's public school student population exceeded 137,500, an enrollment never eclipsed since. The number of students at the Latin schools swelled proportionately to 2,300 at Boston Latin and 1,100 at Girls Latin.

For students at the other end of the economic spectrum, the situation was dire. Many students who could not afford the five-cent trolley fare were forced to leave Girls' Latin. Finances were limited, and the prospects for paying for college had become much dimmer than in any previous decade. Many senior girls had to choose between buying their $7.00 class ring or a yearbook. "Old Man Depression has had a finger in everybody's pie, so it would seem. Even our illustrious yearbook has had to feel the dreaded clutches of his hand," wrote the 1932 yearbook staff.[7] They cut down on content and traded the leather-bound cover for paper to save money. Constantly admonished by teachers, "*Labor omnia vincit!*" GLS graduates were also told to equip themselves to weather the economic crisis.

From the standpoint of governance, however, the 1930s started out well for Boston's schools. Patrick Campbell, who had proven to be an exceptional headmaster of Boston Latin, resigned his position in 1929 to become assistant superintendent and then in 1931 superintendent of

Enrollment in Boston Public Schools, 1878–1933

YEAR	TOTAL STUDENTS	BLS	GLS
1878	55,412	388	28
1880	49,075	353	102
1890	58,587	419	181
1900	77,742	578	344
1910	100,059	761	620
1920	112,802	1,069	820
1930	132,870	2,352	1,146
1933	137,521	2,239	1,149

Source: Records of the School Committee of the City of Boston. Boston City Archives

Plus ça change . . .

Entrance into the courtyard from Huntington Avenue; Girls' Latin School is at right.

the Boston Public Schools. True to his sumus primi training, Campbell quipped, "I got one of those Irish promotions. . . . I was made Superintendent of Schools, but that is not a promotion. There is no promotion from the headmaster's chair of Boston Latin School."[8] Hapgood was especially relieved. He knew the Latin schools would be safe under Campbell's leadership, and he hoped that he would not have to navigate any more political incidents or assaults on standards.

At Campbell's invitation, Hapgood readied Girls' Latin School to help mark the BLS Tercentenary Celebration, which was held in the auditorium at Avenue Louis Pasteur on Monday, April 21, 1935. Along with Hapgood, 18 other headmasters presented Headmaster Powers with small gifts to commemorate the occasion. They were entertained by a play—a series of scenes from the important elements of Boston Latin's history.

Afterward, an article in *The Jabberwock* noted that "the Tercentennial Celebration of the founding of the Public Latin School was of great import to us, for with it came an invitation to attend an assembly there in April. We were addressed by Superintendent Patrick D. Campbell, one of the greatest educators of America. The uniforms and white gloves of the ushers made a lasting impression on us."[9]

The pageant was followed two days later by the BLS Tercentenary Dinner at the Copley Plaza Boston Hotel. Every single class from 1877 to 1935 was represented, as were several classes from between 1858 and

1876. What George Santayana BLS '82, founder of the school's newspaper, *The Register*, wrote on the occasion was also pertinent to Girls' Latin:

> To have existed for three hundred years, as things go, is remarkable; much more remarkable to have been constant, through those three hundred years, to one purpose and one function... the Latin School, supported by the people of Boston, has kept the embers of traditional learning alive.... This fidelity to tradition, I am confident, has and will have its rewards."[10]

BARBARA POLK WASHBURN

In Girls' Latin's class of 1931, the vivacious Barbara Polk was always among the three or four students who scored the highest marks on tests and report cards. She loved the school: "I felt I was with smart girls; it was hard but I loved every bit of it. I had a great sense of pride and honor to be able to go to Girls' Latin."[11] She remembers Hapgood calling her to the office to congratulate her for receiving an approbation. Having no idea what that was, she was relieved to find out it was an award. She got into trouble only once, while in the assembly hall waiting for a speaker to commence. She cracked a joke that made her friends laugh. Mr. Hapgood asked her to leave the assembly hall and stand outside in the corridor.

Her math teacher was Mr. Merserve, who scared her to death because she wasn't very good in that subject. Toward the end of her senior year, she went to a dance and did not return home until 4 A.M. the next morning. She was due to take a final exam in French a few hours later and did very poorly on it. Her French teacher, knowing she had been admitted to Smith, told her, "Barbara, if you are going to Smith College, do not take French." Barbara wound up majoring in French and was glad she did not take the teacher's advice.

After graduating from Smith College in 1935, she attended secretarial school and eventually got an administrative job in the biology department at Harvard University. One day the mailman came in and asked her to interview with the new director of Harvard's Museum of Natural History because the director was searching for a secretary. Brad Washburn, the director, was energetic and persistent, and Barbara—although she'd always been bored by the museum when she visited it as a child—thought it might be interesting work. So she took the position and eventually married him. Brad went on to become the founding director of the Boston Museum of Science, in which role he served from 1939 to 1980. He also performed the first-recorded ascents of eight different North American mountains. Barbara accompanied her husband on many of his climbing and surveying expeditions and became the first woman to ascend Mount McKinley, the highest mountain in North America, on June 6, 1947. She wrote a book about her life called *The Accidental Adventurer*.

In 1947, Barbara Polk Washburn became the first woman to conquer Mount McKinley.

The decade of the 1930s can be best characterized as a time when Girls' Latin School hit its full stride. Although the Depression affected much of the economy, the quality of GLS's outstanding teaching staff was immune. Of its 35 teachers, 19 had graduated from Ivy League institutions.[12] GLS teachers were acutely aware that more and more women were entering college, and they strove to develop the best students possible in light of the increased competition for places in institutions of higher learning.

GLS COPES WITH WORLD WAR II

On Sunday, December 7, 1941, the Japanese attacked Pearl Harbor. The next day, in a seven-minute speech, President Franklin Delano Roosevelt asked a joint session of Congress for a declaration of war against Japan, and within an hour of his request it passed in both houses. The United States had officially entered World War II. "Japan treacherously attacked our Pacific possessions today. We lay helpless, as Gulliver must have lain when pinioned to the ground by the ropes of the Lilliputians."[13]

Headmaster Hapgood decided that President Roosevelt's radio broadcast declaring a state of war was a moment in history that GLS students should experience in person, and the following Tuesday, he assembled the entire school in Tetlow Hall, where the recorded speech was replayed. It was a solemn moment: Hapgood studied the faces of his young students and wondered if they fully understood the import of the president's decision. As one student recounted in the January 1942 issue of *The Jabberwock*, "The most impressive address we have ever had occurred on December ninth, when the entire school assembled to hear President Roosevelt's message to Congress, requesting a declaration of war against Japan."[14] The headmaster took enormous pride in noting that his students seemed, rather than downcast, filled with resolve. One student remarked: "Heard our President's stirring declaration of war upon Japan. They deserved it, and our boys are going to make them wish they'd stayed home peacefully in their own backyards."[15]

During the war years, shifting college vacations, heat problems, and wartime blackouts pushed the GLS Alumnae Association meetings into the late spring.[16] To curtail expenses the alumnae opted not to hold annual dinners but to serve punch and cookies. Afterward, they donated their own silver—punch bowls, ladles, goblets, plates, and vases—to the war effort. Much discussion ensued before it was decided not to let go of the two

Girls' Latin School teaching staff, 1930–1931 (left to right):
Front row (seated): Janet Crawford, Raymond S. Tobey, Harrison G. Meserve, William T. Williams, Kathryn McNamara
Second row: Zabelle D. Tahmizian, Cora F. Roper, Adeline G. Simmons, Elizabeth P. Condon, Catherine M. Morley, Dorothea Jones, Mary R. Stark, Ellen B. Esau, Margaret J. Griffith
Third row: Grace E. Lingham, Ida A. Cohen, Alice M. Smith, Sibyl B. Aldrich, Helen A. Stuart, Ernest G. Hapgood, Margaret E. Lundell, Catherine M. Crowley, Carolyn M. Gerrish, Mary E. Greene, Marjorie W. Woodhead
Back row: Gladys M. Heyl, Marion I. Lithgow, Helen A. Austin, Mabel S. Morse, Marion C. Moreland, Eva Z. Prichard, Helen S. Miller, Helen G. Holland, Gertrude M. Hall, Elinor J. Fowle, Blanch W. Harding, Marie E. Glennon

ornate sterling silver flower bowls inscribed "Girls' Latin School Alumnae— In Memoriam." The bowls had been purchased in 1940 by Eleanor Creed L'Ecuyer '16, president of the association, upon the retirement of Carolyn N. Gerrish, and given to the school. They were passed from president to president and sometimes were referred to as the "President's Bowls."[17]

At the meeting, Mr. Hapgood spoke movingly of the "contribution that the school, through its alumnae, teachers, and student body, is making to the war effort of our country."

> The Girls' Latin School is and will be ready to respond to whatever demands are made upon it in this time of stress and strain and worldwide upheaval. It takes something more than physical courage to endure

Plus ça change . . .

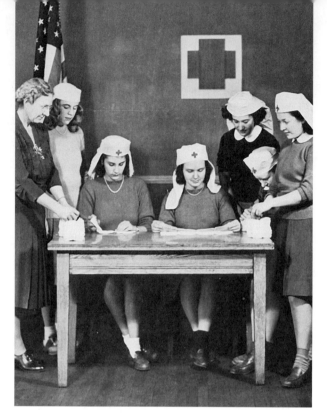

Adeline Lubell Naeiman '42 recalled, "The war broke out my senior year, and we learned to roll bandages."

in such a time as this; it takes high mental fiber and moral courage. We have many girls serving in all sorts of posts with the F.B.I. and in the research departments of the Army and Navy. Mr. Meserve, who came to our school in 1919 after his service to the last war, has just been called for service in this war, and has reported for duty in Niantic, Connecticut. Our teachers have assisted in the various draft registrations, and will shortly undertake registration in the nationwide sugar rationing.[18]

During the war, as the steam boilers at the school were powered by coal, fuel rationing often caused students to come to school late and take numerous days off. Air-raid drills were frequent occurrences, and many students avidly purchased war bonds. Things that had become commodities began to disappear from store shelves, as the factories that had produced them were converted to produce armaments and materiel instead. "The war hits home; we feel the absence of those priceless little gadgets—zippers . . . all that is left for us to do is find zippers in pre-war clothes and transfer them," wrote one student.[19]

Boston Latin School became a draft registration center and many alumni answered the call of the Army, Navy, and Air Force. Bostonians scoured the newspapers for announcements by the War Department on missing and wounded Massachusetts' soldiers, and dreaded the receipt of official notice that a loved one had been killed.

Diana Laskin Siegal, class of 1948, commented on how many wartime burdens were unspoken and unshared:

> The harsh realities of the Holocaust and deaths of servicemen, perhaps even affecting our own families, were never discussed. One event which did touch us was the rumored death of Miss Elizabeth Condon's fiancé. Miss Condon was one of the history teachers and one of the youngest, liveliest, and most attractive of the teachers. This rumor was never openly confirmed, but Miss Condon's obvious sadness and, in our eyes, sudden aging, seemed to confirm the rumor.[20]

In the 1943 yearbook, one GLS student is quoted as remarking that "it's a year now. The news sounds pretty hopeful, doesn't it, with the Russians on one side and our Yanks on the other, scaring all the fight out of a certain A. Hitler?"[21]

The socialization of GLS students with those attending BLS grew much stronger, and the wartime economy resulted in a shared senior prom in 1945, not long before World War II ended. Such semiformals and dances were filled with young men in crisp navy blue and white sailor's uniforms.[22]

By May of 1945, Germany was defeated. Emperor Hirohito acknowledged the surrender of Japan to Supreme Allied Commander Douglas MacArthur and so, "[GLS started the] school year on September 18, 1945, to the truly happy tune of world peace."[23] At the traditional

Seniors from Girls' Latin and Boys Latin Schools dance, 1945

A BLS/GLS LOVE AFFAIR

In 1948, after her family moved to Boston from Maine, Colleen Linscott was accepted to Girls' Latin School. Accustomed to receiving straight-*A* report cards, she had weathered the shock of receiving *B*s, *C*s, and the occasional failing grade in chemistry at GLS. Colleen and chemistry were two things that did not seem to go together. She kept failing, despite help from her friends, and struggled to get a passing grade. In her final year, Colleen was informed that she would need to pass a chemistry proficiency exam in order to graduate. Her classmates sat by the fountain in the courtyard beneath the window where Colleen was taking the exam; one said novenas, another worked a rosary, and they all prayed together that Colleen would pass. It worked, and Linscott graduated a proud member of the class of 1951.

Jack Berrigan graduated Boston Latin School in the class of 1948. In the summer of 1950, he and Colleen met when she was visiting her friend and fellow GLS student Mary Gill at the Gill family's cottage on Lake Winnipesauke in New Hampshire, and Mary's boyfriend Arthur brought Jack to the cottage as a date for Colleen. Beginning that weekend, they started dating on and off. They would drive to the Totem Pole at Norumbega Park in Newton or to Moseley's in Dedham and dance away the nights. Jack took Colleen to the GLS Christmas dance and her senior prom. Colleen took a job as an usher at the Boston Opera House, and Jack saw every opera and play for a year and half.

Jack graduated Boston College and Boston College Law School, enlisted in the Marines, and married Colleen. After his tour of duty was completed and he had passed the bar exams for both Massachusetts and New Hampshire, the couple settled in New Hampshire, where Jack opened a small law firm. They adopted three children and shared more than 50 years of marriage. Colleen died of ovarian cancer in 2003, and in December 2007, Jack donated $25,000 to establish the Colleen Linscott Berrigan Chemistry Scholarship for the female student achieving the highest grade in chemistry. Cancer took him as well, and he died in 2013.

Born in Roslindale on August 22, 1918, Mary McGrory served as business manager of *The Jabberwock* during her senior year at GLS, but contributed little writing for the publication. Her writing skills would emerge and change prolifically, however. She enrolled in Girls' Latin in September 1929. Her father, Edward Patrick McGrory, was a postal worker, although not by choice: in his senior year of high school, he won a scholarship to Dartmouth College, but before he could graduate high school, his father died, and Edward had to cut short his schooling in order to support his mother and seven siblings. "He never complained, and he never took it out on anybody," his sister Mary recalled. "He taught my brother and me to recite poetry and to treasure words—and to enjoy the small things of life, like walking and talking and nice dogs and fresh raspberries and blueberries and things like that."[24]

Mary McGrory almost immediately came under the magical influence of Girls' Latin School's English teachers, who set her on course to become an elegant and incisive writer. In 1992, she described her education:

At Boston's Girls' Latin School, which was a kind of educational boot camp, we, at age 11, trudged through Gaul with Julius Caesar—with the baggage, the bridges, the ablative absolute, Vercingetorix, the Helvetians, the prisoners, the gerundives, and the past imperfect.... We had to translate 50 lines of Virgil every night, and no visual aids or field trips.[25]

Another recollection offers a glimpse of a classical education during the 1930s.

Girls' Latin School drew girls from all over the city because its certain classical training held out hope of passing the college boards, or even a scholarship to Radcliffe.... The tone of Girls' Latin was set in its forbidding entrance. Around the hall stood plaster casts of the Caryatides, the Greek maidens who held up the temple porch on their heads. We often felt comparably oppressed. We threw up before midyears, and some girls even had nervous breakdowns under the terrible threat of "flunking out." But we were unabashed elitists and sustained by feelings of superiority to girls who went to their local high schools where the "standards," which were constantly held up to us, were not so high—or so we thought.[26]

The razor-sharp observation for which McGrory became known informs her thoughts on socialization among GLS students:

In our class there were two black girls, "colored" as we called them. One was Corinne Howe, who was tall and smiling. The other, whose name I have forgotten, was delicate and graceful. They were always together, or little apart. We were smugly tolerant and, I suppose, treated them like mascots. They were a novelty.

Corinne Howe (above) and Georgine Russell, both class of 1935

We never saw colored people, except as we hurried down Columbus Avenue, a grim section of the city, as we headed downtown....

At Girls' Latin School, many of my classmates were Jewish. They were, it was at once apparent, stupendous students, avid for learning. They never groaned like the rest of us when assignments were given out. They saved their allowances for the Boston Symphony Orchestra and the Theatre Guild plays. They set the pace and came closest to meeting those unattainable standards we were measured by. I think even then, in our silly adolescent way, we perceived that they were as responsible for our education as our demanding teachers.[27]

McGrory graduated from Boston's Emmanuel College in 1939. Her love of writing spurred her toward working for a newspaper, but at that time a woman's place in newspapers meant writing either book reviews or features for the women's section. She took a job as an assistant to the book editor of the *Boston Herald Traveler*, and before long was writing her own book reviews, which caught the attention of editors in New York and Washington. In 1947, she landed a position as second book reviewer at the *Washington Evening Star*, then Washington's dominant newspaper. In 1954 the *Star*'s executive editor, Newbold Noyes Jr., who had a keen eye for talent, dispatched her to Capitol Hill to help cover the Army–McCarthy hearings, and it was this assignment that brought her incisive voice to national prominence. During the 1960s she fiercely opposed the Vietnam War and was on Richard Nixon's enemies list. In 1975, in recognition of her articles about Watergate, McGrory became the first woman to win the Pulitzer Prize for commentary. After the *Star* closed in 1981, she went to work for the *Washington Post*. "I don't mind if you call me a liberal," McGrory wrote in 1988. "I still think it's a respectable word. Its root is *liber*, the Latin word for *free*."[28]

She spoke glowingly of her experience at GLS in various articles over the years. In April 1975, after receiving the Pulitzer, she wrote to the GLS Alumnae Association, "Girls' Latin School fostered and even demanded excellence. It was trying at the time, but I have been glad of it ever since. No journalism award could mean more to me than my GLS diploma."[29] In March 2003 she suffered a stroke that left her unable to write or speak, and she died on April 20, 2004, at the age of 85.

first assembly, Hapgood welcomed all with a bright smile and short speech. When he informed them they would be dismissed following registration in their homerooms, the hall burst into applause. The trees were still green, and had not yet begun to flame different colors, the temperatures hovered in the 70s. It seemed a normal start to the school year and a glorious fall again on Huntington Avenue.

Days later, however, personal tragedy struck Headmaster Hapgood. His wife, Edith (Kinne) Hapgood, passed away on Thursday, September 27, 1945, at Newton Hospital. Mrs. Hapgood was keenly interested in drama and always made time to attend theater productions at the school. She was also in regular attendance at the GLS Alumnae Association meetings. Along with their headmaster, the entire student body grieved her loss.

From left to right: Jane Bushmiller, Marcia Coppleman, and Yole Campagna, Class of 1947 Graduation Day from Huntington Avenue Tetlow Hall.

HAPGOOD RETIRES

Although Headmaster Hapgood had endured a great personal loss, in 1947, he married Edith's close friend and sorority sister, Kate Lewis, a Phi Beta Kappa graduate of Tufts University. Lewis had a long career as a reporter for the *Boston Herald* and editor for the *Boston American*. Ernest Hapgood also loved to play bridge, and most days, upon leaving school, he headed straight for the University Club on Trinity Place to engage in a game or two. In the summers, he relished playing golf with friends at the Woodland Golf Club in Auburndale.

A WAR HERO ADDRESSES GLS

In 1946, John F. Kennedy was running for the U.S. congressional seat from Massachusetts' 11th district. Still recuperating from the injuries and malaria he sustained and contracted in the Pacific during World War II, he was thin, walked with a cane, and bore a yellowish hue, none of which detracted from his handsome looks and engaging manner. When Kennedy arrived at Huntington Avenue, Miss Tahmizian greeted him at the door, then led him in where an audience of screaming, clapping, and loudly giggling girls enthusiastically welcomed the war hero. He was deeply embarrassed, and his aides had to push the blushing future president back to the podium.

Testimonial banquet for recently retired Headmaster Hapgood and the GLS seventieth-anniversary celebration, April 1948

But in December 1947, he suffered a minor stroke, which he took as a signal to stop working. Although he knew he wanted to play more golf and bridge and spend more time with his new wife, he nevertheless was reluctant in making the decision to retire from his position as the second headmaster of Girls' Latin School, effective January 31, 1948. An interim headmaster was appointed for the remainder of the year.

From September 1910 to January 1948, the man with a "ringing laugh and expansive smile" had watched over Girls' Latin School.[30] Fatherly, friendly, approachable, caring, yet at all times mindful of the school's standards, Hapgood quietly expanded the school's reputation for outstanding academic preparation. Upon his retirement, just 4,724 girls had graduated Girls' Latin. Hapgood had polished the school's pedigree, and its academic star had never sparkled more brightly. In its first 70 years of existence, Girls' Latin had only had two headmasters. On April 15, 1948, hundreds of well-wishers gathered in the GLS gym for a testimonial dinner.

Headmaster Ernest G. Hapgood, drawing by Xos Stern '47

Plus ça change

1944
George D. Strayer releases his report on the Boston Public Schools.

1947
James Michael Curley is convicted of mail fraud and sentenced to five months in prison.

1948
Ernest G. Hapgood retires and is succeeded by Louis A. McCoy.

George L. McKim succeeds Powers as BLS headmaster.

1949 ▶
John B. Hynes defeats Curley to become mayor of Boston.

1951
Attorney Eleanor L'Ecuyer '39 elected president of the Girls' Latin School Alumnae Association.

1952
The Boston School Committee votes to close the Teachers College of the City of Boston.

Girls' Latin School's Huntington Avenue building is deeded to the state.

1953
Ernest G. Hapgood dies on April 3 at the age of 75.

Girls' Latin School celebrates its 75th anniversary.

1954
The State Board of Education refuses to extend Girls' Latin School's use permit at the Huntington Avenue building.

John J. Doyle replaces McKim at BLS.

Vida Scudder, last surviving member of the first GLS graduating class, dies on October 10.

1955
Girls' Latin School is relocated to Codman Square and the former Dorchester High School building.

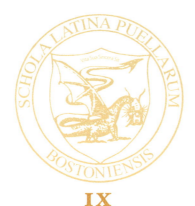

IX

The End of Our Fenway Wonderland, or *Alea Iacta Est*

The gates to the Huntington Avenue campus, which Girls' Latin School was forced to leave

In April 1948, Louis McCoy, headmaster of Girls' High School, was called to a meeting with Boston Public Schools Superintendent Arthur Gould. As he stepped quickly up Beacon Street, McCoy glanced at the Massachusetts State House, and his eyes swept over the bustling Boston Common. Turning the handle on the ornate front entrance door at 15 Beacon Street, he entered the Boston School Committee's headquarters.

McCoy had been an invaluable asset to the school system. He was a kindly, happy-go-lucky man who had come up through the ranks of Boston's schools, first as math teacher at English High School and Roxbury Memorial High School before finally landing in the headmaster's chair.

McCoy silently entered the lobby of 15 Beacon Street resplendent with its brass railings and newel post and took the building's original caged elevator up to Gould's office. He wondered why he was being summoned to School Committee headquarters in the middle of the school year. Gould greeted him, and they sat down.

"So how long have you been headmaster at Girls' High now?"

"Ten years, Arthur."

"You've done a fine job, too, and we all appreciate your efforts."

"Thanks."

"But I need you somewhere else."

"Oh?"

"I want you to take over Girls' Latin School." Gould explained that Hapgood had had a stroke in December, decided to retire, and tendered his resignation in January. "Will you accept the position?"

"For how much extra money?" asked McCoy.

Gould smiled and replied, "None."

"Well, I don't think I will go," McCoy said, thinking to himself, "especially without more pay."

"We'll talk about it."

They talked for a long time, and at the end of it, Gould had somehow persuaded McCoy to take charge of Girls' Latin.

"You will have no problems there. It is a school with tremendous prestige throughout the country, and after you go, you will never be sorry," Gould told him.

For a few more minutes, Gould and McCoy discussed the details of the announcement of the new position. They shook hands, and McCoy turned to leave.

"Louis?"

"Yes?" Gould locked eyes with McCoy.

"Take care of Girls' Latin School, and don't let them do anything to it."[1]

Louis A. McCoy, circa 1949

MCCOY TAKES THE HELM

Effective May 17, 1948, Louis A. McCoy was transferred from Girls' High School to Girls' Latin School, where he became only the third headmaster in 70 years. Born in Pawtucket, Rhode Island, on August 14, 1887, he graduated from Pawtucket High School in 1905. Like Tetlow, he also was a graduate of Brown University, where he earned an A.M. degree. He married Marguerite H. McGlone on July 12, 1916, and they had two daughters, Marguerite and Virginia, the latter of whom also became a teacher in the Boston public schools. Early on, he became a professional baseball player and once he began teaching high school, he continued to coach baseball, football, and track. McCoy taught math and coached Bulkeley High School in New London, Connecticut, from

1910 to 1915; taught math at New Haven High School from 1915 to 1917; and then served as junior master in the math department at English High School through 1928, before becoming head of the mathematics department at Roxbury Memorial High School. In 1938, he was promoted to headmaster at Girls' High.

Upon assuming the headmaster's chair, McCoy said, "The present administration of the Girls' Latin School is striving with all its energy, and whatever ability it has, to keep up the high standards of this school. . . . If we can keep up the high standards, maybe improve them a little, and cut down on the percentage of withdrawals, we shall indeed accomplish a substantial performance."[2]

Under the strong hand of Ernest Hapgood, Girls' Latin had grown from 620 students in 1910 to more than 1,000 by 1948, the year of his retirement. Between 1935 and 1945, however, the number of pupils enrolled in the Boston public school system overall shrank from 134,000 to 94,000. Boston had become run down during the war. Many of the elegant brownstones that lined Commonwealth Avenue were boarded up, offering a symbol of the city's lost wealth. After World War II, the textile, leather, and shoe companies that had made up Boston's industrial base began leaving Massachusetts for nonunion states. The commonwealth would lose 200,000 jobs, and Boston's population would peak in 1950 at 800,000.

In 1944, after the city's school system had lost 30 percent of its pupils, the Boston Finance Commission asked George D. Strayer, professor emeritus at Columbia University's Teachers College, to prepare a comprehensive report on the cost and efficiency of the Boston public school system.[3] His 1,100-page report recommended the closing of more than 35 schools and sharply criticized the inefficiency of having seven all-boys and seven all-girls high schools.[4] The report also took aim at the Teachers College of the City of Boston, which occupied the north building of the Huntington Avenue complex and had been called the Normal School until 1924. The city was spending more than $234,000 per year to operate this college;[5] the Strayer report stated that "no valid reasons exist for the maintenance of a local teachers college in Boston," and recommended closing it to save Boston money.[6] Superintendent Arthur Gould and the School Committee, unwilling to make the changes, called upon their Board of Superintendents to review and prepare a response to the report. The rebuttal was printed by the School Committee and distributed, and for years the Strayer report languished.

Boston taxes and its proportion of public- to private-sector employees were among the highest in the nation. Boston City Hospital and the municipal fire and police departments were full of politically won positions. Bribes riddled the system of city licensing. In 1946, James Michael Curley had been elected mayor for the fourth time. His shamrock-shuttered home on the Jamaicaway, with its gold-plated fixtures, marble fireplaces, and carved mahogany doors, was allegedly built largely on the graft accumulated during his first three terms as mayor. Convicted of mail fraud in June 1947, he served five months in a federal prison in Connecticut.

During Curley's incarceration, Governor Bradford appointed City Clerk John B. Hynes to serve as acting mayor. On the first day Curley returned to office, he told reporters, "I have accomplished more in one day than the clerk has done in the five months."[7] Hynes had intentionally left $30 million in contracts in limbo until Curley's return from prison so the mayor could handle them himself. Insulted by the comment, Hynes decided to run for mayor in the 1949 election. Proposing better city management and an end to corruption, the soft-spoken, bespectacled Hynes beat Curley 138,000 votes to 126,000. He went on to win two more elections and serve as Boston's mayor until 1960. Spurred by a declining city tax base and voter revolt over government waste, the era of patronage and machine politics was ending and an era of technocratic planning, budgeting, and administration was beginning—a regime that would have its own perils, as Girls' Latin School was soon to learn.

BUILDINGS ARE SOLD—NO ONE NOTICES

Some four and a half years after McCoy's discussion with Gould, another meeting critical to the future of GLS took place at 15 Beacon Street. In August 1952, School Committee Chairman Isadore H. Y. Muchnick presided over a meeting the agenda of which consisted largely of legal matters. He was extremely comfortable in these waters. Nicely dressed in suit and tie, his frameless glasses and neatly combed dark hair gave him an appearance of a very organized individual.

The previous January, after being elected the committee's chairman, Muchnick told a *Boston Globe* reporter that he planned to wage war on the political favoritism that had plagued the school system, declaring: "From here on in merit alone will count. The slogan must be changed back from whom you know to what you know."[8] He envisioned a new Boston School system regaining its position of leadership for education in the United States.

Muchnick graduated Harvard College in 1928 and Harvard Law School in 1932. This hard-nosed attorney and former city councilor from Dorchester held corruption, waste, and discrimination in great disdain. It was he who, in 1945, refused to issue a license for the Red Sox to play Sunday baseball until they permitted Jackie Robinson to try out for the team.[9] With Hynes as mayor, a group of reform-minded candidates had been elected to the School Committee alongside Muchnick: Alice Lyons of Jamaica Plain, wife of the headmaster of the Mary E. Curley School; Mary K. Fitzgerald of South Boston, an antidiscrimination activist; William Carr of South Boston; and Dr. Patrick J. Foley, a dentist from South Boston who had run as an independent candidate. He and Lyons helped to vote Muchnick chairman.

Immediately upon taking office, the new chairman had cleansed the committee's agendas of discussion of minutiae, such as teachers' leaves of absence and vacations, and aggressively began to implement recommendations of the Strayer report. Already he had managed to close seventeen elementary schools and two high schools, and he was about to take aim at another school he regarded as a complete waste of the taxpayer's money.

A representative from the city's legal department had come to the meeting to explain the documents the committee members were to sign that evening. The groundwork for these documents had been laid carefully. In May, the Boston School Committee voted to discontinue the Teachers College of the City of Boston effective August 31, 1952.[10] In return, the Massachusetts Board of Education agreed to take over the responsibility of operating the teachers college to provide financial relief to the City of Boston. The transfer, however, was contingent upon the state obtaining ownership of the entire Huntington Avenue complex including the land and buildings of Girls' Latin School.

To execute the deal, Mayor Hynes circumvented the Boston School Committee, which retained the legal authority to transfer the buildings to the state, and went straight to the legislature. The City of Boston, acting through its mayor, petitioned the state to enact special legislation in the form of Chapter 618 of the Acts of 1952, which provided the legal mechanism for the city to "convey certain real estate and certain personal property to the Commonwealth."[11]

The End of Our Fenway Wonderland

RACE AND GIRLS' LATIN SCHOOL IN THE 1940S AND 1950S

In the 1944 yearbook, Joyce Alexander is described as "slim and trim . . . a shining star in chemistry . . . where did she get that Harvard accent?" No mention of her racial heritage is needed, as even then it was not an issue at a school where each student was measured solely on merit. It would not always be that way.

Her husband, George Wein—a white, Jewish jazz aficionado—wrote about the first flush of romance with her in his autobiography, *Myself among Others: A Life in Music*:[12]

> Joyce had been raised in a brownstone at 23 Braddock Park on Boston's South End. The second-youngest of seven children, she had entered kindergarten when she was three years old (she was promptly sent home for being too young, but was admitted a few weeks later, on her fourth birthday). At age nine, she transferred to Boston Girls' Latin School, one of the best public schools in the nation, (with a student body predominantly white). She not only survived that institution's grueling curriculum, she graduated at age fifteen and matriculated to Simmons College, one of the finer women's colleges in the area.
>
> Joyce came to my bon voyage party, which was held the night before I left to summer in Europe for 1949. At party's end, I drove her home to Braddock Park. Arriving there, we sat in the idle car for a few minutes, exchanging pleasantries. Finally, I leaned across the seat and pressed my lips softly against hers. It was our first kiss. I don't remember exactly what I said, but it was probably something like, "I am a Jewish kid from Newton, Massachusetts. I should probably be in love with a nice Jewish girl. But I think I am falling in love with you." Joyce offered no reply.
>
> Our relationship, in fact, did resume, and deepen, upon my return from France. I was intrigued by her intellectual acuity, her curiosity, her wit. She had a keener interest in aesthetic and cultural life than any girl I had known.

Against the wishes of Wein's parents, they were married in 1959 by a justice of the peace. In 1954, Wein introduced the Newport Jazz Festival.

In Dorothy West's 1995 bestselling novel *The Wedding*, a key character—Shelby Coles—was patterned after Alexander, whom West knew. (George Wein is called Meade Wyler.) In this novel, published in 1995 and set on Martha's Vineyard in the upper middle class black community at Oak Bluffs, which centers on "the Oval," West writes:

> But how Shelby, who could have had her pick of the best breed in her own race, could marry outside her race, outside her father's profession [doctor], and throw her life away on a nameless, faceless white man who wrote jazz, a frivolous occupation without office, title, or foreseeable future, was beyond the Oval's understanding.[13]

Dorothy West was born in Boston on June 2, 1907, to Isaac and Rachel Benson West. A former Virginia slave and an extremely ambitious man, Isaac became a very successful banana merchant and owned a grocery store and ice cream parlor. Like her father, Dorothy demonstrated a strong will to succeed. "The gifts he had given me were endurance and strength of will," she later wrote.[14] West attended the Martin School in Boston's Mission Hill district, and at the age of twelve she entered the Girls' Latin School. Two years later, her short story "Promise and Fulfillment" won the *Boston Post*'s weekly fiction-writing contest. Although she did not graduate from GLS, she attended both Boston and Columbia

Universities and while living in New York became active in the Harlem Renaissance. Her first novel, *The Living Is Easy*, concerned middle class African Americans in Boston and was published in 1948. She next published *The Wedding*, which she wrote 47 years later. Dorothy West died August 16, 1998.

Gloria L. Johnson, class of 1954

The first African American to graduate first Girls' Latin School, then Mount Holyoke College, Gloria L. Johnson had the strength of her convictions—not all of which were in concert with the expectations for the behavior of a student at GLS. As a young girl, her mother, Elizabeth Hendren, had come from Virginia to Boston to escape Southern racism. She married Walter William Johnson, who sometimes worked two or three jobs in order to support his four young children. During Elizabeth's pregnancy with her fifth child, Walter died tragically in an auto accident. Elizabeth found work as a domestic servant and was able to obtain welfare at a time when very few blacks were accepted into the program.[15]

Elizabeth Johnson monitored her children's education closely and made sure all were accepted to the best schools in Boston. Her daughter Gloria, her third child, was clearly the most academically gifted, however, and she was accepted by Girls' Latin School. In her junior year, she began to question religion, God, and her allegiance to the United States. By the time she had entered senior year, Johnson was at the top of the class, possibly first, and a lock for the National Honor Society. She was popular among her peers, but her challenges to the status quo continued to antagonize faculty and administration at Girls' Latin, where everyone was expected to follow the rules.

Gloria refused to stand and say the pledge of allegiance and to sing songs of prayer. Her homeroom teacher took her to the guidance counselor, who in turn remanded her to Headmaster McCoy, who did not view her actions as intellectual individualism and threatened to send letters to all the colleges that had accepted her and offered her scholarships. He warned her if he expressed his concerns to them about her nonconformance to school rules, she would lose her scholarships. McCoy suspended Johnson for a day for unpatriotic behavior and told her to return with her mother.

When Elizabeth Johnson returned with her daughter, she effectively took control by telling McCoy the meeting would last only a half hour. Without giving McCoy the opportunity to speak, she calmly explained her daughter's right to freedom of worship, how ridiculous it was for an educator to punish intellectual individualism, and, lastly, that writing recommending Gloria's scholarships be retracted would seriously damage his own credibility with the various departments of admission. This bold, assertive mother subdued McCoy, something parents rarely, if ever, accomplished. Although no letters were sent, McCoy did remove Johnson from the National Honor Society.

Johnson graduated Mount Holyoke in 1958 with a B.A. in economics and received her M.D. in 1962 from Meharry Medical College in Nashville, Tennessee. She completed her residency at UCLA and was on the faculty there for fifteen years before joining the Harvard Medical School (where she was on the faculty for ten years).

She married Rodney Powell and became a professor of child psychiatry. Gloria Johnson-Powell, MD, is also an important figure in the American civil rights movement and was one of the first African American women to attain tenure at Harvard Medical School. She later became associate dean for cultural diversity and a professor of psychiatry and pediatrics at the University of Wisconsin School of Medicine and Public Health.

The library of Girls' Latin School, Huntington Avenue

At the meeting with Muchnick that evening were Carr, Fitzgerald, and Lyons as well as Superintendent Dennis C. Haley, who had replaced Arthur Gould as superintendent on September 1, 1948, and a few others from his office. As a procedural matter, this portion of the meeting needed to be public, and the minutes were therefore recorded. (Although the meeting was open to the public, no public testimony is recorded in the minutes.) The legal department representative explained the purpose of the votes the School Committee was about to take: that Chapter 618 provided for (1) a State Teachers College in Boston; (2) the conveyance of certain city real estate to the state via an act of the mayor; and (3) an allowance for the city to continue to use the property to be transferred for the operation of Girls' Latin School until the state needed it for the teachers college. Upon Muchnick's request, the deed conveying the realty was read into the minutes:

> WHEREAS Section 4 of Chapter 618 of the Acts of 1952 empowers the City of Boston, acting by its Mayor, to convey to the Commonwealth of Massachusetts, without consideration, all land held by said City for school purposes within the area of said city bounded by Huntington Avenue, Longwood Avenue, Worthington Street, Tetlow Street, and Evans Way; provided that such conveyance is authorized by the School Committee of said city by a four-fifths vote of all of its members; and WHEREAS such conveyance has been authorized by the School Committee of said City by a four-fifths vote of all of its members; and WHEREAS such conveyance is a condition precedent to the establishment of a State Teachers College in the City on September 1, 1952, which would be of great benefit to the City; NOW, THEREFORE, THE CITY OF BOSTON . . . does hereby convey to THE COMMONWEALTH OF MASSACHUSETTS, without consideration, [this] land in the City of Boston.

Carr then moved that the mayor be authorized to carry out the conveyance, and all four members present (Muchnick, Carr, Fitzgerald, and Lyons) voted in favor of the motion.[16] At this point the public meeting was recessed, and the committee went into private conference. However, in the recorded School Committee proceedings of the same date is the vote on the use permit for Girls' Latin School. It stated in part, "Permission is hereby given by the Commonwealth of Massachusetts to the City of Boston to use for the purposes of Girls' Latin School until June 30, 1953, and from year to year thereafter, until the State Department of Education shall determine."[17] Again, all four committee members voted in favor of this motion.

The next day, the deed for the Girls' Latin School's Huntington Avenue building was recorded at the Suffolk Registry of Deeds.[18]

With the recording of the deed and the use permit, the City of Boston forever relinquished control of the Girls' Latin School building. The GLS community remained uninformed about what had just transpired because of the vague wording of the use permit: "until the State Department of Education shall determine."

THE DIAMOND JUBILEE: GLS CELEBRATES 75 YEARS

On Saturday, April 11, 1953, the scent of spring flowers from many bouquets permeated the air of the Girls' Latin School's library. Around the long oak table that dominated the room stood a dozen or more New England sack-back wooden chairs, and upon it stood four handsome brass reading lamps with green-glass conical shades. At one end of the library were two enormous windows, and at the other a cozy fireplace. The walls were lined with dark stained-oak bookcases, into one of which was built an exquisitely carved frame of leaves and acorns surrounding the Ipsen portrait of John Tetlow.

Diamond Jubilee Alumnae Banquet in GLS gymnasium, April 11, 1953

The End of Our Fenway Wonderland

Right: Eleanor Creed L'Ecuyer (standing, fourth from left) with members of the GLS class of 1916

GLS students present a play based on the history of the school to celebrate its Diamond Jubilee.

GLS Alumnae Association president Eleanor L'Ecuyer '39 mingled with guests and chatted gaily with other GLS board members. L'Ecuyer's family had deep ties to Girls' Latin School. Her mother, Eleanor Creed '16, had formerly served as the association's president, and both of her sisters had graduated GLS: Virginia in 1940 and Rosalie in 1951. Eleanor was born in Dorchester on June 13, 1922, graduated Suffolk University in 1944 and Suffolk Law School in 1950, and was admitted to the Massachusetts bar the following year.

After an hour's reception in the library, the guests moved to the assembly hall for a presentation of a play based on the history of the school. The play recreated scenes representing significant moments in GLS history: Congressman Claflin's Mount Vernon Street home in 1877, the School Committee office in 1877, and Classroom A4B at GLS in 1888 with Abbie Farwell Brown and classmates. The play was followed by a sumptuous dinner in the gym, which had been filled with long tables and chairs. Waitresses in neat white uniforms and aprons bustled between rows of alumnae representing classes from 1897 to 1953. The ceiling above was festooned with colorful crepe-paper streamers and balloons.

The Alumnae Banquet program had been printed just a few days before. Listed as guests at the head table were all five members of the Boston School Committee: Carr, Fitzgerald, Foley, Lyons, and Muchnick. Also included were Mr. and Mrs. Louis McCoy, Misses Frances and Helen Tetlow, and, by herself, Mrs. Ernest Hapgood. Her husband, who was born the same week as GLS's first day of classes and had been its second headmaster, had died at age 75 of heart disease on April 3 at Newton-Wellesley Hospital, one week before the school's Diamond Jubilee celebration.

Eleanor Creed L'Ecuyer's daughters, all GLS alumnae (left to right): Eleanor '39, Virginia '40, and Rosalie '51

Following L'Ecuyer's welcome, Marjorie Taylor Sanderson spoke in tribute to Hapgood and reminded the assembly that as headmaster he had "demanded the highest standards of scholarship and was largely responsible for the enviable scholastic reputation of the Girls' Latin School."[19] The week-long diamond jubilee celebration reminded all that four generations of devoted and inspired teachers had labored to create, from every point of view, an outstanding college preparatory school.

GLS PROTESTS REMOVAL FROM THE HUNTINGTON AVENUE BUILDING

Dennis C. Haley knew that what he was about to say at the January 26, 1954, School Committee meeting would not be well received. He was required to announce that Girls' Latin, which had been in the Fenway for almost 50 years, would have to move out in the fall. In December 1953, the Massachusetts commissioner of education notified the Boston School Committee that the state would be reclaiming seven rooms at the Huntington Avenue site's Collins Building, which was used by GLS. The commissioner's intent was to devote this space to the newly created State Teachers College. The School Committee had asked the State to extend GLS's use permit, but the Massachusetts Board of Education refused.

GLS would be reduced in size from 30 to 23 classrooms, a harbinger of the end. Haley in particular seemed to regret the way the transfer agreement had played out. He had spoken out at a meeting of the Boston School Committee the previous May, after the state had taken charge of the property:

> It was found that the heating units and ventilating units and all the service units were joined between the Teachers College building and

The End of Our Fenway Wonderland

Boston-area newspapers gave significant coverage to the School Committee hearing of February 24, 1954. The following day, the Daily Record *gave over the entire front-page, above-the-fold space to a banner headline (top); the* Boston Herald *ran a photo of Eleanor L'Ecuyer's presentation of a stack of petitions to School Committee Chairman Carr (bottom).*

the Girls' Latin School building. Following that time it was agreed by the School Committee to give the complete unit to the State, and I objected to it, on the basis that the Girls' Latin School was traditional and that we needed the facilities for that particular building and that in my opinion, as I said at the time, it was very unwise to do.[20]

The prospect of losing the Huntington Avenue building had suddenly become a reality for the GLS community. A storm had been brewing over this matter, and now it was about to unleash like a nor'easter. Weeks later, GLS demanded a public hearing. That hearing took place at School Committee headquarters on February 24, 1954. Headmaster McCoy and Eleanor L'Ecuyer moved purposefully toward the table where the members of the School Committee were seated. Attorney L'Ecuyer '39 wore a belted three-quarter-sleeve dress with a white collar, a matching pancake-style hat, and on her left wrist a small gold watch. Although dainty in appearance, L'Ecuyer had earned her law degree from Suffolk Law School in 1950, and had served in the U.S. Coast Guard Reserve during World War II. She later went on to to become the first female captain of the Coast Guard to retire from active duty. Both she and McCoy shared a fierce determination to retain the GLS building at any cost.

Behind the headmaster and the attorney, the auditorium was filled with GLS parents, alumnae, and students. Attorney L'Ecuyer had done a masterful job of recruiting more than 350 people to attend the 2:00 P.M. hearing to persuade the School Committee that Girls' Latin School should remain in its home on Huntington Avenue rather than relocate to the vacant Dorchester High School in Codman Square. People packed the auditorium, and many were forced to stand.

The Girls' Latin community was still struggling to understand what had happened. Most of the hearing's attendees were unaware that GLS's building had already been transferred permanently to the state. Members of the School Committee and Superintendent Haley were there to try to explain.

In early 1954, three new members took seats on the School Committee. Curley protégé Mike Ward of Roxbury topped the ticket to oust Muchnick, largely in response to the latter's support of the Strayer agenda. Patrick J. Foley and Alice Lyons had been ousted by Louis F. Musco and Joseph Lee. Faced with pointed questions from the audience, recently reelected School Committee member Ward was confused and appealed to Haley for clarification.

Mr. Ward: No, I was not here the last two years, as you know, but I was here the two years before that. However, as a member of the Council, we voted $5,000,000 each year for new school buildings in the long-range program. Did you have in your plans, Mr. Superintendent, a plan for a new Girls' Latin School?

Superintendent Haley: No, Mr. Chairman. In the long-range program there are plans... for a new English High School, for a new Girls' High School, and a new Boys' Technical High School, because of the age of the buildings. There was not any plan for a new Girls' Latin School. In fact, Mr. Chairman, if the state did not take over the entire unit of the Teachers College and the Girls' Latin School, we wouldn't be confronted as of the present time with this particular problem.

Mr. Ward: Did the state take it over?

Superintendent Haley: Under an act of the legislature, the state took over the entire unit for a dollar, I think.

Mr. Ward: By an act of the legislature?

Superintendent Haley: Yes.[21]

The first of dozens of speakers was City Councilor Gabriel F. Piemonte, a resident of the North End and father of a GLS student: "If the school system in Boston is great . . . it is great because somewhere far in the past somebody had the vision to set up in Boston a school such as the Girls' Latin and Boys' Latin Schools. It is around the Latin schools that our school system and our reputation has been built."

Representative Anthony J. Farren of Dorchester had walked down from Beacon Hill to testify at the hearing. He spoke in favor of the relocation—the only speaker to do so—telling the crowd he supported the move to Dorchester High School in Codman Square and pointing out that it would save the cost of rent at Huntington Avenue. Built in 1901, Dorchester High had been closed since the previous year and was used to store furniture and machinery from the 29 Boston schools that had already been already closed. It was a vacant monster of a building sitting in the middle of Farren's district.

As Farren pointed out the benefits, murmurs rose from the crowd. Chairman Carr rapped his gavel loudly to regain order. When Farren tried to discuss how the school would benefit by attracting more girls from Dorchester, the crowd hissed and booed. Shouts of "Get out!" could be heard as he explained that he had to return to Beacon Hill for a roll call. "I hope I get out of here alive!" he quipped.

After several more people had testified, L'Ecuyer rose to present a petition signed by about 1,500 alumnae opposing the relocation of GLS to Codman Square, saying that the statement "was drawn up particularly to insist upon the standards of the school being maintained, by the traditions of the school being upheld, and the only possible way we can see it be done is to leave it, in spite of our representative, in the Fenway district." Photographers asked her to pose with Chairman Carr for a picture. The stack of signatures was more than a foot thick, and L'Ecuyer strained to smile as she held the weighty stack.

Many of the hearing's attendees wanted to know why the City couldn't continue to make lease payments to the state so the school could remain in the present building. Many others who spoke urged the School Committee to move GLS to the building currently occupied by the soon-to-be-closed High School of Commerce, across the street from Boston Latin, into which the committee was considering moving English High School. One attendee stated, "Transferring Girls' Latin School from the Fenway to Dorchester would be like moving the Ritz-Carlton from its present site." Discussion was raised concerning the overcrowded conditions at GLS, which required some students to remain standing during classes, and questions as to whether the School Committee was aware of these overcrowded conditions. In all, public testimony would amount to 81 pages. One of the most probing speakers was Mrs. Rose Dordetsky of West Roxbury, whose daughter Rose was a GLS student. She was one of the last to speak.

> *Mrs. Dordetsky*: After listening to all these remarks, I think it is quite evident that Latin School means a great deal not only to the mothers, the alumnae, but to all concerned.... There is only one thing that came to my mind during this whole discussion. How come and for what reason was it ever sold, or why did we ever sell out Girls' Latin School for one dollar?
>
> *Chairman Carr*: I think it was explained by one of the women from the audience.
>
> *Mrs. Dordetsky*: It was explained?

Chairman Carr: Yes.

Mrs. Dordetsky: It was a legal thing, I know, but wasn't it silly?

Chairman Carr: Not necessarily. The State Government was trying to set up a State Teachers College here in Boston. The previous committee felt that the taxpayers of Boston were supporting an institution at a great expense, and the figures showed that out of the whole graduating class they retained about ten graduates a year in the Boston School System. We were doing a great job of educating teachers for the surrounding cities and towns. The majority of them were finding employment there.

Mrs. Dordetsky: But what were they planning to do with the Girls' Latin School, remove that, when they sold the building?

Chairman Carr: I think they were given assurances at that time that they would have use of that particular building. Isn't that right, Mr. Superintendent?

Superintendent Haley: I would think, in general, that was so.

Mrs. Dordetsky: That was kind of selling them short and not having any place for them, because Girls' Latin School has meant something, not only here, but any girls or anybody who has had an attachment for the—

Chairman Carr: I think it is obvious to the committee that the Girls' Latin School means a great deal to the people here... [Applause.]

Mrs. Dordetsky: There were a great number of rooms in the Teachers College which could have been absorbed, which you people didn't do. You just sold out to the state. Now they want more. We understood, when you sold that out, that Girls' Latin was going to remain there.

Miss Fitzgerald: That was our understanding. Our understanding was that the Girls' Latin School would be able to remain there indefinitely. Otherwise, it would certainly not have been done. That is all we can say. [Fitzgerald had in fact voted for the use permit that stated "until the State Department of Education shall determine."]

Mrs. Dordetsky: Well, then, somebody missed the boat on the whole deal right from the beginning.

The End of Our Fenway Wonderland

THE STRUGGLE CONTINUES, AND OTHER VOICES WEIGH IN

Those who wished Girls' Latin School to remain where it was thought they had achieved a measure of victory a few weeks later, when the School Committee, by a vote of 3 to 2, decided to leave the school in its Fenway location. The triumph was short lived, however. In November 1954, the state commissioner of education notified the Boston School Committee that the state would take an additional eight rooms from GLS for use by the State Teachers College. The school, which had already been reduced in size from 30 to 23 classrooms and was operating on a staggered schedule, was now to be allotted just 15 classrooms. This order would make continued operation in the Huntington Avenue building impossible.

Although Boston was in desperate need of new schools, it had many old school buildings that were not being used efficiently. Superintendent Haley had revealed a plan to save $12 million by consolidating and reshuffling schools, which was the basis for the School Committee's recommendation to move Girls' Latin to Dorchester High School. The Municipal Research Bureau, which had contributed to the plan's recommendations, wrote that separate schools for girls and boys made adjusting class sizes less efficient. The Sargent report, an exhaustive survey of the Boston schools carried out by the Harvard Center for Field Studies, recommended that the two Latin schools be combined in one building, but this recommendation was also turned down.

The School Committee had the opportunity in 1954 to transfer Girls' Latin School to the building located across from Boston Latin on Avenue Louis Pasteur. That building had been vacated when the School Committee closed down the High School of Commerce. In a decision that would in the end preclude GLS ever coming back to the Fenway, the building was awarded to English High School instead.

It was clear the 1955 incarnation of the School Committee was not going to give up easily and would fight to keep Girls' Latin School in its building. At the same time, the state Department of Education was likewise determined in its claims. Shortly after the 1955 School Committee was sworn into office, the Boston Finance Committee issued to the mayor and city council a "Communication in Regard to the Girls' Latin School Location in Future."[22] It described how the impasse had come about and noted sympathetically that GLS enrollment had recently increased by 11 percent. The letter continued:

Boston (the School Committee), therefore, is faced with three alternatives. Boston must close out entirely and permanently the Girls' Latin School; or Boston must provide an entirely different building for the school. The first of these alternatives is, to many, unthinkable; the second might cause an unexpected expenditure of over $3,000,000.

The School Committee has suggested, as the solution to this dilemma, the use of the now closed Dorchester High School for Girls as the new Girls' Latin School. However, a storm of protest from alumnae of the Latin School . . . has halted consummation of that idea. What makes this solution of the difficulty attractive from a financial standpoint is that the maximum cost of it would be no more than $75,000.

It is questionable if the School Committee can make any other use of the Dorchester property. It cost the city (land and building) approximately $500,000 many years ago. . . . It is now in sound condition, needing only internal repairs to make it as good as new. The Dorchester High School has been closed for over a year. When the building is closed, deterioration proceeds at an alarming rate.[23]

At the regular meeting of the Boston School Committee on February 7, 1955, committee members placed into the record a communication from Massachusetts Governor Christian A. Herter, which read:

Since receiving your letter of January 4, I have conferred with Commissioner Desmond with respect to occupancy by the Girls' Latin School of classrooms in the State Teachers College of Boston. I am in receipt of a communication from Commissioner Desmond, a copy of which is enclosed, in which are set forth very clearly his views as to why the State cannot modify the agreement entered into in 1952. I concur with Mr. Desmond's views.[24]

Commissioner John J. Desmond's letter of January 20, 1955, stated in part:

In order that the State might be protected from a large capital outlay expense which would result from an increased enrollment in the State Teacher's College of Boston when it became a state institution, the Board of Education stipulated that in addition to the property occupied by the Teachers College that the whole property including that occupied by the Girls' Latin School be acquired by deed by the State.... At the time when the "Use Permit" was drafted, the City of Boston understood that progressively the increased enrollment in the State Teachers College at Boston would necessitate the reduction in the number of rooms to be occupied by the Girls' Latin School, and it was further understood that some provision would be made for the housing of the school in other school property of the City of Boston.... It was obvious that this situation was well understood by the School Committee of Boston in 1952 when they had under consideration plans for the accommodation of Girls' Latin School students.... In view of the complete meeting of the minds at the time when this legislation was passed in 1952, it would appear that the interest of the Commonwealth would not be served by refusing admittance of hundreds of prospective teachers in the Greater Boston area.[25]

Having exhausted all options, the Boston School Committee then ordered that beginning September 1, 1955, the school would be housed in the building formerly known as the Dorchester High School for Girls. The School Committee appropriated a total of $75,000 to renovate the building and summarized its position in the proceedings of a meeting in February 1955:

> Circumstances beyond the control of this School Committee give us no immediate alternative but to re-locate Girls' Latin School for a temporary period. If the Alumnae Association, the students, teachers, and Headmaster will cooperate with us, we can try to impress the Mayor and the City Council, the Governor, and the Legislature with the need for funds to build a new Girls' Latin School in the Fenway area. Here is our only hope.... Even if we had in hands the funds and the site on the Fenway for a new building, we would need the time in which to build it. As things stand, we either have to move Girls' Latin or suspend its life. The Committee finds this re-location an unpleasant but necessary step to preserve the life of a school which brings honor to our City's education system.... The School Committee urges all who are concerned with Girls' Latin School to demonstrate the qualities of character the school teaches. We feel they will.[26]

MOVING DAY

Thirty of the 35 buildings listed in the Strayer report had now been closed. The last building to be closed was Girls' Latin School, making 31 in total. With that done, the venerable counterpart of the Boston Latin School was separated from the only building ever built exclusively for it.

Friday, June 24, 1955, was the final day of classes at the building. Almost every room was filled with folding cartons. Decades of school records, all the statues, and hundreds of boxes filled "with everything from books to Bunsen burners" were packed up and shipped to Codman Square.[27] "It is very hard to leave the old building," said Marion Moreland, math and science teacher. "I was here the day the building opened in 1907. I can remember bringing up a folding chair to sit on for the first class."[28] English teacher Zabelle Tahmizian said, "I've read my class some famous poems of leave-taking but none of them quite expressed the sadness we felt."[29]

An editorial in *The Jabberwock* took a philosophical view:

Girls' Latin School's destination in June 1955, its new home at Codman Square in Dorchester

> Next September we shall be in a new building in another section of the city. Until now we have used all of our resources in a valiant effort to remain in our present location. The decision, however, has been made; we must go. . . . Thus, ironically, we learn the lesson that a thing is not fully appreciated until it is lost. Our next thought should be that of carrying on our curriculum, traditions, and school spirit the best way we are able and fixing them firmly in our new abode. Let us, therefore, "Stand by her gallantly and fight for her valiantly, in all times and places her greatness proclaim."[30]

◀ 1955
Girls' Latin School relocates to Codman Square in Dorchester.

◀ 1957
Louis McCoy retires as GLS headmaster and Thomas F. Gately takes the helm.

◀ 1960
The first Girls' Latin School building on West Newton Street is demolished.

1961
Ray Kroc introduces McDonald's and fast food.

1963 ▶
President John F. Kennedy is assassinated.

1964 ▶
The Prudential Tower is built on Boylston Street in Boston's Back Bay.

Gulf of Tonkin Resolution leads to a vast expansion of the number of U.S. troops in Vietnam.

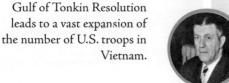

1964
Wilfred O'Leary becomes headmaster of Boston Latin School, succeeding John J. Doyle.

◀ 1965
Headmaster Thomas Gately retires and is replaced by William T. Miller.

Louis McCoy dies.

◀ 1966
Miller leaves, and Margaret C. Carroll becomes first female headmaster.

1968
Robert Kennedy and Martin Luther King are assassinated.

Kevin White becomes mayor ▶ of Boston.

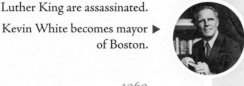

1969
Woodstock music festival takes place in upstate New York.

X

The Yellow-Brick Building

Entryway arch into Dorchester High School shortly after GLS moved to Codman Square, Dorchester

By the time the former Dorchester High School became the fourth location for Girls' Latin School, in 1955, Codman Square, Dorchester, was a run-down financial and retail district struggling to keep storefronts occupied. The First National Bank was perhaps its most prominent tenant.

The district was dominated by two very different buildings. The Second Church of Dorchester, today the second-oldest church remaining in Boston, was a stunning example of Federal frame architecture. Its graceful clocktower originally boasted a bell cast by Paul Revere & Son. The square was named after its first minister, Reverend John Codman (1808–1847). The delicate religious building was dwarfed by the contiguous yellow-buff brick building, the former Dorchester High School, but now repurposed as Girls' Latin School.

Dorchester High School had been in use for more than five decades before it was awarded to GLS. Completed on June 3, 1901, both boy and girl students had occupied it.[1] In 1925, the boys moved to a new building, and this one became the Dorchester High School for Girls. In 1953, however, the girls moved to rejoin the boys in their school on Dunbar Avenue, making Dorchester High coeducational once again, but the

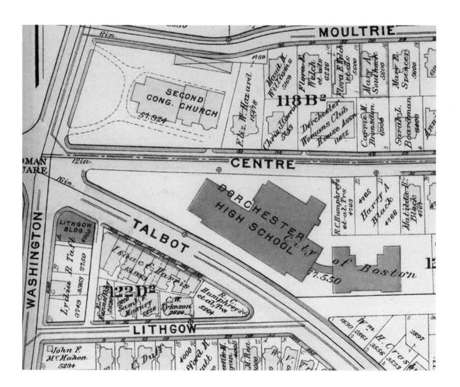

The school building in Codman Square sat on a triangle of land, the apex of which extended out to the middle of the square at Washington Street; Talbot Avenue provided the hypotenuse and Centre Street formed the third side.

Before and after: the frieze on the Codman Square school building

Codman Square building was left empty for two years before being awarded to Girls' Latin.[2]

The Dorchester High building sat on a tight triangle of land, the apex of which extended out to the middle of Codman Square at Washington Street. The city purchased the land in 1896, but construction of the school building did not start for two years due to the difficult shape of the 60,000-square-foot site. The first proposal for the building was rejected, and the later, Renaissance-revival—approved—design was by Hartwell, Richardson & Driver. The building's exterior was clad in a distinctive yellow brick, called "buff brick," which was accented by limestone lintels and trim. Over both entrances, a black sign with *Girls' Latin School* in gold lettering was placed over the words *Dorchester High School*, the original inscription in the limestone. Through a small yard enclosed by a black wrought-iron fence, students followed a stone-lined walkway into the building's side entrance, which faced Codman Square.

Inside, on each of its four floors, a wide main corridor running parallel to Talbot Avenue extended the length of the building. Two broad sets of stairs with elaborate designs on the risers and balusters climbed from the basement to the fourth floor. On the first floor was the headmaster's office, reception office, and several classrooms; the second floor held the library and assembly hall. Both the second and third floors had fully equipped laboratories, and the fourth floor had two art rooms. Once an annex to the main building was constructed in 1908, a total of 58 classrooms were available.

SETTLING IN, MOVING ON

Reluctantly, during the summer of 1955, Headmaster McCoy arrived to set up his new office. He was grateful to the many teachers who volunteered to help unpack boxes, arrange furniture, and restore order at the new Girls' Latin School. Its many pieces of artwork, so evocative of its long history and singular mission, traveled from Huntington Avenue to Codman Square. The replica frieze of Luca della Robbia's *Singing Boys* was placed opposite the headmaster's office. The caryatids were situated against a wall at the top of the stairs on the second floor, Joan of Arc graced the landing between the second and third floors, and other busts and statues were distributed throughout the building. In an editorial in an early post-move issue of *The Jabberwock*, a student mused:

> Well, after many arguments pro and con, here we are in Dorchester.... It is certainly wonderful to have the rest of our statues here, but where is the Parthenon Frieze? ... In spite of these disadvantages, there are some improvements. Although the building is not situated in as convenient surroundings, it is much larger. We certainly do not miss that feeling of being packed into each room like so many sardines.... However there is another silver lining to our cloud, and that is the wonderful teachers came in and prepared the building for us. They gave up part of their well-earned vacation to [do this.] ... In summing up all these advantages and disadvantages, we must keep one thing in mind: the discomforts of exile last only a short time...

One of the massive staircases connecting floors in the Codman Square building

The Yellow-Brick Building

and are forgotten in the joy of returning home, which joy we hope to experience in the very near future.³

From the beginning of their tenure at Codman Square, GLS students were isolated from the local community. In 1971, Judith Brody class of 1963, at the time a staff writer for the *Boston Globe*, contributed an article that summarized the situation.

> The Dorchester neighborhood where the school is located has become more run down but still has a lively, lusty quality to it. Girls' Latin School seems strangely out of place in Codman Square, psychologically walled off from the fast-moving cars and the people weaving in and out between them.
>
> As a student I had no contact with the people in the neighborhood. I was only dimly aware of their existence. For when I entered the school each day, I entered another world, one that is symbolized by the white statues in the Latin School Hall—the Caryatides, priestesses in the Temple of Diana.
>
> We students were, in a way, like the priestesses, sheltered from the harsher realities of life. In the Latin School world, innocence was possible, and friendships among women could be deep and long lasting because there were no men to compete for. It was a world of discipline, of singleness of purpose.⁴

Louis McCoy, Headmaster of Girls' Latin School, *painted by Griswold Tyng, 1957*

By early 1957, Louis McCoy was approaching his seventieth birthday and his forty-seventh year of teaching. Long before he had committed himself to carrying out Superintendent Gould's request to protect and preserve Girls' Latin, but now it was time for him to pass along the reins. The school's prestige and academic reputation had survived the move undamaged, and in the end these qualities were what could not be taken away, the way a building could. After all, he thought, GLS was an institution that would survive anything. McCoy had watched over it carefully during the two-year transition at Codman Square and was sure he had done his best. The GLS Alumnae Association honored the retiring headmaster with a banquet at which his portrait was unveiled. It had been painted by Griswold Tyng, the artist who also made the portrait of Orville Farnham of Roxbury Latin.

HEADMASTERS IN TRANSITION

Between 1957 and 1966, Girls' Latin School made transitions through three headmasters.

Thomas F. Gately, who succeeded Louis McCoy in 1957, was born in 1895 and served in the U.S. Navy in World War I. He was a graduate of Boston College High School and earned both a bachelor's and a master's degree in classics from Boston College in

Thomas Gately's retirement portrait, 1965

William T. Miller, 1966

1920.[5] While at Boston College, he played varsity basketball. He taught at Jamaica Plain High School before becoming headmaster at Roslindale High School and then transferring to GLS. Upon his arrival, *The Jabberwock* reported, "His chief aim... is to make the future of G.L.S. more illustrious than her past, if possible."[6]

As was customary, Mr. Gately addressed the students at the school's opening assembly in the autumn of 1957: "As it says in Virgil, *Labor omnia vincit*—Labor conquers all things. To each and every student of Girls' Latin School, I urge you to find your goal and work, work, work."[7] On June 1, 1965, the same date that Gately retired after eight years as headmaster, he was honored at a reception held by the GLS Alumnae Association at the school, and he was presented his portrait, which was painted by Glenn MacNutt, father of Karen MacNutt '67.

William T. Miller, who was the shortest-tenured headmaster in GLS history, graduated Boston College in 1929 and earned an M.S. in 1932. He was headmaster of South Boston High School from 1958 until 1965, when he began his stint at GLS, which lasted only until the close of school the following June.

Then, for the first time in its history, Girls' Latin was led by a female headmaster. Margaret C. Carroll was born June 17, 1908, in Boston and graduated from Girls' High School. She earned a B.S. degree from Teachers College Boston and an M.A. in education from Teachers College and Boston University. After teaching science at Girls' High from 1931 to 1950, she became head of the Dorchester High School science department from 1950 until 1957, followed by headmaster at Roxbury Memorial High School for Girls from 1951 until 1959. She was in charge of Boston Business School from 1959 until her arrival at GLS in 1966.

Margaret C. Carroll, 1967

THE ROCK 'N' ROLL 50s

After World War II, for ten cents you could buy a hotdog and soda at Joe and Nemo's or take the Commonwealth Avenue trolley to Norumbega Park in Newton, where, in the Totem Pole Ballroom, you could dance the night away to big band music for $1.35. Men still wore overcoats and fedoras; women, white gloves and small hats. A decade later, however, this carefree postwar era was evaporating.

For students, the rock 'n' roll fifties were front and center. Girls found lipstick colors to present the most pressing issue of the times: Which was best: petal pink, pink peppermint, pink dahlia, or regal red? Elvis stole everyone's heart. New hairdos—the flip, the beehive, and the bouffant, for example—raged into style. Fashions were changing tremendously and rapidly. Saddle shoes and the infamous bobby socks Mr. Hapgood had disallowed were finally approved.

Students gathered on the front steps to GLS in Codman Square, ca. 1960

Cardigan sweater sets and wool-and-corduroy skirts reigned supreme. But at least for girls' school wear, pants remained taboo.

In September 1957, Thomas F. Gately took over Louis McCoy's former office. Having majored in classics at Boston College, he was fairly comfortable in his new role. His first priority was to meet with each class and become more familiar with some of the students.

Gately readily embraced the challenge of maintaining the school's academic standards and poured his support enthusiastically into its traditions, such as the Athenian Club, *The Jabberwock*, and Baby Day. About 10 percent of each class was being accepted to one of the Seven Sisters colleges. He recognized that each year, as more students from more and more of the United States strove to capture those seats, GLS's standards had to move forward in stride with the burgeoning competition.

For eight years, Gately quietly guided GLS and the school continued its excellent showing in acceptances to the Seven Sisters colleges. In 1965, however, Gately decided to retire. William T. Miller took the helm, but for only one year. Then the baton was passed to the first female headmaster of Girls' Latin School.

THE TURBULENT 1960s

On September 5, 1968, Headmaster Margaret C. Carroll readied to leave the main office and head to the assembly hall. This year, the first day of school was picture perfect: temperatures hovered in the 60s and there was a welcome breeze to keep the air circulating through the non-air-conditioned building. This was the third year she had opened the school, and she had grown accustomed to her unenviable role as strict guardian of GLS's academic traditions and standards.

Outside the office, she heard new members of the Sixth Class asking for directions and, from somewhere further down the corridor, older students hissing "*SSSSSSixxxies*," as had become a privilege for girls in the upper classes. This minor taunting was allowed, but not encouraged.

Before becoming headmaster at GLS, the last time Carroll had taught at a Boston public high school was in 1959. Since then, she had overseen Boston Business School—colloquially known as Boston Clerical—a public school that provided training to students who sought secretarial or other administrative-assistant positions. It provided a sharp contrast to GLS's strictly college-preparatory course.

GLS's total enrollment at this time was about 1,250 students, which matched the seating capacity of the building. Students carried five major subjects each year—six in Class Three—and were expected to participate in extracurricular activities. Having inherited a dedicated staff, Carroll managed six heads of departments, three guidance counselors, one

THE GLS PROGRAM OF STUDY IN THE SIXTIES

CLASS SIX:
English, Latin, Pre-Algebra, World Geography, Art, Music, and Physical Education

CLASS FIVE:
English, Latin, Algebra, Physical Science, American History, Music, and Physical Education

CLASS FOUR:
English, Latin, Geometry, Ancient History, German or French, Music, and Physical Education

CLASS THREE:
English, Latin, Algebra II, World History, Biology, German or French, Music, and Physical Education

CLASS TWO:
English, Latin, Trigonometry/Geometry, U.S. History, German or French, Music, and Physical Education

CLASS ONE:
English, Calculus, Physical Education, and three of the following electives: Latin, French, German, International Relations, Western Cultures, Physics, or Chemistry

nurse, one librarian, and 52 faculty. She was aware of the chatter that claimed that a graduate of Girls' High and former head of Boston Clerical simply was not qualified to lead Girls' Latin School, but she would prove them wrong. Carroll defined and asserted her authority right from the outset, and the first assembly of the new school year, which took place in front of the entire student body, was the perfect forum both for greeting the school and reinforcing its mission. She hoped her speech would be remembered by all students who heard it.

Over the summer, as usual, she had sent out letters of acceptance to the girls who had successfully gained admission. The letter read:

Dear Candidate for Admission to Girls' Latin School:

It is a pleasure for me to tell you that as a result of your entrance examination you will be admitted to Girls' Latin School in September of 1968 if you successfully complete Grade VI.

You should report to the Assembly Hall of the Girls' Latin School on Thursday, September 5, 1968 at 8:00 A.M. This letter does not reserve a seat for you and therefore if you are not present on Thursday, September 5, 1968, your place will be assigned to the next girl on the list.

Although a great many girls did well in the examination, we shall be able to admit only a limited number of the top scores because of the size of our building. It is therefore imperative that you complete the form below and return it to me immediately, so that if you are not planning to attend, we can ask another girl.

My best wishes for success in your school work.

Located on the second floor, the assembly hall was two stories high and crowned with a ceiling of massive, exposed arched timbers. Students were seated on hard wooden club chairs in order by class. The Sixth Class sat in the balcony above the main floor at the very rear of the assembly hall. The Fifth Class was on the floor level beneath the balcony. Then there was an aisle, from which chairs extended all the way up to a stage. Beginning with the Fourth Class, then the Third Class seated in front of them, followed next by the juniors, the sequence finally closed with the seniors, who occupied the front rows closest to the stage. A large black piano sat up front on the left.

Headmaster Carroll was petite, but stocky. Her blue eyes were piercing. Her wavy, dark hair peppered with grey was pulled tightly into a chignon at the back of her neck. She used no makeup, but often wore a pearl choker and a matching gold-and-pearl pin to accent the tailored suits in hues of cobalt, navy, hydrangea, or light blue. Her black pumps tied with black laces.

Entering the assembly hall and heading for the stage, Carroll quickly reached the podium. She looked up and, though she did not utter a syllable, the raucous hall noise of 1,200 talkative teenage girls dropped to complete silence. Not only was this expected, Carroll insisted upon it.

At the podium, she took a few seconds to survey the hall. Her head turned slowly, like an owl's. When speaking, she held her bifocals in her right hand by their bows. When she read from notes, she peered over them in order to make eye contact. An aura of Puritan strictness emanated from her, and her demeanor rivaled that of any queen of England. After brief introductory remarks, she asked, "Sixth Class, please stand up." Looking at her notes, she said,[8]

The Assembly Hall in the school building at Codman Square upon its completion in 1901 (top) and filled with GLS students in 1968 (bottom)

> The education you are about to receive is priceless. Those who do not value it will find themselves dismissed. Please take a very long look at the young lady to your right and the one to your left, and remember them. You can be almost certain that one of them will not be there when you graduate. You are all girls of excellent intellectual ability, but now you will be asked to accomplish tasks seemingly impossible. Only the best and the brightest girls will be able to rise to meet the academic rigors and demands of Girls' Latin. The rest of you will fail. When you fail to live up to our standards, you will return to your neighborhood high school. I and all of our teaching staff are here to assure that only the best graduate Girls' Latin School. Now please be seated.[9]

After dismissing the students back to their homerooms, Carroll returned to her office to handle the myriad of assignment problems that were typically encountered on the first day of school. All of these

The Yellow-Brick Building

problems were generally within her control. She was less optimistic about the social revolution going on, threatening the school with changes with which she knew inevitably she would have to cope.

The 1960s brought both major upheaval for women and brought wave after wave of change to American culture. Polaroid would introduce "instant" color film that developed in 60 seconds, and IBM introduced the Selectric typewriter, which completely changed office work. Elvis still topped the charts, but now he was rivaled by Chubby Checker, who sparked a dance craze called the Twist. Everyone watched American Bandstand, Father Knows Best, and Leave It to Beaver, then swooned

ZABELLE TAHMIZIAN, CLASS OF 1919

Born June 13, 1903, to an immigrant Armenian family, Zabelle Dickran Tahmizian grew up in Roxbury and graduated in 1919 from Girls' Latin School. Four years later, in 1923—at the age of 19—she received her bachelor's degree from Radcliffe College, where she had majored in English literature. Although her Radcliffe yearbook told of her boundless love "for all kinds of people, of all stations and nationalities,"[10] her students at GLS knew this without reading it in a yearbook. Many recalled her story of the day she had to fill out a form that asked for her race. She told her students, "I wrote *human*."[11]

Miss Tahmizian taught English, and her goal was simple: every one of her students would learn how to write the language clearly and properly. Although she was short in stature, her imperious voice left little doubt about her intellectual powers or the respect she commanded from students. She began teaching at Girls' Latin School immediately after graduating Radcliffe, and her devotion to the school grew as time went on. For many decades she remained the strongest link, as alumna and teacher, to the school's past. Many GLS teachers could be held up as exemplars of excellence, but perhaps none more so than Tahmizian. Her standards were the highest, and her commitment to the teaching of fluent and expressive English was second to none.

Two former students eloquently convey what made her so outstanding. Diana Laskin Siegal '48 recalled:

> Miss Tahmizian was very strict and demanding. She gave out horizontal 5" × 7" thin-lined paper each day and assigned a one-paragraph topic to write quickly. She corrected them each evening and passed them back the next day marked in red ink for spelling, grammar, punctuation, and syntax. The paragraph had to have an opening sentence, development of

Zabelle Tahmizian, ca. 1916, while a student at GLS

Tahmizian's Radcliffe yearbook portrait, 1923

over the Beatles' performance on the Ed Sullivan Show. Fans worshipped Frankie Avalon, Herman's Hermits, the Supremes, or even Mitch Miller, but mobs of teenage girls screaming over male singing groups was exactly the sort of behavior Carroll would not abide.

On the national front, the United States grieved over the assassinations of President John F. Kennedy in 1963, Malcolm X in 1965, and Martin Luther King and Bobby Kennedy in 1968. These assassinations and the Vietnam War ignited a period of civil disobedience the likes of which the country had never before seen. The 1960s may have changed permanently how U.S. citizens saw themselves and the world, but Carroll was resolute

the theme, and a closing sentence. She was demanding, but I never learned so much. In all six years at GLS, I don't remember ever writing more than a few papers. But a long paper is, after all, just a collection of paragraphs, and Miss Tahmizian taught us how to write a paragraph.... I also remember Miss Tahmizian reading Robert Browning's "My Last Duchess" to us. She read so beautifully, with such dramatic flair, that the poem and the painting about which he wrote came alive to me.[12]

Theresa Gulinello Raymond '70 remembers Tahmizian as "one of the best teachers I ever had."

She was very, very demanding, but my feeling was she believed in us. Some found her demeaning. I never did, even when she told me as a Sixie that if I stood up straight, cut my hair, and forgot about the Beatles, I would win a scholarship in Class I. Alas, I still slouch and have longish hair, but I did win a four-year full scholarship in Class I. She was the first to see something in me and bring it out. I am forever grateful.[13]

In the spring of 1964, Tahmizian was teaching in her classroom when the fire alarm sounded. It was

Fire at Girls' Latin School, May 1964

not a pre-announced drill but a real alarm: a fire had erupted in a fourth-floor storage room, and all students and teachers were to be evacuated. Miss Tahmizian, however, refused to leave the building. The firefighters almost had to carry her out. Indignantly, she fumed, "I have spent my entire life from sixth grade in this school, except for the four years I was at Radcliffe. I will go down with my school."[14]

Zabelle Tahmizian retired in 1970 and died in October 1972.

that there would be no struggle at Girls' Latin—she would hold steadfastly to its traditions and keep the school firmly rooted in its proud past.

Locally, by 1950 the number of African Americans living in Boston had doubled, although they still made up less than 10 percent of the city's population. Most lived in the South and West Ends, and both neighborhoods were considered slums. In the early 1960s, the Boston branch of the National Association for the Advancement of Colored People (NAACP) began to discuss ways to alleviate racial imbalance in Boston's schools. Richard Banks, vice president of the NAACP, reported to *The Jabberwock* the three ways he envisioned the alleviation of this imbalance: (1) shift zones a few blocks either way in Roxbury; (2) make it known to the black community that there were underused schools in other parts of Boston; and (3) if possible, establish a busing system to provide transportation to those particular schools. This conversation began to reverberate throughout Boston.

One-hundred percent of Girls' Latin School's graduates were admitted to college, and that statistic drove her to maintain the status quo that produced such results. Carroll continually defended the curriculum, "The strength of a Latin School education is the broad base of information which you acquire. You touch on all areas of knowledge."[15]

However, she soon would be shocked, as was the student body, when Girls' Latin's protective inner sanctum was pierced. Dorchester had evolved into a neighborhood progressively more in favor of civil rights. Martin Luther King Jr. lived there for a time when he attended Boston University to get his Ph.D., and his sermons served as a catalyst for change in this community, which was in transition from being predominantly Jewish to African American. Militant groups formed to discuss the need for change, and during the first few weeks of school in 1969, one group found the cachet of Girls' Latin School to represent an opportunity to publicize its cause.

The *Boston Globe* reported:

5 SDS Organizers Invade Classroom

Five female organizers for Students for a Democratic Society staged a brief takeover of a Girls' Latin School teacher's classroom yesterday morning. Miss Helen Mannix, 57, head of the English Department, told police that while 26 members of a senior class watched helplessly,

The 1967 prom at GLS

five young girls invaded her classroom shortly before 11 A.M. Miss Mannix said that she was held captive by one girl while two other guarded the classroom exits and a fourth watched the telephone so no calls could be made from the room. She said that the fifth member of the group then lectured the class on the merits of staging a revolution against the school system and overthrowing the establishment. She also distributed pamphlets to the class. When the 11 A.M. bell rang to indicate the change of classes, the five girls, four white and one black, escaped unnoticed as students filing out of adjoining classrooms.[16]

Elaine Milton, class of 1970, was in that classroom:

I sure remember the SDS visit to Miss Mannix's English class. I don't think I will ever forget the look on her face and just remember her repeating "get your hand off my watch" to the girl holding her wrist. I think we were all in shock. We sat there in stunned silence as they spoke to us. At last the bell rang. With raised fists they shouted, "Power to the people," and disappeared into the crowded hall. The few newsletters they left behind had a headline that said "The Fire Next Time" prompting much discussion while we tried to figure out what was going on.[17]

Despite the currents of change, tradition and the past remained vividly alive for GLS students and alumnae. A 1966 alumnae newsletter included messages from Edith Wheeler Ripley '92, classmate of Mabel Hay Barrows. In her contribution, Ethel Johnson Mersel '08—whose class was the first to graduate at the Huntington Avenue building and who would became the first African American graduate of GLS to graduate from Radcliffe—expressed a desire to visit the Codman Square building. Anne Roberts Gleason '14 reported seeing the original frieze of the Parthenon in London and remembered Mr. Tetlow explaining the copy in the GLS assembly hall. The year 1966 also marked the fiftieth reunion of the class of 1916, and a celebratory tea was planned by Eleanor Creed L'Ecuyer, former president of the Alumnae Association. The newsletter noted that Helen Schmidt '29 had been head of the math department at GLS since 1963 and that Lillian Greene Lapidus, who graduated in the same class as Schmidt, had been teaching history at GLS since 1960.

FINALLY, BACK TO THE FENWAY ... PERHAPS

The Boston Public Facilities Commission was established in 1966 to oversee the construction of public buildings. At that time, a new school complex for 5,500 students was under construction at Madison Park in Roxbury, and it was proposed that English High School, which was located across the street from Boston Latin School, move to Madison

JULIANNE GLOWACKI

The Civil Air Patrol cadet smiling at JFK is Julianne Glowacki '62, who recalled the circumstances surrounding this photograph, which was taken in May of her senior year.

I am that cadet—Major Glowacki. Civil Air Patrol was important in my development, giving me experiences in teaching courses such as "Power for Aircraft" and "Navigation and Weather," giving me leadership training, and teaching me the importance of service to community in light of the many search missions we undertook. Those tools provided a foundation for both career and citizenship. I was primarily part of the unit at the Naval Air Station in Weymouth, Massachusetts, and also participated in activities with the unit at the Fargo Building in Boston, Massachusetts. Can you imagine the thrill for an inner-city high school girl to become Massachusetts Cadet of the Year and visit the White House and Congress? As the cadet representing Massachusetts, I vividly remember my conversation with President Kennedy at the moment of that photo on May 7, 1962. He shook my hand and asked where I went to school (Girls' Latin School) and where I lived (Dorchester). He commented that his mother and I were neighbors! He asked about my aspirations (a career in medical research) and wished me well.[18]

Glowacki received her B.A. from Boston University in 1966 and her Ph.D. in biological chemistry from Harvard in 1973. She went on to establish the Plastic Surgery Research Laboratory at Boston Children's Hospital and become an internationally recognized scientist in the field of orthopedic research. She is currently director of skeletal biology at Brigham and Women's Hospital, professor of orthopedic surgery at Harvard Medical School, and professor of oral and maxillofacial surgery at Harvard School of Dental Medicine.

Glowacki in 2012, upon being named among the Outstanding GLS Alumnae

Park. On December 18, 1967, the Boston School Committee voted that English High should become part of the Madison Park complex and that Girls' Latin should be relocated to a renovated English High building on Avenue Louis Pasteur.

> ORDERED that the Girls' Latin School be relocated in the present English High School when English High is relocated in the Madison High complex and that the renovation of the present English High School be so planned.
>
> Yeas: 5 Thomas S. Eisenstadt, Louise Day Hicks, Joseph Lee, William E. O' Connor, and John J. McDonough; Nays: 0

Carroll was elated and began to have conference calls and correspondence about a Girls' Latin returning to the Fenway, across from Boston Latin. On April 8, 1968, Malcolm E. Dudley, director of the Public Facilities Commission Department, wrote to Superintendent William H. Ohrenberger to report that the department had determined it was not feasible to renovate the English High Building and had decided instead that it should be torn down and a new school built. The Boston School Committee in turn reported to the state Board of Education that it had elected new construction instead of renovation on the English High site, and that the new building was to be used by Girls' Latin School. In her history of Girls' Latin School, Carroll recalled the plans that were made once the idea gained traction.

> Beginning in 1966, the School Committee became actively aware of the fact that Girls' Latin School needed to be relocated. In the School Committee meeting of December 18, 1967, it was ordered that the Girls' Latin School be located in the English High School building when English High School were relocated in what was being called the Madison Park Complex, and that any renovations to the present English High School building be so planned. Later it was decided to construct a high-rise building behind the existing English High School with the intention of removing the old building when the new building was completed. The architects discussed the plans with Miss Margaret C. Carroll, the Head Master, and later they were presented by Public Facilities and the Architect to a regular meeting of the Girls' Latin Home and School Association.[19]

Gym class, 1968

The state Board of Education was responsible for overseeing state funding for school projects through the state Building Assistance Bureau. In January 1971, the state wrote to the Boston School Committee and explained that, in order to be eligible for 65-percent state funding for the project, the proposed new building would have to house English High School and the school's student population would have to be racially balanced. On January 13, 1971, the deputy commissioner of the state Board of Education, Thomas J. Curtin, wrote to the superintendent of schools, asking him to confirm the appropriate funding level for English High School. On February 12, 1971, Edward J. Winter, secretary of the Boston School Committee, replied to Curtin that they would build the school in compliance with the state's Racial Imbalance Act and would need 65-percent funding. The state Board of Education approved the funding ($15,655,250 of $24,085,000 total) on March 23, 1971. The Public Facilities Department wrote to Commissioner of Education Neil Sullivan on March 18, 1971, urging the Department of Education to move forward quickly with arrangements for financing the balance of the English High School construction project.

It is unclear why, but the School Committee never formally voted on this project. Winter had issued the February 12 letter communicating back to the state's Building Assistance Bureau that English High School would occupy the facility and would be racially balanced. Almost no one anticipated that the statement contained in Winter's letter, even though the project was not voted on by the School Committee, would become binding.[20]

THE DRESS CODE GETS AN ALTERATION

Margaret Carroll was obsessed with two things when she saw her students: how many books they were bringing home and, given the fashion revolution of the early 1970s, how they were dressed when they arrived at school. To carry home 25 pounds of books every day was not uncommon for each student, so rebuke for the former infraction was infrequent. The dress code, however, received a serious test at Girls' Latin School.

Debra Holland '71, a National Merit Finalist, recalled Carroll's censure for dress code violations:

> In the spring of '68, my mother had bought me a new outfit. It was a large blue and white houndstooth check—a sleeveless long vest, over a sheer—yes, see-through—long-sleeved navy blouse that tied in a bow at the neck, with culottes that were so full they looked like a skirt! Although the vest totally covered the see-through bodice, if I took it off,

"IT'S THE BEST SCHOOL IN AMERICA FOR GIRLS!"

Shirley Barsamian entered the school as a member of the Sixth Class—or seventh grade—in 1969. Here she tells about her father's decision process:

It was the spring of 1969. My little sixth-grade classroom was abuzz about the fact that nearly all the students would be heading off to the Latin schools. It would be Girls' Latin for all of the girls and Boston Latin for the boys, with one or two attending the private Roxbury Latin, too. I wasn't very happy though, since my dear childhood friend wasn't going to Girls' Latin, but to a parochial girls' school. Feeling a bit sad, I trudged home, my worn green schoolbag slung over my shoulder, shoes scuffing on the sidewalk, thinking about how everything was changing.

My father, noticing my mood that evening, wanted to know what was the matter with me. I was his eldest child and had always been a strong student, delivering the As that were the required standard in our house. A little over a dozen years earlier, he and my mother had embarked on their great adventure, traveling by ship to the United States where they could both continue their careers in medicine. As countercultural as it may have been at the time, education, even for their girl children, was paramount. The forward thinking of my maternal grandparents that had educated my mother as a nurse in the early 1950s (in the Middle East, no less) combined with the liberal outlook of my father—again influenced by his strong, well-educated mother—left little wiggle room for me and my attendance at Girls' Latin School.

He brought me to his desk and sat me down in the chair next to him. Puffing on his pipe, he riffled through the papers, searching for the newspaper clipping he had saved. Finding it, he smiled and leaned over to me, pointing at the headline with his beautiful surgeon's hand—"Girls' Latin No. 1 School in U.S.," it said. "See, Shirley, it's the best school in America for girls!" his melodious accented English stressing the point. "You will go there." And that, as they say, was that.

Seniors from the class of 1970 wearing "dresses and skirts only"

someone could have seen through it, so it was interdicted. "Does your mother know that you came to school like that?" Miss Carroll asked me. I replied, "Of course; she bought it for me!" At that time, my mother was all of 37 years old, and more fashion conscious than I would ever be. (She cottoned on to the culottes, though, which were verboten under the no-pants rule.) After that, I wore a heavy white turtleneck with that suit.[21]

In 1969, students finally were allowed to wear dress slacks, although denim and jeans still were not allowed. Even so, this was a significant change when one considers that the boys at Boston Latin still were required to wear shirts, ties, and sports coats. (Nehru jackets were prohibited.) By October 1971, the School Committee felt it necessary to issue a dress code that could be enforced at the discretion of the headmaster, and required students to come to school "clad in clothes that present the wearer as ready to learn. . . and which are not disturbing to the learning process." Hot pants, tube tops, miniskirts, and platform shoes were prohibited at Girls' Latin School as were dresses or skirts with hemlines more than three inches above the knee.

UPHOLDING THE TRADITION OF EXCELLENCE

In the autumn of 1970, Headmaster Carroll anxiously opened her school's official results from the National Merit Scholarship Corporation. Earlier that year, 710,000 high school juniors across the United States had taken the National Merit Qualifying Test, and 14,750 (or 2 percent) were named National Merit Semi-Finalists; 429 Massachusetts students made the cut. The letter she received informed Carroll that the GLS class of 1971 had 16 semi-finalists, the second-largest number of students from any single school (Phillips Academy in Andover had 18). Boston Latin School had three, and Roxbury Latin had eight.[22] Margaret Carroll quickly wrote up the results for the next morning's daily bulletin.

Thomas Gosnell, GLS Latin teacher, ca. 1970

> I have now the official report from the National Merit Scholarship program. Among the public schools in the state, Girls' Latin, with 16

semi-finalists, is in the top position and quite by itself since the next highest number is ten semi-finalists.... While we all can be proud of this achievement, we cannot be satisfied. There is still much we have to learn. Knowledge—all kinds of information—will give each one of us the ability to cope with the many problems we have in today's world when in turn we become adults."[23]

All 16 students were also finalists. From the class of 1971, 12 students went to Ivy League and Seven Sisters colleges: three went to Vassar; two to MIT; and one each to Barnard, Cornell, Mount Holyoke, Radcliffe, Smith, Wellesley, and Yale. In aggregate, members of the class were awarded approximately $1 million in scholarships.

During the mid-1960s, GLS students' Scholastic Aptitude Test (SAT) scores were particularly impressive: in 1965, for example, 11 students received perfect scores of 800, which surpassed the standing record for a single school. The class of 1966 was close behind, with 9 perfect scores and one 799. Another indication of academic excellence is the acceptance rates of GLS students by Seven Sisters colleges and Ivy League universities (see below).

Measuring Academic Achievement at GLS, 1962–1970

	1962	1963	1964	1965	1966	1967	1968	1969	1970	TOTAL
Barnard College	2	1	2			2	3	1	2	13
Bryn Mawr College				2	1	2				5
Cornell University			1		1		1		1	4
Mount Holyoke College	4	2		2		2	1	3	1	15
Princeton University								1		1
Radcliffe College	2	4	4	4	4	3	3	5	5	34
Smith College	1	1	2	1	1	3	3	1	3	16
Vassar College					2			2	2	6
Wellesley College	1		2	1	3			1	1	9
Yale University								1		1
Total	10	8	9	11	10	15	11	14	16	104

Source: "Headmaster's Circulars," 1965, 1966 (Records of Girls' Latin School, Schlesinger Library, Radcliffe Institute for Advanced Study, Harvard University)

1970
Civil Liberties Union of Massachusetts charges that the Boston school system does not provide an equal opportunity for girls to prepare for college.

1971
Massachusetts law is enacted stating no child may be excluded from admission to a public school on the basis of sex.

1971
Edith W. Fine contends that separate Boston Latin and Girls' Latin Schools are illegal and both must become coeducational.

1972 ▶
Matina Souretis Horner '57 becomes the youngest president of Radcliffe College in its 93-year history.

1972
29 boys admitted to Girls' Latin School and 92 girls to Boston Latin School.

1973
The Boston School Committee votes to use the new $33 million, ten-story, 380,000-square-foot building on Avenue Louis Pasteur for Girls' Latin School.

◀ The Massachusetts Supreme Judicial Court rules that the Boston Public Schools cannot turn the facility over to Girls' Latin; English High School is awarded the new building.

◀ **1975**
Boston School Committee orders that the name of Girls' Latin School be changed to *Boston Latin Academy*.

1976
The last all-girls class graduates from Girls' Latin School.

◀ **1977**
For the first time the GLS diplomas read *Boston Latin Academy*.

◀ **1978**
Margaret C. Carroll retires as headmaster.

GLS celebrates its 100th anniversary.

XI

Brevis Est Vita
The Ironic Undoing of GLS by the Women's Equal Rights Movement

Bicentennial Parade of Sail, Boston Harbor, 1976

Weekend after weekend, the graceful green lawns that carpet the Boston Common were filled with Anti-Vietnam War and civil right rallies. On April 15, 1970—Moratorium Day—100,000 protesters from across Massachusetts gathered there making the green lawn invisible from the air. As the protesters listened to the numerous speakers, planes skywrote peace symbols and long-haired demonstrators wearing love beads and peace pins applauded in support.[1] At the same time the Black Panther Party, Students for a Democratic Society, and the Women's Liberation Front were all making headlines. In answer to segregation in Boston's neighborhood schools, the hue and cry for racial integration of the city's schools rang louder and louder.

Headmaster Carroll recalled, "In the late 1960s and 1970s there developed in the City of Boston intense differences of opinion among the parents and members of the school committee. Many strongly supported the idea of assigning students to neighborhood schools with the exception of a few high schools which were city-wide schools such as Boston Latin School, Girls' Latin School. . . . Other parents felt very strongly it was more important to have the schools racially balanced."[2]

For years, Girls' Latin bore slight resemblance to the Brahmin-dominated institution of Abbie Farwell Brown's era: a group of pampered, privileged, wealthy girls with a few ethnic, poor, or otherwise underprivileged students sprinkled among them. Although the perception that it was an institution for "advantaged" girls persisted, the only advantage for most Girls' Latin School students was their intelligence. Very fortunately, each GLS student earned a high score on one test—the school's entrance examination—and that changed the trajectory of their lives.

In the 1960s and 1970s, Girls' Latin School students were a diverse ethnic group from a broad socioeconomic range. They were largely disadvantaged girls, many on welfare or some type of public assistance, who came from some of the toughest Boston neighborhoods. Most were daughters or granddaughters of immigrants and came from Irish, Catholic, Italian, Jewish, Asian, Lebanese, Greek, or another one-dimensionally ethnic neighborhoods. Few of their parents had graduated from college. The cultural worlds of these neighborhoods were narrow, and these students first attended public grammar schools with a predominance of their same ethnic group. From this homogeneous experience, they were thrown into the Girls' Latin School's melting pot, where they met girls from other cultures, races, and religions for the very first time.

When Margaret Carroll was called to attend a public hearing before the Boston School Committee on June 17, 1970, she did not suspect that the critical entrance examination would be at issue, and she could not have seen that, ironically, the disparity over the number of students admitted by this exam would be the beginning of the end of Girls' Latin School.

PRIMI SUNT, MELIORES SUMUS (THEY ARE FIRST, WE ARE BETTER)

During the decades between 1950 and 1970, it was a little-known fact that applicants to Girls' Latin were held to a higher admissions standard than their male counterparts applying to Boston Latin. It also seldom was noted that, for the most part, the number of students admitted to both Latin schools was determined by the size of their buildings. Boston

Latin School's 2,400-student enrollment was approximately twice that of Girls' Latin, which resulted directly from the relative sizes of the schools' buildings: Boston Latin School on Avenue Louis Pasteur had been expanded three times since it opened early in the century, while Girls' Latin, now housed in the former Dorchester High School, had not grown at all.

On March 6, 1970,[3] the exam prepared by the Boston School Committee Board of Examiners was administered to candidates who wished to be accepted to Boston Latin or Girls' Latin. Starting with John Tetlow's entrance exam of 1878, this or a similar test of academic skill in math and English had been administered at Girls' Latin in one form or another for 92 years. That year, Boston Latin admitted 420 boys; Girls' Latin admitted 215 girls.

Because Girls' Latin School admitted fewer students, in 1970, 177 girls scored high enough to be admitted to Boston Latin, but their scores were not sufficient to admit them to Girls' Latin. Out of 200 total points, 133 points were required to enter Girls' Latin; the cutoff at Boston Latin was 120 points.

GLS caryatids, 1968

Janice Bray, Sandra Wright, Marie Musto, and Sandra LaRoca each scored between 124 and 128 points, and they felt that denial of admission to Girls' Latin had significantly diminished their chances of attending college. Their parents, as well as those of the other 173 who were denied admission, were represented by attorneys provided by the Civil Liberties Union of Massachusetts, W. Jay Skinner and Matthew Feinberg, who charged that the Boston school system did not provide equal opportunity for girls to prepare for college.[4]

The upshot was the public hearing to discuss the issue scheduled by the School Committee for June 17. From her office, Margaret Carroll spoke on the phone with Headmaster Wilfred O'Leary of Boston Latin School, and to her the conversation seemed almost surreal. Could they really make the Latin schools coeducational? It was as outlandish an idea in 1970 as admitting girls to public Latin school had been in 1877. This time, however, the legal and political systems would fail to hold the growing tide against them.

Again, the Girls' Latin School Alumnae Association and the Boston Latin School Association tried to rally support to oppose the measure. Much would depend on the public hearing. Once again, the schools' headmasters found themselves at 15 Beacon Street.

Breva Est Vita

At this time, the Boston School Committee consisted of Chairman Joseph Lee,[5] John J. Craven Jr. (Ward 18, Mattapan), James W. Hennigan Jr. (Ward 19, West Roxbury), John J. Kerrigan (Ward 16, Dorchester), and Attorney Paul R. Tierney (Ward 18, Hyde Park). Both Margaret Carroll and Wilfred O'Leary would testify against making the schools coeducational.

The first person to speak at the hearing was John Chandler, a parent of seven children, five of whom were girls, in the Boston public schools, who lived in the South End. Speaking as a representative of the Committee to End Discrimination in the Boston Public Schools, he read a statement: "Discrimination in education is one of the most damaging injustices women suffer. It denies them equal education."[6] When would the School Committee take steps to end *sexual* segregation in the Boston public schools? he asked.

HELEN CUMMINGS, CLASS OF 1950 AND FRENCH TEACHER

I arrived at Girls' Latin School in 1946 as a "beezie" [student first enrolled in Class IV, or ninth grade] because my father felt that my taking the MTA at age 11 was not wise. (Actually, at age 13 it wasn't much better.) My father and his brothers—sons of Irish immigrants—had all graduated from Boston Latin School, so there was no question that I would go anywhere but GLS.

I loved being a student at GLS from the very beginning. I remember being shocked that I earned Bs and Cs in the beginning, but things began to turn around, and my junior and senior marks were so improved that I was a member of the National Honor Society. I have only fond memories of my four years there, enjoying all the challenges and the competition—French classes of course; Mr. Tierney's weekly music classes on Fridays; glee club; annual Gilbert and Sullivan shows in the BLS auditorium; playing *Pomp and Circumstance* as the class of 1949 marched in, again in the BLS auditorium.

In Miss McNamara's Latin class, first year, when we were located on the first floor, and huge windows allowed us to gaze at the uniformed BLS students practicing their drills for the annual schoolboy parade. Miss Earle, our homeroom teacher, was not happy teaching us a once-a-month health class. She frequently assigned us to visit Mrs. Jack Gardner's Palace [the Isabella Stewart Gardner Museum], this being better for our health than sitting in a classroom.

When I look back over the years now, it is amazing how much of my life has been spent in the Fenway/Longwood area of Boston: GLS, Emmanuel College, and Boston State College. Then, in 1995, I was a patient at the Dana-Farber Cancer Institute—and today I am still gratefully in remission.

I spent 1955–1956 in Besançon in Franche-Comté—one of the happiest years of my life. I lived with a wonderful family, and in the course of my 18 trips to Europe I always returned to spend time in Besançon.

In 1956, on my return, I began teaching French in middle school, where I learned a great deal about disciplining that age group! Then, in 1957, I became a

Hennigan rebutted, "I'd like to point out for the public record that although the examination was the same given for both applicants for Boys' Latin and Girls' Latin, the passing score was different. The reason for the difference in the score was not based on discrimination by reason of sex but rather on the physical capacity of the schools. The Latin School was certified by the Department of Public Safety as having a much larger capacity than Girls' Latin School."

Hennigan went on to suggest that instead of attacking "an institution which sends 99.9 percent of our boys and girls onto college, they should have been down helping us get an addition to the [Boston Public Schools] addition and repair [the] budget," to add additional seating to Girls' Latin School in order to accommodate the 177 girls who were turned away. But Joseph Lee, a graduate of the private Nobles School, was in clear disagreement.

permanent teacher at Boston Technical High School, at that time the only woman on the staff. My colleagues were extremely supportive. In today's world, I might be considered a trailblazer, but it didn't seem like that to me. In January 1964, I was named department head of foreign languages at Girls' High School—the youngest department head in the history of the Boston Public Schools, they said. In 1968, Miss Miller, GLS's department head of modern foreign languages, wrote to me and said she was going to retire. She praised my qualifications and requested that I apply for her position. So I became the foreign language department head at GLS, responsible for the French and German programs. I was welcomed by Miss Carroll and colleagues, some of whom were there when I was a student, including my French teacher in 1951–1952. That was a delicate situation!

I was very conscious of the excellent achievement of our students and was determined that it should continue. It was a challenge and a pleasure at the same time. My schedule always included freshman and senior classes, plus either sophomore or junior classes, from French I to French IV—four classes and a homeroom.

It is clear to me that my formative years at GLS were the key to all that followed. In my yearbook, the statement about me says that one day I would return to teach French at GLS. My goodness! How predictable. To work with the outstanding students at GLS/BLA from 1968 to 1983 was the most fulfilling experience, both professionally and personally. I am grateful for everything.[7]

Chairman Lee: I have seen too many people, and some of them have sat at this table, whose personalities were pinched and warped, were dried out, sacrificed on the alter of the Latin School... whose careers were over the day they left the school and then found the world wasn't open to them by merely application of the Latin School diploma.... I have never seen a girl come out of the Latin School who did not feel crushed and hurt by the experience and stifled. And if I am unique in saying that, which I am sure I am not, how come the administration that runs these Boston Schools for years has been trying to get changes at those two schools and has been balked by that percentage of alumni who have survived the ordeal and want to justify their own over-rigid education?

Mr. Paul Tierney: Mr. Chairman, I might take issue with what you have described as the typical graduate of the Boston Latin School. I had the distinct privilege and pleasure recently of addressing the graduates of Boston Latin School and I have found them to be [among] the finest young men I have met anywhere... they are the pride of the Boston Public School System.... In fact, we look to them to lead this country in the future and help solve many pressing problems. They are our future leaders....

Chairman Lee: If the Latin School is right then all of the rest of the school system is wrong because we have gone off on a tack of flexibility, experimentation, innovation and different methods of teaching.

Mr. Tierney: The Latin School is not rigid. It has flexibility. It has innovation.... It's far from rigid.

Chairman Lee: Let Dr. O'Leary tell us about that.

Dr. Wilfrid O'Leary: ... I am happy to have the opportunity to speak after this illuminating session.... I went to the Latin School myself. I am a graduate in the year 1925, and I have not come out with any incubus and it hasn't hurt me. In fact I am very grateful for the opportunity.... I won't bore you with others so that the youngsters who come from all walks of life, from all types and classes of people, races and colors would have an opportunity and do have the opportunity to come to school. It is not elite in the true sense of the word.... Rather the Latin School has been a beacon of light for all those youngsters who had the motivation to want to get ahead, to grow up in the system.... If you take and destroy the identity of these two schools, then of course you are going to deprive these youngsters of the wonderful opportunity to come along....

If the two Latin schools [buildings] were opposite each other, you could meld certain classes [drama].... We now have girl cheer leaders from Girls' Latin School. Our boys are very popular in the [Girls'] Latin School proms.... You could have them in music and art classes. In this way you could have the leavening that Mr. Lee refers to in substance and you would fulfill a fine goal in giving these boys and girls the icing on the cake.

Chairman Lee: Miss Carroll from Girls' Latin School, are you here?

Miss Margaret G. Carroll: I have not come here prepared to speak, but I do feel the Girls' Latin School is serving a very definite purpose and giving the opportunity of the girls in the school to carry on to the full potential that is important to them. I see no advantage to combining the two schools because they each serving their own individual purpose as they are today. Is there something else?

Mr. John J. Craven: Miss Carroll, is it true you would be happy if we could get your building opposite the boys' Latin School?

Miss Carroll: The crux of the whole matter seems to be that I cannot admit as many girls as Dr. O'Leary has been able to, due to the physical limitation of our present building. As Dr. O'Leary pointed out to you, if we were larger we could take in a larger number of girls. If we were near each other we could certainly share programs which would be to the advantage of boys and girls. We are quite a long distance apart from each other, and this makes it very hard; but we would like to share programs. There is no reason why girls shouldn't take programs with us and still keep the identity of the boys' and girls' schools separate. This is done at many of the colleges and it works out successfully.

Chairman Lee: You heard most of what I said, I presume.

Miss Carroll: Yes I did.

Chairman Lee: I think it is much too rigid for girls. Perhaps *rigid* is the wrong word, but boys, given an equally exacting schedule as they are at Latin School, can take it better. Boys have reserves of horseplay and agreeable obscenities and other forms of relation by which they are pretty good at making progress; but as Mr. Kipling's poem, which I read in part, indicated, a women is a person of much more single purpose.[8] . . . I don't think Girls' Latin is good for those girls, and when we had a hearing that somehow involved the graduates of the Practical Arts High School and Girls' Latin School . . . I don't remember what is was but the Practical Arts girls who made no pretension of going anywhere near college were far more calm, far more poised, far more rational, far more persuasive, whereas the graduates of Girls' Latin School were hysterical, screaming, irrational. It was pathetic. Because girls aren't made like men and there is no sense of trying to make women like men, and that is what the Girls' Latin School does. It

MATINA SOURETIS HORNER '57: PRESIDENT OF RADCLIFFE COLLEGE

Graduation photo of Matina Souretis, 1957

In 1972, Girls' Latin School graduate Matina Souretis Horner, class of 1957, became president of Radcliffe College. Through this role, she would have a major impact on both the women's movement and achieving parity for women at Harvard.

Beginning with classes at the Harvard Annex in 1879, Radcliffe students had been taught by male Harvard professors. It was not until 1948 that a woman professor was first granted tenure at Harvard; in 1950, the first woman was admitted to Harvard Law School. In 1963, Radcliffe graduates were finally awarded Harvard degrees and a woman was accepted to the MBA program for the first time. Women gained equal access to sports and, in 1975, varsity letters were awarded to female athletes at Radcliffe for the first time.

In 1972, when Horner assumed the mantle of president, 1,452 students were enrolled at Radcliffe, making the ratio of Harvard to Radcliffe students 4 to 1. Horner inquired whether Harvard alumni also had daughters and, her point taken, the college agreed to change their admissions policy. By 1987, the Harvard-Radcliffe ratio was 1.44 to 1.

Matina Souretis was born on July 28, 1939, in Roxbury, Massachusetts, to parents Demetre and Christine, who had come from Greece during World War II and decided to remain. Petite, with short dark hair and dark brown eyes, Souretis was both the business manager for *The Jabberwock* and a member of S.T.A.C. After her sophomore year, the class moved to Codman Square, where they became only the second class to graduate from that location.

She was accepted at Bryn Mawr College where she studied experimental psychology. It was at Bryn Mawr that she met and married Joseph L. Horner. They graduated in 1961 and both went on to do graduate work at the University of Michigan. Matina Horner earned her Ph.D. in 1968.

On July 1, 1972, the 32-year-old mother of three became the youngest president in Radcliffe College's doesn't make girls more feminine.... While I can accept Dr. O'Leary's case for Boston Latin School as at least being a good presentation and there is much to be said for it, I can't accept such a case applied to Girls' Latin School....

Miss Carroll: I can't speak for fifteen years ago, Mr. Lee, but I think it's quite different today.... There is a very happy feeling in the school, and if you had been with us today you would have to have had an experience with that.

Chairman Lee: Well. All right.... I think if we can believe the evidence I get from talking to students and graduates, that overlordly attitude is in most of those teachers at the Latin School. They take a top-lofty

93-year history. The Radcliffe Archives summarizes her rise and achievement in this position:

> Horner's research concentrated on intelligence, motivation, and achievement. She hypothesized that high anxiety levels found in women she tested were caused not by fear of failure, but by the possibility of success. Horner's "fear of success" theory became a potent tool in the women's movement. In 1969 Horner joined the faculty of Harvard University as a lecturer in the Department of Social Relations. The following year she was named assistant professor in the Department of Psychology.
>
> In 1972 Horner was named the sixth (and youngest) president of Radcliffe. She inherited a complex relationship with Harvard. Under her predecessor, Mary Bunting, this relationship had evolved into what was known as the "non-merger merger." Responsibility for students had largely been transferred to Harvard, though women students were still admitted to Radcliffe by a separate Admissions and Financial Aid Office. Radcliffe had delegated some business operations (payroll, accounting, dining halls, library, and buildings and grounds) to Harvard, but had retained control of and administered its own educational, research and alumnae programs. In 1977 Horner negotiated a new agreement with Harvard that reestablished Radcliffe's financial independence, with its own administration, governing board, research programs, and redefined an oversight role and special programs for undergraduate women.
>
> In her inaugural address, Horner spoke of a broad mission for Radcliffe: "to do the right thing for its undergraduates, its alumnae, and for women generally," and she succeeded in bringing a new focus at the college to the concerns of women and women's rights.
>
> Horner served on the boards of Time Inc., the Federal Reserve Bank of Boston, and President Jimmy Carter in 1979 appointed her to the President's Commission for the National Agenda for the 1980s and the following year asked her to serve as chairperson of the Task Force on the Quality of American Life.[9]

position and they think that the learning of Latin School should be the god of every girl's idolatry.... As we said here a year ago or earlier, educating the heart is more important than educating the mind.... I don't think the Latin School goes out to educate the heart. I should think all our schools should, but certainly our all girls' school should. I think we have fallen down.

Miss Carroll: I think there is a different relationship between students and the teachers in the school as I know it. They are understanding of the girls and very much concerned about the girl not only as a student but as a person too, Mr. Lee....

Chairman Lee: Well you are a nice person yourself.

Miss Carroll: Thank you very much.

Chairman Lee: Perhaps you are not a graduate of Latin School. You had better not answer.

Miss Carroll: No, I am a graduate of Girls' High School.

Chairman Lee: There you are.

ESCALATION: THE CASE GOES TO COURT

The Massachusetts Law Chapter 622 of the Acts of 1971[10] was known as the equal educational opportunities law. It was filed by three Representatives including Speaker of the House David Bartley, who said the legislation was designed primarily to open to girls the opportunities presently reserved for boys. The bill, which was meant to end sex discrimination, was supported by women's rights groups throughout the state. The new law, which was enacted in November 1971, stated: "No child shall be excluded from or discriminated against in admission to a public school of any town, or in obtaining the advantages, privileges and course of study of such public school on account of race, color, sex, religion, or national origin."

Shortly after its passage, the parents of the four seventh graders who had been denied admission to Girls' Latin School formally filed a complaint in U.S. District Court. They charged that their daughters had been victims of sexual discrimination under Massachusetts Law Chapter 622. The suit was brought before the court on Friday August 13, 1971.[11]

Both Latin Schools remained hopeful they would be exempted from the legislation because of their special histories. Under the title "Should the Latin Schools Become Co-ed?" a *Jabberwock* editorial by Marcia Masters dealt with the issue:

> There are many more arguments against than for mixing the Latin Schools. Tradition plays an important role. GLS has always been an all-girl high school with high standing and national recognition. . . . The Latin Schools should be placed near each other. Certain classes in all grades should be able to be combined. . . I do not think total ruination would come to GLS nor BLS. . . . However, to avoid the anger and opposition to those staunchly against the law, a compromise should be made to satisfy all who will be affected.[12]

On the heels of this sexual discrimination lawsuit followed the most pivotal night in the history of busing in Boston. The School Committee had voted 3 to 2 to redraw district lines so none of Boston's three new elementary schools would be more than 50 percent nonwhite. But at a meeting in September 1971 at the O'Hearn School in Dorchester, John Craven changed his mind, leaving Paul Tierney and James Hennigan cheated from the compromise that had been forged. When the committee changed the boundaries of the new Joseph Lee Elementary School in Dorchester to forestall its integration, Judge W. Arthur Garrity determined that the Boston School Committee was culpable of segregating Boston's public schools. Hennigan recalled in 2006, "That vote that night . . . it did more damage to this city than anything else."[13]

In an unanticipated twist, principally as a result of the civil suit brought by the four girls' parents, Edith W. Fine, assistant corporation counsel for the City of Boston, contended that separate Boston Latin and Girls' Latin Schools could not be maintained. One of only five women in her law school graduating class, Fine had received her LL.B. from Harvard in 1957.

At a conference of the School Committee held on Tuesday, November 16, 1971, School Committee members Tierney (now chairman), Craven, Hennigan, Lee, and Kerrigan heard "Ruling of the Law Department on the opinion of segregated schools on a co-educational basis."

Chairman Tierney: I want to get at Item No. 10, ruling of the Law Department.... This holds a great deal of interest for all of us. Mrs. Fine, will you come forward, please? It is my understanding that a recent state statute no longer makes valid the maintaining of sex-segregated schools. What effect does this statute have on the Boston Public School System?

Mrs. Edith W. Fine: Yes, Mr. Chairman. It is Chapter 622 of the Acts of 1971, which in relevant part, provides: "No child shall be excluded from or discriminated against in admission to a public school of any town, or in obtaining the advantages, privileges and course of study of such public school on account of race, color, sex, religion, or national origin." I would say based on this statute that unless you could show that a boys' school and a girls' school were exactly equal in terms of program and facilities, a sex-segregated school starting in September, 1972, would be illegal.

Chairman Tierney: So this, then, would have a direct effect on our Latin Schools beginning in September of 1972?

Mrs. Fine: That is correct....

Mr. Joseph Lee: ... I think this is the greatest thing that we have seen in six years. This says no child shall be excluded from or discriminated against in admission to a public school or in obtaining advantages because of race. Now that certainly supersedes the old racial balance law of 1965. Am I right Mrs. Fine?

Mrs. Fine: ... But I would like to point out that this is the only amendment to the present existing statute that added the word "sex." This statute with the word "race" has been in existence for a long time pre-dating the Racial Imbalance Act.[14]

The following day, the *Boston Globe* stated, "Mrs. Fine... ruled out the chance that the schools could claim to be equal."[15] The same article reported that security patrols were needed at the King, Timilty, Holmes, and Lewis Schools, underscoring the complex issues that seemed far greater at the time. No one appeared willing to make the necessary changes so that both Girls' Latin and Boston Latin were "equal" in curriculum and facilities. The next day Judith Brody, a GLS graduate in the class of 1963, reported in the *Globe*, "Famed Boston Latin School—founded in 1635 to educate boys in classical languages—will fall before the tide of coeducation next September."¹⁶

The *Boston Herald* reported:

> The Boston School Committee was told yesterday that the city's sex-segregated high schools, including the prestigious all-male Boston Latin School, will have to become coeducational—presumably by next fall—to comply with state law.... The ruling was announced by Atty. Edith Fine of the city corporation counsel's office at the regular school meeting. She said separate schools can no longer be maintained unless they have identical programs, and she ruled out that the schools could claim to be equal. Mrs. Fine's opinion was based on an amendment to discrimination legislation enacted by the state legislature in August.¹⁷

Because it would be impossible to implement the new law by September 1971, the schools were given a one-year moratorium.

On January 11, 1972, the School Committee voted to revise admission requirements for the Latin Schools as mandated by Chapter 622. It also ordered that all candidates who took the SSAT entrance examination at the Latin Schools be numerically ranked, "and the candidates offered admission to Boston Latin School and Girls' Latin... [would be determined]... solely on the basis of rank order until all pupil stations are filled."¹⁸ On January 14, Superintendent William H. Ohrenberger issued a memo to the headmasters concerning the revised admissions procedures:

> In accordance with Massachusetts Law (Chapter 622 of the Acts of 1971) no child may be excluded from admission to a public school on the basis of sex. Therefore, a boy or girl may apply for admission to either Latin School.... A single list of candidates for both schools will be established. A student will be admitted to the school of his or her choice in the order of his or her position on the list according to score, until the capacity of one of the schools has been reached.¹⁹

The headmaster of Boston Latin School still argued for keeping the schools separate: "I'm not against co-educational schooling by any

Linda Mazzoni and Karen Mastrobattista in Boston Latin School cheerleading uniforms, 1973

Breva Est Vita

means, but I feel the inclusion of girls will deprive many boys of a high quality education."[20]

Some school officials suggested that the 7th and 8th grades be combined at the Codman Square building and the 9th through 12th grades be moved to Avenue Louis Pasteur. This plan was abandoned because the upper grades from Girls' Latin would be transferred to a new faculty and would not have sufficient facilities for extracurricular activities. At the time, a plan to integrate each school from within seemed the less disruptive way to adopt the mandated change. But the most important reason for no outcry rising to integrate both Latin Schools was that Girls' Latin had been told by the School Committee they would soon move to a new building across the street from BLS.

In an effort to preserve the Latin Schools, Boston City Councilor Lawrence S. DiCara proposed a home-rule bill that would have kept the schools segregated by sex, which Mayor Kevin White refused to sign.

The headlines that blanketed the *Boston Globe* the first week of September 1972 included the murder of eleven Israeli athletes at the Munich Olympics, Mark Spitz's unprecedented capture of seven Olympic gold medals in swimming, and Bobby Fisher's victory over Boris Spassky at the World Chess Championship. On September 7, 1972, boys were admitted to Girls' Latin and girls to Boston Latin. Buried on the same page as Ann Lander's advice column was an article entitled, "The Day English and Latin Went Coed." It made little news and few waves. BLS admitted 92 girls and GLS admitted 29 boys.

To the general public, the issue was not significant. For the guardians of tradition, however, the change was sacrilege. "When the girls came in," stated Headmaster O'Leary, "old Ezekial Cheever rolled over in his grave."[21] Cheever, who lived from 1614 to 1708, was BLS's most renowned headmaster.

After the first boys were admitted, *Jabberwock* Associate Editor Janice Goodman wrote:

> Girls' Latin School is now a coeducational institution. The ninety-seven year old tradition has died and no one is asking why.... Are the two Latin schools equal? Has forced coeducation improved the quality of our education?... Obviously, those representatives who voted in favor of abolishing single-sex schools because they were unconstitutional and provided unequal opportunities for acquiring the best high

school education possible, had an ulterior motive. Any child... can tell that coeducation has not brought the Latin Schools the "equality" that all so righteously called for.[22]

Helen Cummings, class of 1950 and later a GLS French teacher, recalled:

Making GLS and BLS both coed was more than unfortunate. There were strong faculty debates then. Miss Carroll did her best, but GLS had to become BLA! When she retired in 1978—she had always succeeded in keeping the standards high—the school suffered. Two weak headmasters followed her. It did not help that the fire department declared the building unsafe. No classes could be held on the top floor. We always believed that the fire department would not have made this decision if Miss Carroll was still the headmaster![23]

School Committee member John J. Kerrigan resigned his chairmanship on December 20, 1972. In his final speech as chairman he noted:

Another matter left to be resolved in the coming year is the question of the future of the Latin schools. The recently enacted legislation preventing operation of Boys' Latin as an all boys school and Girls' Latin as an all girls school could well lead to monumental confusion next year. The confusion is unavoidable. I have examined the question at some length. In my opinion it is absolutely necessary for the Girls' Latin School to be relocated to the Fens area so that it may be operated with some measure with the Boys' Latin School. I shall continue to interest myself with this matter as a School Committee-man.[24]

Two years later, on April 23, 1973, the School Committee voted to use the new $33 million, 10-story, 380,000-square-foot building on Avenue Louis Pasteur, which was due to open in September, for Girls' Latin School. It seemed all of GLS's decades of prayers finally had been answered. Girls' Latin School, after almost 20 years in Dorchester, would return to the Fenway to a brand new school directly across the Street from Boston Latin School.

When the Boston School Committee voted to give the building to Girls' Latin, however, three separate lawsuits were filed to stop the action, including one by the state Board of Education, which charged that the building had been constructed with the written agreement that English High would be assigned to it in an effort to reduce racial imbalance in the Boston schools.

On July 16, 1973, the Massachusetts Supreme Judicial Court reviewed the three lawsuits and agreed. Using Winter's letter as evidence of the binding agreement, the court ruled that because the School Committee had agreed to construct the school as part of a plan to alleviate racial imbalance in the high schools, and because the building qualified for increased state financial assistance, the Boston Public Schools could not turn the facility over to Girls Latin. English High School was awarded the new building.[25]

Judge Garrity alluded to this award as a strong example of the lack of cooperation of the School Committee with the efforts to racially balance the Boston Public Schools:

Boston's Latin and English High Schools shared close proximity near Huntington and Longwood Avenues: English High School (1) faced Boston Latin School (2) across Avenue Louis Pasteur; Girls' Latin School (3) was situated closer to Huntington Avenue.

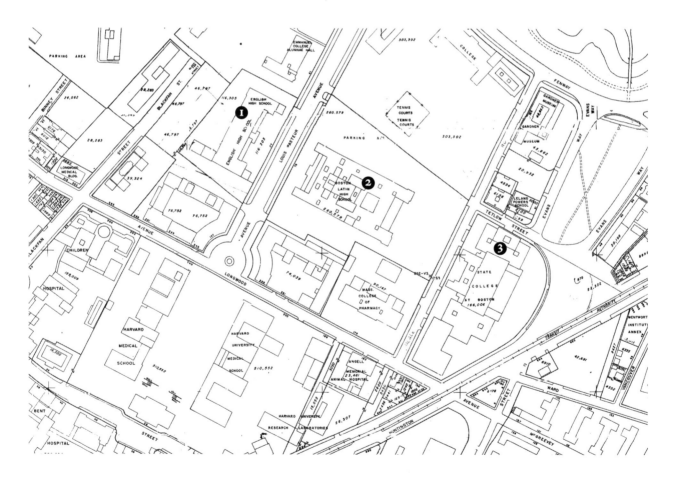

> Similarly in the case of the new building for the English High School, that school was going to be opened as a balanced school, and it was to be a magnet school. That was why this new, expensive, high quality facility was built, and there again the School Committee did not follow through, despite their promises, and in that case it was not a question of inability, they just decided it would be appropriate to put another school in that area.[26]

The new English High School building was closed in 1989, after just 16 years of use, and the school moved to the former Jamaica Plain High School. In 1993, the building on Avenue Louis Pasteur was sold for $12 million to Harvard University, which converted it for use as research space.

Ironically, had the School Committee chosen in 1971 to build the school with 40 percent funds from the state, they would have had every legal right to award it to GLS.

On March 15, 1972, the Harvard Center for Law and Education filed suit against the City of Boston's School Committee alleging de jure segregation in the Boston Public Schools. The case, called *Morgan v. Hennigan* (Talullah Morgan v. James Hennigan Chairman Boston School Committee D.C. Mass., June 21, 1974), was filed on behalf of 15 parents and their 43 children. It is named for the lead plaintiff (Morgan) and the defendant (Hennigan), who was chairman of the Boston School Committee at that time. The case charged that Boston had violated the 14th Amendment and long had segregated its schools. The NAACP filed suit on behalf of black parents and against the Boston School Committee, its individual members, the superintendent of the Boston Public Schools, the Board of Education of the Commonwealth of Massachusetts, and the commissioner of education.

Judge Garrity decided the case in favor of the plaintiffs on June 21, 1974, and when the court released its decision, he concluded that the Boston School Committee had segregated the Boston Public Schools, including the examination schools, "with the purpose or intent to [do so]." He then assumed for the U.S. District Court oversight of the Boston Public Schools. In October 1973, the Massachusetts Supreme Court ordered the Boston School Committee to implement Glenn's plan starting in September of 1974.

Among the issues that Judge Garrity addressed in *Morgan v. Hennigan* was black enrollment in the examination schools. A review of the "Information on Student Enrollment" prepared by the School

Enrollment of Black Students in GLS and BLS, 1967–1972

	1967	1968	1969	1970	1971	1972
Boston Latin	3.2%	3.0%	2.6%	2.3%	1.9%	2.2%
Girls' Latin	3.5%	6.1%	6.3%	5.3%	5.4%	5.0%

Source: Boston School Committee

The valedictory drawing from and the cover of the last Liber Annalis, *the GLS yearbook*

Committee for 1972–73 showed the total enrollment for Boston Latin School to be 1,914 students, of whom 92.4 percent were white. The official capacity of the building was listed as 2,803, and 906 seats were unoccupied. Similarly, of the 1,190 at GLS, 88 percent were white; of its 1,400 seats, 210 remained unoccupied.[27] Less than 5 percent of 1,200 students were black at Girls' Latin and at Boston Latin only 2.2 percent of 2,000 were black—far fewer than the 1972 citywide enrollment reflected: 32 percent black and 7 percent Hispanic students.

On September 12, 1974, court-ordered bussing commenced, fulfilling the U.S. District Court's ruling that attempted to achieve desegregation of the Boston schools. In February 1975, Attorney William F. Looney Jr. submitted to the United States District Court a document entitled "Memorandum of the Boston Latin School Association and the Girls' Latin School Association in Support of Its Proposal Regarding Student Assignment to the Examination Schools." In it he wrote, "If the Court imposes an admissions program on these schools based on racial quota rather than based upon sound educational criteria, it will not only be doing a disservice to the school but it will not be acting in conformance with federal law." Margaret Carroll agreed, adding the warning that changing the present academic requirements of the school would destroy its academic excellence.[28] F. Washington Jarvis, headmaster of Roxbury Latin School also weighed in, sending a letter of support to Headmaster O'Leary that stated, "What a scandal and tragedy, if, in the guise of improving the schools of Boston, that which is already proven and demonstrably excellent is crushed and destroyed."[29] Shortly afterward, Judge Garrity formulated a desegregation plan for the examination schools. His Student Desegregation Plan, issued on May 10, 1975, stated:

> Boston Latin School and Boston Latin Academy will continue for the school year 1975–76 to provide a six-grade program to accept

both 7th and 9th grade students. At least 35% of each of the entering classes at Boston Latin School, Boston Latin Academy and Boston Technical High in September 1975 shall be composed of black and Hispanic students.[30]

A law prohibiting Massachusetts public school names from reflecting sex was passed by the state legislature in the summer of 1973, and on March 24 of the following year, the Boston School Committee ordered Girls' High School, the oldest high school for girls in the United States, to change its name to Roxbury High School.[31] It was not until February 25, 1975, however, that the School Committee put the matter of changing the name of Girls' Latin on its agenda. GLS Alumnae Association

BOSTON SCHOOL SYSTEM POLITICS: TWO STEPS AHEAD, THREE BACK

In September 1985, issuing his 415th and final court order, Judge Garrity returned the governance of Boston's public schools to the School Committee.

Ten years later, in August 1995, Julia McLaughlin, a white seventh-grade student, filed suit against the Boston School Committee, alleging that unconstitutionally she had been denied admission to Boston Latin due to the 35-percent set-aside for black and Hispanic students then in effect. Judge Garrity initially denied a motion for a preliminary injunction, which sought to admit Julia to Boston Latin for the 1995–96 school year; on August 22, 1996, however, he granted it, admitting Julia to Boston Latin for the 1996–97 year. On December 10, 1996, in light of the Boston School Committee's decisions to permit Julia to remain at Boston Latin and to adopt a new admissions policy that would eliminate the 35-percent set-aside, Judge Garrity dismissed the McLaughlin case as moot.

That same month, the School Committee abandoned the 20-year-old racial quotas that had reserved 35 percent of exam school seats for African Americans and Hispanics at Boston's three examination schools. The new policy authorized admission of 50 percent of students based solely on tests and grades. The remaining students were admitted according to the proportion of their racial group in the remaining applicant pool.

In November 1998, a Federal Appeals court struck down this system of racial quotas as a result of a suit filed on behalf of Sarah Wessmann and the policy that admitted half of each class solely on the basis of "composite score" ranking and replaced it with "flexible racial/ethnic guidelines." With this decision, every legal limitation as to admission for the two Latin schools set by the courts had been reversed—except one.

In 2007, Boston Mayor Thomas Menino and Superintendent of Schools Carol Johnson proposed that the city should reinstate single-sex schools. Because of the 1971 legislation banning such schools, the Massachusetts legislature must pass a new law allowing such schools. This legislation is called "An Act Providing for Same Sex Schools and Classes" House Bill 352.

In August of 2010, a second bill—House Bill 4989—was filed. This one was a study order for the Bill 352. As of this writing, both bills languish in committee. The legal implications, together with the potential loss of federal funding due to Title IX, have made it very unlikely that this measure will ever be passed.

President Rosemary L. Reilly had conducted a poll of alumnae and expressed in a letter dated February 14 that Miss Carroll and the Alumnae Association's board supported the name *Boston Latin School*, "since the co-education law has in effect created one school from the two schools."[32]

Headmaster Carroll later reflected about the situation: "In 1972, the School Committee recognized the State law which ended sex discrimination in public schools and thereafter all schools became coeducational. For most schools this change was not a problem. However, for Girls' Latin School, it was a problem because it meant after almost one hundred years, the name of the school had to be changed."[33]

During the February 25 meeting, on the recommendation of four students, the School Committee ordered that the name of the school be changed to Boston Latin Academy. It also ordered that, for the last time, diplomas issued in 1975 and 1976 would be granted under the name *Latina Puellarum Schola Bostoniensis*—Girls' Latin School of Boston.

SEEKING ASSISTANCE ACROSS A CENTURY

Early in 1975, GLS Alumnae Association President Paula Wheelock Garrity '56 approached Headmaster John Tetlow's second daughter Helen, then close to 100 years old, with a request that she lend her support to the association's proposal. Garrity received the following letter, dated April 25, 1975—shortly after the School Committee turned down the proposal—in response.[34]

Miss Frances H. Tetlow
8 Craigie Circle
Cambridge, Ma 02138

Dear Mrs. Garrity,
You will understand, I am sure, that at ninety-eight my sister [Helen] does not feel equal to answering your letter, and wishes me to write for her.

The Latin School of say 1890–1903 was a nineteenth-century college-preparatory school. We learned self-discipline, to prepare lessons thoroughly, to answer questions honestly, and we passed college entrance examinations. The years of Latin and Greek gave us grounding in the meaning, exact and derived, of English words, and the study of formal sentence structure gave us ease in clear expression, rare in today's high school students.

The proposals I would think of as an interim arrangement pending equalization of educational opportunities for all. We accept but think seats should be available for all of quality. I am glad the Alumnae Association is taking this active role and I wish you understanding and cooperation.

Sincerely yours,
Frances H. Tetlow

The following was presented by David Keenan Student School Committee member:
ORDERED, That the name of Girls' Latin School be changed to Boston Latin Academy.
On roll call the order passed by a 4-0 vote.
ORDERED, That the diplomas to be granted to the 1975 and 1976 classes of Boston Latin Academy shall show the name of the school as Girls' Latin School.
On roll call the order passed by a 4-0 vote.[35]

On April 28, 1975, Judge Garrity ordered:

In connection with formulating a plan for desegregation of the examination schools, Boston Latin School and Boston Latin Academy, and Boston Technical School, and appropriate admissions criteria with respect to these schools for the 1975–76 school year and for future years.... Therefore it is ORDERED that the city defendants compile and deliver... the number and race of students.... the result of 1975 SSAT examinations....[36]

Further adjustments were made to the racial quota systems at all three schools.

Robert Dentler, dean of Boston University and a member of Boston's Secondary School Commission, recommended in January 1977 that Boston Latin School and Boston Latin Academy be merged, with grades nine through twelve attending at Latin School on Avenue Louis Pasteur and grades six through eight attending at Roslindale High School. Parents from both schools voiced opposition to the proposal and Superintendent of Schools Marion Fahey withdrew her proposal.

Two months later, the new president of the GLS Alumnae Association petitioned the School Committee to rescind the order changing Girls' Latin School to Boston Latin Academy: "The Association, while keenly disappointed over the name chosen for the school in 1975, has not spoken before, but," she continued, "the constant barrage of criticism from our Alumnae" had prompted the association to try once again to change the name to Boston Latin School. The petition was unsuccessful.[37] The school song changed from "Hail Girls' Latin School!" to "Hail Latin Academy!" The first class to include boys graduated in 1977. For the first time, the school's diplomas read *Boston Latin Academy*.

In 1978, Girls' Latin School/Boston Latin Academy celebrated its one-hundredth anniversary. Alumnae Association President Paula Wheelock Garrity '56 wrote, "Girls' Latin School represents an opportunity for girls from all backgrounds to study, work, and associate together. . . . We learned to value others for their intelligence, achievements and standards—not for their stations in life."[38]

Margaret Carroll wrote: "While during the past twelve years of the one-hundred-year history of the school, many changes occurred which were in sharp contrast to the past, the school continued the strong tradition of achievement in the classical education of students who attended."[39]

In 2007, *U.S. News & World Report* published its first ranking of the top 100 public high schools in America. (The rankings do not include the more than 3,000 independent high schools in the United States.) Selected from 22,000 schools, Boston Latin School ranked at 19; in 2012, the number was 38. In the magazine's 2014 listing of the country's best public high schools, Boston Latin School ranked at 56, and Boston Latin Academy came in at 353, behind the John D. O'Bryant School of Mathematics and Science (formerly Boston Technical High School), which stood at number 213.

In 2014, only 57,000 students were enrolled in Boston's public schools—nearly the same quantity as when Girls' Latin started in 1878 and 40 percent fewer than in 1970.

Endnotes

ABBREVIATIONS

ARM	Archives and Records Management, Office of the City Clerk, City of Boston
Barrows papers:	Barrows Family Papers, Houghton Library, Harvard University
BLS:Cat—1866	*The Boston Latin School Catalogue: Scholars in the Public Latin Grammar School in Boston, Mass., from October 1859 through November 1866*
BLS:Cat—1886	*Catalogue of the Boston Public Latin School, Established 1635: With an Historical Sketch*, prepared by Henry F. Jenks (Boston: Boston Latin School Association, 1886)
BLSA	BLSA Minutes, Rare Books and Manuscripts, Boston Public Library
BPL	Rare Books and Manuscripts, Boston Public Library
Carroll	Margaret C. Carroll, "History of Girls' Latin School & Boston Latin Academy" [unpublished MS]. The Records of Girls Latin School, Arthur and Elizabeth Schlesinger Library on the History of Women in America, Radcliffe Institute for Advanced Study, Harvard University
GLSRec	The Records of Girls Latin School. Arthur and Elizabeth Schlesinger Library on the History of Women in America, Radcliffe Institute for Advanced Study, Harvard University
Gotlieb	Howard Gotlieb Archival Research Center, Boston University
Gutman	Munroe C. Gutman Library, Harvard University
Houghton	Houghton Library, Harvard University
Jab	*The Jabberwock*, Girls' Latin School
Liber Annalis	*Liber Annalis: The Yearbook of the Girls' Latin School*
Register	*The Register*, Boston Latin School
RLSA	Roxbury Latin School Archives
SCCB:Ann	*Annual Report of the School Committee of the City of Boston* [date]
SCCB:Pro	*Proceedings of the School Committee of Boston* [date] (Boston: Rockwell and Churchill, [date])
SCCB:Rep	*Report of the School Committee of the City of Boston* [date]
Schlesinger	Arthur and Elizabeth Schlesinger Library on the History of Women in America, Radcliffe Institute for Advanced Study, Harvard University
Talbot	Marion Talbot, "The Boston Girls' Latin School by Emily Talbot," original manuscript typed by Miss Marion Talbot, June 5, 1901 (Talbot, Marion, BU MS 1478 Box 2). Howard Gotlieb Archival Research Center, Boston University
Tetlow papers	Tetlow, John, 1843–1911. Papers (MS Am 1986). Houghton Library, Harvard University
Tripod	*The Tripod*, Roxbury Latin School

CHAPTER I

1   The exact date of construction is unknown but assumed to be between 1645 and 1652. From 1635 until 1638, the school was conducted in the home of Philemon Pormort and, from 1638 until August 1645, in the home of the second headmaster Daniel Maude.

2   Oliver W. Holmes, *Elsie Venner: A Romance of Destiny* (Boston: Ticknor and Fields, 1861), p. 19. Contrary to popular belief, however, it was not the wealthy Protestants Holmes was describing, but the intellectual elite, particularly the scholars of Harvard College. "The scholar is, in a large proportion of cases, the son of scholars or scholarly persons. . . . He comes of the Brahmin caste of New England," wrote Holmes. He was also the father of Oliver Wendell Holmes Jr., who went on to serve from 1902 to 1932 on the U.S. Supreme Court and is regarded as one of its greatest justices.

3   Boston Latin School's name has changed over time. Originally Public Latin School (1831), it became Boston Latin School the following year. Succeeding names include Latin Grammar School (1853–1872), Public Latin School (1874–1884), and Boston Public Latin School. Later catalogues list the name as Public Latin School (1920s–1948), although the name Boston Latin School was in simultaneous use. Beginning in 1949, the school began to call itself Boston Latin School exclusively.

4   "People's Views: The Girls' Latin School," *Boston Daily Globe*, February 6, 1878, p. 3.

5   Ibid.

6   Built by Charles K. Kirby in 1870, 66 Marlborough Street was one of eight contiguous three-story houses. It first was occupied by famed architect Gridley J. F. Bryant, who sold the home to Dr. Israel Talbot on September 9, 1876.

7   Talbot, p. 1; another copy is in BPL, Ms f. Res 4351.157.

8   Lucy R. Woods, *A History of the Girls' High School of Boston, 1852–1902* (Boston: Printed by Riverside Press, 1904), p. 2.

9   Talbot, p. 1.

10   *SCCB:Ann* 1873 (Boston: Rockwell & Churchill, 1874), pp. 238–241. Also, *SCCB:Ann* 1902, appendix, p. 41 [Boston: ARM].

11   Edith Talbot Jackson, "Life of Dr. I. T. Talbot," 1943, p. 26. Emily Talbot Vertical File [Gotlieb].

12   *Proceedings of the Massachusetts Homeopathic Medical Society* (Boston: Daniel Gunn & Co., 1901), vol. 14, p. 49.

13   Israel Talbot developed impressive skills as a surgeon, and he is credited with performing the first successful tracheotomy in the United States on June 5, 1855.

14   L[orenzo] S[ayles] Fairbanks, *Genealogy of the Fairbanks Family in America, 1633–1897* (Boston: The author, 1897), p. 281. The Talbots had six children: Marion b. July 31, 1858; Edith b. August 21, 1860; Agnes Woodman b. May 31, 1862, d. December 24, 1862; Emily b. January 7, 1864, d. August 6, 1864; Winthrop b. April 11, 1866; and Henry R. September 3, 1872. Agnes and Emily both died before turning one year old.

15   Letter from Emily Talbot to daughters. Talbot, Marion, BU MS 1478 Box 2, Family 1865–1868 [Gotlieb].

16   "Will Be Sincerely Mourned–Death of Mrs. Emily Talbot Comes as Severe Blow to Many Friends in Boston," *Boston Globe*, November 1, 1900, p. 17.

17   "Personal," *Boston Evening Transcript*, November 3, 1900, p. 4.

18   Robert A. McCaughey, *Josiah Quincy, 1772–1864: The Last Federalist* (Cambridge, MA: Harvard University Press, 1974), pp. 123–125; Woods, p. 5.

19   *SCCB:Ann* 1873, pp. 238–241. Also, *SCCB:Ann* 1902, appendix, p. 41

20   Woods, *History of the Girls' High School of Boston*, p. 5.

21   Mary Caroline Crawford, *Romantic Days in Old Boston* (Boston: Little, Brown and Company, 1922), p. 9.

22   Talbot, p. 3.

23   *SCCB:Ann* 1873, pp. 238–241. Also, *SCCB:Ann* 1902, appendix, p. 41.

24   Thomas Cushing, *Catalogue of Graduates/Historical Sketch of the Chauncy Hall School 1828–1894* (Boston: David Clapp & Son, 1895), p. 165. The catalogue lists all four Talbot children: Marion (1873) and Edith (1874), who attended from the eighth grade; Winthrop T. (1875) and Henry R. (1882) attended from the fourth grade. (Parenthetical numbers denote year of entry into the school.)

25   *Girls' High School Admissions and Discharges*, vols. 1–3: *Examinations for Admissions* [ARM].

26   Marion Talbot and Lois Kimball Mathews Rosenberry, *The History of the American Association of University Women, 1881–1931* (Boston: Houghton Mifflin, 1931), p. 4.

27   Ibid.

28   Ibid.

29   The Boston Latin School catalogues first list Winthrop under the year 1877 and for the last time in 1883. According to the catalogues, he entered BLS in fall 1877 in Class VII (Division B). He proceeded to Class VI (Division A) in 1878, Class V (Division A) in 1879, Class III in 1880 (skipping Class IV), Class II in 1881, and Class I in 1882, completing his schooling in June 1883. The school offered a six-year program from 1852 to 1876, and then for two years, from 1876 to 1878, it offered an eight-year course, which reverted back to six years in 1879. Thus Winthrop Talbot attended BLS during years of transition. Furthermore, it appears that at least some students including Winthrop Talbot finished their studies in less than the prescribed number of years through "due exertion."

30   Talbot and Rosenberry, *History of the American Association of University Women*, p. 6.

31   Ibid.

32 Excluding homes of headmasters prior to John Lovell; see *BLS:Cat—1886*, p. 6. In 1877, Boston Latin was located on Bedford between Chauncy and Washington Streets. Bedford terminated on Washington Street directly opposite West Street.

33 Charles W. Eliot, "Contributions to the History of American Teachings," *Educational Review* vol. 42 (June–December 1911), pp. 348–349.

34 The Boston Latin School Battalion was organized in 1865, at the close of the Civil War. Military drill continued as part of the prescribed curriculum, and an annual exhibition was held on the Common.

35 "A Great Calamity: The Richest Business Portion of Boston Consumed," *Boston Evening Transcript*, November 11, 1872, p. 1

36 *Register* vol. 5, no. 8 (April 1886): p. 3.

37 When Julia Ward Howe's poem "The Battle Hymn of the Republic" was published in 1861, it brought her instant celebrity, and the song eventually made her one of the most famous women in the nineteenth-century United States. In her memoirs, Howe later noted that "the change in the position of women" that took place during her lifetime could be traced to "the hour in which the first university received women graduates." (See her *Modern Society* [Boston: Roberts Brothers, 1881], pp. 83–84.)

38 Flyer announcing opening of the club, June 8, 1868, and 19f and 20vf photographs. New England Women's Club Records 1843–1970, MC 175 M-145, 10v Historian's records [Schlesinger].

39 Record Book of Weekly Social Meetings, Monday, December 16, 1872, 4:30 P.M., vol. 40, microfilm reel 9, pp. 8–9. New England Women's Club Records 1843–1970, MC 175 M-145, 39v [Schlesinger].

40 Ibid.

41 Edward Hammond Clarke, *Sex in Education; or, A Fair Chance for Girls* (Boston: James R. Osgood and Company, 1873), p. 23.

42 Ibid., p. 31.

43 Ibid., pp. 102–104.

44 Ibid., pp. 105–106.

45 Ibid., pp. 80–81. Also, Alida C. Avery, "Testimony from [Vassar] College," in Julia Ward Howe, ed. *Sex and Education: A Reply to Dr. E. H. Clarke's "Sex in Education"* (Boston: Roberts Bros., 1874) p. 194.

46 Boston University was founded in 1869 by Isaac Rich, Jacob Sleeper, and Lee Claflin.

47 Information on Durant is compiled primarily from Florence Morse Kingsley's *The Life of Henry Fowle Durant, Founder of Wellesley College* (New York: Century, 1924).

48 The Massachusetts Homeopathic Hospital was incorporated in 1855, and from the beginning Dr. Israel Talbot had been deeply involved, serving as both surgeon and secretary of the corporation. He helped plan a new hospital building, completed in 1877, on East Concord Street. A surgical wing was completed in 1884.

49 Talbot Marion BUMS1478 Box 2, p. 11 [Gotlieb].

50 "Women's Participation in Higher Education, 1870–2000," in *Encyclopedia of Women and Gender* (San Diego, CA: Academic Press, 2002), pp. 17–19. Of 52,286 enrolled in institutions of higher education, 21.3 percent were women in 1870. However, only 3,000 were enrolled in degree-granting institutions. About 2,200 were enrolled in women's colleges, 600 in coeducational colleges, and 200 at state universities.

51 Talbot, p. 11.

52 Ibid.

53 The meeting on January 7 was attended by Mrs. Wilbur F. (Mary A.) Claflin; Elizabeth P. Peabody; Mrs. Kate Garnett Wells, author; Mrs. Thomas Talbot, whose husband was lieutenant governor in 1872 and 1873 and was elected governor in 1878; Elizabeth S. Phelps, author; Mrs. James F. Hunnewell; and Miss Annie E. Johnson, principal of the Bradford Academy. Also attending were William F. Warren's wife; Mrs. Borden (Kate W.) P. Bowne, whose husband was a professor of philosophy, ethics, and history at BU, and Mrs. Augustus (Elizabeth) H. Buck, who was married to the former headmaster of the Roxbury Latin School, master at Boston Latin, and now professor of Greek and German at BU. Mentioned as standing in support were Miss Ellen M. Richards, Mrs. Julia Ward Howe, Mrs. Alice Freeman Palmer, Mr. Carroll D. Wright, Mrs. Mary A. Livermore, and Professor Richard G. Moulton. List of Attendees. Massachusetts Society for the University Education of Women Papers, Box 1, MSUEW 1877 [Gotlieb].

54 Talbot, p. 12.

55 In the fall of 1875, 314 courageous young female students had arrived at College Hall to take the Wellesley College entrance exam; of them, only 30 were deemed prepared to start as freshmen. The rest of the girls were asked to take further preparatory courses in hopes they could enter the second freshman class the following fall.

56 Talbot, p. 12.

57 Ibid.

58 Ibid.

59 *Jab* vol. 32, no.3 (December 1918), p. 6.

60 *First Annual Report of the MSUEW 1877* (Boston: Cochrane & Sampson Printers, 1878), p. 5. Massachusetts Society for the University Education of Women Papers, Box 1 [Gotlieb].

61 Talbot, p. 13.

62 Talbot, p. 15.

63 SR [Sarah Rodriguez] and CJ [Colton Johnson], "Florence Cushing," in *Vassar Encyclopedia*. http://vcencyclopedia.vassar.edu/alumni/florence-cushing.html

64 Talbot, p. 16.

65 BLSA, 1844–1887, MS598 [BPL]. The meetings of the BLSA were held once a year in May. In the record for May 2, 1877, there is no mention of Girls' Latin School. In the record for May 1, 1878, Secretary Joseph Healy

gave the following report: "In anticipation of a full report from the standing committee, the report of the Secretary will merely congratulate the association that the building of a new and commodious schoolhouse is now an assured fact; the foundations are laid; and the contract for the masonry has been awarded. The important events of the year have been the movement to admit girls to the school, which the school committee failed to approve; the dinner in November, which exceeded our anticipations in its brilliancy and the number of distinguished alumni who were present."

66   For a detailed history of education in Boston, see Charles Dillaway, "Education Past, Present and Future," in Justin Winsor, *The Memorial History of Boston*, vol. 4, (Boston: James R. Osgood and Company, 1883), pp. 235–255. Dillaway includes his explanation of the founding of Girls' Latin School.

67   *Second Report of the Record Commissioners of the City of Boston Containing the Boston Records, 1634–1660, and the Book of Possessions*, 2nd ed. (Boston: Rockwell and Churchill, 1881), pp. 4–5. Also, *BLS:Cat—1886*, p. 3.

68   *BLS:Cat—1886*, p. 5.

69   Ibid., p. 308; and *Catalogue of the Graduates of the Public Latin School in Boston, 1816–1917* (Boston: Boston Latin School Association, 1918), p. 28.

70   Boston Latin School was located on three different sites between 1645 and 1877. The first building (1645–1704) was built on the north side of School Street (now occupied by the rear of King's Chapel and Old City Hall); that building was renovated/rebuilt and in use from 1704 to 1748. The second site (1748–1812) was the south side of School Street (now occupied by the Parker House); a second schoolhouse (1812–1844) was built on the same site. The third site was Bedford Street (1844–1881).

71   *Barnard's American Journal of Education* (Hartford, CT: Henry Barnard, 1881), International Series, p. 410.

72   Ibid.

73   Talbot, p. 16.

74   Ibid.

75   Communication from the Women's Education Association, June 29, 1877, The School Committee Papers, 1877 Sept–Oct, Ms. Bos. SC.2.I. October 9, 1877 [BPL]. The first letter, dated June 29, 1877, was sent to the Boston School Committee, and read in part, "The Women's Education Association respectfully represent that the opportunities in this city for girls to fit for college are inadequate and not equal to those provided for boys, or provided for girls in the neighboring cities, and they pray that their wants be supplied." The next correspondence was from the Trustees of Boston University, which read, "The Trustees of Boston University respectfully petition your honorable Board that the same provision be made for the classical education of girls in the Boston Latin School as is now made for boys" It was signed by William Claflin, president. The trustees of Smith College and Wellesley College also sent letters expressing their support.

76   Talbot, pp. 16–17. Talbot personally wrote to many friends to garner support for the movement, although not every one was in favor. Mrs. Augustus (Mary) Hemenway, widow of one of Boston's wealthiest and most influential merchants, wrote the following:

I have been thinking about the petition to make arrangements for girls at the new Latin School. I feel that I have not followed the matter closely enough to give my name as you requested, for I am not quite clear in my own mind whether I should not feel more hesitation in putting girls and boys together, say when about 14 years of age than when more mature. At all events it is an important matter to decide off handed and I have not reached the absolute conclusion in the matter I might before affixing my name.

I am sorry to disappoint you.

Believe me.

Letter from Mary Hemenway to Emily Talbot, June 19, 1877. Talbot Marion BU MS 1478 Box 1 [Department of Special Collections, Gotlieb].

77   Literary Scraps: Cuttings from Newspapers, Extracts, Miscellaneous, etc., BLSA 224, BLSA vol. 1, 1876–1881 [BPL].

78   A reference to girls having their period one week per month.

79   Literary Scraps: Cuttings from Newspapers, Extracts, Miscellaneous, etc., BLSA 224, BLSA vol 1, 1876–1881 [BPL].

80   Talbot, p. 17.

81   "After careful consideration nominate as candidates to the headmastership of the Latin School Moses Merrill and J. M. Whiton. Whole number of votes 24. J. M. Whiton had 4. Moses Merrill had 20 and was accordingly declared elected. Term of service to commence September 1, 1877." Minutes of the Boston School Committee June 29, 1977. Also *BLSA:Cat—1886*, p. 58. "Henry Augustine Gay . . . was made headmaster in June 1876; but was taken ill soon after summer vacation, and could only attend to his work for a short time until November, when he suddenly died. For the next six months the school was under the charge of Moses Merrill. . . who was appointed headmaster in June, 1877." Also *BLSA:Cat—1886*, p. 10.

Moses Merrill was born in Methuen, Massachusetts, in 1833 to Washington and Abiah Merrill. He prepared for college at Phillips Academy, Andover, Massachusetts, and entered Dartmouth in 1852. After two years he transferred to Harvard, from which he graduated in 1856. He was principal of the Shepard Grammar School in Cambridge from 1856 until 1858. In October 1858 he was appointed an usher at Boston Latin School, became submaster in 1867, master in 1869, and headmaster in 1877. In 1857 he married Sarah Ann White of Methuen, and they had four children.

82   Emily Talbot, "The Boston Latin School for Girls," *Jab* vol. 11, no. 5 (February 1898): 3, 17.

83   Helen Magill is not listed in the Boston Latin School Catalogue during the years her father taught there, which confirms that she was not formally admitted (*BLSA:Cat—1866* [Gutman]). In a letter to the Boston Latin School Association dated June 7, 1895 (and later published

in the Boston Latin School Class of 1870's twenty-fifth reunion booklet), Magill stated that she did attend classes from 1862 to 1866 and laments that she did not graduate with "her" class. She left the school in 1867 when her father resigned to take a two-year sabbatical abroad. Later she married Andrew Dickson White, who cofounded Cornell University and would become the U.S. ambassador to Germany.

84 "Miss Nellie Magill, the only lady who has ever received her preparatory education in the Latin School, visited our new building last week. She is the daughter of the former teacher in the school, Mr. E. H. Magill, who is now President of Swarthmore College, Pennsylvania. She has since continued her studies at Boston University." "Editor's Slate," *Register* vol. 1, no. 6 (February 1882), p. 3.

85 Letter from Edward H. Magill, n.d. William F. Warren Papers, BU 1476, Box 4, Folder 40 [Department of Special Collections, Gotlieb].

86 *The Laws and Liberties of Massachusetts, Reprinted from the Copy of the 1648 Edition* (Cambridge, MA: Harvard University Press, 1929).

87 In 1842, John Philbrick graduated from Dartmouth College and became a teacher at the Roxbury Latin School. Two years later he left to teach at English High School of Boston, followed by the Mayhew School in Boston, and then the Quincy School of Boston in 1847. In 1853, he became principal of the Connecticut State Normal School at New Britain, and in 1855, superintendent of the public schools for the State of Connecticut. After one year, he became superintendent of the Boston Public Schools, to which office he was elected annually from 1856 to 1874 and from 1876 to 1878, serving in that position 20 years in all. Philbrick was born May 27, 1818, and died on February 2, 1886.

88 Philbrick strongly believed that, in education, specialized work required specialized functions, and he favored a normal school to prepare teachers, Latin schools to prepare university-bound students, and so forth. "This same principle also held him as a firm advocate of the establishment of a separate Latin school for girls, instead of having the work of fitting girls for college done in a regular high school for girls where the chief business is giving a general education." (Larkin Dunton, ed., *A Memorial of the Life and Services of John D. Philbrick* [Boston: New England Pub. Co., 1887], p. 48.)

89 Talbot, p. 18.

90 John D. Philbrick, *The Thirty-Second Semi-Annual Report of the Office of Superintendent of Boston Public Schools, September 27, 1877* [ARM]. He stated, "The education of women in colleges creates a demand for that instruction of girls which is required for the admission. . . . It is no longer a question in this country whether provision shall be made for the collegiate education of women. It has been made. . . . The reorganization of the high school system, which went into operation in 1876, abolished all the [college] preparatory functions of all schools except the Boston Latin School. . . . There is now no longer existing in the [Boston] system a school or class where a girl could fit for college." Also, "Classical Education for Girls," *New York Times*, October 4, 1877.

91 "The Petitioners for a Classical Department for Girls in the Public School System: Their Arguments before the School Committee Yesterday: No Opposition Manifested," *Boston Daily Globe*, October 6, 1877, p. 8.

92 "The Classical Education of Girls: The Admission of Girls to the Latin School before the Committee on High Schools: The Views of Prominent Citizens," *Boston Evening Transcript*, October 6, 1877, p. 2.

93 Ibid.

94 Sally Schwager, *"Harvard Women": A History of the Founding of Radcliffe College* (Cambridge, MA: Harvard University Press, 1982), p. 107.

95 "The Petitioners for a Classical Department for Girls. . . ," p. 8.

96 "The Classical Education of Girls. . . ," p. 2.

97 In all, five public hearings were held: Friday, October 5, 1877; Monday, October 15, 1877; Wednesday, October 24, 1877; Thursday, November 1, 1877; and Monday, November 5, 1877; all began at 3:00 P.M.

98 Talbot, p. 21.

99 "The Classical Education of Girls: Female Students in the Latin School: The School Board's Hearing Continued; Wendell Phillips, Rev. Dr. Miner, Samuel Eliot, Homer B. Sprague, Joseph Healy, Amos Noyes," *Boston Evening Transcript*, October 16, 1877, p. 1. [Portions paraphrased from reporter's statement.]

100 "The Classical Education of Girls: The Latin School Third Public Hearing; Views by Charles K. Dillaway, Joseph Healy, President Porter, William Everett, Henry F. Durant, William Grey, and Dr. Reynolds," *Boston Evening Transcript*, October 25, 1877, p. 2. [Portions paraphrased from reporter's statement.]

101 Ibid.

102 "The Classical Education of Girls: The Admission of Girls to the Latin School; Opposition by Superintendent Philbrick, Mr. Collar of the Roxbury Latin School, and President Bartlett of Dartmouth College," *Boston Evening Transcript*, November 2, 1877, p. 2. [Portions paraphrased from reporter's statement.]

103 Ibid.

104 Ibid.

105 Ibid.

106 "Girls with Boys in the Boston Latin School: Still Another Hearing; Diverse Views Expressed and No Decision Yet Reached," *Boston Daily Globe*, November 6, 1877, p. 3.

107 Ibid.

108 Ibid.

109 "The Girls and the Latin School," *Boston Journal*, November 6, 1877. Literary Scraps: Cuttings from Newspapers, Extracts, Miscellaneous, etc. BLSA 224, BLSA col. 1, 1876–1881 [BPL].

110 "The Classical Education of Girls," *Boston Evening Transcript*, November 6, 1877, p. 1.

111 Ibid.

112 Ibid.

113 Thomas Wentworth Higginson, "Argument of President Warren on the Admission of Girls to Boston Latin School," Dep. 559, No. P 30 951, pp. 1–8, Special Collections, Boston Public Library.

114 "The Latin School Alumni: The Annual Dinner at the Parker House," *Boston Evening Transcript*, November 16, 1877, p. 2.

115 "The Latin School: A Very Pleasant Commencement Dinner, A Feast of Reason," *Boston Globe*, November 16, 1877, p. 8.

116 *BLSA:Cat—1886*, p. 313.

117 *SCCB:Pro* 1877; School Document no. 4, *Thirty-Third Semi-Annual Report of the Superintendent of Public Schools of the City of Boston, March 1878*, pp. 17–19 [ARM].

118 Ibid.

119 School Committee Papers, MS.Bos.Sc.2.I, November 27, 1877, BPL. Minutes of the Boston School Committee, November 27, 1877, p. 197 [ARM].

120 Talbot, p. 22.

121 Abby May offered the following as a substitute:

Ordered that the Committee on High schools be authorized to organize a class for girls who are desirous to prepare for college and to employ a competent teacher for the same with the rank of sub-master: the course of study for said class, and the direction of the same for the present school year, to be made under the charge of the head master of the Latin School. Lost.

Mr. Hutchins offered the following as a substitute:

Ordered that the Committee on High Schools be authorized to furnish classical education to girls in connection with the Latin School and in such rooms as they may deem best suited for the purpose. Lost.

122 "Order to Approve a Latin School for Girls, November 27, 1877," School Committee Papers MS.Bos.Sc.2.I [BPL].

123 *Thirty-Third Semi-Annual Report of the Superintendent of Public Schools* (1878), pp. 17–19.

124 Talbot and Rosenberry, *The History of the American Association of University Women*, p. 6. Also, Rosalind Rosenberg, *Beyond Separate Spheres: Intellectual Roots of Modern Feminism* (New Haven, CT: Yale University Press, 1983).

125 Talbot and Rosenberry, *The History of the American Association of University Women*, p. 1, note 2. "In Philadelphia no girl could be prepared for college in a public high school before 1893. . . . In Baltimore, two girls high schools were still, in 1900, unable to prepare girls for college." GLS was the fourth all-girls public school established in America—the first was Normal and Girls' High of Boston (1826/1852); the second, Western High School in Baltimore, Maryland (1844); and the third, Philadelphia High School for Girls (1848). The concept of Girls' Latin School would be imitated, however, when Girls' Latin School Baltimore was established in 1890.

CHAPTER II

1 Tetlow papers: Series VII, Other Papers, Box 109, Houghton.

2 *Minutes of the Boston School Committee, January 22, 1878* (Boston: Rockwell and Churchill), p. 10 [ARM].

3 The Normal School was formally separated from Girls' High School in 1872. *SCCB:Ann 1903*, pp. 40–41.

4 "From a Classmate," *Jab* vol. 24, no. 1 (October 1910), p. 13.

5 Lucy R. Woods, *A History of the Girls' High School of Boston 1852–1902* (Boston: Riverside Press, 1904), p. 29.

6 "Boston's Schoolmasters," *Boston Daily Globe*, June 14, 1891, p. 24.

7 Vida D. Scudder, "'Tis Twenty Years Since," *Jab* vol. 11, no. 5 (February 1898), p. 4.

8 Mary C.C. Goddard, "Dear Jabberwock." *Jab* vol. 21, no. 5 (February 1908), p. 12.

9 "The Latin School for Girls," *Boston Evening Transcript*, February 4, 1878, p. 1.

10 John Tetlow, "The Girls' Latin School Passes Its Twentieth Mile-Stone," *Jab* vol. 11, no. 5 (February 1898), p. 4.

11 Ibid. Also, "Girls' Latin School: Mrs. Emily Talbot and Mr. John Tetlow Tell History of Its Beginnings; Twenty-Fifth Anniversary Next Week," *Boston Evening Transcript*, January 29, 1903, p. 11.

12 Author's paraphrase based on written statements and records.

13 *SCCB:Pro* 1878, June 11, 1878, pp. 101–102 [ARM].

14 "The Girls' Latin School," *Boston Daily Globe*, February 6, 1878, p. 3.

15 "The Girls' Latin School: One Girl Expresses Her Opinion on the Subject and Favors the Study of Classical Works," *Boston Daily Globe*, February 8, 1878, p. 3.

16 "The Girls' Latin School: He Believes That the Study of Domestic Duties Is Better Than That of the Old Masters," *Boston Daily Globe*, February 15, 1878, p. 3.

17 "Girls' Latin School: Mrs. Emily Talbot and Mr. John Tetlow Tell History of Its Beginnings; Twenty-Fifth Anniversary Next Week", *Boston Evening Transcript*, January 29, 1903, p. 11.

18 *Minutes of the Boston School Committee, June 11, 1878*, pp. 101–102; also, *SCCB:Pro 1878*, p. 65 [ARM].

19 "Superintendent's Report," *SCCB:Rep 1886*, p. 31 [ARM].

20 Because there were fewer than 100 students, on June 11, 1878 the School Committee ordered "that the salary of the Principal of the Girls Latin School be fixed at the rate of $3,000 per annum." When the school reached 150 students, Tetlow's salary would be increased to $3,780. In comparison, the salary of the headmasters of other high schools was set at $3,500 for the first year and $4,000 thereafter for 1878.

21 Tetlow, "The Girls' Latin School Passes Its Twentieth Mile-Stone," p. 5.

22   Vida D. Scudder, "Mr. Tetlow as I Knew Him," *Jab* vol. 25, no. 5 (February 1912), p. 8. Also, Vida D. Scudder, "Mr. Tetlow as I Knew Him," reprinted in *Jab* vol. 41, no. 6 (March 1928), p. 15.

23   In 1884, Tetlow published a textbook that would become a standard in Latin classrooms, *A Progressive Series of Inductive Lessons in Latin*. He also wrote a translation of the *Aeneid*.

24   [Paraphrase of] Dorothy Worrell, "With the Latin School as a Background," *Jab* vol. 41, no. 6 (March 1928), p. 28.

25   Tetlow, "The Girls' Latin School Passes Its Twentieth Mile-Stone," p. 4. Also, *SCCB:Pro 1878*, p. 99.

26   Vida Dutton Scudder, *On Journey. Part I: Childhood and Adolescence 1861–1887* (Boston: Dutton, 1937), p. 58.

27   Scudder, "Mr. Tetlow as I Knew Him" (1928), p. 15.

28   Scudder, *On Journey*, p. 59.

29   Alice M. Mills, "Jabberwock Letter Box," *Jab* vol. 41, no. 6 (March 1928), p. 32.

30   Scudder, *On Journey*, p. 60.

31   Ibid., p. 58.

32   Ibid.

33   Mary J. Foley, "John Tetlow as Seen by Student and Teacher," *Jab* vol. 41, no. 6 (March 1928), p. 15.

34   Scudder, *On Journey*, pp. 59–60.

35   Scudder, "'Tis Twenty Years Since," *Jab* vol. 11, no. 5 (February 1898), pp. 3–4.

36   Quoted in Dorothy Elia Howells, *A Century to Celebrate: Radcliffe College 1879–1979* (Cambridge, MA: Radcliffe College, 1978), p. viii.

37   "Girls of Harvard Annex," *Milwaukee Journal*, May 12, 1891, p. 4. Also, "Women at Harvard Annex," *The Arrow of Pi Beta Phi* vol. 11, no. 1 (October 1892), p. 94; and Lucy Allen Paton, *Elizabeth Cary Agassiz: A Biography* (Boston: Houghton Mifflin, 1919), pp. 203–204.

38   Other accounts attribute the name to "a witty Cambridge lady." See Elizabeth Cady Stanton, Susan B. Anthony, and Matilda Joslyn Gage, eds., *History of Woman Suffrage* (Rochester, NY: Susan B. Anthony, 1886), vol. 3, p. 295.

39   *Reports for the Society for the Collegiate Instruction of Women, Twelfth Year, 1891* (Cambridge, MA.: W.H. Wheeler, 1891), pp. 8–12.

40   Howells, *A Century to Celebrate*, p. 3.

41   "Memoirs of Lucretia Crocker and Abby W. May," part 2: "Abby Williams May" (Boston: prepared for private circulation by Mrs. Edna Dow Cheney, 1893), p. 34.

42   "Mrs. Talbot and the Girls' Latin School," *Boston Home Journal*, December 2, 1879. Boston Latin School Association vol. 1, 1876–1881, BLSA 224 [BPL].

43   Editor's statement in reply to "Mrs. Talbot and the Girls' Latin School," *Boston Daily Advertiser*, December 9, 1879. Boston Latin School Association vol. 1, 1876–1881, BLSA 224 [BPL].

44   Marion Talbot diary 1879–1880. Marion Talbot Papers 1854–1948, Series 2: Diaries, Articles, and Books, Box 6 Folder 1. Special Collections Research Center, University of Chicago Library, University of Chicago.

45   Ibid.

46   Ibid.

47   "Voting in Massachusetts; The Bay State's Experiment with Female Suffrage," *New York Times*, December 9, 1879.

48   *SCCB:Ann 1879*, School Document no. 30, p. 52 [ARM].

49   "Superintendent's Report," *SCCB:Ann 1879*, School Document No. 2, p. 53.

50   Elizabeth P. Tetlow, "A Message from Mrs. Tetlow: Memories 1878," *Jab* vol. 41, no. 6 (March 1928), p. 18.

51   Charlotte W. Rogers, "Jabberwock Letter Box," *Jab* vol. 41, no. 6 (March 1928), p. 35.

52   Scudder, *On Journey*, p. 61.

53   "Abby Leach" in Radcliffe College Student Files 1890–1985, Abby Leach Papers, RA.A/L434 [Schlesinger].

54   Foley, "John Tetlow as Seen by Student and Teacher," pp. 16–17.

55   Ibid.

56   "Mary J. Foley" in Radcliffe College Student Files 1890–1985 [Schlesinger]; also "Mary Josephine Foley, A.B. 1888," Radcliffe College Student Biographies [Schlesinger]; Records of the Office of the Registrar, 1874–1966, RG XII, Series 1, Academic Record Books, Graduates and Undergraduates 1879–1898, Radcliffe College, Harvard University.

57   Foley, "John Tetlow as Seen by Student and Teacher," p. 17.

58   "Mary Josephine Foley," Radcliffe College Student Files 1890–1985 [Schlesinger].

59   Alice Cunningham Lacey, "Mary Josephine Foley," *Jab* vol. 42, no. 1 (October 1928), p. 5.

60   *Jab* vol 42, no. 8 (May 1929), p. 21.

61   "The Duty of Scholarship," in Thomas J. Morgan, ed., *Educational Mosaics: A Collection from Many Writers (Chiefly Modern) of Thoughts Bearing on Educational Questions of the Day* (Boston: Silver, Rogers & Co., 1887), p. 245.

62   John Tetlow, "Some Aspects of the Higher Education of Women," in *Proceedings of the Annual Meeting of the American Institute of Instruction*, Saratoga, New York, July 11–14, 1882 (Boston: American Institute of Instruction, 1883), p. 100.

63   "Vida Scudder In Memoriam," *Jab* vol. 68, no. 1 (November 1954), pp. 5–6.

64   Vida D. Scudder, Faculty Record, Wellesley College Archives, Wellesley College.

65   Mary L. Mason, Class of 1884, Smith College Alumnae Records, Smith College Archives, Smith College.

66   Alice Mountfort Mills, Class of 1884, Smith College Alumnae Records, Smith College Archives, Smith College; also Death Certificate #2568, Year 1944, vol. 10, p. 466. Massachusetts Office of Vital Statistics, City of Boston.

67   Mrs. Edwin T. Brewster. Radcliffe College Student Files 1890–1985, RGXXI Series 1 [Schlesinger].

68   Charlotte Rogers. Radcliffe College Student Files 1890–1985, RGXXI Series 1 [Schlesinger]; also, Death Certificate, Year 1943, vol. 48, p. 488. Massachusetts Office of Vital Statistics, City of Boston.

69   Miriam Witherspoon, nongraduate, Smith College Alumnae Records, Smith College Archives, Smith College; also, Death Certificate, Year 1949, vol. 100, p. 95. Massachusetts Office of Vital Statistics, City of Boston.

70   "The Duty of Scholarship," p. 245.

71   *SCCB:Pro 1885*, pp. 142–143 [ARM]. "The committee having attended to that duty, reported the whole number of votes to be 18; necessary for a choice under the rule, 13. John Tetlow had 18 votes, and was accordingly declared principal of the Girls' High School with the rank of head-master from September 7, 1885."

72   Mary J. Foley, "Early Days at the Girls' Latin School," *Jab* vol. 25, no. 5 (February 1912), p. 12.

CHAPTER III

1   Sibyl Collar Holbrook, "Abbie Farwell Brown and Josephine Preston Peabody," *Jab* vol. 41, no. 6 (March 1928), pp. 11–12.

2   Mabel Hay Barrows, "Jabberwock Letter Box," *Jab* vol. 41, no. 6 (March 1928), p. 31.

3   Abbie Farwell Brown, "The Early Jabberwock," *Jab* vol. 21, no. 5 (February 1908), p. 9.

4   Holbrook, "Abbie Farwell Brown and Josephine Preston Peabody," pp. 11–12.

5   Charles Lutwidge Dodgson's pen name was Lewis Carroll—a play on his real name: *Lewis* is the anglicized form of *Ludovicus*, the Latin for *Lutwidge*; and *Carroll* is an Irish surname similar to the Latin *Carolus*, from which comes the name *Charles*.

6   Abbie Farwell Brown, "The Passing of Lewis Carroll," *Jab* vol. 11, no. 5 (February 1898), pp. 1–2.

7   Brown, "The Early Jabberwock," p. 9.

8   Barrows, "Jabberwock Letter Box," p. 31.

9   Flyer inserted into *The Jabberwock* vol. 1, no. 1 (February 1888).

10   Tetlow papers: Series VII Other Papers Box 109, Memoriam Booklet, Speech by William Coe Collar, April 1911.

11   "The Intimate Letters of William Coe Collar," typed and donated to the archives by Mary Sibyl Collar Holbrook, Introduction, Letter from William Coe Collar to Mrs. Mary (T.O.) Eliot, pp. 33–34 [RLSA].

12   Ibid., p. 38.

13   Ibid.

14   Passport, United States of America, No. 8659, issued June 14, 1899. (Sibyl was born October 29, 1873; her father's second wife was born May 8, 1865.)

15   "Holbrook-Collar, Daughter of Principal of Roxbury Latin School Married in First Church," *Boston Globe*, Wednesday, July 1, 1896, p. 18.

16   William Collar (1900), Carolyn Averill (1901), Elizabeth Ridgeway (1906–1907), Frances Lodge (1907–1916), and John (1909).

17   "Intimate Letters of William Coe Collar," pp. 133 and 146.

18   Letter, "To Whom It May Concern," April 22, 1957, from Sibyl Collar Holbrook. Box 10, Headmaster File 7 [RLSA].

19   Brown, "The Early Jabberwock," p. 9.

20   Brown, Abbie Farwell Papers d. 1927, 1859–1927, Box 1, A-12 3 Biographical Material, Letter from Benjamin Brown [Schlesinger].

21   Brown, Abbie Farwell Papers d. 1927, 1859–1927, Call No. A-12, Box 1 No. 12, Early School Papers and No. 14, "Valedictory" Class of 1886. Bowdoin School [Schlesinger].

22   Sibyl Collar Holbrook, "Abbie Farwell Brown and Josephine Preston Peabody," *Jab* vol. 41, no. 6 (March 1928), pp. 11–15.

23   Brown, Abbie Farwell Brown Papers d. 1927, 1859–1927, Call no. A-12, Box 43, *The Book of Saints and Friendly Beasts*, 1900.

24   *G.L.S. Alumnae Association*, pp. 1–113 containing summary of each meeting and pp. 114–199 blank. This book is a handwritten record of the minutes of each Alumnae Association meeting from May 21, 1909, through 1942. Records of Girls' Latin School [Schlesinger].

25   Brown, Abbie Farwell Brown Papers d. 1927, 1859–1927, Box 1, 9, Ticknor, Caroline, Memorial Tribute *Boston Transcript* (March 23, 1927) [Schlesinger].

26   "A Letter From Mr. Carroll," *Jab* vol. 1, no. 2 (March 1888), p. 1. The location of this first letter is not known, although *Jabberwock* editors recall it later being kept in a box at the school's Codman Square location. A second letter, which includes a poem, was at one time in the school library at Codman Square, but was misplaced when the school moved to Ipswich Street. Two other original Carroll letters were donated by the Barrows family to Harvard's Houghton Library.

27   Brown, "The Passing of Lewis Carroll," pp. 1–2.

28   "The Jabberwock," *Jab* vol. 1, no. 1 (February 1888), p. 1.

29   Ibid.

30 Elias Grossman, "Editorials," *Register* vol. 7, no. 7 (March 1888), p. 4.

31 "Exchanges," *Jab* vol. 2., no. 8 (April 1889), p. 7.

32 "Why They Will Be Thankful," *Jab* vol. 4, no. 3 (November 1890), p. 2.

33 Anthony Mitchell Sammarco Dorchester Collection II, Collection 119 Box 7, Letters by Virginia Holbrook, F-21. Joseph P. Healey Library, University of Massachusetts Boston.

34 United States of America Passport No. 25437, issued June 8, 1906, to Virginia Holbrook, 35 years old, of 20 Percival Street, Dorchester, Massachusetts.

35 "Marriages: Virginia Holbrook to Dr. Ernst Dick at Berne, Switzerland, August 7, 1906," *Harvard Graduates Magazine* vol. 15 (1906–1907), p. 297.

36 "Intimate Letters of William Coe Collar," p. 143.

37 Isabel Chapin Barrows, *A Sunny Life: The Biography of Samuel June Barrows* (Boston: Little, Brown and Company, 1913), p. 88.

38 Sarah Tappan Coe, "Mabel Hay Barrows Mussey," *Jab* vol. 45, no. 4 (January 1932), p. 4.

39 Barrows, *A Sunny Life*, p. 111.

40 Coe, "Mabel Hay Barrows Mussey," p. 4.

41 Tetlow papers: Series II, (66), Letter to Samuel June Barrows, January 6, 1887.

42 Barrows, *A Sunny Life*, p. 112.

43 "Boston Girl's Classic Triumph," *Boston Globe*, December 3, 1899, p. 15.

44 "A Camp Wedding," *Boston Transcript*, July 6, 1905.

45 Coe, "Mabel Hay Barrows Mussey," p. 4.

46 Mabel Hay Barrows, "Jabberwock Letter Box," *Jab* vol. 41, no. 6 (March 1928), p. 31.

47 "Editorial Notes," *Jab* vol. 2, no. 3 (November 1888), p. 3.

48 "Editors Desk," *Register* vol. 8, no. 3 (November 1888), p. 1.

49 Barrows papers: Two letters: 1888–1889; no. 2 not signed, no. 1 signed by secretary. Letters to Mabel Hay (Barrows) Mussey (129) from Dodgson, Charles Lutwidge, 1832–1898. bMS Am 1807.2.

50 "A Friend Worth Having," *Jab* vol. 1, no. 5 (June 1888), p. 1.

51 Ibid.

52 Ibid., p. 2.

53 Ibid.

54 Ibid.

55 Barrows papers: Two letters: 1888–1889; no. 2 not signed, no. 1 signed by secretary. Letters to Mabel Hay (Barrows) Mussey (129) from Dodgson, Charles Lutwidge, 1832–1898. bMS Am 1807.2.

56 Barrows papers: Letter from John Tetlow (58) to Isabel Chapin Barrows. MS Am 1807.2.

57 Barrows papers: Letter from Mabel Hay (Barrows) Mussey to Isabel Chapin Barrows, 1845–1913, recipient, (396), Folder 2 of 58; 1892, May 18, 1892, Dorchester, Mass. MS Am 1807.1, Series: III.

58 In 1945, *Time* magazine published an article about Lewis Carroll and, in a subsequent issue, a letter to the editor from a Mrs. Anne Y. Copeland recalling that her school magazine was named after one of his characters. Mary King '46 of *The Jabberwock* staff wrote to ask Copeland if she had attended GLS. Mrs. Copeland turned out to be Annie H. Young, class of 1892, who, on October 10, 1899, married William Rogers Copeland.

59 Barrows papers: Letter from Mabel Hay (Barrows) Mussey to Isabel Chapin Barrows, 1845–1913, recipient, (396), Folder 2 of 58; 1892, June 26, 1892. MS Am 1807.1, Series: III.

60 Barrows papers: Letter from Mabel Hay (Barrows) Mussey to Isabel Chapin Barrows, 1845–1913, recipient, (396), Folder 2 of 58; 1892, June 30, 1892. MS Am 1807.1, Series: III.

61 "Discovering Great Britain," in "The Intimate Letters of William Coe Collar," Section II, p. 90; typed by and donated to the archives by Mary Sibyl Collar Holbrook [RLSA].

62 Barrows papers: Letters to Mabel Hay (Barrows) Mussey, (484) Sheldon, Jennie R. 1890. bMS Am 1807.2.

63 "Our Party," *Jab* vol. 2, no. 5 (January 1889), p. 5.

64 Coe, "Mabel Hay Barrows Mussey," p. 4.

65 *Boston Globe* and *Boston Post* quoted in "Comments of the Press," *Jab* vol. 3, no. 6 (February 1890), p. 3.

66 "The Feast of Dido," *Register* vol. 9, no. 7 (March 1890), pp. 103–104.

67 *Tripod* vol. 2, no. 6 (March 1890), p. 4.

68 "The Feast of Dido," *Jab* vol. 3, no. 8 (April 1890), p. 1.

69 Barrows papers: Letter Sawyer Ave., Boston, May 17, 1890. Letters from Mabel Hay (Barrows) Mussey to Isabel Chapin Barrows, 1845–1913, recipient, (396), Folder 1 of 58; 1886 MS Am 1807.1, Series: III.

70 "Good Times for the School Girls," *Jab* vol. 3, no. 10 (June 1890), p. 1.

71 At the time Barrows wrote this postcard to her mother, Greek remained a required course by order of the Boston School Committee, and it would remain so until June 12, 1894, when the committee agreed to allow German to be taken instead. Barrows papers: Letter Thursday, June 1890. Letters from Mabel Hay (Barrows) Mussey to Isabel Chapin Barrows, 1845–1913, recipient (396), Folder 1 of 58; 1886. MS Am 1807.1, Series: III.

72 *Jab* vol. 4, no. 1 (September 1890), p. 6.

73 "The Intimate Letters of William Coe Collar," Part III: 1891–1908, p. 107.

74 Holbrook, "Abbie Farwell Brown and Josephine Preston Peabody," pp. 11–15.

75 "New England Women," *Boston Globe*, October 8, 1915, p. 12.

76 "Vale," *Jab* vol. 4, no. 10 (June 1891), p. 1.

77 GLSRec.

78 Holbrook, "Abbie Farwell Brown and Josephine Preston Peabody," pp. 11–15.

79 Ibid.

80 "A Class Prophecy for '91," *Jab* vol. 4, no. 10 (June 1891), pp. 2–3.

81 "One Step Ahead," *Boston Globe*, June 24, 1891, p. 4.

82 Florence Alden Gragg, "Memories," *Jab* vol. 41, no. 6 (March 1928), p. 20.

83 "The Intimate Letters of William Coe Collar," Part III, 1891–1908, p. 107.

84 "Notes," *Jab* vol. 4, no. 10 (June 1891), p. 7.

85 "Jabberwock at Home: High School Papers and Their Editors," *Boston Sunday Globe*, June 12, 1892, p. 26.

86 Barrows papers: Letter from John Tetlow. Letters to Mabel Hay (Barrows) Mussey from various correspondents. (534) Series: V. bMS Am 1807.2.

87 Abbie Farwell Brown Papers 1859–1927, Box 2, Letters [Schlesinger].

88 Barrows papers: Letter Sawyer Ave., Dorchester, March 28, 1892. Letters from Mabel Hay (Barrows) Mussey to Isabel Chapin Barrows, 1845–1913, recipient, (396), Folder 2 of 58; 1892, MS Am 1807.1, Series: III.

89 Tetlow papers: Letter to Samuel June Barrows, January 6, 1887. Series II, Box 66 [Houghton].

90 Although admitted to the Harvard Annex, these students would be among the first to graduate from Radcliffe College, which received its charter from the Commonwealth of Massachusetts in 1894.

CHAPTER IV

1 E. E. Smith "and twenty others" noted the following in the minutes of an 1897 meeting of the School Committee: "The membership of the Girls' Latin School has increased 127 percent within the last eleven years, and this year the number of students has risen to 338. . . . The building occupied by Girls' High School and Girls' Latin School is none too large for Girls' High School alone. Although it was originally designed for 925 pupils, it now contains nearly 1300." SCCB:*Pro* 1897, p. 15 [ARM].

2 "Co-education in the Public Schools," *Boston Evening Transcript*, October 22, 1890, p. 3.

3 Ibid.

4 *Boston Globe*, December 11, 1896, p. 22. Tetlow referred to the city's expenditures to build Frederick Law Olmsted's park system known as the Emerald Necklace; McKim, Mead, and White's new Boston Public Library; and its mural series, *The Triumph of Religion*, by John Singer Sargent.

5 "Overcrowding," *Boston Globe*, September 8, 1897, p. 19.

6 SCCB:*Pro* 1881, p. 12 [ARM].

7 Reported by Thomas W. Bicknell in *Education: An International Magazine* vol. 1 (September 1880–July 1881), p. 401.

8 SCCB:*Ann* 1881, p. 11 [ARM].

9 John D. Philbrick, "Description of the Building," in *Memorial of the Dedication of the Public Latin and English High School-House* (Boston: Rockwell & Churchill, 1881), p. 107.

10 "Our Building," *Register* vol. 1, no. 7 (March 1882), p. 2. The students of Boston Latin School seemed much more willing to entertain the thought of Girls' Latin School occupying the building, however. This issue of the *Register* also reported, "Who could wish to see our beautiful building become to a great extent a mere store-house for musty volumes! . . . If there are any Latin School boys among the powers that be, we appeal to them to raise their voices in our behalf. Perhaps the more recent suggestion to take the Girls' High School building and transfer its occupants hither may meet with more favor. Certainly, our opposition will not be quite so bitter."

11 BLSA, 1844–1887, MS598 [BPL].

12 "Co-education in the Public Schools," *Boston Evening Transcript*, October 22, 1890, p. 3.

13 "The Following Orders Were Presented," *Boston Daily Globe*, November 29, 1882, p. 2.

14 SCCB:*Pro* 1882, pp. 240–241 [ARM]. Although the Latin schools may not have shared buildings, the boys of Boston Latin seemed to have formed an affinity with the girls at their sister school already. In September 1882, the *Register* asked the girls to help them: "We do not propose to publish this paper as the outcome of any class organization or literary society, but rather as the unanimous effort of a school whose every hope is for the good and final success of its work. With this idea in view let none refuse to aid us in any manner his or her (for we claim the young ladies of Girls' Latin) talents may enable them."

15 *Jab* vol. 59, no. 5 (June 1946), p. 9.

16 David L. Angus and Jeffrey E. Mirel, *The Failed Promise of the American High School, 1890–1995* (New York: Teachers College Press, 1999), p. 8.

17 Ibid.

18 *Report of the Committee of Ten on Secondary School Studies* (New York: published for the National Educational Association of the United States by the American Book Co., 1894), p. 4.

19 Tetlow papers: Speech by William Coe Collar, Memoriam Booklet, April 1911. Series VII, Other Papers Box 109.

20   Appendix, "Diplomas of Graduation, The Winthrop School (Girls)," *SCCB:Ann* 1898, p. 266. Also, "Mary Antin Taught by Maine Women," *Lewiston Evening Journal*, October 10, 1914, p. 5; in this article her teacher, Mrs. Dwight D. Ball, states that Antin entered grammar school in 1894 and completed nine years of work in four years.

21   Mary Antin, *The Promised Land* (Boston: Houghton Mifflin Company, 1912), pp. 292–293.

22   Ibid., pp. 183–184.

23   Ibid., p. 291.

24   Ibid., p. 292.

25   Ibid., p. 293.

26   Ibid.

27   Ibid.

28   The name of Antin's town of origin in Poland, Polotzk, was misspelled in the book's title.

29   Tetlow papers: Series II, (54) Antin, Mary, recipient. 1 letter; 1899.

30   Letter to Israel Zangwill (September 17, 1899), in Evelyn Salz, ed. *Selected Letters of Mary Antin* (Syracuse, NY: Syracuse University Press, 2000), p. 15.

31   Ibid, p. 32.

32   Antin, *The Promised Land*, p. 186.

33   "Tributes to Work of Jewish Council," *New York Times*, December 9, 1912.

34   Ken Gewertz, "Revisiting 'The Promised Land': Werner Sollors Edits New Edition of Premier Immigrant Autobiography," *Harvard Gazette*, March 6, 1997.

35   Antin, *The Promised Land*, pp. 294–295.

36   Ibid., p. 295.

37   Ibid., pp. 342–343.

38   "Supplement Report of Ellis Peterson, Supervisor," *Documents of the School Committee of the City of Boston for the Year 1898*, p. 53 [ARM].

39   "Supplement Report of Mr. John Tetlow, Head-master of the Girls' Latin School," *SCCB:Ann* 1903, pp. 183–187, [ARM].

40   *SCCB:Pro* January 26, 1897, p. 42 [ARM]. The chair read a petition signed by Henry L. Higginson and 3,050 others relating to a new building for Girls' Latin School. Referred to the Committee on School Houses.

41   "Want New Building: Girls' High and Latin School Overcrowded," *Boston Globe*, January 28, 1897, p. 2.

42   John Tetlow, "The Girls' Latin School Passes Its Twentieth Milestone," *Jab* vol. 11, no. 5 (February 1898), p. 5.

43   Mary C.C. Goddard, "Dear Jabberwock," *Jab* vol. 21, no. 5 (February 1908), p. 12.

44   *Jab* vol. 11, no. 6 (March 1898), p. 1.

45   Nan Guernsey, "Gay L'il Skola, 1880," *Jab* vol. 61, no. 3 (January 1948), pp. 3–4.

46   "First in New Building Graduation Exercise in the New Home of the Girls' Latin School," *Boston Evening Transcript*, June 28, 1898, p. 8.

47   *SCCB:Pro* 1899, p. 469 [ARM].

48   *SCCB:Pro* 1902, pp. 447–448 [ARM].

49   Supplement, "Report of Mr. John Tetlow, Head-master of the Girls' Latin School," *SCCB:Ann* 1903, pp. 183–187.

50   "Founded 25 Years. Observances by the Girls' Latin School," *Boston Globe*, February 5, 1903, p. 6.

51   "Education of Girls," *Boston Evening Transcript*, February 5, 1903, p. 8.

52   Ibid.

53   This statue, cast in a variety of materials, was popular throughout France after 1900. Approximately four feet high and three feet in diameter, it shows Joan sitting with hands folded on her knee. Chapu represented Joan of Arc not as a warrior but as a shepherdess from Lorraine listening to the voices that instruct her to help her king liberate his kingdom. As of this writing, the statue, which became dear to the hearts of alumni of both Girls' Latin School and Boston Latin Academy (BLA), is located in the BLA library at Townsend Street.

54   Tetlow papers: Seaver, Edward Pliny, 1 letter, February 3, 1903. Series I, (40).

55   Vida Scudder '80 and Elizabeth Mason '82 (Smith College); Sarah Briggs '83 and Mary Josephine Foley '83 (Harvard Annex); Sarah Ida Shaw '85 (Boston University); Grace M. Coleman '90, Katrina Sanborn '92, Elizabeth Tetlow '92, Florence Gragg '95, Henriette Heinzen '95, Carlotta Wiswall '97, Rosalie Abbott '98, Helen McCleary '00, and Annie Walley '00 (Radcliffe College); and Valeria Goodenow '96 and Elise Mendell '97 (Vassar College).

56   Letter from Helen Magill White dated June 7, 1895, to her BLS class of 1870. MS BLS 123–125, pp. 1–3 [BPL].

57   *SCCB:Pro* 1904, School Document No. 13-1904: Appendix, p. 116 [ARM].

58   Tetlow papers: Series II, (60) Harkins, Daniel S., 1 letter; 1904.

59   Tetlow papers: Series I, (18) Harkins, Daniel S., 1 letter; 1904.

60   "Editorial," *Jab* vol. 20, no. 8 (June 1907), p. 1.

CHAPTER V

1   "The Latin Awards," *Boston Evening Transcript*, June 1, 1906, p. 2.

2   Ibid.

3   Arthur Irving Fiske was born August 19, 1848, in Holliston, Massachusetts. In 1869, having just graduated Harvard, he stayed on at the college as a tutor in Greek until 1873; from then until 1901 he

was a master at Boston Latin School. Fiske married in 1879 and had two daughters. Upon the death of Moses Merrill in 1902, he became BLS headmaster, in which position he remained for eight years. Illness caused him to resign early in 1910, and on February 18 of that year he died in Portland, Connecticut.

4   *Two Hundred and Seventy-Fifth Anniversary of the Boston Latin School: 1635–1910* (Boston: Boston Latin School Association, 1910), pp. 40–41.

5   "Tercentenary Dinner Speech of Dr. Patrick Thomas Campbell," in Lee J. Dunn, ed., *Proceedings and Addresses of the Boston Latin School Tercentenary, 1635–1935* (Boston: Boston Latin School Association, 1937), pp. 180–181.

6   Finance Commission of the City of Boston, "A Chronology of the Boston Public Schools" (Boston: Printing Department, 1912), p. 15.

7   "200 Parents Vote to Fight Removal of Miss Griswold," *Boston Herald*, January 8, 1908, p. 2.

8   Constance Bridges, "The Function of the Classical School," *Jab* vol. 26, no. 8 (May 1913), p. 9.

9   "Supplement Report of Mr. John Tetlow, Head-master of the Girls' Latin School," *SCCB:Ann* 1903, pp. 185–186 [ARM].

10   Finance Commission of the City of Boston, *Report on the Boston School System*, October 7, 1911. *Reports and Communications* vol. 7 (Boston: City of Boston Printing, 1912), p. 16.

11   *SCCB:Pro* 1906, March 12, 1906, p. 70.

12   *Reports of Proceedings of the City Council of Boston* (Boston: Municipal Printing Office, 1907), p. 512.

13   *Annual Report of the Superintendent of Schools 1907*, Documents of the School Committee of the City of Boston, no. 13 (Boston: Municipal Printing Office, 1907), p. 9.

14   "Letters to the Editor," *Boston Evening Transcript*, January 20, 1908, p. 12.

15   "200 Parents Vote to Fight Removal of Miss Griswold," p. 2.

16   "Brooks Refused to Specify—Tetlow," *Boston Herald*, Sunday, January 12, 1908, p. 2.

17   *SCCB:Pro* 1908, January 20, 1908, pp. 7–9. Also January 27, 1908, p. 20 [Gutman].

18   Tetlow papers: Series II, Letters from John Tetlow (56) Brooks, Stratton Duluth, 2 letters, 1907.

19   Tetlow papers: Series I (50) Letters upon resigning from Girls' Latin School, 3 folders.

20   Ibid.

21   Ibid.

22   Ibid.

23   Tetlow papers: Series I, (46) Walker, Albert Perry, 1 letter; 1907.

24   Tetlow papers: Series I, (48) Letters concerning the case of Stratton Duluth Brooks versus Ellen Chase Griswold: 12 folders.

25   *SCCB:Pro* 1908, January 27, 1908, p. 20 [Special Collections, Gutman].

26   Tetlow papers: Series I, (48) Letters concerning the case of Stratton Duluth Brooks versus Ellen Chase Griswold: 12 folders.

27   Ibid.

28   Ibid.

29   "Supt. Brooks Brands Rumors Contemptible," *Boston Post*, January 3, 1903, p. 5.

30   Tetlow papers: Series I, (48) Letters concerning the case of Stratton Duluth Brooks versus Ellen Chase Griswold: 12 folders.

31   "200 Parents Vote to Fight Removal of Miss Griswold," p. 2.

32   *SCCB:Pro* 1908, January 20, 1908, pp. 7–9 [Special Collections, Gutman].

33   "Brooks' Aid Asked for Miss Griswold," *Boston Herald*, January 2, 1908, p. 4.

34   "Teacher's Case Is Left Untouched," *Boston Herald*, January 4, 1908, p. 5.

35   *SCCB:Pro* 1908, January 27, 1908, p. 21 [Special Collections, Gutman].

36   "Pupils Petition for Miss Griswold," *Boston Herald*, January 3, 1908, p. 2.

37   Ibid.

38   "200 Parents Vote to Fight Removal of Miss Griswold," pp. 1–2.

39   Ibid.

40   Ibid.

41   "Messrs. Crawford and Filene Opposed Hasty Action by Parents," *Boston Herald*, January 8, 1908, p. 2.

42   "Brooks Refused To Specify—Tetlow," p. 2.

43   Ibid.

44   "Filene, Crawford Reply to Tetlow," *Boston Herald*, January 13, 1908, p. 3.

45   "[Parents' Committee] Names Eleven to Aid Miss Griswold," *Boston Herald*, January 14, 1908, p. 7.

46   "Mr. Brooks Answers Alumnae President," *Boston Herald*, January 17, 1908, p. 4.

47   "Ignored by Brooks Declare Alumnae," *Boston Herald*, January 16, 1908, p. 4.

48   *SCCB:Pro* 1908, January 20, 1908, pp. 7–9 [Special Collections, Gutman].

49   Ibid., pp. 17–21.

50 "Griswold Removal Attacked," *Boston Post*, January 21, 1908, p. 12.

51 *SCCB:Pro* 1908, January 27, 1908, p. 20 [Special Collections, Gutman].

52 Ibid., pp. 20–21.

53 Tetlow papers: Series II, Letters from John Tetlow (59); Mary C. C. Goddard, 1 letter, 1908.

54 Ibid.

55 Tetlow papers: Series II, Letters from John Tetlow (57) Ellis, David A., 1 letter 1908.

56 "In Memoriam Ellen Chase Griswold," *Jab* vol. 22, no. 4 (January 1909), p. 2.

57 "The College," *Radcliffe Bulletin* 15 (August 1909), p. 8.

58 Tetlow papers: Series I, (40) Letters received from Seaver, Edwin Pliny 1838–1917, 3 letters 1903–1908.

59 Mary J. Foley, "John Tetlow as Seen by Student and Teacher," *Jab* vol. 41, no. 6 (March 1928), p. 17.

60 Mary Underhill, "Jabberwock Letter Box," *Jab* vol. 41, no. 6 (March 1928), p. 33.

CHAPTER VI

1 John Tetlow, "The Girls' Latin School," *Jab* vol. 21, no. 5 (February 1908), p. 5.

2 *SCCB:Pro* 1907, September 9, 1907, p. 118.

3 Mary C.C. Goddard, "Dear Jabberwock," *Jab* vol. 21, no. 5 (February 1908), p. 12.

4 *Boston Globe*, April 4, 1891, p. 4.

5 "History of the Class of 1908", *Jab* vol. 21, no. 8 (May 1908), p. 2.

6 *Boston Daily Globe*, August 16, 1897, p. 1.

7 "Mrs. Alfred W. Ingalls," *Jab* vol. 59, no. 5 (June 1946), p. 9.

8 Tetlow, "The Girls' Latin School," p. 4.

9 Ibid., pp. 4–5.

10 "From a Classmate," *Jab* vol. 24, no. 1 (October 1910), p.14.

11 Tetlow papers: Series I (50). Letters upon resigning from Girls' Latin School, 3 folders.

12 Ibid.

13 "Mrs. Alfred W. Ingalls," p. 9.

14 Records of the Girls' Latin School, 1876–2003, 2009-M154, GLS Alumnae Association Meeting Records, book with handwritten record of meeting minutes from May 21, 1909, through 1942 [Schlesinger].

15 John Tetlow, "Response to Helen A. Stuart," *Jab* vol. 24, no. 1 (October 1910), p.18.

16 Tetlow papers: Series II, (65) Letters from John Tetlow to Tetlow, Helen Ingersoll, recipient. 13 letters; 1911.

17 *Jab* vol. 25, no. 1 (October 1911), p. 6.

18 Tetlow papers: Series VII. Other papers, (108) Newspaper Clippings. *The Boston Transcript*, December 11, 1910, p. 3.

19 *Jab* vol. 25, no. 5 (February 1912), p. 2.

20 Elizabeth Proctor Howard Tetlow survived her husband by more than 30 years. Her funeral took place on March 23, 1942.

21 Tetlow papers: Series III (68) Letters to Elizabeth Howard Tetlow, letters upon Tetlow's death.

22 *SCCB:Ann* 1911, p. 80. Also, Tetlow papers: Series VII, (107) Memorabilia, folder 1 of 2.

23 Tetlow papers: Series II (66) Fragments.

24 James Greenleaf Croswell, *Letters and Writings of James Greenleaf Croswell* (Boston: Houghton Mifflin, 1917), pp. 218–219.

25 Tetlow papers: Series II (66) Fragments.

26 Ibid.

27 Helen Ingersoll Tetlow, "John Tetlow," *Jab* vol. 66, no. 3 (May 1953), p. 24.

CHAPTER VII

1 "Mr. Hapgood: A Tribute, by the Alumnae," *Jab* vol. 66, no. 3 (May 1953), p. 5.

2 "Student Handbook," p. 13. Records of Girls' Latin School, 2009-M154, Carton 1 112.4.08 [Schlesinger].

3 Helen B. Bagley, "First Impressions of the Latin School," *Jab* vol. 27, no. 1 (October 1913), p. 4.

4 Lee J. Dunn, ed., *Proceedings and Addresses of the Boston Latin School Tercentenary, 1635–1935* (Boston: Boston Latin School Association, 1937), p. 149.

5 Frederic Cople Jaher, *The Urban Establishment: Upper Strata in Boston, New York, Charleston, Chicago, and Los Angeles* (Champaign: University of Illinois Press, 1982), p. 102.

6 Cleveland Amory, *The Proper Bostonians* (New York: E. P. Dutton, 1947), p. 144.

7 Joseph Marr Cronin, *Reforming Boston Schools, 1930 to the Present: Overcoming Corruption and Racial Segregation* (New York: Palgrave Macmillan, 2008), p. 7.

8 James Michael Jr. (1907), Mary D. (1908), Dorothea (1910), Paul Gerard (1913), Leo Francis (1915), George J. (1919), John and Joseph (1921), and Francis X. (1923). Based on a review of BLS *Catalogues* from 1918–1940, BLS Archivist Valerie Uber confirms that five of his sons attended BLS for a period of time, although only two would graduate: James Michael Jr. entered 1918 (attended six years and graduated 1924); Paul entered 1925 (attended five years, but did not graduate);

Leo entered 1926 (attended six years and graduated 1932); George entered 1930 (attended only three years); and Francis, who entered 1937 (attended only two years).

9   *Jab* vol. 32, no. 8 (May 1919), p. 19.

10   "Boston Latin Wins Admissions Award," *Harvard Crimson Magazine*, December 5, 1925.

11   "Students in College Come from 832 Schools," *Harvard Crimson Magazine*, May 24, 1926.

12   Hapgood's list of graduates, which he marked with Rs (for Radcliffe), in his copy of "Closing Exercises of the Boston Girls' Latin School, Friday, June 26, 1925" [GLSRec].

13   Ernest G. Hapgood, "Efficiency in the Public Secondary School," *Education: A Monthly Magazine Devoted to the Science, Art, Philosophy, and Literature of Education* vol. 35, no. 1 (September 1914), p. 651.

14   "Course of Study for the Latin Schools," Documents of the School Committee of the City of Boston for the Year 1911, School Document No. 6–1911 (Boston: City of Boston Printing Department, 1911), p. 4.

15   School Committee of the City of Boston, *Annual Report of the Business Agent for the Year Ending January 31, 1917*, p. 81. Also *Annual Statistics of the Boston Public Schools*, p. 33 [ARM].

16   Quotations from author's interviews with GLS alumnae.

17   Elizabeth Frank, *Louise Bogan: A Portrait* (New York: Columbia University Press, 1986), p. 11.

18   Ibid., pp. 25–27.

19   Ibid.

20   Margaret A. Lowe, *Looking Good: College Women and Body Image, 1875–1930* (Baltimore: Johns Hopkins University Press, 2003), p. 2.

21   Ibid.

22   Mary-Ann DeVita, "Alumnae, by Mary-Ann DeVita '56," *Jab* vol. 67, no. 3 (April 1956), p. 9.

23   *Jab*, vol. 27, no. 7 (April 1915), p. 4.

24   *Girls' Latin School 1978—Boston Latin Academy 1978* (Boston: Centennial Committee of the Girls' Latin School—Boston Latin Academy, 1978), p. 12.

25   *Jab* vol. 38, no. 5 (February 1925), p. 5.

26   Ibid.

27   "Hail Girls' Latin School," *Jab* vol. 40, no. 3 (December 1926), p. 8.

28   Ibid.

29   "Roslindale Sisters Write New Song with Irish Air for Girls' Latin School," *Boston Sunday Post*, December 5, 1926, p. T.

30   Sibyl Collar Holbrook, "Abbie Farwell Brown and Josephine Preston Peabody," *Jab* vol. 41, no. 6 (March 1928), p. 12.

31   Ibid.

32   *Superintendent's Report 1928*, Documents of the School Committee of the City of Boston for the Year 1927 (Boston: City of Boston Printing Department, 1928), p. 29.

33   "Says America Has Outgrown Audacity," *Boston Daily Globe* (April 1, 1928), p. A22.

34   "Girls' Latin at 50th Anniversary," *Boston Daily Globe* (March 25, 1928), p. B14.

35   "Domi," *Jab* vol. 41, no. 5 (February 1928), p. 19.

36   "Foreword," *Jab* vol. 41, no. 6 (March 1928), p. 5.

37   *Jab* vol. 37, no. 2 (November 1923), p. 4.

38   "Domi," *Jab* vol. 41, no. 5 (February 1928), p. 19.

39   Sally Ellis, "Skating Family Has Reunion on Ice," *Boston Sunday Post*, July 7, 1946.

40   "Sonja Always Dimmed Maribel's Title Hopes," [Omaha, Nebraska] *Evening World Herald*, February 16, 1961. Deceased Alumnae Files, ca. 1894–2004, RG IX, Series 2, Box 236, Owen, Maribel Vinson '33, Clippings 1961–1980 [Schlesinger].

41   Student Files 1890–1985, Maribel Vinson [Schlesinger].

42   "Maribel Y. Vinson," *Jab* vol. 51, no. 5 (February 1938), p. 17.

43   "Laurence Owen: 1961 U.S. National Championships Freeskate," CBS Broadcast.

CHAPTER VIII

1   In the early twenty-first century, the building was converted into a boutique hotel, its Beaux Arts façade carefully preserved.

2   In 1928, the School Committee consisted of Edward M. Sullivan, Jennie Loitman Barron, Francis C. Gray, Joseph J. Hurley, and Joseph V. Lyons, DMD.

3   Special Meeting of the School Committee, May 1, 1928, in *SCCB:Pro* 1953, pp. 87–114 [ARM].

4   Hapgood's testimony fills three pages of transcript characterized by similarly confrontational and grueling questioning.

5   Boston Latin School's score of 90 percent won it top honors again in 1928, but in 1929 Exeter would best BLS, 90.3 to 89.8; two years later, in 1930, BLS ran second to the Lawrenceville School in New Jersey; in 1931 BLS placed third behind Exeter and Lawrenceville.

6   Joseph Marr Cronin, *Reforming Boston Schools, 1930 to the Present: Overcoming Corruption and Racial Segregation* (New York: Palgrave Macmillan, 2008), p. 21.

7   *Liber Annalis* 1932, p. 74.

8   Boston Latin School Association. *Proceedings and Addresses of the*

Boston Latin School Tercentenary 1635–1935, comp. and ed., Lee J. Dunn (Boston: Best Printers, 1937), p. 183.

9   *Jab* vol. 68, no. 5 (May 1935), p. 23.

10   Boston Latin School Association, *Proceedings and Addresses of the . . . Tercentenary*, p. 110.

11   Author's interview with Barbara Polk Washburn.

12   Alma maters of GLS faculty in the 1930s: Brown University: Ernest Hapgood and Mary R. Stark—Harvard College: Harrison G. Meserve and Raymond S. Tobey—Mount Holyoke College: Marion I. Lithgow—Radcliffe College: Margaret C. Cotter, Catharine T. Fennessey, Margaret J. Griffith, Blanche W. Harding, Gladys M. Heyl, Mary Marnell, Marion C. Moreland, Cora F. Roper, Helen A. Stuart, and Zabelle D. Tahmizian—Smith College: Adeline G. Simmons—Vassar College: Mary E. Greene—Wellesley College: Gertrude M. Hall and Eva Z. Prichard. Other colleges not known or listed: Sibyl B. Aldrich, Ida A. Cohen, Alice M. Smith, and Marjorie W. Woodhead.

13   "Dear Diary, December 7, 1941," *Liber Annalis*, 1943, p. 18.

14   "Domi," *Jab* vol. 55, no.2 (January 1942)

15   "Dear Diary, December 8, 1941," *Liber Annalis*, 1943, p. 18.

16   GLS Alumnae Association minutes for the years 1940–1942, Girls' Latin School Records, M255, Carton 1, 113.2.07 [GLSRec].

17   They were last seen in 1979 at the hotel where the GLS Alumnae Association met for the unveiling of Margaret Carroll's portrait. Inadvertently, the bowls were left after the meeting, and although inquiries were made, the hotel staff was unable to find them.

18   GLS Alumnae Association Meeting Minutes [GLSRec].

19   "Orange Patches. . . Green Suspenders," *Jab* vol. 57, no. 4 (May 1944), p. 16

20   Author's interview with Diana Laskin Siegal.

21   "Dear Diary, December 7, 1942," *Liber Annalis*, 1943, p.19.

22   *Jab* vol. 57, no. 16 (May 4, 1944), p. 16.

23   *Jab* vol 58, no. 1 (September 1945), p. 18.

24   Mary McGrory, *The Best of Mary McGrory: A Half-Century of Washington Commentary*, ed. Phil Gailey (Kansas City, MO: Andrews McMeel, 2006), p. xv.

25   Mary McGrory, "Meet J. Danforth Prole," *Washington Post*, October 4, 1992.

26   Mary McGrory, " 'Magnet School' Hope of Boston," *Eugene [OR] Register Guard*, September 15, 1975, p. 8.

27   Ibid.

28   "Mary McGrory, 85; Washington Post Columnist Covered Scandal and War," *Los Angeles Times*, April 23, 2004, Obituaries.

29   Mary McGrory to GLS Alumnae Association [GLSRec].

30   "Mr. Hapgood: A Tribute by the Alumnae," *Jab* vol. 66, no. 3 (May 1953), pp. 5–6.

CHAPTER IX

1   Conference minutes, Monday, August 11, 1952, p. 54 [ARM].

2   Mary M. Mallard, *History of Girls' Latin School, 1878–1953* ([n.p.], 1953), pp. 48–49.

3   *Report of a Survey of the Public Schools of Boston, Massachusetts conducted under the Auspices of the Finance Commission of the City of Boston*; George D. Strayer, Director of Survey (Boston: Printing Dept., 1944).

4   Ibid., p. 623. Of 11,357 boys in the high schools, 71 percent are in boys schools, and of 12,820 girls, 64 percent are segregated in girls schools.

5   Ibid., p. 43.

6   Ibid., p. 838.

7   William M. Bulger, *James Michael Curley: A Short Biography with Personal Remembrances* (Beverly, MA: Commonwealth Editions, 2009), p. 78.

8   "Muchnick Wants Sweeping Reform in School System: Demands End to Political Manuevering," *Boston Daily Globe*, January 8, 1952, p. 7.

9   Joseph Marr Cronin, *Reforming Boston Schools, 1930 to the Present: Overcoming Corruption and Racial Segregation* (New York: Palgrave Macmillan, 2008), p. 53.

10   "Proceedings of the School Committee, May 5, 1952," in *SCCB:Rep* 1952, p. 99 [ARM].

11   Conference of the Boston School Committee, August 11, 1952, in *SCCB:Rep* 1952, p. 2 [ARM].

12   George Wein, *Myself among Others: A Life in Music* (Cambridge, MA: Da Capo Press, 2003), pp. 64–67.

13   Dorothy West, *The Wedding* (New York: Random House, 1995), p. 4.

14   Dorothy West, *The Richer, The Poorer: Stories, Sketches and Reminiscences* (New York: Doubleday, 1995); quoted in "Dorothy West," *Encyclopedia of World Biography*: http://www.notablebiographies.com/supp/Supplement-Sp-Z/West-Dorothy.html#ixzz32ToE4cEi

15   David Halberstam, *The Children* (New York: Random House, 1998), pp. 168–175.

16   Conference of the Boston School Committee, August 11, 1952, pp. 1–5.

17   Ibid., p. 211.

18   Deed [ARM].

19   "Mr. Hapgood: A Tribute by the Alumnae," *Jab* vol. 66, no. 3 (May 1953), pp. 5–6

20   Report for May 13, 1953, in *SCCB:Pro* 1953, p. 335 [ARM].

21 All quotations from the February 24, 1954, School Committee hearing are from transcripts published as "Excerpts from the Boston School Committee Hearing on High School Relocations, February 25, 1954," in *SCCB:Rep* 1954, p. 7 [ARM].

22 Boston Finance Commission, "Communication in Regard to the Girls' Latin School Location in Future," January 5, 1955, in *Boston Finance Commission Reports* vol. 51 (1955), pp. 39–43 [ARM].

23 Ibid.

24 *SCCOM:Pro* February 7, 1955 (Boston: Printing Department), p. 66 [ARM].

25 Ibid., pp. 66–67.

26 *SCCB:Pro* February 21, 1955, p. 85 [ARM].

27 "Silence, Sadness Mark Closing of Girls' Latin," *Boston Traveler*, June 24, 1955, p. 21.

28 Ibid.

29 Ibid.

30 Dorothy Elia, "Ad Astra Per Aspera [To the stars through difficulty]," *Jab* vol. 68, no. 4 (June 1955), p. 4.

CHAPTER X

1 "Dedication of the Dorchester High School-House," December 5, 1901, *SCCB:Rep* 1901, Appendix pp. 361–367 [ARM].

2 Ibid.

3 "Home away from Home," *Jab* vol. 67, no. 1 (November 1955), p. 7.

4 Judith Brody, "Boy, Its Tough at Girls' Latin," *Boston Globe*, February 11, 1971, p. 1.

5 Kerry Reilly, "Welcome Mr. Gately," *Jab* vol. 68, no. 5 (November 1957), p. 4.

6 Ibid.

7 Ibid.

8 Paraphrased from author's notes and memory of the experience.

9 Contrast this to the 1964 school-year opening speech Dr. O'Leary, headmaster of Boston Latin School, delivered: "On behalf of the faculty and as your Head Master, I bid you welcome to the Boston Latin School. Many years ago I was welcomed to this venerable institution of learning by then Head Master, the great and learned Dr. Patrick T. Campbell. Like you I was in awe of this school with its grand traditions, and like you I wondered if I ever would be a graduate. As I made it so can you. . . . We hold no brief for the cult of mediocrity so prevalent in our society today. . . . The only aristocracy we have is the aristocracy of the intellect. You will be free from the so-called curriculum of Modern Progressive Education, which in essence permits the student to pursue any end in education which he chooses so long as he is happy. We further believe work coupled with desires insures success in any endeavor of life." [BLSA]

10 Author's interview with GLS alumna.

11 Ibid.

12 Author's interview with Diana Laskin Seigal.

13 Author's interview with Theresa Gulinello Raymond.

14 Author's interview with GLS alumna.

15 Brody, "Boy, Its Tough at Girls' Latin," p. 1.

16 *Boston Globe*, September 18, 1969, p. 3.

17 Author's interview with Elaine Milton.

18 Author's interview with Julianne Glowacki.

19 Carroll, p. 7.

20 United States District Court, District of Massachusetts, *Tallulah Morgan et al., Plaintiffs v. John J. Kerrigan et al., Defendants*, Civil Action Nos. 74-1251. Accession No. 92-042, Record Type: Desegregation Files, January 1975–June 1976, Box 3 of 6, April–May 1975, Volume II. On Appeal from Orders of the United States District Court for the District of Massachusetts, Supreme Judicial Court, Suffolk, No. 73-91 Eq., *Nancy Bradshaw et al. v. Paul R. Tierney et al., City of Boston et al., v. Paul R. Tierney et al., Board of Education of the Commonwealth of Massachusetts et al., v. School Committee of the City of Boston*. No. 73-106 Eq., Bales et al., parents of the pupils of Girls' Latin School are interveners, pp. 1074–1089 [ARM].

21 Author's interview with Debra Holland.

22 "From Bay State High Schools 429 in Merit Scholar Finals," *Boston Herald Traveler*, September 19, 1970, p. 6.

23 Margaret Carroll, "Headmaster's Bulletin" no. 29 (October 5, 1970) [GLSRec].

CHAPTER XI

1 Patricia Wyckoff, '72, "Moratorium Day," *Jab* vol. 22, no. 2, (June 1970), p. 11.

2 Carroll, p. 8.

3 *SCCB:Pro* November 17, 1969, p. 323 [ARM].

4 Minutes, June 17, 1970, *SCCB:Pro*, Acc. no. 92-003: "Minutes 1/5/70–8/11/70," p. 51–120 [ARM].

5 Lee had served on the committee for more than 30 years. His grandfather was a Boston banker, and Lee grew up with his three siblings in Brookline. From 1910 through 1937, Joseph Lee's father and namesake, graduate of Harvard University and Harvard Law School, served on the Boston School Committee, then Lee took his father's seat in 1937. The son was described as an outspoken, independently wealthy Brahmin.

6 All quotations from the June 17, 1970, School Committee hearing are from the transcript in *SCCB:Pro*, Acc. no. 92-003: "Minutes 1/5/70–8/11/70" [ARM].

7   Author's interview with Helen Cummings.

8   Rudyard Kipling's poem "The Female of the Species" returns again and again to "For the female of the species is more deadly than the male," in what becomes almost a refrain. See his *The Years Between* (London: Methuen, 1911), p. 128.

9   Finding Aid for the Records of the President of Radcliffe College, Matina Horner. Schlesinger Library RG II, Series 5, Hollis Number 011522441 [Schlesinger].

10   The Boston City Archives De-segregation Era Collection summarizes the timeline of events from 1956 leading up to passage of Massachusetts Law Chapter 622 of the Acts of 1971.

11   "US Court to Hear Suit Charging Boston Schools with Sex Bias," *Boston Herald Traveler*, August 10, 1971, p 40.

12   Marcia Masters, "Should the Latin Schools Become Co-ed?" *Jab* vol. 34, no. 1 (December 1972), p. 3.

13   John Wolfson, "The Road to Perdition," *Boston Magazine*, May 16, 2006.

14   *SCCB:Pro* November 16, 1971, Minutes #40, pp. 47–50 [ARM].

15   "Coed Enrollment Ordered for 7 Boston Schools," *Boston Globe*, November 17, 1971, p. 4.

16   "All Hub Schools Must Go Coed, City Lawyer Says", *Boston Globe*, November 17, 1971, p. 3.

17   All-Boy, Girl Hub Schools Out", *Boston Herald Traveler*, November 17, 1971, pp. 1 and 5.

18   *SCCB:Pro* May 9, 1972, pp. 152–153 [ARM].

19   Examinations for Admissions to Boston Latin School and Girls' Latin School, January 14, 1972, Superintendents Circulars 1971–1972 [ARM].

20   *SCCB:Pro* June 17, 1970, Minutes, pp. 98–102.

21   Otile McManus, "The Day English and Latin Went Coed," *Boston Globe* (September 7, 1972), p. 33.

22   Janice Goodman, "Should the Latin Schools Become Co-ed?" *Jab* vol. 34, no. 1 (December 1972), p. 3.

23   Author's interview with Helen Cummings.

24   *SCCB:Pro* June 17, 1970, Minutes, pp. 98–102.

25   Commonwealth of Massachusetts, Supreme Judicial Court, Suffolk, ss., No. 73-91 Eq., *Nancy Bradshaw, et al v. Paul R. Tierney, et al, City of Boston et al., v. Paul R. Tierney, et al, Board of Education of the Commonwealth of Massachusetts, et al, v. School Committee of the City of Boston*. No. 73-106 Eq., Bales et al., parents of the pupils of Girls' Latin School, are interveners [ARM].

26   United States District Court, District of Massachusetts. *Tallulah Morgan et al., Plaintiffs v. John J. Kerrigan et al., Defendants*, Civil Action Nos. 75-1194, 75-1197, On Appeal from Orders of the United States District Court for the District of Massachusetts. Accession No.: 92-042, Record Type: Desegregation Files, January 1975–June 1976, Box 3 of 6, April–May 1975, Appendix, Stenographic Transcript of Proceedings, p. 394 [ARM].

27   *Tallulah Morgan et al., Plaintiffs v. John J. Kerrigan et al., Defendants*, Civil Action No. 74-1251. Accession No.: 92-042, Record Type: Desegregation Files, January 1975–June 1976, Box 3 of 6, April–May 1975, Volume II, Exhibit, pp. 817–824 [ARM].

28   United States District Court, District of Massachusetts, No. 72-911-G, p. 17.

29   F. Washington Jarvis to Wilfrid O'Leary, letter, April 3, 1975, author's files.

30   *Tallulah Morgan et al., Plaintiffs v. John J. Kerrigan et al., Defendants*, Civil Action No. 74-1251. Accession No. 92-042, Record Type: Desegregation Files, January 1975–June 1976, Box 3 of 6, April–May 1975, Volume II, Exhibit, pp. 47–48 [ARM].

31   *SCCB:Pro* March 27, 1974, p. 67 [ARM].

32   GLSRec.

33   Carroll, p. 7.

34   GLSRec.

35   *SCCB:Pro* February 25, 1975 [ARM].

36   *SCCB:Pro* April 28, 1975, p. 457 [ARM]. Also, *Tallulah Morgan et al., Plaintiffs v. John J. Kerrigan et al., Defendants*, Civil Action No. 74-1251. Accession No. 92-042, Record Type: Desegregation Files, January 1975–June 1976, Box 3 of 6, April–May 1975 [ARM].

37   *SCCB:Pro* May 9, 1972, pp. 152–153 [ARM].

38   "100th Anniversary Brochure" (Boston: Centennial Committee of the GLS/BLA Association, 1978), p. 3.

39   Carroll, pp. 9–10.

Picture Credits

Key to position designations:

a — all
b — bottom
c — center
l — left
r — right
t — top

numbers indicate vertical position (e.g., 2nd, 3rd, etc.)

For example: "27r" refers to the righthand photo on page 27; "27bl" would be the bottom lefthand photo on page 27; and "27[2t]" would be the second picture from the top on page 27.

City of Boston
    Division of Archives and Records Management: 164[3t], 184[2t], 190, 220b, 223, 229t
    School Building Photographs: 128[3t], 150t, 153b, 156–157a, 200[3b]
    Topographic and Planimetric Survey 1962 (prepared under Direction of Boston Redevelopment Authority, sheet No. 21N-8E): 256

Boston Globe (May 7, 1964): 231

Boston Latin Academy: 225l, 240[2b]

Courtesy of the Boston Latin School Archives: 150[4t], 184t

Courtesy of the Trustees of the Boston Public Library: 2[t, 2b, and 3b], 11, 130
    Folsom Collection: 40[t, 3t], 45a, 104t, 107a, 108a, 109–113a, 131t
    Leslie Jones Collection: 150b, 200[3t]
    Norman B. Leventhal Map Center: 1
    Print Department: 3, 36, 104[2t, 2b], 105, 129, 150[2b], 165

Boston University, Howard Gotlieb Archival Research Center: 6, 8l, 22r, 70t

The Bostonian Society: 40b, 43, 220[3t]

Bromley, George W., and Walter S. Bromley, *Atlas of the City of Boston: Boston Proper and Back Bay from Actual Surveys and Official Plans* (Philadelphia: Bromley, 1908): 200b, 222t

———, *Atlas of the City of Boston from Architectural Surveys and Official Plans* (Philadelphia: Bromley, 1931): 152

Brown University Archives, Class of 1864 Photographs: 40t, 44

Catalogue of the Boston Normal School for the Year 1906: Architect's Renderings for the City of Boston's Schoolhouse Department, School Document No. 3 (Boston: Municipal Printing Office, 1907): 156a

Catalogue of the Boston Public Latin School, Established 1635: With an Historical Sketch, prepared by Henry F. Jenks (Boston: Boston Latin School Association, 1886): 2[2t and 3t]

Glenna Collett: 158

Karen D. Curran: front cover, ii, 77, 98b, 104b, 148a, 163, 164[4t], 178b, 181a, 198, 212a, 222[2b], 228, 234r

Dorchester Historical Society: 81

Harvard University
    Archives: 25r, 29a
    Arthur and Elizabeth Schlesinger Library on the History of Women in America, Radcliffe Institute for Advanced Study: 56, 76, 97, 98t, 150[3b], 159, 160, 164b, 182, 183
    Abbie Farwell Brown Papers: 70[2b], 76–78, 79t, 90, 92, 98t
    Girls' High School Archives: 48
    Radcliffe College Archives: 40[2b], 56, 64, 65r, 99, 128b, 135, 141a, 182, 230r, 240t
    Records of Girls' Latin School: 104[3b], 121, 174, 178t, 181c, 199, 210t, 224, 230l
    Houghton Library: Barrows Family Papers, 70b, 82, 85, 87, 88, 89, 90, 102, 103
    Theodore Roosevelt Collection, 115

The Jabberwock: 70[3t], 80; vol. 66, no. 3 (May 1953): 210b, 211l

Jarvis, F. Washington, *Schola illustris: The Roxbury Latin School 1645–1995* (Boston: David Godine, 1995): 75

John F. Kennedy Presidential Library and Museum, Archives: 234l

King, Moses, *King's Handbook of Boston* (Cambridge, Mass.: King, 1881): 2b

Liber Annalis (Girls' Latin School yearbooks)
    1931: 191, 193
    1935: 196, 197[t-a]
    1937: 184[3t], 187
    1938: 166, 208
    1940: 164[3b], 177, 211c
    1942: 153t
    1943: 184[2b], 194
    1945: 195
    1948: 199b, 200[2b]
    1949: 200[2t], 202
    1951: 201, 211r
    1952: 164t
    1953: 209, 210b
    1957: 248
    1959: 220[2t]
    1960: 219
    1966: 220[3b], 225c, 227

Liber Annalis (continued)
  1967: 220[2b], 225b, 232, 240b
  1968: 229b, 236, 243
  1969: 245
  1970: 169b, 238a
  1974: 221, 222b, 253, 261
  1976: 258a

Library of Congress
  Mary McGrory Papers: 197b
  Prints and Photographs Division: 70[2t, 3b], 71, 86, 128[2b], 164[2t]

Lightstream, photograph by Al Mallette: 180, back cover

Massachusetts Historical Society: 22l, 65[l, c]

Museum of Fine Arts, Boston, detail of *Portrait of C. K. Dillaway with Hanabusa Kotaro, Hiraga Isasaburo, Tsuge Zengo, and Aoki Yoshihira*: 25l

poetryfoundation.org: 172

Courtesy of The Roxbury Latin School: 74, 164[2b], 184b

Seventieth Birthday of James Freeman Clarke: Memorial of the Celebration (Boston: Church of the Disciples, 1880): 22r

Smith College Archives: 40[2t], 47a, 52c, 61, 142
  Alumnae Files: Mason, Howes, Goodwin: 52l, 52r

Swarthmore College Archives: 27, 124

University of Chicago, Special Collections: Edith Talbot Papers: 8r
  Marion Talbot Papers: 7

University of Oklahoma Sooner Yearbook (1916): 128t, 131b

Vassar College Library, Special Collections: 21, 154

Courtesy of the Wellesley College Archives: 16, 19, 155

Wikimedia Commons
  license CC-BY-SA 2.0: 241 (William Murphy, photographer)
  license CC-PD-Mark [public domain]: 2[3t], 41 (Baldwin Coolidge, photographer), 79b, 150[2t], 151, 220[4t, 4b]

Wikipedia (license CC-BY-SA 3.0): 2[4t], 22[2r], 26, 40[3b], 240[2t]

Woods, Lucy R., *A History of the Girls' High School of Boston, 1852–1902* (Boston: Printed by Riverside Press, 1904): 28

Best efforts were made to determine rights holders and to request permission to reprint the pictures in this book. The publisher welcomes information identifying uncredited photographs.

Index

Abbot, Rosalie, 171, 179
admission exam. *See* entrance exams
"advisor of girls," 185–186
African Americans, 196–197, 232, 257–258, 259
    at GLS, 154–155, 206–207, 233, 258
Agassiz, Elizabeth, 99
Aldrich, Sybil, 171, 193, 277(n12)
Alexander, Curt, 173
Alexander, Joyce, 206
Allis, Annie Amelia, 61
Alumnae Association, GLS, 65, 77, 124–125, 137, 277(n17)
    annual meeting (1936) of, 187
    Diamond Jubilee celebration by, 210–211
    50th-anniversary celebration by, 175, 177–180
    first president of, 67
    and Griswold's transfer, 144
    J. Peabody and, 97
    opposition to making Latin Schools coeducational, 243
    opposition to moving GLS to Dorchester, 214
    Parthenon frieze donated to GLS by, 156
    retirement reception for Gately by, 225
    during Tetlow's tenure, 159
    World War II and, 192
American Association of University Women, 21, 135
Ames, Edith, 100
Ames, Mrs. Charles G., 98, 100
Antin, Maryashe, 111–117, 273(n20)
Association of Colleges and Secondary Schools of New England, 110
Association of Collegiate Alumnae, 7, 21
Athenian Club (GLS), 172, 174
Atherton, Edward, 171
athletics. *See* sports
Austin, Helen A., 193
Avenue Louis Pasteur (Boston), 169, 216, 235–236, 255

Baby Day (GLS), 169
Ball, Mrs. Dwight D., 273(n20)
Banks, Richard, 232
Barnard College, 239
Barnes, Clara, 102, 103
Barron, Jennie Loitman, 276(n2)
Barrows, Isabel Chapin, 73, 82, 87, 88–89, 90, 93–94, 101, 106
Barrows, Mabel Hay, 72–77, 78, 88–95, 100–101, 102, 103, 233
    life details, 82–83
Barrows, Samuel, 82–83, 102, 106
Barsamian, Shirley, 237
Bartlett, Samuel D., 31–32
Bartley, David, 250
Beaman, Barbara G., 181
Bedford Street (Boston), 10, 11
Berrigan, Jack, 195
Bigelow, Blanche, 102, 103
Bishop, Nathan, 8–9
BLSA (Boston Latin School Association), 10, 22, 35–36, 124
Board of Education, Mass., 205
Board of Supervisors, Boston, 131
Bogan, Louise, 172–173, 174
Boston, Massachusetts. *See also* public schools, Boston
    African Americans living in, 232
    during Great Depression, 188
    in early 1900s, 168
    Hispanic students in, 259
    influence on education throughout U.S. of, 8–9
    percentage of students graduating high school in 1920s, 169–170
    political favoritism in, 204–205
    racial segregation in, 241
    school population in, 121, 189
Boston City Archives De-segregation Era Collection, 279(n10)
Boston Finance Commission, 203, 216–217
Boston Interscholastic Press Association, 94
Boston Latin Academy, 259–260, 262
Boston Latin School (BLS), 22–25, 130, 158
    academic equality with GLS of, 123
    admission of girls to, 3–4, 20, 25–27, 30, 31–35, 254–255
    admissions policy of, 243, 259
    African American student enrollment at, 258
    alumni of, 10, 22, 35–36, 124
    among best high schools in U.S., 262
    annex to, approval to build, 188
    annual meetings of, 265–266(n65)
    on Avenue Louis Pasteur, 169
    on Bedford Street, 10–11, 12
    coeducation and, 106, 244–250
    College Board Entrance Exams at, 187
    Curley and, 188
    curriculum at, 23
    dress code at, 238
    enrollment at, 169, 175, 188, 189
    entrance exam for, 245
    establishment of, 23
    first female to study at, 26–27
    GLS, sharing with, 109, 272(n10), 272(n14)
    GLS, socialization with girls from, 195
    graduates accepted at Harvard, 68, 170
    graduation rate of, controversy over, 130
    locations of, 266(n70)
    names of, 264(n3)
    O'Leary's opening day speech to (1964), 278(n9)
    The Register, 79, 84, 93, 94, 191
    teachers at, 149, 171
    Tercentenary Celebration of, 190–191
    on Warren Avenue, 12, 105, 107–109
    during World War II, 194
Boston Latin School Association (BLSA), 10, 22, 35–36, 124
Boston Normal School, 9, 29, 120, 152, 203
Boston Public Library, 104, 105, 115, 116, 119, 172, 272(n4)
Boston Technical School, 245, 261
Boston University, 7, 15–16, 18–19, 120, 266(n75)
    GLS graduates admitted to, 68, 99, 173, 183
Bowditch, Henry P., 28
bowls, silver, 193, 277(n17)
Bowne, Kate W., 265(n53)
Bray, Janice, 243
Brett, John A., 120
Brewster, Alice S. *See* Rollins, Alice S.
Briggs, Sarah Elizabeth, 68, 124

Brock, George E., 133
Brody, Judith, 224, 252–253
Brooks, Grace, 88, 89, 103
Brooks, Helen, 133, 138
Brooks, Marion, 133, 138, 142
Brooks, Stratton, 129–133
   as Boston school superintendent, 133
   changes proposed to GLS teachers by, 134
   as critical of GLS, 131, 144–145
   Griswold transfered to Dorchester High by, 137–149
   investigates high attrition at GLS, 134
   meets with GLS parents, 140–141
   stated mission for Latin Schools of, 134–135
   Tetlow honored by, 162
Brown, Abbie Farwell, 72–77, 78, 85, 88, 89, 91, 92, 94, 95–96, 98–99, 101, 144, 177, 180, 210, 242
   life details, 76–77
Brown, Mary Frances, 93, 103
Brown University, 110, 277(n12)
Bryant, John D., 139
Bryn Mawr College, 248
Buck, Elizabeth H., 265(n53)
Building Assistance Bureau, Mass., 236
Bunting, Mary, 249
Burke, Jeremiah, 179
Bushmiller, Jane, 198
busing, court-ordered, 232, 251, 258

Calderwood, Samuel H., 120
Cambridge Latin School, 94
Campagna, Yole, 198
Campbell, Patrick, 130, 189–190, 278(n9)
Capen, Charles J., 159
Capen, Edward W., 93, 94
Carr, William, 205, 208–209, 210, 212, 214–215
Carroll, Lewis, 70, 73, 78–79, 84–87, 104, 270(nn5, 26), 271(n57)
Carroll, Margaret C., 225, 226–231, 244, 261
   on coeducational Latin Schools, 247–250
   curriculum at GLS defended by, 232
   dress code and, 237–238
   on GLS entrance exams, 242–243
   on GLS return to Fenway area, 235
   school segregation and, 241–242
Carter, Jimmy, 249
caryatids, 156, 196, 223, 224, 243
Caution-Davis, Ethel, 154, 155
CEEB (College Entrance Examination Board), 110, 187
Cercle Français, Le (GLS), 174

Chandler, John, 244
Chapter 618 law, Mass., 208
Chapter 622 law, Mass., 250–257
Chauncy Hall School (Boston), 9, 94, 118–120, 121, 122
Church, Blanche Bonnelle, 144
Civil Air Patrol, 234
Civil Liberties Union of Massachusetts, 243
civil rights movement, 207, 232
Claflin, Mary B., 15, 18–19, 265(n53)
Claflin, William, 15–16, 266(n75)
Clarke, Edward H., 13–14
Clarke, James Freeman, 21, 22, 29, 63
class rings, GLS, 181
classics, study of, 51–52
Cliff, Gertrude, 182
clubs at GLS, 174
Codman Square (Boston). *See* Dorchester High School
Coe, Sarah Tappan, 83
coeducation, 24, 57, 106, 243–261. *See also* single-sex schools
Coes, Mary, 158
Cohen, Ida A., 193, 277(n12)
Collar, Hannah C. Averill, 74
Collar, (Mary) Sibyl, 71–77, 78, 81, 88, 90–91, 95, 97, 98, 99, 101, 158–159
   at 50th-anniversary celebration, 177–178, 179–180
   life details, 74–75
Collar, William Coe, 31, 71, 74, 75, 80, 90, 98, 110, 158
College Entrance Examination Board (CEEB), 110, 187
College Board Entrance Exams, 187
college preparatory education, 108, 170–171
Committee on High Schools, Boston, 120
Committee on Latin and High Schools, Boston, 27–35, 38
Committee to End Discrimination in the Boston Public Schools, 244–245
Comstock, Ada, 179
Condon, Elizabeth P., 193, 194
Conley, George H., 132
Copeland, Anne Y. *See* Young, Annie
Copley Square (Boston), 119, 120, 125
Coppleman, Marcia, 198
Cornell University, 239
Cotter, Margaret C., 277(n12)
Cowan, Fred, 171
Cowen, Philip, 114, 115
Craven, John J. Jr., 244, 247, 251
Crawford, Cora, 141, 142–143
Crawford, Janet, 193

Crawford, Mary Caroline, 8
Crawford, William C., 140
Creed, Eleanor. *See* L'Ecuyer, Eleanor Creed
Crocker, Lucretia, 58
Cross, Barbara, 181
Croswell, James Greenleaf, 162
Crowley, Catherine M., 193
Cummings, Helen, 244–245, 255
Cunningham, Alice, 65, 177
Curley, James Michael, 168–169, 188, 204, 275(n8)
Curley, Leo, 188, 275(n8)
Curley, Mary, 168
Curley, Paul, 188, 275(n8)
Curtin, Thomas J., 236
Curtis, Augusta, 63
Cushing, Florence, 7, 20–21, 28, 63, 106

Daniels, Mabel, 77
Davenport, Mary, 171
DeNormandie, Sarah, 161
Dentler, Robert, 261
desegregation, 258, 260–261. *See also* segregation
Desmond, John J., 217–218
Deutsche Gesellschaft, Die (The German Society, GLS), 174
Diamond Jubilee, GLS, 209–211
DiCara, Lawrence S., 254
Dick, Virginia Holbrook. *See* Holbrook, Virginia
Dickerson, Diane M., 181
Dillaway, Charles, 17, 23, 25–26, 31, 108
discrimination in Boston public schools
   race-based, 154–155, 206–207, 250, 252, 261
   sex-based, 244–245, 250–257, 258–259
Distaff, The (Girls' High School), 94
Dix, Florence, 171
Dixwell, Epes Sargent, 10, 23
Dodgson, Charles Lutwidge. *See* Carroll Lewis
Dorchester High School (Codman Square, Boston)
   GLS moves into, 212, 213–214, 217, 221–239
   Griswold affair and, 137–149
Dordetsky, Rose, 214–215
dramatic productions, GLS, 91–94
dress code, GLS, 237–238
Dudley, Malcolm E., 235
Durant, Henry, 16–17, 18, 19–20

Earle, Miss, 244
Eisenstadt, Thomas S., 235
Eliot, Charles, 10–11, 29, 31, 56–57, 68–69,

110, 158, 159
Eliot, Samuel, 61–62
Elliott, Lucy C., 52
Ellis, David, 133, 147
Emerson, Ralph Waldo, 108
Emmanuel College, 197
English High School (Boston), 94, 105, 108, 216, 234–235, 256–257
entrance exams, 242, 245, 253
    for admission to BLS or GLS, 243
    earliest, 46–49
equal educational opportunities law, 250–257
equal opportunity, 243, 248–249
equal rights movement, 241–261
Esau, Ellen B., 193
Everett, Martha E., 52
exam schools. See Latin Schools
extracurricular activities, 174, 178–79, 227. See also Jabberwock, The; sports; and entries for individual clubs

faculty, GLS. See teachers, GLS
Fahey, Marion, 261
Fairbanks, Emily. See Talbot, Emily Fairbanks
Farren, Anthony J., 213–214
Faunce, William, 179
"fear of success" theory (Horner), 249
Feast of Dido, The, 91–94
Feinberg, Matthew, 243
Fennessey, Catharine T., 277(n12)
Fenway (Boston), 125, 169, 211, 234–236. See also Avenue Louis Pasteur; Huntington Avenue, GLS location on
Fields, Annie Adams, 20, 22, 67
figure skating, 182–183
Filene, A. Lincoln, 140, 142–143
Filene, Catherine, 140, 141
Filene, Edward A., 140
Fine, Edith W., 251, 252, 253
Finney, William H., 42
Fiske, Arthur I., 123, 129, 130, 149, 158, 273(n3)
Fitzgerald, John F. "Honey Fitz," 167
Fitzgerald, Mary K., 205, 208, 210, 215
Flannagan, Rena, 174
Flint, Charles L., 26, 28, 30, 46
Foley, Martha, 173, 210
Foley, Mary J., 64–65, 66–67, 68, 149, 171, 179
Foley, Patrick J., 205, 212
Fowle, Elinore J., 193
Fox, Mollie, 88
Francis, George H., 161

Frank, Elizabeth, 172
Fraser, Mathilda, 171
friezes, classical (reproductions), 45, 156, 223, 233

Gardner, Isabella Stewart, 15, 104, 125, 152, 244
Garrity, Arthur, 251, 256–257, 258–259, 260–261
Garrity, Paula Wheelock, 260, 261
Gately, Thomas F., 225, 226
Gay, Henry Augustine, 266(n81)
Gerrish, Carolyn M., 172, 173, 174, 193
gifts from GLS classes to alma mater, 156–157, 180
Gill, Mary, 195
Gilman, Arthur, 57
Girdwood, Jessie, 63, 65
Girls' High School (Boston), 5, 9, 29, 43, 45–46, 58, 64, 108, 202, 245
    college-preparatory department at, 30
    Distaff, The, 94
    headmaster of, 68, 136–137
    on West Newton Street, 105
Girls' Latin School (GLS; Boston), 267(n88)
    academic achievement at, 239
    academic reputation of, 68–69, 131, 186, 237
    admission standards for, 242–243
    "advisor of girls" and, 185–186
    African American students at, 154–155, 206–207, 233, 258
    Alumnae Association. See Alumnae Association, GLS
    attrition rate at, 131
    as BLS's academic equal, 123
    and BLS Tercentenary Celebration, 190–191
    and Boston Normal School, 120
    boys admitted to, 254–255
    Brooks' criticism of failing grades at, 145
    buildings of. See Chauncey Hall School; Dorchester High School; Huntington Avenue, GLS location on; West Newton Street
    class gifts given to, 156–157, 180
    clubs at, 174
    college admissions for graduates of, 68, 173, 232. See also entries for specific colleges
    curriculum at, 51, 227, 232
    Diamond Jubilee of, 209–211
    dress code at, 237–238
    during 1930s and 1940s, 185–199

    during 1950s, 226
    during 1960s, 226–233
    enrollment at, 105, 117, 151, 158, 175, 189, 203, 227, 243, 272(n1)
    entrance exams for, 46–49, 242, 245
    extracurricular activities at, 174, 178–79, 227
    50th anniversary of, 173, 175, 177–180
    fire at, 231
    first graduating class (1880) at, 56
    first students of, 53–56
    first-year classes begin, 49–56
    founding of, 4–9
    Golden Jubilee celebration of, 177–180
    grading system at, 138
    graduates admitted to Harvard Annex, 63–68, 99–100
    graduates' honors and awards, 187
    graduation at. See graduation(s)
    in gymnastic meet, 178–179
    Hapgood's tenure at, 165–183
    headmasters of, 225. See also entries for specific individuals
    homework assigned at, 51
    Huntington Avenue building. See Huntington Avenue, GLS location on
    logo of, 79, 84
    made coeducational, 244–250
    mementos from, 181
    move to Dorchester High, 219
    name change for, 259–260
    National Merit Scholarship program at, 238–239
    organization of, decision for, 38–39
    racial issues at, 206–207
    regulations for, 49, 51
    SAT scores (1970s) at, 239
    school paper. See Jabberwock, The
    school song at, 175–177
    70th anniversary celebration at, 199
    75th anniversary of, 162
    sex-discrimination complaint filed against, 250–257
    socialization among students at, 196–197
    socialization of students with BLS boys, 195
    struggle over control and direction of, 129–149
    teachers at. See teachers, GLS
    and Teachers College of the City of Boston, 205, 208–209
    Tetlow and. See Tetlow, John
    30th anniversary of, 158
    25th birthday celebration at, 122–124

women's equal rights movement and, 241–261
and World War II, 192–195
year-end examinations at, 94–96
Gleason, Anne Roberts, 233
Glennon, Marie E., 193
Glowacki, Julianne, 234
Goddard, Mary C. C., 136, 153–154
Goodman, Janice, 254–255
Goodwin, Fannie, 52
Goodwin, William M., 56, 64
Gosnell, Thomas, 238
Gould, Arthur, 201–202, 203, 208
Grabau, Amadeus William, 114, 115
graduation(s), GLS
    1891 class, 96, 98–99
    1898 class, 120
    1904 class, 127
    1910 class, 159
Gragg, Florence, 99
Grant, Frances Olivia, 154
Gray, Francis C., 276(n2)
Great Depression, 188–189
Greek (study of), 51–52, 271(n70)
Greene, Mary E., 193, 277(n12)
Greenough, James B., 56, 57
Griffith, Margaret J., 193, 277(n12)
Griswold, Ellen C., 99–100, 106, 131, 135–136, 162, 179
    accused of insubordination, 142
    death of, 148
    public sentiment about transfer of, 140
    transferred to Dorchester High, 137–149
gymnastic meets, GLS in, 178–179

Hale, Lucretia B., 58, 59
Haley, Dennis C., 208, 211–213, 215, 216
Hall, Gertrude M., 193, 277(n12)
Hammond, Claire, 98, 99
Hammond, Eleanor, 102, 103
Hapgood, Ernest G., 115, 162, 165–166, 187, 193, 198, 277(n12)
    on "advisor of girls" position, 186
    enrollment growth at GLS during tenure of, 203
    50th anniversary celebration at GLS and, 179–180
    life details, 167
    reputation of, 186–187
    retirement of, 198–199
    teaching staff doubled by, 171
    Tetlow and, 160
    and World War II, 192
Hapgood, Mrs. Ernest, 210

Harding, Blanche W., 193, 277(n12)
Harlem Renaissance, 207
Harper, Carrie, 103
Harris, William T., 110
Harvard Annex, 57–58, 248. *See also* Radcliffe College
    beginnings of, 63–68
    class of 1891 at, 99–100
    GLS graduates admitted to, 65, 68, 69, 77, 99, 102
    renamed Radcliffe College, 75
Harvard University, 29, 158, 170, 249, 257, 277(n12). *See also* Radcliffe College
    admission of women to, 56–57
    BLS graduates admitted to, 68, 179
    entrance exam for, 132
Headmasters Association of the United States, 110, 162
Healy, Joseph, 22–23, 25–26, 29–34, 265(n65)
Hecht, Hattie, 114
Hemenway, Mary (Mrs. Augustus), 266(n76)
Hemmings, Anita, 154
Hennigan, James W. Jr., 244, 245, 251, 257–258
Herter, Christian A., 217
Heyl, Gladys M., 193, 277(n12)
Hicks, Louise Day, 235
Higginson, Henry Lee, 117–118
High School of Commerce (Boston), 216
Hispanic students in Boston, 259
Holbrook, Alice, 94, 101
Holbrook, Pickney, 75, 81
Holbrook, Sibyl. *See* Collar, (Mary) Sibyl
Holbrook, Virginia, 72–77, 88, 89–90, 95, 99
    life details, 81
Holland, Debra, 237–238
Holland, Helen G., 193
Horner, Joseph L., 248
Horner, Matina Souretis, 248–249
Howard, Alice, 88
Howard, Elizabeth Proctor, 62–63
Howe, Corrine, 196–197
Howe, Julia Ward, 13, 14, 15, 128, 265(n37), 265(n53)
Howes, Abby C., 48, 123, 136, 171, 179
Howison, George H., 29
Hunnewell, Mrs. James F., 265(n53)
Huntington Avenue (Boston), GLS location on, 127
    GLS forced to leave, 201–219
    potential return to, 234, 255–257
    removal from, protests about, 211–215
    struggle to obtain, 105–127

students' feelings about, when new, 154–155
Hurley, Joseph J., 186, 276(n2)
Hurling, Ray C., 110
Hutchins, Edward, 38, 268(n121)
Hynes, John B., 204, 205

immigrants, 145
    Antin's story and, 111–112, 114, 115
    as GLS students, 167–168, 230, 242
Ipsen, Ernest L., 159
Ivy League universities, 192, 239

Jabberwock, The, 71–103, 173
    Athenian Club and, 174
    beginnings of, 177
    on coeducation, 251, 254–255
    finances of, 80, 84
    first issue of, 78–84
    format of, 80
    founding editresses of, 101
    fundraising for, 91–94
    at GLS 50th anniversary, 180
    gymnastics meet covered by, 178–179
    Lewis Carroll's interest in, 84–87
    on move to Dorchester, 219, 223–224
    name of, origin, 73
    office of, in Copley Square building, 119
    officers of, 89–91, 100
    on school pin, 181
    on school song, 176
    Tetlow letter to, 160
Jabberwock Dance (GLS), 91
Jackson, F. G., 84
Jaher, Frederic, 168
Jewish students (GLS), 112, 114, 115, 196–197
Joan of Arc (sculpture), 123, 157, 223, 273(n52)
Johnson, Annie, 265(n53)
Johnson, Carol, 259
Johnson, Ethel, 154, 155, 233
Johnson, Gloria, 207
Johnson-Powell, Gloria, 207
Jones, Dorothea, 193
Jones, Frances, 103
Jones, Nellie, 103
Jutten, Emma, 103

Keenan, David, 260
Kemp, Elise, 157
Kennedy, John F., 198
Kenny, Thomas J., 133
Kenny, William S., 133
Kerrigan, John J., 244, 255
King, Martin Luther Jr., 232

Lacey, Alice Cunningham, 65, 177
Lane, Daniel, 130
Lane, Grace, 102, 103
Lane, Sarah, 59
lapel pins (GLS), 181
Lapidus, Lilian Greene, 233
LaRoca, Sandra, 243
Latin Schools. *See also entries for specific schools*
   authority to build new one, 169
   Brooks' mission for, 134–135
   coeducation and, 216, 243–261
   during Great Depression, enrollment in, 189
   entrance exams for, 245, 253, 257–258
   girls admitted to, 27, 34–35
   graduation rate at, 170
   high dismissal rate at, 134
   integration from within, plan for, 254
   teachers at, 249–250
Leach, Abby, 56, 63–66
L'Ecuyer, Eleanor Creed, 193, 210, 211, 212, 214, 233
L'Ecuyer, Rosalie, 210, 211
L'Ecuyer, Virginia, 210, 211
Lee, Joseph, 212, 235, 244, 245–250, 278(n5)
Lehmann, Jacob, 171, 174
Lewis, Kate, 198
Lincoln, Charles J., 137
Lincoln, Marion, 103
Lingham, Grace E., 193
Linscott, Colleen, 195
Lithgow, Marion I., 193, 277(n12)
Livermore, Mary A., 265(n53)
logo (GLS), 79, 84
Long, John D., 107
Lovett, Emily, 103
Lowell, Amy, 77
Luce, Miss, 91
Lundell, Margaret E., 193
Lynch, Barbara, 175–177
Lynch, Carrie V., 144
Lynch, Ruth, 175–177
Lyons, Alice, 205, 208, 210, 212
Lyons, Joseph V., 186, 276(n2)

MacNutt, Glenn, 225
MacNutt, Karen, 225
Madison Park complex (Roxbury), 234–235
Magill, Helen "Nellie," 26–27, 33, 34, 124–125, 266(n83), 267(n84)
Mannix, Helen, 232–233
Marble, S. P., 110–111

Marks, Lionel S., 97
Marnell, Mary, 277(n12)
Mason, Elizabeth S., 52, 68
Mason, Mary, 47, 54, 61, 66–67
Massachusetts College of Art, 156
Massachusetts Institute of Technology (MIT), 18, 239
Massachusetts Schoolmasters Club, 110
Massachusetts Society for the University Education of Women (MSUEW), 20–21, 22, 26
Masters, Marcia, 251
Mastrobattista, Karen, 253
Maude, Daniel, 264(n1)
May, Abby W., 28, 37, 38, 46, 58, 59, 268(n121)
Mazzoni, Linda, 253
McCoy, Louis, 201–204, 212, 223, 224, 225
McCoy, Mrs. Louis, 210
McCullough, Leo F., 133
McDonough, John J., 235
McGrory, Mary, 196–197
McLaughlin, Julia, 259
McNamara, Kathryn, 193
McNamara, Miss, 244
Menino, Thomas, 259
Merrill, Moses, 23, 25, 26, 55, 108, 130, 266(n81), 274(n3)
   death of, 122–123
   feelings about coeducation of, 106, 109
Mersel, Ethel Johnson. *See* Johnson, Ethel
Meserve, Harrison G., 191, 193, 194, 277(n12)
Miller, Helen S., 193
Miller, Miss, 245
Miller, William T., 225, 226
Mills, Alice, 47, 53, 54, 61, 67, 124, 179
Milton, Elaine, 233
MIT (Massachusetts Institute of Technology), 18, 239
Moore, Isabella, 99
Moreland, Marion C., 176, 179, 193, 219, 277(n12)
Morgan, Talullah, 257–258
Morgan v. Hennigan, 257–258
Morley, Catherine M., 193
Morse, Godfrey, 28, 29, 32, 34
Morse, Mabel, 178, 193
Mott-Smith, Ida, 99–100
Moulton, Claxton B., 187
Moulton, Richard G., 265(n53)
Mount Holyoke College, 18, 207, 239, 277(n12)
MSUEW (Massachusetts Society for the University Education of Women), 20–21, 22, 26
Muchnick, Isadore H. Y., 204–205, 208–209, 210
Musco, Louis F., 212
Mussey, Henry Raymond, 83
Mussey, Mabel Barrows. *See* Barrows, Mabel Hay
Musto, Marie, 243
Myrick, Hannah, 103
Myrick, Nan, 88

NAACP (National Association for the Advancement of Colored People), 232, 257
Naeiman, Adeline Lubell, 194
National Education Association, 110, 131
National Merit Scholarship program, 238–239
New England Female Medical College of Massachusetts, 17–18
New England Poetry Club, 77
New England Women's Club, 13–14, 16
Newton High School (Newton, Mass.), 94
Nickels, Edith, 102, 103
Normal School. *See* Boston Normal School
"Nursery, the," 119

O'Connell, Elizabeth M., 177
O'Connor, William E., 235
Ohrenberger, William H., 235, 253
O'Leary, Wilfred, 243, 244, 246–247, 278(n9)
Olympic Games, 182–183
Ordway, Julia, 171
Owen, Guy, 183
Owen, Maribel Vinson. *See* Vinson, Maribel

Paine, Robert Treat, 130
Palmer, Alice Freeman, 265(n53)
Parthenon (Athens, Greece), frieze from, 45, 156, 223, 233
Peabody, Elizabeth Palmer, 18–19, 20, 265(n51)
Peabody, Josephine Preston, 77, 95–96, 99, 177, 180
   life details, 97
Peabody, Lucia M., 58
Phelps, Elizabeth S., 265(n53)
Phi Beta Kappa, 52, 68, 124, 186–187
Philbrick, John, 24, 27, 31, 36–37, 51, 59, 61, 108, 267(nn 87, 88, 90)
Piemonte, Gabriel E., 213
pins (GLS), 181
Polk, Barbara, 191
Pormort, Philemon, 264(n1)
Porter, Noah, 31
Powell, Rodney, 207

Pozen Center, Massachusetts College of Art, 156
President's Bowls, 193, 277(n17)
Prichard, Eva Z., 193, 277(n12)
Prince, Frederick O., 24, 26, 35, 107–108
prom(s), 195, 232
public schools, Boston
   early education of girls in, 5, 8–9
   enrollment in, 189, 203
   girls' education, as legally required of, 21
   governance of, 189–190. *See also* School Committee, Boston
   racial imbalance in, 232, 236, 242, 252, 256–257
   segregation in, 241, 251, 257–258
   single-sex schools among, 203
   wealthy families' withdrawal from, 168
Pulitzer Prize, 197

quotas, racial, 259, 261

race, 206–207, 236. *See also* African Americans
   education imbalance based on, 232, 236, 242, 252, 256–257
   quotas based on, 259, 261
Radcliffe College, 67, 75, 81, 120, 158, 173, 248–249, 272(n89), 277(n12). *See also* Harvard Annex
   Alumnae Association for, 135
   early beginnings of, 56–58
   GLS graduates admitted to, 83, 97, 102, 124, 132, 154, 170, 175, 179, 182, 230, 233, 239
Raymond, Theresa Gulinello, 231
Register, The (BLS), 79, 84, 93, 94, 191
Reilly, Rosemary L., 258–259
Rice, Charles, 126
Richards, Ellen M., 265(n51)
rings, class (GLS), 181
Ripley, Edith Wheeler. *See* Wheeler, Edith
Robinson, Adelaide Sears, 154
Robinson, Katherine Naomi, 154
Rogers, Charlotte W., 54, 61, 63, 67
Rogers, Ethel, 99
Rollins, Alice S., 54, 67
Roper, Cora F., 179, 193, 277(n12)
Roxbury (Boston), 234–235
Roxbury Latin School, 31, 71, 74, 75, 80, 93, 94, 108, 110, 158
Runkle, John D., 21, 22
Russell, Duncan, 140, 143–144
Russell, Georgine, 197

Sanborn, Esther, 98, 99
Sanborn, Josephine, 88, 92, 94, 98, 99
Sanborn, Kathrina, 102, 103
Sanderson, Marjorie, 166, 187, 211
Santayana, George, 79, 191
Sargent report, 216
SAT (Scholastic Aptitude Test), 110, 239
Schmidt, Helen, 233
Scholastic Aptitude Test (SAT), 110, 239
School Committee, Boston, 131, 276(n2)
   "advisor of girls" position and, 186
   appropriates money to build new Latin School, 169
   approves land acquisition for GLS, 121
   Brooks appointed superintendent by, 133
   coeducational Latin Schools, attitude toward, 244–250
   decides GLS remains in Fenway, 216
   dress code for schools and, 238
   Emily Talbot runs for, 58–61
   fights to keep GLS in Huntington Avenue building, 216
   Foley appointed temporary teacher by, 65
   GLS attrition and, concerns about, 131–132
   GLS entrance exams and, 242–243
   GLS name change and, 259–260
   GLS's purpose, statement by, 170–171
   on Griswold's transfer to Dorchester High, 137, 140, 144–146
   Latin Schools admissions and, 253–254
   organizes Latin school for girls, 38–39
   public hearings about admitting girls to Latin School, 28–34
   public schools' segregation and, 251
   reforms in, 205
   regulations for GLS by, 51
   and segregation, 257–258
   space for GLS, decision to obtain additional, 118
   State Teachers College and, 204–205, 208–209, 212
   Tetlow requests new building before, 121–122
   Tetlow honored by, 159–160, 162
   votes to relocate GLS to English High building, 235–236, 255
   W. C. Collar and, 74
   wants GLS to move to Dorchester High building, 217
   wants GLS to remain in Copley Square, 125
   women's right to serve on, 58–64
School Editors' Club (SEC), 94
school song (GLS), 175–177

"Scribblers, The," 72–77
Scudder, Vida, 47, 53–56, 61, 66, 68, 98, 157, 161–162
SDS (Students for a Democratic Society), 232–233
Seaver, Edwin, 63, 107, 123–124, 126, 131, 147, 149
SEC (School Editors' Club), 94
Seelye, Julius H., 31, 62, 123
segregation, 241, 244–245, 251, 257–258. *See also* desegregation
Seven Sisters colleges, 68, 173, 175, 226, 239
sex discrimination in Boston schools, 244–245, 250–257, 258–259
Shaw, Caroline B., 144
Sheldon, Jane, 52, 63, 65, 71, 90–91
Siegal, Diana Laskin, 194, 230–231
Simmons, Adeline G., 141, 142, 171, 193, 277(n12)
Simmons College, 125, 206
single-sex schools, 38–39, 203, 216, 259. *See also* coeducation
Skinner, W. Jay, 243
Smith, Alice M., 171, 193, 277(n12)
Smith, Mabel "Belle," 88, 91, 98, 99
Smith, Robert D., 21, 28
Smith College, 18, 277(n12)
   class of 1884, 61, 62, 66–67
   GLS graduates admitted to, 52, 68, 75, 99, 102, 191, 239, 266(n75)
Society for the Collegiate Instruction of Women, 57–58
song, school (GLS), 175–177
Souretis, Matina. *See* Horner, Matina Souretis
sports
   figure skating, 182–183
   at GLS, 178–179
   at Radcliffe, 248
   in student publications, 80
Sports Illustrated, 183
Sprague, Howard, 68
S.T.A.C. (Student Teacher Advisory Council), 174, 248
Stanwood, Dorothy, 140, 141
Stark, Mary R., 171, 185–186, 193, 277(n12)
State Teachers College (Mass.), 203, 204–205, 208–209, 211–216
Steere, Julia, 174
Stern, Xos, 199
Stillings, Katherine E., 156–157
Storrow, James J., 130, 133, 139, 141, 149, 167
Strayer, George D., report by
   buildings closed due to, 219

single-sex schools criticized in, 203
recommendations of, 205
Stuart, Helen A., 99, 159, 171, 179, 193, 277(n12)
student publications, 94. *See also entries for individual periodicals' titles*
Student Teacher Advisory Council (S.T.A.C.), 174, 248
Students for a Democratic Society (SDS), 232–233
suffrage, women's, 74
Sullivan, Edward M., 276(n2)
Sullivan, Neil, 236

Tahmizian, Zabelle D., 193, 219, 230–231, 277(n12)
Talbot, Agnes, 264(n14)
Talbot, Edith, 6, 7, 8, 9, 10, 26, 264(n24), 265(n14)
Talbot, Emily Fairbanks, 4–9, 13, 14–15, 15–16, 20, 21, 264(n14), 266(n76)
addresses public hearing, 28–29
life details, 6–7
enrolls daughter in Latin School, 26
petition for girls' entrance to BLS, 25
runs for Boston School Committee, 58–61
Talbot, Henry R., 6, 264(n24), 264(n14)
Talbot, Israel Tisdale, 4, 6, 7, 17–18, 32–34, 264(n13), 265(n47)
Talbot, Marion, 6–7, 8, 9, 21, 60, 264(nn 14, 24)
Talbot, Mrs. Thomas, 265(n53)
Talbot, Winthrop T., 6, 9–10, 26, 264(nn 14, 24, 29)
Tappan, Sarah "Sadie," 83, 88, 89, 91, 92, 99, 103
teachers (GLS), 52, 62, 63–66, 65, 90–91, 135–136, 171–175, 192, 193, 230, 249–250, 277(n12). *See also entries for names of specific teachers*
feelings about Tetlow of, 68, 110, 146–147
meet with Brooks, 134
pay for, 171
Teachers College of the City of Boston. *See* State Teachers College (Mass.)
Tetlow, Elizabeth Proctor Howard, 44, 62–63, 91, 275(n20)
Tetlow, Elsie, 44, 102, 103, 160
Tetlow, Frances, 160, 210, 260
Tetlow, Helen, 44, 160, 162, 210, 260
Tetlow, John, 41–69, 98, 100, 162
Antin and, 111–117
appointed headmaster of Girls' High, 68
characteristics of, 46–47
chastised by School Committee, 146
on coeducation, 106
death of, 161–163
at dedication of BLS's sixth building, 108
disagreement with Brooks concerning Latin schools' mission, 134–135
educators' respect for, 110
faculty's feelings about, 68, 110, 146–147
family of, 102
fights for new GLS building, 105–127
Foley asked to teach by, 66–67
friendship with C. Eliot, 68–69
friendship with S. Barrows, 102
at GLS's 25th birthday celebration, 123–124
and Griswold's transfer to Dorchester High, 137–149
at Harvard Annex graduation (1891), 99–100
honors and awards bestowed upon, 110, 159–160, 162
and *The Jabberwock*, 87
Latin textbook by, 269(n23)
marries Elizabeth Howard, 62–63
memorial tribute to, 177
near-resignation from GLS of, 134–137
retirement of, 157–160
salary of, 268(n20)
and Scholastic Aptitude Test, 110
School Committee and, 121–122, 132
Seaver and, 147, 149
standards for students set by, 82–83
Storrow meets with, 141
students' opinion of, 55–56
as teacher, 64–65
and W. C. Collar, 74
Thayer, George A., 28
Thayer, Gideon F., 118
Thomas, Prudence, 103
Ticknor, Caroline, 77
Tierney, Daniel D., 177, 244
Tierney, Paul R., 244, 246, 251, 252
Title IX (U.S. law), 259
Tobey, Raymond S., 193, 277(n12)
Tripod, The (Roxbury Latin), 80, 93, 94
Tyng, Griswold, 224

U.S. News & World Report, 262
Underhill, Mary, 149
University of Michigan, 99

Vassar College, 18, 20–21, 29, 63–64, 277(n12)
GLS graduates admitted to, 102, 154, 239

Vinson, Maribel, 182–183

Waite, Elizabeth "Bessie," 88, 98–99, 101
Walker, Albert Perry, 136–137
Ward, Mike, 212–213
Warren, Lucy, 99
Warren, William F., 18–19, 20, 22, 34–35
Warren, Mrs. William, 265(n53)
Warren Avenue (Boston), 11–12, 105, 107–109
Washburn, Barbara Polk, 191
Wein, George, 206
Wellesley College, 15, 17, 18–19, 19–20, 66, 97, 120, 266(n75), 277(n12)
entrance exam for, 265(n55)
GLS graduates admitted to, 68, 99, 102, 154, 155, 239
Wells, Kate Garnett, 265(n53)
Wessmann, Sarah, 259
West, Dorothy, 206–207
West Newton Street (Boston), 43, 46, 68, 72, 105, 118–119, 122
Wheeler, Edith, 103, 233
White, Andrew Dickson, 267(n83)
White, Kevin, 254
White, Max, 140
Whitman, Alma, 103
Whiton, J. M., 266(n81)
Wilder, Helen, 99
Williams, William T., 193
Willis, May, 99
Winn, Charles, 140
Winter, Edward J., 236
Winthrop, Robert C., 35, 108
Witherspoon, Miriam S., 54, 61, 67
Women's Education Association, 16, 58
women's movement, 241–261
women's suffrage, 74
Woodhead, Marjorie W., 193, 277(n12)
World War II, 192–195
Wright, Carroll D., 265(n53)
Wright, Sandra, 243

Yale University, 239
Yates, Iola D., 154, 155
yearbooks (GLS), 181
Young, Annie H., 88, 89, 91, 92, 102, 103, 271(n57)
Young, Royal B., 142
Young, Sibyl, 141

Zangwill, Israel, 114
Ziegler, Annie, 103